Technology and Problem-Based Learning

Lorna Uden
Staffordshire University, UK

Chris Beaumont
Liverpool Hope University, UK

 Information Science Publishing

Hershey • London • Melbourne • Singapore

Acquisitions Editor:	Michelle Potter
Development Editor:	Kristin Roth
Senior Managing Editor:	Amanda Appicello
Managing Editor:	Jennifer Neidig
Copy Editor:	Morgan Horton
Typesetter:	Diane Huskinson
Cover Design:	Lisa Tosheff
Printed at:	Yurchak Printing Inc.

Published in the United States of America by
      Information Science Publishing (an imprint of Idea Group Inc.)
      701 E. Chocolate Avenue
      Hershey PA 17033
      Tel: 717-533-8845
      Fax: 717-533-8661
      E-mail: cust@idea-group.com
      Web site: http://www.idea-group.com

and in the United Kingdom by
      Information Science Publishing (an imprint of Idea Group Inc.)
      3 Henrietta Street
      Covent Garden
      London WC2E 8LU
      Tel: 44 20 7240 0856
      Fax: 44 20 7379 0609
      Web site: http://www.eurospanonline.com

Library of Congress Cataloging-in-Publication Data

Uden, Lorna, 1946-
  Technology and problem-based learning / Lorna Uden and Chris Beaumont.
     p. cm.
  Summary: "This book is aimed at educators who may be considering introducing problem-based learning and need to know what it involves, its benefits and the practical details of how to implement it"--Provided by publisher.
  Includes bibliographical references and index.
  ISBN 1-59140-744-3 (hardcover) -- ISBN 1-59140-745-1 (softcover) -- ISBN 1-59140-746-X (ebook)
  1. Problem-based learning. 2. Educational technology. I. Beaumont, Chris, 1955- II. Title.
  LB1027.42.U53 2006
  371.39--dc22
                        2005023872

British Cataloguing in Publication Data
A Cataloguing in Publication record for this book is available from the British Library.

Technology and Problem-Based Learning

Table of Contents

Preface

Readers may wonder why there is another book on problem-based learning (PBL). Let us give the reasons how this book came about.

Many tutors are experiencing problems with their students. The students are not learning what they should and many have no idea how to learn. Students find problem solving, critical thinking and self-directed learning difficult. In order to overcome this problem, many tutors have been turning to problem-based learning as a means of teaching their students in their respective disciplines. We have been implementing PBL since 1996 as a means to help students to learn better. Our experiences with PBL have been very positive and encouraging. Students have benefited enormously from the study.

Since then, we have been very keen to promote PBL as a powerful way for students to learn problem-solving, critical thinking and self-directed learning skills in workshops for colleges teaching computer science and engineering subjects. Those who came to the workshops were very encouraged by what we shared with them about our experiences with PBL for our students. Many wanted to learn more about PBL and told us that they could not find any books that actually helped them to start. Most of the books are written for the medical profession, but none of them are really ideal for someone who is new to PBL. As far as we know, there is no book written about PBL for technology teaching. Those who have read the PBL books told us that many of the books talk about what PBL is and the benefits of it, but there is little information about how to conduct PBL. Our colleagues then urged us to write a book that would help them to learn about PBL and how best to conduct it. This book is the outcome of that challenge.

PBL occurs in any environment in which the problems drive the learning. Many educators in higher education and schools are contemplating incorporating PBL in their curriculum. However, to achieve its full potential, PBL needs to be well designed and the tutors employing the method need intensive preparation through hands-on educational experiences. This book is designed to help anyone who wants to learn how to implement PBL and understand the different phases of how PBL is conducted. It also prepares staff to consider the implications of moving to PBL and assists in preparing for the practicalities of the introduction of PBL into the curriculum.

The chapters focus on the following areas:

- Chapter I: Traditional versus cognitive learning
- Chapter II: What is problem-based learning?
- Chapter III: Why PBL?
- Chapter IV: Role of the tutor
- Chapter V: Preparing students for PBL
- Chapter VI: Developing problems /triggers
- Chapter VII: The PBL tutorial process
- Chapter VIII: Assessment
- Chapter IX: Integrating e-learning technology
- Chapter X: Curriculum and organisational issues
- Chapter XI: Lessons learned and tips
- Chapter XII: Postscript

The first three chapters of the book explain the rationale for problem-based learning, define PBL, and explain why there is growing interest and how it is aligned with current thinking about learning in higher education.

These chapters underpin the practice of PBL. The book then proceeds to explain the practical details of implementation, with examples and checklists which are intended to help readers deal with important issues. Problem-based learning is a fundamental shift away from a traditional teacher-led model of education, and this has considerable impact on all aspects of teaching, learning and assessment. Chapters IV through VIII discuss these points in detail. Chapter IX examines the variety of ways in which e-learning technology can be used to support PBL e-learning is currently the focus of much attention, and it is by no means obvious that PBL and e-learning are closely aligned. Finally, after examining the details, we turn to the wider issues of curriculum design in Chapter X. There are some advocates for a curriculum that is 100% PBL, yet some institutions introduce it into single course modules. Is there a best way? In Chapter

XI we reflect on our PBL experiences and share some of the insights we have learned. We also provide some useful guidelines to some of the issues discussed. Each of the chapters is now briefly reviewed.

Chapter I:
Traditional vs. Cognitive Learning

Traditional teaching is generally known as didactic instruction in which information is presented to students by the tutor in a class. The teacher is the sole information-giver, undertaking lectures to a large group of students The students sit passively to receive the information from the tutor. Very often there is little interaction between tutor and students. Classes are typically driven by teacher talk—or as information giver—and depend heavily on textbooks for the structure of the course. It is generally accepted that there is a subject content that the students must come to know. Information is often divided into discrete parts and builds into a whole concept. The tutor's objective is to transmit their thoughts and meanings to passive students.

Learning by students is often detached from real world cases. This is because knowledge is often taught as context-independent. Students find it very difficult to transfer what they have learned to solve problems in the real world. They tend to memorise content without understanding the concepts learned and knowledge of how to apply it to actual problems. How can we make the need and reason to learn content apparent? How can we help students actually apply the information they learn?

Although there is no consensus among educators on how learning occurs, we believe that it is important to have a look at learning—what it is, how it occurs, and the different types of learning—before addressing these issues. This chapter looks at learning in general and the three main learning theories: behavioural, cognitive, and constructivist learning. Behavioural learning is described as a change in the observable behaviour of a learner, made as a function of events in the environment. Learning in behaviourism is equated with changes in either the form or frequency of observable performance..

Cognitive learning is equated with discrete changes between states of knowledge rather than with changes in the probability of response. In cognitive learning, the issues of how information is received, organised, stored, and retrieved by the mind are important. Learning is concerned not so much with what learners do, but with what they know and how they came to acquire that knowledge. The most dominant of the cognitive learning theories is based on an information-processing approach. Cognitive learning theories have been challenged by the currently popular constructivist learning. The philosophical assumptions for both behavioural and cognitive theories are primarily objectivistic. The objectivist philosophy, or world view, holds that there is an objective world that we perceive more or less accurately through our senses. Knowledge in objectivist learning is thought to exist independently of the learners. Learning consists of transferring that knowledge from outside to within the learner. Constructivist learning theory on the other hand is based on the assumption that knowledge is constructed by learners as they attempt to make sense of their experiences. Learners actively construct knowledge based on prior experiences, and they are not empty vessels waiting to be filled.

There are several approaches advocated by researchers that have been shown to be effective in promoting constructivist learning. These include cognitive apprenticeship (Collins et al., 1989), cognitive flexibility theory (Spiro et al., 1991), anchored instruction (CTGV, 1991) and problem-based learning (Barrows, 1992).

Chapter II:
What is Problem-Based Learning?

A search on the educational databases will confirm the rapid and extensive proliferation of PBL as an instructional method in many different disciplines. So, what is problem-based learning? Problem-based learning (PBL) is an instructional approach borrowed from the medical field. In PBL, students working in groups take on the responsibility of solving a professional problem. The underlying assumptions in traditional learning contrast sharply with those in PBL. The traditional approach views teaching as transmission of knowledge and learning as acquisition of that knowledge. In the traditional approach, it is generally assumed that knowledge is learned most effectively when it is organised around the disciplines and taught through lectures. In PBL, learning involves both knowing and doing. Knowledge and the use of that knowledge are both important. Students bring prior knowledge to their learning in PBL. The problem is used as the stimulus for learning. Problems are typically messy, ill-defined, and representative of the problems that students will face in real life. In PBL, students are assigned to groups that are responsible for framing the problem and deciding how to use the knowledge found to solve the problem. Each group usually has five or six members. The problem challenges students to learn-to-learn, working collaboratively in groups to seek solutions. It also engages students to initiate learning the subject content. PBL requires students to find and use appropriate resources and prepares them to think critically and analytically. The aims of implementing PBL are: to integrate knowledge and skills from a range of multidisciplinary modules; to teach students how to work as a team; and to develop problem solving, critical thinking, and learning-to-learn skills.

Chapter III:
Why Problem-Based Learning?

There is much literature written in support of the assertion that, relative to conventional lecture-based curriculum, PBL offers several benefits to students. Its curricula improves student problem-solving skills and enhances understanding and retention of concepts learned as well as the development of critical thinking skills. PBL makes students more motivated and engaged in their learning. It offers students a reason they are learning the materials that they are currently working on. This is because students can see that the problem they are working on is based on a real life problem. Students in PBL develop high-order thinking skills that enable them to know why they are getting the right answers to the problem. PBL also promotes metacognition and self-regulated learning by asking students to generate their own strategies for problem definition, information gathering, data-analysis, and hypothesis-building and testing, comparing these strategies against and sharing them with other students' and mentors' strategies.

Students in PBL appear to enjoy learning and are more actively involved in their own learning. Reports on the benefits of PBL on students' performance on national examinations vary greatly. Some showed that no harm was done when moving to a PBL curriculum to reports of improved performance for students in PBL curricula. Our personal experiences using PBL have been very positive, showing students in general benefited from PBL and they also enjoyed doing so.

Chapter IV: The Tutor's Role

Traditional lecture-based learning is tutor directed. It is generally acknowledged by tutors that knowledge consists of facts that need to be disseminated to students because students have a deficit. The tutor's role is simply the transmission of knowledge to the students. Tutors in a problem-based learning curriculum need to alter their traditional teaching methods of lectures, discussions, and asking students to memorise materials for tests. Problem-based learning begins with the introduction of an ill-structured problem on which all learning centres. The tutor assumes the role of coach or facilitator rather than knowledge-holder and disseminator. Instead of a disseminator of knowledge to students, tutors are co-learners with the students. They monitor the learning by probing and challenging students' thinking. Tutors focus their attention on questioning student logic and beliefs, providing hints to correct erroneous student reasoning, providing resources for student research, and keeping students on task. Another important role of the tutor is to manage group dynamics of the students making sure that the tutorial process keeps moving. As the students become more proficient, the tutor's role gradually fades away.

Chapter V: Preparing Students for PBL

Students in PBL assume the role of active problem-solvers, decision-makers, and meaning-makers, rather than passive listeners. They are given an ill-structured problem that mirrors real-world problems. The problem is messy and complex in nature. In PBL, students simultaneously develop problem solving strategies, disciplinary knowledge bases, and critical-thinking skills. Students in PBL are required to inquire, gather information, and reflect on the solution. They are active participants and engage in the learning process by constructing meaning. In problem-based learning, students assume increasing responsibility for their learning, giving them more motivation and more feelings of accomplishment, setting the pattern for them to become successful life-long learners. PBL requires students to take on active learning strategies and adopt self-directed learning dispositions. Some students find it difficult to cope when asked to transform into active critical thinkers.

Students who are new to a PBL classroom environment may find it, initially, very difficult. This is because they have been asked to take responsibility for their own learning, to work on ill-structured problems where there is not a pre-established right answer and where they are expected to structure their own approach to acquiring and using information to solve problems. Group work is an integral part of PBL. Students need to learn how to make optimal use of their time and resources, while working in groups. Working effectively in groups involves knowing how to organise the work, distribute responsibility, break up complex tasks, and provide useful feedback on work that is done. Students must learn how to work in groups.

When faced with a problem, students often find it difficult to identify the critical issues and to generate a coherent solution. Students are often unclear about how they can relate what they are currently reading to what they already know. They are also unfamiliar with different stages of the problem solving process, such as generating hypotheses, providing logical arguments, and transforming data into a product.

Helping students to enter this new type of learning environment requires that students are prepared for it. It is important for students to understand what they are getting themselves into. This chapter describes how to prepare students to accept risk and uncertainty and to become self-directed learners.

Chapter VI: Developing Problem Statements/Triggers

In many ways, the problem statement, or trigger, is the key to successful PBL. If it does not stimulate the students' interest, or enable students to generate learning issues that relate closely to the desired learning outcomes, then there are likely to be difficulties with both team work and achieving cognitive learning outcomes. It also needs to ensure students cannot simply adopt a "divide and conquer" approach, since this often means students do not integrate their knowledge or elaborate on their findings.

In this chapter, we explore the issues around the development of problem statements and collect advice from a variety of experienced practitioners on what makes an effective problem statement as well as what to avoid. We will also describe a possible process for the development of problem statements (triggers) and discuss examples. The chapter concludes with a number of examples from computing, management, and psychology to illustrate how triggers can be constructed and analysed.

Chapter VII: The Tutorial Process

The tutorial process is the hub of all learning in PBL. During the tutorial session, which typically lasts an hour, the teaching role of the tutor becomes one of questioning, probing, encouraging, critical appraisal, balancing emphasis, promoting interaction, and prompting students to become aware of the reasoning skills they are using. As the group works through the problem, students' progress is monitored by the tutor, and feedback is delivered along with identified research topics for the group. As the process progresses, ideas are challenged by other group members or by the teacher, if necessary. The process is cyclical, and it is repeated several times as new information is learned and ideas have been modified to generate new learning needs. Solving the problem is not the most important objective; the power of PBL is found within the learning process itself through student-directed inquiry. Facts and concepts are not taught directly, but integrated within the learning process. The tutorial process consists of several steps. The problem is presented and read by group members. A member of the group acts as scribe to write down *facts* as identified by group. Students discuss what is known (the facts). They brainstorm their ideas and formulate their hypotheses. Students then identify what they need to learn in order to prove or disprove their ideas. Students share research findings with their peers. The steps are repeated until the problem is solved. During the tutorial process, the tutor uses open-ended questions to foster student metacognitive growth. If necessary, ask questions like: What is going on here?; What do we need to know more about?; What is your evidence?; and Can you tell me more about it? As students participate in PBL over time, they become self-directed learners who are able to ask their own questions and identify what they need to know to continue their learning.

Chapter VIII: Assessment

Assessment probably has a more important effect on student learning than anything else. For the student, high grades and good qualifications signify success and open better opportunities in life. This chapter critically examines the issues for assessment in problem-based learning. Traditional examinations and coursework are not aligned well with the PBL approach and can undermine student learning if not adapted carefully. This chapter first considers the reasons why we should assess and then discusses the place of formative and summative assessment. We proceed to discuss what should be assessed. In particular, we argue that it is essential to assess the process skills involved in PBL in addition to subject knowledge and skills, since this adds credibility to our claim that they are important. Having determined what to assess, the next fundamental question is how we should assess and what techniques and assessment criteria we can use that are particularly relevant to PBL. A particularly thorny issue is the balance of team and individual assessment. Finally, we consider the timing of assessment and raise the issues of who should assess. Should students take part in assessing each other and themselves?

Chapter IX:
Integrating E-Learning Technology

Information technology has been used in teaching, learning, and assessment for many years, from programmed learning and on-line tutorials, which are teaching-centred at one end of the spectrum, to computer-supported collaborative environments, which are learning-centred. The term e-learning has developed over recent years to subsume these and related terms.

In this chapter, we will focus on the pedagogy and identify relevant aspects of e-learning technology that we believe are particularly relevant to problem-based learning. The chapter commences by discussing a model from Ron Oliver, identifying three essential components: learning tasks, learning resources, and learning supports. We then move on to focus on PBL specifically, adapting a framework from Ronteltap and Eurelings and using this model as the structure to analyse the use of e-learning technologies to support PBL. These include information related activities such as providing resources for faculty and students, structuring the PBL case, and the role of wireless networking. The second aspect of this model concerns communication-related activities, and we discuss the development of asynchronous and synchronous communication tools, such as virtual learning environments, wikis, video-conferencing, intelligent learning companions, and their role in the PBL case. The final sections discuss the blended learning approach and how e-learning technologies can support assessment activities in PBL.

Chapter X: Curriculum and Organisational Issues

The subject of problem-based learning can raise some surprisingly strong emotions, both in terms of the right process to use and the right curriculum model. For example, on the PBL Initiative Web site (director, Howard Barrows), the minimum essentials for PBL are stated, and include: *"Problem-based learning should not occur within a single discipline or subject."*

This requires a large scale intervention, obtaining commitment, collaboration, and consensus from staff in multiple subject areas, followed by much planning and training. It can be quite intimidating for a teacher who can see many benefits in the PBL approach and would like to try out PBL "in the small."

While there are numerous benefits from implementing PBL throughout a curriculum, which are discussed in this chapter, there is an alternative view of PBL as a pedagogical approach. It can be applied at several levels, from a single session to a fully integrated curriculum.

In this chapter, we explore some of the curriculum and organisational issues of implementing PBL, both "in the small," that is at module level, and "in the large," throughout the curriculum. The chapter discusses student preparation, issues of team size, facilitation models, classroom facilities, and how PBL can be introduced within an otherwise traditional lecture-based model. The later section of the chapter analyses the benefits and requirements for introducing PBL throughout the curriculum and describes a model for systematically developing the framework.

Chapter XI: Lessons Learned and Tips

Many books and articles have been written about tutors' experiences of PBL in various subjects. Our experiences may have many features similar to others. We have enjoyed implementing PBL to help our students to learn better in Computing Science teaching. Although we have been very pleased with the outcomes of our PBL experiences, it was by no means easy to start with. Since 1996, we have been learning and researching how we can improve our PBL process to help students to cope with the change of mindset they needed to better cope with PBL. This chapter is an attempt to show some of the insights we have learned.

Chapter XII: Postscript

The final chapter is presented as a postscript, a collection of advice from experienced practitioners. Since learning is complex, institutional contexts differ widely, and PBL changes many aspects of the learning system. We posed the following question to a wide range of PBL researchers and practitioners: *"What is the most important advice you could give someone just starting to use PBL?"*

The responses identified three themes: preparation and planning, the inevitability of criticism and difficulties, and the importance of adaptation to local context.

We trust that this book will contribute to the advancement of PBL and generate interest to promote learning among students so that they might become better learners.

Lorna Uden and Chris Beaumont
September 2005

Acknowledgments

We would like to thank many of our colleagues and friends who have encouraged us to write this book so that others will benefit from learning about problem-based learning.

Our thanks also go to the many current and past students who have given us very positive feedback about their experiences of problem-based learning and how it has helped them in their studies and careers. There have also been many students who have participated in the research that led to this book.

We would like to thank Chew Swee Cheng for her wealth of experience and understanding of problem-based learning and for sharing so much in the many hours that we discussed PBL issues. We would particularly like to thank Carol Swift, for her encouragement and comments on the manuscript.

We would also like to express our thanks to our respective spouses, Ian Uden and Sara Beaumont, who have encouraged and supported us throughout.

Last, but not least, we would like to express our gratitude to God who has given us the grace and strength to undertake a difficult task during a very busy teaching schedule.

Chapter I

Traditional vs. Cognitive Learning

Introduction

In order to help our readers to have a better understanding of the PBL process, we feel that it is important first to understand something about traditional methods of learning and cognitive learning. Since the focus of PBL is to help students to learn better, an understanding of learning itself would give a better perspective of the process in PBL. This chapter will look at traditional approaches in learning and compare them with cognitive learning. This is followed by constructivist learning, a type of cognitive learning. Several models of constructivist learning are briefly reviewed.

What is the Difference between Instruction and Learning?

While learning is defined as a change in human performance or performance potential that results from practice or other experience and endures over time, instruction refers to that which is done to help students learn (Newby, Stepich, Lehman, & Russell, 1996). In schooling, instruction and learning often go hand in hand. Instruction is often associated with teaching. It is the creation and use of environments in which learning is facilitated (Alessi & Trollip, 2001).

According to Alessi and Trollip (2001), typical instruction consists of four phases: (1) presenting information; (2) guiding the learner; (3) practising; and (4) assessing learning. In order to help students to learn better, it is important to have an understanding and appreciation of the principles of how people learn.

Traditional Teaching

Teaching has come under tremendous scrutiny by parents, students, and government lately because of widespread dissatisfaction with the results. Traditional teaching is typically characterised as didactic instruction in which information is presented to students to learn with little consideration of how that information is used. The students sitting in the classroom are passive recipients of information. The teacher is the sole information giver, undertaking lectures to a large group of students. The students are empty vessels waiting to be filled with information from the teacher. From personal experience, the authors found that most students tend to lose concentration after 15 minutes. There is no interaction between teacher and students, or between students themselves. The typical classroom resembles a one-person show with a captive, but bored, audience. Classes are typically driven by teacher talk, or as information giver, and depend heavily on textbooks for the structure of the course. It is generally accepted that there is a subject content that the students must come to know. Information is often divided into discrete parts and builds into a whole concept. The tutors' objective is to transmit their thoughts and meanings to passive students. The goal of learning in this setting is to regurgitate the accepted explanation or methodology expostulated by the teacher (Caprio, 1994).

Another problem associated with this type of learning is that students often perceive what they have learned as detached from real-world cases. This is because knowledge is often taught as context-independent. There is evidence that unless students learn something in a way that includes an understanding of its significance or function, they may experience restricted access, even when applicable situations arise (Bransford, Sherwood, Vye, & Reiser, 1986). This is generally referred to as a transfer problem or the problem of inert knowledge. It is therefore important that students are given problems to do that allow them to practice skills in environments similar to those in which the skills will be used. The learning situation should promote application and manipulation of knowledge within the context of the ordinary practices of the target task. There is a vast difference between being told about a task's relevance and actually experiencing the relevance of new information first hand. We believe that the ultimate goal of education is to help students become masters of their own learning. In most situations, content is often presented to the learner in simplified, discontextualised, isolated chunks that encourage memorisation rather than problem-solving or higher-level thinking. Students often cannot see interrelationships among content areas, the inherent complexity of the content, and the content's applicability to actual problems and meaningful situations (Dunlop & Grabinger, 1994). It is important to consider two issues:

- How can we make the need and reason to learn content apparent?
- How can we help students actually apply the information they learn?

How, then, would we overcome the above paradigm of teaching and help students to become independent learners? Before we address these issues, it is important that we first have a look at learning: what it is, how it occurs, and the different types of learning.

What is Learning?

According to Driscoll (1993), learning is defined as a persisting change in human performance or performance potential. There should be a change in performance brought about as a result of the learner's interaction with the environment. There are other definitions of learning apart from Driscoll's. Schunk (1991, p. 2) defines the process of learning as:

1. A change, or the capacity for such a change, occurs in the learner's behaviour.
2. The change, or its capacity, results from practice or other forms of experience (e.g., observing others).
3. The change, or its capacity, endures over time (i.e., it is not something temporarily induced by fatigue, drugs, or illness).

These two definitions of learning show that for learning to occur, there should be a change in one's level of ability or knowledge. Learning is measured by the amount of change that occurs in an individual's level of performance or behaviour. This change occurs over time and results from specific experiences such as practice (Newby et al., 1996).

Why Bother to Study Learning?

Learning is important for both those who will be learning and those who will be helping, guiding, and facilitating learning in others. It is important to understand learning because there are specific actions and technologies that can have an impact on the quality and quantity of what is learned. Therefore, learning what learning is, how it occurs, and what factors combine to influence the learning process, enables us to change and influence the levels of ability and knowledge in the learner.

Unfortunately, there is no consensus among educators on how learning occurs. Views concerning the properties of learning among educators and psychologists have changed significantly throughout the 20th century. There are various theories that have been advocated by different theorists concerning how learning occurs. A theory is a set of related principles explaining the cause-and-effect relationship among events (Richey, 1986). Theories are important because of their ability to predict (i.e. theories inform practice) (Driscoll, 1993). Principles of theories can be translated into practical guidelines. Therefore, theories have practical value for learning. The theory that has relevance here is that of learning.

Learning theory is a set of related principles explaining changes in human performance potential in terms of the causes of those changes (Newby et al., 1996). It is the cornerstone of our educational systems. The way we teach is governed by what we know about how people learn. Because learning is a complex process, there is not a single learning theory that can explain the process (Driscoll, 1993). Although this is the case, three broad approaches are generally acknowledged (Newby et al., 1996; Alessi & Trollip, 2001). These are behavioural, cognitive, and constructivist theories. Each of these is now briefly reviewed.

Behavioural Learning

Behavioural learning is closely associated with the work of B. F. Skinner (1974), which maintains that learning should be described as a change in the observable behaviour of a learner made as a function of events in the environment. The primary focus of the behavioural perspective is on behaviour and the influence of the external environment in shaping the individual's behaviour (Newby et al., 1996). Learning in behaviourism is equated with changes in either the form or frequency of observable performance. It is accomplished when a proper response is demonstrated following the presentation of a specific environmental stimulus. Take, for example, the question, "What is 2 + 2?" The learner responds with "4." The question is the stimulus and the answer is the associated response (Ertmer & Newby, 1993).

The learner, in behavioural learning, is characterised as being reactive to conditions in the environment as opposed to taking an active role in discovering the environment. Memory is not typically addressed in behavioural learning. According to Ertmer and Newby (1993), behavioural learning is generally effective in facilitating learning that involves discriminations (recalling facts), generalisations (defining and illustrating concepts), associations (applying explanations), and chaining (automatically performing a specified procedure). However, this is not sufficient to explain the acquisition of higher-order thinking skills. The goal of learning in behaviourism is to elicit the desired response from the learner who is presented with a stimulus. Instruction is typically target-structured around the presentation of the target stimulus and the provision of opportunities for the learner to practise making the proper response (Ertmer & Newby, 1993). Learning in behaviourism is defined as a change in the probability of an observable behaviour. The traditional approach to learning in the classroom is largely based on behavioural learning. The emphasis is on specifying behavioural objectives or learning outcomes (what the students will be able to do at the end of the instruction) analysing learning tasks and activities and teaching to specific levels of learner performance.

Behavioural learning is useful to help us manage the way instruction is carried out. Just as we can set goals for appropriate behaviour, we can also express in behavioural terms the outcomes that we desire students to achieve. The only evidence of learning in behaviourism comes from the students' behaviour—what they do after instruction that they could not do before. Because of this, it is important to specify desired instructional outcomes in terms of clear, observable behaviour. These goal statements are generally referred to as behavioural objectives, instructional objectives, or performance objectives. Behavioural learning has contributed to many instructional innovations. Its principles continue to be a useful way to design instruction.

One of the main limitations of behavioural learning is that it ignores important unobservable learning such as thinking, problem solving, and reasoning, etc. Behavioural learning tends to put too much emphasis on the teacher and instructional materials and too little attention is paid to the learner. This limitation has led to a search for a new way of explaining human behaviour.

Cognitive Learning

Learning theory began to make a move away from behavioural learning models in the early 1960s and began to focus on learning theories and models from cognitive sciences. The emphases placed on observable behaviour are replaced by stressing, instead, more cognitive processes such as thinking, concept formation, reasoning, and problem solving.

Cognitive theory replaces behavioural learning in order to compensate for the inadequacy of behaviourism to explain many aspects of human activity. One of the main criticisms of behavioural learning is that learning is assumed to be the product of causal links between instructional stimuli and student responses that are strengthened and weakened through reinforcement (Hannafin & Hooper, 1993). Different responses to the same stimulus are attributed to complex stimulus-response-reinforcement networks that establish conditional associations and not to student mediation. Learning in cognitivism emphasises learning as a process and the role of the student in mediating learning. Learners in cognitive learning organise knowledge and meaning by modifying mental representation. Stimuli become inputs and behaviours become outputs in cognitive learning. The metaphor of the information processing system is often used to illustrate the process.

Cognitive learning is equated with discrete changes between states of knowledge rather than with changes in the probability of response. In cognitive learning, the issues of how information is received, organised, stored, and retrieved by the mind is important. Learning is concerned not so much with what learners do, but with what they know and how they came to acquire that knowledge (Jonassen, 1991). The most dominant of the cognitive learning theories is based on an information-processing approach. Whilst behavioural learning is defined as a change in the probability of an observable behaviour, emphasising the influence of the external environment, the information-processing theory has an internal focus.

Information Processing Theory

In the information-processing view, the learner is perceived as a processor of information in the same way as a computer. Learning occurs when information is input from the environment, processed, and stored in memory and output in the form of some learned capability. Learning is therefore perceived as information processing. Central to this is the role of memory as shown in Figure 1.1 (from Driscoll, 1993, p. 69). Stimulation from the learner's environment is transmitted as information to the information processing system. The information is briefly registered in one of the sensory memories. Sensory memory represents the first stage of information processing. There is a separate sensory memory associated with each of the five senses, but all are assumed to operate in the same way.

The information from the sensory memory is then transformed into recognisable patterns and enters the short-term memory (STM). This transformation is known

Figure 1.1. Information-processing model (Driscoll, 1993)

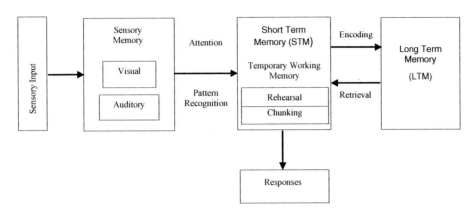

as selective perception, or feature perception (Gagné, Briggs, & Wager, 1988). This is when visually presented marks on a page of print become letters such as C, A, T, and so on, when they are stored in STM. Working memory only holds information for a very limited amount of time. The duration is typically less than 20 seconds unless it is rehearsed. Imagine trying to remember a nine-digit telephone number to dial it. Once it is dialled, it disappears from STM. Miller's (1956) chunking concept describes the capacity of STM. According to Miller's theory, a person can remember seven, plus or minus two, items in their STM, where an item can be a number, a face, a word, or any unit. Short-term memory only holds a limited amount of information, often as few as four items.

Information from the STM is again transformed by a process called semantic encoding to a form that enters the long-term memory (LTM) (Gagné et al., 1988). Encoding occurs when new and existing information is integrated in working memory (STM) and transferred into long-term memory. Long-term memory represents the permanent storage of information. Things to be remembered must be transferred from STM to LTM. There are two types of LTM: episodic and semantic memory. Episodic memory is memory for specific events. For example, you remember the circumstances surrounding how you learned a poem. On the other hand, semantic memory refers to all the general information stored in memory that can be recalled independently of how it was learned. You may not remember how you learned the poem because the circumstances surrounding the event were not particularly memorable, however, you do remember the skill. Long-term memory comprises schemata, organised networks of related knowledge. Each schema provides slots into which new knowledge is placed. Schemata also provide a framework within which related, but unfamiliar knowledge may be subsumed (Hannafin & Hooper, 1993). As a result, schemata are constantly refreshed and restructured through new knowledge, while additional connections among related schemata are made.

Information from LTM may return to STM through the process of retrieval. Retrieval requires the activation among various schemata that are cued based upon ongoing cognitive demands. The retrieved items may combine with others to bring about new kinds of learning. The STM is often known as working memory in this process. Some of the important principles of information processing theory for learning are discussed below.

The Importance of Prior Knowledge

Prior knowledge is often characterised, metaphorically, as schemata—organised networks of prior knowledge. Bartlett (1932) introduced the term "schemata" in his study of memory. According to Bartlett, schemas or schemata are the basis of all knowledge. Schemata provide a means by which learners can compare and contrast to-be-learned information with existing knowledge, assimilate new information meaningfully within existing knowledge, and continually restructure knowledge accordingly (Hannafin & Hooper, 1993). Availability of schemata improves metacognition (Flavell, 1979). More recently, schemas have been used to explain people's memories for stories.

Cognitive Engagement

The concept of cognitive engagement styles has a number of important implications for learning and teaching. Corno & Mandinach (1983) suggest that we can observe learners when they are giving sustained, engaged attention to a task requiring mental effort. Authentic, useful learning is produced by extending engagement in optimally complex cognitive activities. Cognitive engagement is inextricably linked with motivation through mental representations, monitoring, and evaluation of responses and strategic thinking (Stoney & Oliver, 1999). According to Schunk (1989), the amount of cognitive effort expended is an appropriate index of motivation as it relies on the learner focusing on mastering the learning task and maintaining a high sense of personal efficacy. Learning improves as the quality of cognitive engagement increases. There are two types of cognitive processing: superficial and deepened. According to Hannafin (1989), cognitive engagement is referred to as the intentional and purposeful processing of lesson content. Hannafin points out that engagement requires strategies that promote manipulation rather than memorisation. Engagement can be achieved by a variety of activities such as inducing cognitive dissonance, posing argumentative questions requiring the development of a supportable position, and causing learners to generate a prediction and rationale during a lesson (Hannafin & Hooper, 1993). Self-regulated learning is a facilitative style of cognitive engagement. It represents the highest form of cognitive engagement.

According to Corno and Mandinach (1983), self-regulated learning refers to the deliberate planning and monitoring of the cognitive and affective processes that are involved in the successful completion of academic tasks. They also suggested that for some learners these metacognitive processes of planning and monitoring may be so well developed that, at times, they appear to occur automatically.

Meaningful Learning Knowledge

It is important to have meaningful information stored in memory. There are three methods by which information may be meaningfully learned. These are: selection, organisation, and integration (Mayer, 1984). Information must be perceived or selected for learning to take place. Perceived information must be organised in working memory before it is stored in LTM. The nature of organisation in working memory determines the meaningfulness of the learning. When there is little guidance given to the learner as to the organisation of the content, the learner is unable to organise the content successfully, resulting in rote learning. Deeper and meaningful learning occurs when learners can organise the information by identifying logical relationships within the content. Integration of organised information with existing familiar knowledge is necessary for meaningful learning. Mayer (1989) also identifies methods that increase the meaningfulness of instruction. He has identified the use of conceptual models to be useful to improve retention and problem solving. Conceptual models help learners to build mental frameworks that focus attention on relevant lesson content and provide a means by which it can be used to generate solutions to unfamiliar problems (Engelbart, 1962).

Based on the information processing theory, learning in cognitive theory is described as a change in knowledge stored in memory (Newby et al., 1996). Memory plays an important role in cognitive learning. Learning results when information is stored in memory in an organised, meaningful manner. In cognition theory, a learner's thoughts, beliefs, attitudes, and values are considered to be influential in the learning process (Winne, 1985). According to Ertmer and Newby (1993), the real focus of the cognitive approach is on changing the learner by encouraging him/her to use appropriate learning strategies.

Because learning results when information is stored in memory in an organised, meaningful way, the emphasis is on students' cognitive processes and the critical role memory plays in helping students to translate new information into a meaningful form that can be remembered and used (Newby et al., 1996). The main role of the teacher is to arrange external conditions that will help the students attend to, encode, and retrieve information. In order to achieve this, Ertmer and Newby (1993) suggest making knowledge meaningful and helping learners organise and relate new information to existing knowledge in memory. Instruction must be based on students' existing mental structures to be effective. The information should be organised in a way that learners are able to connect new information with existing knowledge in some meaningful way.

Constructivist Learning

Cognitive learning theories have been challenged by the currently popular constructivist learning. The philosophical assumptions for both behavioural and cognitive theories are primarily objectivistic. The objectivist philosophy, or world view, holds that there is an objective world that we perceive more or less accurately through our senses. Learning is the process of correctly interpreting our senses and responding correctly to objects and events in the objective (real) world (Alessi & Trollip, 2001). According to Alessi and Trollip (2001), teaching through the objectivist view is the process of helping the learner correctly interpret and operate within the real world. Knowledge in objectivist learning is thought to exist independently of the learners. Learning consists of transferring that knowledge from outside to within the learner. Constructivist learning theory, on the other hand, is based on the assumption that knowledge is constructed by learners as they attempt to make sense of their experiences. Learners actively construct knowledge based on prior experiences and they are not empty vessels waiting to be filled. In constructivism, constructive processes operate and learners form, elaborate, and test candidate mental structures until a satisfactory one emerges (Perkins, 1991).

In constructivism, meaning is created by ourselves rather than existing in the world independently of us. There are many ways to structure the world and there are many meanings or perspectives for any event or concept. Meaning, in the constructivist view, is indexed by experience (Brown, Collins, & Duguid, 1989). Whilst objectivism emphasises the object of our knowledge, constructivism is concerned with how we construct knowledge. The construction of knowledge is a function of the prior experience, mental structures and beliefs that one uses to interpret objects and events. Constructivism does not preclude the existence of an external reality. It merely claims that each of us constructs our own reality—our interpretation of our perceptual experiences of the external world (Jonassen, 1991).

The constructivist assumptions of learning can be described as follows (Uden, 2004):

1. All knowledge is constructed (albeit socially) and not transmitted.
2. Knowledge and meanings result from activity and are embedded in activity systems.
3. Knowledge is distributed in persons, tools, and other cultural artefacts.
4. Meaning arises out of interpretation and, thus, multiple perspectives are recognised.
5. Meaning construction is prompted by problems, questions, issues, and authentic tasks.

Although there are several characteristics associated with constructivism, two stand out: good problems and collaboration (Newby et al., 1996).

Good problems are important because they are good for stimulating the explanation and reflection necessary for knowledge construction. A good problem (Brooks & Brooks, 1993) is one that:

*   Is realistically complex—Complex problems are more likely to trigger the different experiences of students and therefore promote different approaches to a solution.

*   Requires students to make and test a prediction—Knowledge is constructed as it is used to explain what has happened and to predict what will happen.

*   Is relevant and interesting to students—Students are likely to invest more effort in problems they perceive as relevant.

*   Allows for collaborative work—The problem should generate dialogue and negotiation that encourage the exploration of alternative implementations.

Collaboration is essential because students learn through interaction with others. There can be two kinds of collaboration in constructivist learning: student-to-student and teacher-with-students. In the first case, students work as peers, applying their combined knowledge to the solution of the problem. The dialogue that results from this combined effort provides students with the opportunity to test and refine their understanding in an ongoing process. Collaboration with the tutor is likened to an apprenticeship (Collins, Brown, & Newman, 1989), in which the teacher participates with the students in the solution of meaningful and realistic problems. Teachers may not know the answer to the problem, but they serve as models and guides, showing students how to reflect upon their evolving knowledge and possible direction when the students are having difficulties. This means that the teacher should pose good problems that are realistically complex and personally meaningful to students.

In the learning, teachers should encourage group activities in which the teacher and the students can participate in a community of inquiry (CTGV, 1993) to explore and apply their combined knowledge. The relationship between student and teacher is that of an apprentice to his master. Students and teacher work together to solve problems, with teacher providing direction, consistent with the experiences and knowledge of the students (Newby et al., 1996). The critical difference between cognitivism and constructivism is that cognitivism views learning as objective, representative of our experience, whereas constructivism defines knowledge as an individual interpretation of experience (Jonassen, 1991).

Learning Goals in Constructivist Learning

Instead of identifying the entities, relations, and attributes that the learners must know in the objectivist approach, constructivist learning identifies learning goals by emphasising learning in context (Duffy & Jonassen, 1991). According to Brown, Collins, and Duguid (1989), knowledge that learners deploy should be developed. This can only be achieved in the context of meaningful activity. Brown, Collins, and Duguid (1989) believe that learning is a continuous, lifelong process resulting from acting in situation. Thinking activities are central to constructivism (CTGV, 1991).

According to Driscoll (1993), problem solving, reasoning, critical thinking, and active use of knowledge constitute the goals of constructivist instruction. How do we bring about these goals? A variety of recommendations are given by researchers, based on the principles of constructivism. Most of these mainly emphasise the process of learning, rather than the products of learning. Driscoll (1993) provides the following recommendations:

- Provide complex learning environments that incorporate authentic activity;
- Provide for social negotiation as an integral part of learning;
- Juxtapose instructional content and include access to multiple modes of representation;
- Nurture reflexivity; and
- Emphasise student-centred learning.

Complex Learning Environments

One of the important principles that constructivists believe is that students should be exposed to complex tasks that they would be expected to face in real life. Real-life problems are typically complex and cannot be solved in a few minutes because they are ill-structured. The solving of the problem requires integration of knowledge and skills from different learning objectives. It is, therefore, important for learning environments to be provided so that learners can experience the full complexity and authenticity of the real problems. This means that the problem given to students should be realistic, reflecting, as accurately as possible, the problem students would be facing in their working lives.

Social Negotiation

Another important aspect of constructivism is that of social negotiation. Social interaction is essential for the development of higher human mental processes. Since social interaction is central to learning and thinking in constructivism, collaboration is considered essential in the learning environment. Collaboration is not about working together in groups or the sharing of individual knowledge between students. On the contrary, collaboration enables insights and solutions that would not otherwise come about to arise synergistically (Driscoll, 1993). An effective learning environment should provide a means for learners to understand perspectives from others. Learners should be given opportunities to defend their viewpoints and recognise those of others. There should be negotiation of viewpoints among learners in order to present alternative solutions.

Juxtaposition of Instructional Content

Many problems are complex and cannot be solved by looking at a simple answer. To solve this type of problem requires having instructional content from different perspectives. According to Spiro, Feltovich, Jacobson, and Coulson (1991), it is important to visit the same materials, at different times, in rearranged contexts, for different purposes, from different conceptual perspectives, for the learning of advanced knowledge acquisition. Driscoll (1993) suggests that using multiple perspective modes of representation serves as a means of juxtaposition.

Nurturance of Reflexivity

Reflexivity is the ability of students to be aware of their own role in the knowledge construction process (Cunningham, 1992). Metacognition is generally described as the awareness of one's own thinking and learning process (Driscoll 1993). It is important to help students to develop metacognition skills if they are to be self-directed learners.

In constructivism, reflexivity is more than metacognition. According to Driscoll (1993), in reflexivity, a critical attitude exists in learners that promotes awareness of how and what structures create meaning. The use of juxtaposition of instructional content and the emphasis on multiple perspectives can be used to support reflexivity.

Student-Centred Instruction

It is important that students take control of their own learning. Students should be actively involved in determining what their own learning needs are and how these needs are best met. It is generally acknowledged that students are not the best judges of their own learning needs. This means that students should be assisted in managing their learning tasks. This can be achieved through scaffolding or coaching. Many students may not have the skills to manage their own learning. It is the responsibility of teachers to encourage students to take this role. It is important that teachers or tutors provide an environment where the students can acquire these skills.

Modes of Implementing Constructivist Learning

The question often asked by teachers is: "How do we develop constructivist methods of instruction to achieve the goals of constructivist learning, such as reasoning, problem solving, retention, understanding, and the use of knowledge and critical thinking, as well as learning how to learn?" "What type of support can we give to students that would enable them to construct meaningful knowledge, based on their experiences in learning?" In constructivist learning, rather than attempting to map the structure of an external reality onto learners, we should help students construct their own meaningful and conceptually functional representation of the external world (Jonassen, 1991).

Since the 1990s, learning theories have been moving from cognitive theories that emphasise individual thinkers and their isolated minds to theories that emphasise the social nature of cognition and meaning (Uden, 2004; Vygotsky, 1978). Vygotsky's theoretical framework is that social interaction plays a fundamental role in the development of cognition. Vygotsky (1978) states, "Every function in the child's cultural development appears twice: first, on the social level, and later, on the individual level; first, between people (interpsychological) and then inside the child (intrapsychological)." According to Brown, Collins, and Duguid (1989), knowing and doing are reciprocal. Knowledge is situated and progressively developed through activity. Knowledge is, thus, contextually situated and is fundamentally influenced by the activity, context, and culture in which it is used.

There are several approaches advocated by researchers that have been shown to be effective in promoting constructivist learning. These include: cognitive apprenticeship (Collins et al., 1989), cognitive flexibility theory (Spiro et al., 1991), anchored instruction (CTGV, 1991), and problem-based learning (Barrows, 1992). Space does not permit a full description of all of these. Interested readers are referred to the appropriate constructivist learning literature for other approaches.

Cognitive Apprenticeship

Teaching and learning were accomplished through apprenticeship in ancient times. Apprenticeship today has largely been replaced with formal schooling, except in language learning for children, some on-the-job training, and graduate education. According to Collins et al., (1989), although formal schools have been relatively successful in organising and conveying conceptual and factual knowledge, standard pedagogical practices have made key aspects of expertise invisible to students. Collins et al. (1989) believe that there is too little attention paid to the process that experts use in carrying out complex or realistic tasks. The processes taught are confined to formulaic methods for solving textbook problems or on the development of low-level sub-skills in relative isolation. There are few resources given to higher-order problem solving activities that require students to actively integrate and appropriately apply sub-skills and conceptual knowledge. The practice of problem solving is not visible to students. Cognitive apprenticeship is a model of instruction, developed by Collins et al. (1989), that makes thinking visible to students in learning. These authors believe that cognitive apprenticeship can be adapted to the teaching and learning of cognitive skills.

The framework proposed by Collins et al. (1989) consists of four dimensions of a learning environment: content, method, sequence, and sociology. Relevant to each of these dimensions is a set of characteristics that should be used in considering or evaluating learning environments. The principles for designing

Table 1.1. Principles for designing cognitive apprenticeship environments (Collins et al., 1991, p. 43)

CONTENT: (types of knowledge required for expertise).	**Domain Knowledge:** Subject matter, specific concepts, facts, and procedures. **Heuristic Strategies:** Generally applicable techniques for accomplishing tasks. **Control Strategies:** General approaches for directing one's solution process. **Learning Strategies:** Knowledge about how to learn new concepts, facts, and procedures.
METHOD: (ways to promote development of expertise).	**Modelling:** Teacher performs a task so students can observe. **Coaching:** Teacher observes and facilitates while students perform a task. **Scaffolding:** Teacher provides supports to help the student perform a task. **Articulation:** Teacher encourages students to verbalise their knowledge and thinking. **Reflection:** Teacher enables students to compare their performance to others. **Exploration:** Teacher invites students to pose and solve their own problems.
SEQUENCING (keys to ordering learning activities).	**Global before Local Skills:** Focus on conceptualising the whole task before executing the parts. **Increasing Complexity:** Meaningful tasks, gradually increasing in difficulty. **Increasing Diversity:** Practice in a variety of situations to emphasise broad application.
SOCIOLOGY (social characteristics of learning environments).	**Situated Learning:** Students learn in the context of working on realistic tasks. **Community of Practice:** Communication about different ways to accomplish meaningful tasks. **Intrinsic Motivation:** Students set personal goals to seek skills and solutions. **Co-Operation:** Students work together to accomplish their goals.

Cognitive Apprenticeship environments are summarised in Table 1.1 (taken from Collins, Brown, & Holum, 1991).

Anchored Instruction

In traditional learning, knowledge is often regarded as an entity that exists independently of the learner or any context. Because knowledge is considered independent of the learner or context, it is typically considered to be objective, absolute, and unconditional. The goal in instruction is met if the students acquire this knowledge, usually transmitted by teaching mechanisms such as a teacher or a tutoring machine. In such an approach, the transmitted process is optimised if the knowledge can be specified and an ideal acquisition sequence identified (CTGV, 1993). Taking this view, cognition is regarded as the rule-based manipulation of symbols via processes that will ultimately be describable through the language of mathematics and logic (Duffy et al., 1993). However, there is a shift in the basic epistemology of schooling in recent years. According to Duffy, Lowyck, and Jonassen (1993), the constructivist epistemology views knowledge not as a collection of discrete entities, but as constructed in the context of the environments in which it is encountered. In constructivism, context is crucial to understanding. Meaning can only be created from context. Knowledge is constructed through social and collaborative interaction. Meaning and under-standing are the result of this social process.

Anchored instruction was developed by the Cognition and Technology Group at Vanderbilt (CTGV) (1993) based on the concept of creating a semantically rich "anchor" that illustrates important problem-solving situations. These anchors create a "macrocontext" that provides a common ground for experts in various areas, as well as teachers and students from diverse backgrounds, to communi-cate and build collective understanding (CTGV, 1993). According to the researchers at CTGV (1993), macrocontexts can be used to integrate concepts across curricula, through which meaningful authentic problems can be posed. The anchors can serve as contexts for collective inquiry in classrooms and in learning research. CTGV (1993) has developed the Jasper series based on the anchored instruction approach. The Jasper series is a set of specially designed, video-based adventures that provide a motivating and realistic context for problem posing, problem solving, and reasoning. The series provides students, teachers, and others the ability to integrate knowledge from a variety of areas, such as mathematics, science, history, and literature. The theoretical framework underlying the Jasper series are built on assumptions about goals and learning. In the Jasper series, the goal of learning emphasises the importance of helping students learn to become independent thinkers, rather than simply to become able to perform basic computations and retrieve simple knowledge facts. Students must learn how to identify and define issues and problems on their own rather than simply to respond to problems that others have posed (CTGV, 1993).

The basic assumption about learning in the Jasper series is based on constructivism. Students must be engaged in generative, rather than passive, learning activities. Central to learning in the Jasper series is the importance of anchoring, or situating, instruction in meaningful, problem-solving contexts that allow one to simulate, in the classroom, some of the advantages of apprenticeship learning (Brown et al., 1989). It is, therefore, important to create shared environments that permit sustained exploration by students and teachers in order to allow them to understand the kinds of problems and opportunities that experts in various areas encounter and the knowledge that these experts use as tools.

Another feature of the Jasper series is the use of co-operative learning and co-operative problem solving by groups. Researchers argue that in co-operation, students have the opportunity to form committees of enquiry that allow them to discuss, explain, and learn with understanding (Vygotsky, 1978). The design principles of the Jasper series are shown in Table 1.2 (CTGV, 1993).

Although implementation of the Jasper series does not require computers, it has included specifically designed multimedia publishing software that allows students and teachers to research various topics (CTGV, 1993).

We believe that cognitive apprenticeship is a useful instructional method for constructivist learning. The model incorporates many of the important characteristics of effective learning and will form many of the principles of problem-based learning. In cognitive apprenticeship, the tutor does not have to take on the role of an expert. Instead, tutors need to encourage students to explore questions that tutors cannot answer and to challenge solutions the experts have found. That is, to allow the role of expert and student to be transferred. Cognitive apprenticeship encourages the student to become the expert (Collins et al., 1989).

It is our belief that the development of cognitive and metacognitive skills is important for students. Several important principles from research in constructivism can be used to teach these skills. Among these are:

- Learning skills should be focused on authentic or real-world problems (Collins et al., 1989);
- The tutor should act as a coach (Collins et al., 1991);
- Support collaborative construction of knowledge through social negotiation (Savery & Duffy, 1995);
- Provide access to expert performance and the modelling process (Collins et al., 1989);
- Stress conceptual interrelatedness, providing multiple representations or perspectives on the content (Jonassen, 1991);
- Promote exploration by formulating the problems to be solved (Collins et al., 1989);
- Promote reflection (Collins et al., 1989);
- Provide coaching (Collins et al., 1989);
- Provide scaffolding (Collins et al., 1989);
- Provide articulation (Collins et al., 1989);
- Provide for assessment, based on authentic tasks; and
- Provide exploration.

Table 1.2. Seven principles underlying the Jasper series

Design Principles	Hypothesised Benefits
Video-based format.	• More motivating. • Easier to search. • Supports complex comprehension. • Especially helpful for poor readers, yet it can also support learning.
Narrative with realistic problem rather than lecture on video.	• Easier to remember. • More engaging. • Primes students to notice the relevant mathematics and reasoning for everyday events.
Generative format (i.e., the stories and students must generate the problems to be solved).	• Motivating to determine the ending. • Teaches students to find and define problems to be solved. • Provides enhanced opportunities for reasoning.
Embedded data design (i.e., all the data needed to solve the problem are in the video).	• Permits reasoned decision making. • Motivating to find. • Puts students on an "even keel" with respect to relevant knowledge. • Clarifies how relevance of data depends on specific goals.
Problem Complexity (i.e., each adventure involves a problem of at least 14 steps).	• Overcomes the tendency to try for a few minutes and then give up. • Introduce levels of complexity characteristic of real problems. • Helps students deal with complexity. • Develop confidence in abilities.
Pairs of related adventures.	• Provides extra practice on core schema. • Helps clarify what can be transferred and what cannot. • Illustrate analytical thinking.
Links across the curriculum.	• Helps extend mathematical thinking to other areas (e.g., history, science). • Encourages the integration of knowledge. • Supports information finding.

Cognitive Flexibility Theory

According to Spiro et al. (1991), effective instruction must simultaneously consider several highly intertwined subjects such as:

• The constructive nature of understanding;
• The complex and ill-structured features of the knowledge domain;

- Patterns of learning; and
- A theory of learning that addresses known patterns of learning failure.

Based on a consideration of the interrelationships between these topics, they have developed a set of principal recommendations for the development of instructional hypertext systems to promote successful learning for difficult subject matter.

Cognitive flexibility theory (CFT) is an integrated theory of learning, mental representation, and instruction. It provides a number of heuristics to design instruction that avoids over-simplification by providing real-world cases, using multiple representations of content in order to enhance transfer and require knowledge construction by the learners, not knowledge retrieval. A central tenet of the theory is that revisiting the same material at different times, for different purposes, and from different conceptual perspectives, is essential for attaining the goals of advanced knowledge acquisition.

The metaphor that is used in cognitive flexibility theory is the criss-crossed landscape. The idea is the suggestion of a non-linear and multidimensional traversal of complex subject matter, returning to the same place in the conceptual landscape on different occasions, coming from different directions. The teaching strategy is the use of hypertexts that allow the students considerable control as they explore and browse through a content domain (Uden, 2004).

How Do We Help Learners to Acquire the Necessary Cognitive and Metacognitive Skills?

The subsequent chapters will show how some of the above principles can be used to help learners in problem-based learning.

Conclusion

There is no definitive answer to the question of how the concept of PBL was developed in relation to educational theories. Researchers suggest that the learning approach is derived from a number of educational theories through the practice of PBL in medical programs, such as McMaster and Case Western reserve programs. The most prominent theoretical principles come from cognitive learning theories such as constructivism. The constructivism orientation emphasises the individual's active construction of knowledge and meaning. Many of the principles of constructivist learning are evidenced in PBL. These principles include: understanding comes from interactions with our environment; and cognitive conflict stimulus learning and knowledge evolves through evaluation of the viability of individual understanding (Savery & Duffy, 1995).

References

Alessi, S. N., & Trollip, S. R., (2001). *Multimedia for learning: methods and development*. Needham Heights, MA: Allyn & Bacon.

Barrows, H. S. (1992). *The tutorial process*. Springfield: Southern Illinois University, School of Medicine.

Bartlett, F. C. (1932). *Remembering*. Cambridge: Cambridge University Press.

Bransford, J. D., Sherwood, R., Vye, N. J., & Reiser, J. (1986). Teaching thinking and problem-solving. *American Psychologist, 41*(10), 1078-1089.

Brooks, J. G. F., & Brooks, M. G. (1993). *In search of understanding: The case of constructivist classroom*. Alexandria, VA: American Society for Curriculum Development.

Brown, J. S., Collins, A., & Duguid, P. (1989). Situated cognition and the culture of learning. *Educational Researcher, 18,* 32-42.

Brown, J. S., & Palincsar, A. S (1989). Guided, co-operative learning and individual knowledge acquisition. In L. B. Resnick (Ed.), *Knowing, learning and instruction: Essays in honor of Robert Glaser* (pp. 393-451). Hillsdale, NJ: Lawrence Erlbaum Associates.

Caprio, M. W. (1994). Easing into constructivism: Connecting meaningful learning with student experience. *Journal of College Science Teaching, 23*(4), 210-212.

Cognition and Technology Group at Vanderbilt (CTGV). (1991). Technology and the design of generative learning environments. *Educational Technology, 31*, 34-40.

Cognition and Technology Group at Vanderbilt (CTGV) (1993). Designing learning environments that support thinking: The Jasper series as a case study. In T. M. Duffy, J. Lowyck, & D. H. Jonassen (Eds.), *Designing environments for constructive learning*. NATO-ASI Series. London: Springer-Verlag.

Collins, A. S., Brown, J. S., & Holum, A. (1991). Cognitive apprenticeship: Making thinking visible. *American Educator Writer, 15*(3), 6-11, 38-46.

Collins, A. S., Brown, J. S., & Newman, S. F. (1989). Cognitive apprenticeship: Teaching the craft of reading, writing and mathematics. In L. B. Resnick (Ed.), *Knowing, learning and instruction: Essays in honor of Robert Glaser* (pp. 453-494). Hillsdale, NJ: Lawrence Erlbaum Associates.

Corno, L., & Mandinach, E. B. (1983). The role of cognitive engagement in classroom learning and motivation. *Educational Psychologist, 18*(2), 88-108.

Cunningham, D. J. (1992). Beyond educational psychology: Steps toward and educational semiotic. *Educational Psychology Review, 4*, 164-194.

Driscoll, M. P. (1993). *Psychology of learning for instruction.* Boston: Allyn & Bacon.

Duffy, T. M., & Jonassen, D. H. (1991). Constructivism: New implications for instructional technology. *Educational Technology, 31*, 7-12.

Duffy, T. M., Lowyck, J., & Jonassen, D. H. (1993). *Designing environments for constructive learning.* London: Springer-Verlag.

Dunlop, J. C., & Grabinger, R. S. (1994). *Rich environments for active learning in the higher education classroom.* NATO-ASI Workshop, Herriott-Watt University, Edinburgh, Scotland.

Engelbart, D. C. (1962). *Augmenting human intellect: A conceptual framework.* Menlo Park, CA: Stanford Research Institute. (Summary report AFOSR-3233). Retrieved September 27, 2003, from http://www.bootstrap.org/augdocs/friedewald030402/augmentinghumanintellect/ahi62index.html

Ertmer, P. A., & Newby, T. J. (1993). Behaviourism, cognitivism, constructivism? Comparing critical features from an instructional design perspective. *Performance Improvement Quarterly, 6*(4), 50-72.

Flavell, J. H. (1979). Metacognition and cognitive monitoring: A new area of cognitive development inquiry. *American Psychologist, 34*, 906-911.

Gagné, R. M., Briggs, L. J., & Wager, W. W. (1988). *Principles of instructional design* (3rd ed.). London: Holt, Rinehart & Winston.

Hannafin, M. J. (1989). Instructional strategies and emerging instructional technologies: Psychological perspectives. *Canadian Journal of Educational Communication, 18*, 167-179.

Hannafin, M. J., & Hooper, S. R. (1993). Learning principles. In M. Fleming & W. Levie (Eds.), *Instructional message design: Principles from behavioural and cognitive sciences* (2nd ed.). Englewood Cliffs, NJ: Educational Technology Publications.

Jonassen, D. H. (1991). Objectivism vs. constructivism: Do we need a philosophical paradigm shift? *Educational Research & Development, 38*(3),
5-14.

Mayer, R. E. (1984). Aids to text comprehension. *Educational Psychologist,
19,* 30-42.

Mayer, R. E. (1989). Models for understanding. *Review of Educational
Research, 59,* 43-64.

Miller, G. A. (1956). The magic number seven, plus minus teo: Limits on our
capacity for processing information. *The Psychological Review, 63,* 81-
97.

Newby, T. J., Stepich, D. A., Lehman, J. D., & Russell, J. D. (1996).
*Instructional technology for teaching and learning: Designing in-
struction, integrating computers, and using media.* Englewood Cliffs,
NJ: Merrill/Prentice-Hall.

Perkins, D. (1991). Technology meets constructivism: Do they make a marriage? *Educational Technology, 35*(5), 18-33.

Richey, R. (1986). *The theoretical and conceptual bases of instructional
design.* London: Kogan-Page.

Savery, J. R., & Duffy, T. M. (1995). Problem-based learning: An instructional
model and its constructivist framework. *Educational Technology, 35,*
31-37.

Schunk, D. (1989). Self- efficacy and cognitive skill learning. In C. Ames & R.
Ames (Eds.), *Research on motivation in education: Goals and cognition* (Vol. 3, pp. 13-44). San Diego: Academic Press.

Schunk, D. H. (1991). *Learning theories: An educational perspective.*
Englewood Cliffs, NJ: Merrill/Prentice-Hall.

Skinner, B. F. (1974). *About behaviourism.* New York: Knoph.

Spiro, R. J., Feltovich, P. J., Jacobson, M. J., & Coulson, R. L. (1991). Cognitive
flexibility, constructivism, and hypertext: Random access instruction for
advanced knowledge acquisition in ill-structured domains. *Educational
Technology, 31,* 24-33.

Stoney, S., & Oliver, R. (1999). Can higher order thinking and cognitive
engagement be enhanced with multimedia? *Interactive Multimedia Electronic journal of Computer-Enhanced Learning, (1)*2.

Uden, L. (2004). Editorial. *International Journal of Learning Technology,
1*(1), 1-15.

Vygotsky, L. S. (1978). *Mind in society: The development of higher psychological processes.* Cambridge, MA: Harvard University Press.

Winne, P. H. (1985). Cognitive processing in the classroom. In T. Husen & T. N. Postlethwaite (Eds.), *The international encyclopaedia of education* (Vol. 2, pp. 795-803). Oxford: Pergamon Press.

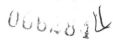

Chapter II

What is Problem-Based Learning?

Introduction

Employers today are demanding communication, team, and problem-solving skills. Few of these skills are evident in the classroom, as students memorise facts for regurgitation. According to Vernon and Blake (1993), problem-based learning is more than a teaching method. It is a complex mixture of general teaching philosophy, learning objectives, and goals. PBL is an instructional approach that uses problems as a context for students to acquire problem-solving skills and knowledge. This chapter describes the shift from traditional teaching methods to PBL. It discusses the characteristics of PBL and explains how it differs from other approaches, such as case-based, project-based, and lecture-based approaches.

Skills Demanded by Employers

Tutors today are facing the continuing challenge to teach pre-professionals to learn to think and solve problems like professions in their fields by linking theory with practice. Employers are now seeking graduates with strong abilities in problem solving, communication, teamwork, and leadership (Carnevale, 2000;

Rao & Sylvester, 2000). Although graduates are entering employment with adequate technical skills, they lack process skills, such as communication and problem solving, that are necessary for successful job performance. These are the skills that are most often lacking (College Placement Council, 1994).

There have been calls for reform in higher education as legislators and national professional associations question the quality of classroom expertise (Braxton, Eimers, & Bayer, 1996).

Before we proceed with redefining the academic learning environments where students can acquire the necessary skills that will prepare them for the job market, it is necessary to examine the problems with our current teaching approach.

Problems with Traditional Learning

University education should, ideally, provide students with the necessary skills, values, and attitudes that are essential to cope with the dynamic complexities of the modern world. On the contrary, employers are complaining that graduates are not prepared with the practical knowledge and skills needed to perform effectively in their professions. It is generally acknowledged by critics that in university learning, the theory students learn is separated from the practice and, thus, there is a lack of deep learning about the complex issues and problems that graduates have to face in the real world.

There has been much criticism leveled at traditional methods of teaching and learning in higher education. In traditional learning, students are often exposed to rule-based models in which they are expected to memorise content in order to prepare for tests and the certifying public examinations. Textbooks do not help students develop problem-solving, critical thinking, and self-directed learning skills. There is virtually no contact with real work environments. It is no surprise, then, that students are unprepared for the ambiguities that exist in the real world.

Another factor contributing to the inability to deliver the sought-after skills demanded by employers is that traditional approaches to computing and engineering education are devoid of cross-disciplinary integration, having insufficient interface with real-life problems and exhibiting insufficient retention of basic knowledge. There is also the problem of students' inability to apply knowledge to actual cases, as well as concerns over the accuracy of their knowledge base. Courses are often fragmented, having very little relationship to one another (Toin, 1997).

Finucane, Johnson, and Prideaux (1998) cited the following criticisms for the traditional approach to learning in medicine:

- It creates an artificial divide between the basic and the clinical sciences;
- Its application of the acquired knowledge can be difficult; and
- Its acquisition and retention of information that has no apparent relevance can be boring and even demoralising for students.

In order to meet the demand of employers for graduates possessing the problem-solving, communication, critical thinking, team work, and self-directed learning skills, there is an urgent need to change the way we teach. There should be reform and a paradigm shift in our learning methods.

A Paradigm Shift

In a traditional class, the teacher is expected to deliver a lecture to the students. Students are required to memorise a large number of facts. The set of facts may or may not be relevant to real-world practice. The students in this learning situation are passive recipients. They may or may not learn the facts in a way that is useful in actual practice or work situations. Students here may pass the examination, but are unable to apply the facts or knowledge to their daily work situations. The teacher is the expert and sage, whose job it is to transmit knowledge to the students. Students are treated as empty vessels to be filled up with knowledge from the teacher. However, while this may have worked in the past, this method of learning is no longer adequate to produce the type of employees that society demands. It is especially true for computing students.

Educating computing students is particularly difficult. The subject undergoes rapid changes each day. There is a large amount of material to be learned and it is conceptually complex. Most of the problems these students face in real life are ill-structured. Information needs to be discovered about the problem. Much of the information is dynamic and changes as the problem emerges. Decisions must be made, and actions taken, in the absence of complete information. Finally, computer technology is advancing at such a rapid rate that students must be able to keep pace with the advancements and acquire the necessary knowledge on demand. This requires the ability to learn. Learning-to-learn is not something that the traditional classroom teaches students. Currently, there is little being done to develop the necessary competencies and skills that employers demand of future graduates.

Critical thinking skills are beginning to be demanded by today's employers of graduate computer engineers. The rapid advances in science and technology, the expanding body of knowledge, and the dynamic and on-demand delivery of projects require computer personnel to think critically. Employees also need to be able to think critically in order to remain competitive in a complex and dynamic world. As educators, we are challenged to teach engineers to learn to think and solve problems like professionals in their field and to link theory to practice. This calls for reform in higher education because traditional methods in education are not preparing students for the job market. Students cannot perform decision-making and problem-solving tasks associated with their profession. It is, therefore, important for us to examine and redefine the academic learning approach.

This is increasing the pressure on higher education establishments, such as universities, especially in the computing, engineering, and technology courses, to reform the way students are taught and the ways in which they learn. The reason given is that traditional teaching practices are not able to deliver the skills demanded of students by employers. A dramatic shift from the traditional view of cognitive development resulting from one's reception of knowledge transmission by teachers should be considered. Problem-based learning (PBL) offers a teaching tool that can provide us with the answer that we urgently need to make the move to achieve the demands of employers.

The attributes of problem-based learning classrooms provide a framework for future learning (Wilson & Cole, 1996). Advocates of PBL argue that it provides an effective environment for future professionals who need to access knowledge across a wide range of disciplines. PBL provides facilities for:

- Encouraging assertion of ideas;
- Not relying on order or training;
- Not fearing failure;
- Providing time and resources;
- Developing expertise;
- Giving positive, constructive feedback that is work or talk focused;
- Encouraging a spirit of play and experimentation;
- Providing a mix of styles and backgrounds with opportunities for group interaction;
- Making a safe place for risk taking;
- Allowing free choice in task engagement; and
- Offering rewards that recognise achievements or enable additional performance, but maintain intrinsic motivation rather than controlling behaviour (Amabile, 1996).

PBL is Constructivist Learning

PBL is a constructivist learning model. It is based on some of the central tenets of constructivism (Savery & Duffy, 1995), which include:

- Construction is in our interaction with the environment. Understanding is an individual construction based upon our experience with content, context, and the learner's goals. It is impossible to separate the knowledge domain from interaction in that domain.

- Cognitive conflict or puzzlement stimulates learning. The goal of the learner is central in considering what is learned. It is not only the stimulus for learning, but it is a primary factor in determining what the learner attends to, what prior experience the learner brings to bear in constructing an understanding.

- Understanding is influenced through the social negotiation of meaning. Knowledge does not represent some ultimate truth, but is simply the most viable interpretation of our experiential world. Social negotiation of meaning and understanding is based on viability.

In PBL there is emphasis on contextualisation of the learning scenario and learning though reflection is an important aspect of PBL. PBL is typically conducted in a small group-based approach, reflecting the constructivist principle of collaborative construction of knowledge by learners as well as the negotiation of meaning. Unlike conventional learning, PBL takes an integrated approach to learning based on the requirements of the problem as perceived by the learners. According to Schmidt (1983), the three essential principles of PBL are:

- Activation of prior learning via the problem;
- Encoding specificity; and
- Elaboration of knowledge via discussion and reflection on consolidated learning experiences.

PBL uses authentic, complex problems as the impetus for learning. It features the acquisition of both disciplinary knowledge and problem-solving skills. An open-ended problem is usually given to the students—similar to those students would face in the workplace. PBL encourages students to develop a context-rich knowledge base and the skills needed to apply that knowledge. Learning in PBL is achieved in an authentic context where students learn how to apply inert knowledge to real problems. These authentic contexts are vital to computing and engineering.

History of PBL

PBL originated in the medical schools at Case Western Reserve University in the United States (1950s) and McMaster University in Canada (1960s). These schools questioned how well traditional preclinical science courses trained physicians to be problem solvers and lifelong learners. Traditional information-laden lectures, given by content experts to large student audiences, seemed disconnected from the practice of medicine that required integration of knowledge, decision making, working with others, and communicating with patients (White, 1996). PBL was used to shift teaching in medical schools from a collection of subjects representing individual disciplines to an integrative programme of study engaging students in problem formulation and solving. Three other medical schools followed the McMaster example and adopted variations of the McMaster model for teaching medicine. These include: the University of Limburg at Maastricht in the Netherlands, the University of New Mexico in the United States, and the University of Newcastle in Australia. Since the 1970s, PBL has spread world wide and moved from medical education into other disciplines. For example, PBL is now being applied in many different subjects, including dentistry, pharmacy, nursing, health science, veterinary medicine, and public health (Camp, 1996). PBL has also been adopted in many other areas, such as architecture, law, engineering, social work (Boud & Feletti, 1991), high school (Barrows & Myers, 1993), education (Duffy, 1994); business (Milter & Stinson, 1993) and others. In recent years, PBL has been implemented in high schools for the teaching of biology and other subjects.

Why PBL is So Popular

One may wonder why, suddenly, there is such an upsurge of interest in an alternative way of learning and teaching. There is a continuing interest in PBL, generated by academia. We believe there are several factors that surround the uptake of PBL among educators in many disciplines other than medicine. These include computing, engineering, and technology learning.

According to Camp (1996), PBL is popular because it was the right solution identified by faculty at the time when there was a great need to overcome the lack of positive learning by medical schools at that time.

It is generally expected that students should be able to learn, remember, and continue to learn when they leave university. However, this is not the case in many situations. Although students can memorise and pass examinations with good grades, they seem unable to integrate or apply knowledge into their working lives. Most interestingly, students resist, or fail to do, any further learning. PBL provides positive results that help students to acquire life-long learning skills.

A contributory factor to the success of PBL as an innovation is that, in the few schools where it was attempted, it was perceived as very successful by faculty and students. This success has given confidence to other medical schools that PBL could be applied universally, or at least at their schools. Once PBL had been successfully implemented by several medical schools, it became a proven teaching method. As PBL began to be implemented more widely in medical schools, there was increasing interest from applicants who had heard about this program as undergraduates and sought admission to schools that had PBL programs (Camp, 1996). Many medical schools are interested in offering curricula that would enhance recruitment of students who have already developed an orientation to self-directed learning.

There is strong evidence that PBL students retain knowledge much longer than students taught using traditional teaching, although their learning may be less than that of traditional students. In studies where integration of basic and clinical knowledge are required, PBL students fared better in providing causal explanations of physiologic process underlying disease. PBL students are also able to transfer concepts and knowledge to new problems. PBL has an impact on students' motivation and self-directed learning skills (Camp, 1996).

To the authors, one of the most important contributing factors that influence the uptake of PBL is that it fits in with the current philosophical views of human learning, especially constructivism. Many of the principles of constructivism are relevant to PBL, including:

- Understanding comes from our interactions with our environment;
- Cognitive conflict stimulates learning;
- Knowledge evolves through social negotiation and evaluation of the viability of individual understanding (Savery & Duffy, 1995);
- Knowledge is constructed by learners, based on their prior experience;
- Reflection is necessary; and
- Coaching and modeling instead of teacher as expert.

There is evidence among academics that faculty and administrators at schools are not willing to be left behind by the new invocation to improve learning. Their desire not to miss the boat could be another factor that spearheads the implementation of PBL in some faculties (Camp, 1996).

The continuing popularity of PBL arises from the recognition that in traditional learning, students retain minimal information and most have great difficulty transferring knowledge learned in classes to solve real world problems.

What is Problem-Based Learning?

Problem-based learning (PBL) results from the process of working towards the understanding of, or resolution of a problem (Barrows & Tamblyn, 1980). The main educational goals of learning are:

- To develop students' thinking or reasoning skills (problem solving, metacognition, and critical thinking) and
- To help students become independent, self-directed learners (learning to learn and learning management).

The origin of PBL can be traced to John Dewey (1916). Dewey believed that students should have experiential, hands-on, direct learning. It is generally accepted that students learn best by doing and thinking through problems

Barrows (1985) believes that the main objective of medical education is to produce doctors capable of managing the health problems of those who seek their services in a competent and humane way. A doctor should have not only the knowledge, but the ability to use it. PBL allows medical students to integrate, use, and reuse newly learned information in the context of patients' problems. The symptoms, signs, laboratory data, course of illness, etc., provide cues to retrieval in the clinical context.

The problems that Barrows (1985) used were conventional case studies. To solve the problems, students have to research a situation, set appropriate hypotheses, develop learning issues, ask appropriate questions, and then produce their plans to solve them. This enables students to develop their clinical reasoning process. Barrows (1985) found that students who had been taught through PBL became self-directed learners. These students had the ability to formulate their needs as learners and also were able to select the best available resources to satisfy those needs. Barrows and Tamblyn (1980) summarised the PBL learning process as follows:

1.   The problem is first encountered in the learning sequence before any preparation or study has occurred.

2.   The problem is presented to the student in the same way as in real life.

3.   The student works with the problem that allows him/her to reason and apply knowledge to be challenged and evaluated as appropriate to his/her level of learning.

4.   Learning issues are identified in the process of working with the problem. These are used as a guide to individual study.

5.   Skills and knowledge learned by this study are applied to the original problem to evaluate the effectiveness of learning and to reinforce learning.

6.   The learning that has occurred in working with the problem and in individualised study is summarised and integrated into the student's existing knowledge and skills. (Barrows & Tamblyn, 1980, pp. 191-192)

Learning—not the completion of the project—is the main aim in PBL. The problem is the means to an end. The main focus of PBL is to confront students with a problem to solve as a stimulus for learning (Boud & Feletti, 1991). The problem does not test skills, but assists in the development of the skills themselves. Problems in PBL have no single solution. They are ill-structured, messy, and complex in nature, requiring problem-solving and critical thinking skills to resolve them. By working through the problems, students learn the necessary skills to deal with real-life problems that they have to face in the real world.

According to Vernon and Blake (1993), PBL is the study of real or hypothetical cases in small discussion groups engaged in collaborative independent study using hyperthetico-deductive reasoning with a style of faculty direction that concentrates on group process rather than the provision of information.

PBL is both a curriculum and a process (Samford, 2003). The curriculum consists of carefully selected and designed problems that demand, from the learner, acquisition of critical knowledge, problem-solving proficiency, self-directed learning strategies, and team participation skills. The processes replicates commonly used approaches to solving problems encountered in real life. In addition to traditional assessment methods, peer and self assessment are also important.

Students in PBL acquire many important skills that are essential in life. PBL encourages students to take an inquisitive and detailed look at all issues, concepts, and problems within the given problem. It also enables students to develop skills, such as literature retrieval, critical appraisal of available information, and ability to seek information from peers and experts. In PBL, students are more involved in their learning and take full responsibility for that learning. We believe that PBL empowers students with:

- Problem-solving skills
- Information skills
- Computing skills
- Thinking skills
- Communication skills
- Team working skills
- Management skills
- Learning-to-learn skills

PBL Differs from Traditional Learning

PBL is a constructivist teaching model that helps students learn how to solve problems and think—skills not often acquired in traditional university learning. The essential feature of PBL is that content is introduced in the context of complex, real world problems. The problem comes first (Boud & Fletti, 1991). This is in contrast with conventional teaching, where concepts are presented before end-of-chapter problems.

In a traditional didactic lecture or tutorial, students are required to apply information provided by the tutor in order to solve the problem and show they have understood the theory or to demonstrate the application of the theory.

In PBL, students work in small groups to identify what they know and what they do not know. Students must learn to solve the problem. These are prerequisite for understanding the problem and making decisions required by the problem. Students in PBL are required to go beyond their textbooks to pursue knowledge in other resources between group meetings (White, 1996).

Unlike a typical classroom, where students work on their own, in PBL, students have to work as a team to solve problems. Co-operation is essential to the learning process. Instead of being passive recipients of information as in traditional lectures, students in PBL are active participants in learning. Students are encouraged to co-operate with other students in learning instead of competing with each other.

Students in PBL learn how to learn and also learn about the subject content. Unlike traditional subject learning, students in PBL not only have to concentrate on knowledge, but also on skills to solve real world problems. Learning how to learn becomes important in addition to acquiring knowledge in subject content. Students in PBL need to move away from a search for a solution for a problem, to identifying what they have to learn and how they can best learn to solve a given problem. They need to know how to identify the necessary information that they need to learn, where to get that information, and how to use the information to solve the problem.

Students have to take control of their own learning. The role of the tutor is very different from traditional learning. Instead of the teacher being a sage, the tutor in PBL acts as a facilitator or coach. Students are given greater control of their learning and expect to be independent rather than dependent on their tutor.

Students in PBL should be motivated by the problem to explore and focus on solving that problem rather than merely learning content. They need to know how they can go about exploring the problem, identify the missing information they do not know, and use the newly acquired information to solve the given problem. By doing so, students are allowed to acquire the learning-to-learn skills that they can transfer to other problems, thus achieving lifelong learning skills needed in their lives.

In subject-based learning, expertise is generally seen in terms of content, most of which is in the form of prepositional knowledge (knowing that). Whilst we do not deny the importance of content in subject-based learning, we do believe that content is best acquired in the solving of a problem. In PBL, the emphasis is placed on what is needed, on the ability to gain prepositional knowledge, as required, and to put it to the most valuable use in a given situation (Margetson, 1991). There is a much greater integration of "knowing that" with "knowing how" required in PBL. For example, the problem of designing an effective e-commerce application requires the integration of knowledge from software engineering, human-computer interaction, systems analysis and design, Web engineering, and project management.

In summary, PBL is an educational method characterised by the use of problem as a context for students to learn problem-solving and acquire knowledge about the basic and clinical science (Finucane et al., 1998). Students in PBL meet in small groups, two or three times per week, for tutorials. They are presented with a problem. In a series of steps, students discuss possible mechanisms and causes and develop a hypothesis and strategies to test the hypothesis. Students are then presented with further information and use this new information to refine their hypothesis, finally reaching a conclusion. The tutor acts as facilitator, guiding students in the group learning process. Students identify both their existing levels and gaps in their knowledge during the course of the exercise. These gaps form the basis for independent learning outside of the PBL tutorials. According to Finucane et al. (1998), the identification and pursuit of learning issues is a key feature of the PBL process.

Characteristics of PBL

Problem-based learning may come under different guises, however, there are certain characteristics that are identified in most PBL courses. First, PBL courses use stimulus material to engage students in considering a problem. Problems are typically presented in the same context as they would be found in real-life situations. In solving the problem, learning also crosses traditional disciplinary boundaries. Second, although resources are available to assist students to clarify what the problem consists of and how they might deal with it, information on how to solve the problem is not given. Students must find out for themselves. Third, PBL students work cooperatively in small groups or teams of five, including a teacher who acts as facilitator to help them in their learning process. Fourth, students must identify the learning issues in order to solve the problem. Fifth, students study resources, some of which may be provided, others that they have located for themselves, and then reapply this learning to the original problem. Finally, learning that has occurred from this process is summarised and integrated into the students' existing knowledge and skills (Boud & Feletti, 1991).

Margetson (1991) also identifies three important characteristics of PBL. These are:

- PBL encourages open-minded, reflective, critical, and active learning.
- PBL is morally defensible in that it pays due respect to both student and teacher, as persons with knowledge, understanding, feeling, and interests, who come together in a shared educational process.
- PBL reflects the nature of knowledge—that is, knowledge is complex and changes as a result of responses by communities of persons to problems they perceive in their worlds.

Before 1980, most of the PBL books focused on medical education. Recently, however, PBL has been applied in many different fields and different countries, as evidenced in the experiences of many different people, whose experiences are documented in the book by Boud and Feletti (1991). Many have reported very positive results. Some of the compelling features of PBL that have generated such interest are:

- It takes account of how students learn. Learning takes place most effectively when students are actively engaged and learn in the context in which the knowledge is to be used.

- We cannot learn all of the knowledge at university because of the rapidly changing society we live in. It is, therefore, important for students to be able to learn effectively when they need it.

- Students need problem solving, critical thinking, and self-directed learning skills in addition to content knowledge.

- Students are expected to become lifelong learners.

- Employers are demanding that students have metacognitive skills.

- No one person can possess all expertise. Employees are expected to work in teams or groups to solve problems.

An effective curriculum consists of a clear conceptual map of the domain of learning, a curriculum structure, a means for students to progress through the material, and a way of checking to see if both the students and the course are achieving what is intended (Boud & Feletti, 1991).

What are the Different Types of PBL Taxonomy?

Barrows (1986) has identified the following different variations that are commonly referred to by teachers as PBL.

Learner-Based Cases

The teacher presents students with information in lectures. Next, a case or two, usually vignettes, are presented to demonstrate the relevance of the information. Learner-based cases are typically used by teachers in their teaching and often referred to as PBL. However, this method does not directly foster any of the objectives required of PBL. Students are typically asked to understand the case presented in terms of information in the lectures and some of the information may be restructured by students. Although some hypothesis generation, data analysis, and limited decision making may be required, there are not any inquiry or case-building skills involved.

Case-Based Lectures

In this method, students are presented with case vignettes or more complete case histories before the lecture. The cases highlight material to be covered. The students must analyse the cases using their prior knowledge, before any new knowledge is provided. This effect causes some oriented structuring of information provided in lectures, as opposed to possible restructuring of information already provided, as may occur in the lecture-demonstration method. This is not self-directed learning.

Case Method

This is a method with a long and venerable history, typically used in business and law education. Students are given a complete case for study and research in preparation for subsequent class discussion. The subsequent interactive case discussion, in class with the teacher, combines both student-directed and teacher-directed learning. There is a stronger challenge to hypothesis generation, data analysis, and decision making with more active structuring of information. The method is also more motivating. However, the case study is already organised and synthesised for the students, thus limiting the amount of reasoning that will occur.

Problem-Based

Students are presented with an authentic problem to solve. They employ all the steps in the tutorial process to establish the database relative to their hypothesis. The teacher uses a coaching or facilitating approach that directly activates students' prior knowledge. A period of self-directed study is completed, students are asked to evaluate the information resources they have used, and then return to the problem as it was presented originally to see how they might better have reasoned their way through it and gained a better understanding on the basis of what they learned in self-directed learning. By doing this, students are also asked to evaluate their prior reasoning and knowledge. Another round of self-directed learning may be needed as a result of this second problem analysis and synthesis. The process is repeated until the problem is solved.

Project-Based and Problem-Based Learning

There appears to be some confusion between the terms problem-based learning and project-based learning. What is the difference? Project-based and problem-based learning share many similarities. Both approaches use problems or projects as the focus of learning. Students in both methods are engaged in real-world tasks to enhance learning. The approach adopted by both methods is student-centred and the role of the tutors is that of facilitators or coaches. Students in both methods work in groups. In both, assessment is peer-based, performance based, and authentic.

Although there are many similarities between problem-based and project-based learning, there are differences. According to Esch (2000), project-based learning typically begins with an end product or "artifact" in mind, the production of which requires specific content knowledge and skills and typically raises one or more problems that students must solve. Students in project-based learning typically use a production model. It consists of (Esch, 2000):

1.   Identify the purpose for the creation of the end product and audience;
2.   Research the topic;
3.   Design the product; and
4.   Create a plan for project management.

Students then begin the project, resolve problems and issues in production, and finish the product. The end product is supposed to be authentic, based on real-world production activities and making use of the students' own ideas and approaches to accomplish the tasks. Students are given time to reflect on and evaluate their work. Although the end product is the driving force in project-based learning, both content and knowledge that are acquired during the production process are important to the success of the project-based learning.

On the other hand, in problem-based learning, the problem is the focus of learning. Problems are often ill-structured to reflect real-life cases. PBL uses an inquiry model rather than a production model. First, students are presented with a problem. They then identify any knowledge they already have or know about the subject. Students also pose additional questions and identify areas that they need to know. A plan is drawn up to gather the information by members of the group. Students conduct necessary research individually and then reconvene to share and summarise their findings and new knowledge with other members of the group. They then present their conclusions. There is time for reflection and evaluation, but unlike project-based learning, the problem is the driving force of the learning.

PBL is often confused with case studies. Many tutors claim they are conducting PBL, but when investigated, what they are actually doing is nothing more than case studies. In PBL, the problem is given to students before they learn the knowledge. In case studies, students use the case to investigate previously learned knowledge. In PBL, the problem is posed so that students discover that they need to learn some new knowledge before they can start to solve the problem. By posing the problem first, before the learning of knowledge, students are motivated to learn. This is because students know why they are learning the new knowledge. Knowing why they must learn the new knowledge allows students to retain the knowledge learned and facilitates better recall. PBL encompasses many of the principles of good teaching. These include active learning, cooperative learning, prompt feedback, self-assessment, and opportunity for personal learning preference.

Objectives of PBL

PBL shares the same educational goals stated by Barrows (1992). They are:

- The development of students' thinking or reasoning skills (problem solving, metacognition, critical thinking).
- To help students become independent, self-directed learners (learning-to-learn, learning management).

The purpose of PBL is to produce students who will (Uden & Dix, 2004):

- Engage a challenge with initiative and enthusiasm;
- Be able to reason accurately, effectively, and creatively from an integrated, usable, and flexible knowledge base;
- Be able to address their own perceived inadequacies in knowledge and skills.
- Collaborate effectively as a team member; and
- Monitor and assess their own learning to achieve the desired outcome.

In addition to the above, other objectives include (Prpic & Hadgraft, 2002):

- Develop skills to identify a problem and design an appropriate solution for it.
- Develop an ability to identify issues that warrant further discussion and self-study within the context of a problem and cultivate skills necessary to become a self-directed learner.
- Recognise, develop, and maintain personal characteristics and attitudes necessary for a career as an engineering professional, including:

- An awareness of personal assets, limitations, and emotional reactions;
- Responsibility and dependability;
- An ability to relate to and show concern for other individuals;
- An ability to evaluate personal progress, that of other group members, and the group process itself.

Conclusion

In today's society, there is a need to foster creative thinking, an entrepreneurial spirit, and lifelong learning skills. Problem-based learning has been advocated by educators as an instructional method that can help students acquire these skills. It is important for educators to realise that education will fail if institutions continue to teach content to students without paying attention to how quickly that content knowledge will become obsolete. Teachers need to reflect on current educational practice and adapt to challenges that will equip students with problem-solving, critical thinking, and life-long learning skills that they need to survive in a competitive and changing society. PBL is an approach that can help us to provide our students with many of the sought-after skills demanded by employers. The PBL environment enables students to develop problem-solving skills as well as the necessary knowledge and skills to be learned in the subject content. It uses real-world problems, not hypothetical case studies with neat convergent outcomes. Students in PBL learn both content and critical thinking skills in the process of solving actual problems.

References

Amabile, T. M. (1996). *Creativity in context.* Boulder, CO: Westview Press.

Barrows, H. (1985). *Designing a problem-based curriculum for the pre-clinical year.* New York: Springer Publishing Company.

Barrows, H. S. (1986) A taxonomy of problem-based learning methods. *Medical Education, 20,* 481-486.

Barrows, H. S., & Tamblyn, R. N. (1977). The portable patient problem pack: A problem-based learning unit. *Journal of Medical Education, 52*(12), 1002-1004.

Barrows, H. S. (1988). *The tutorial process.* Springfield, IL: Southern Illinois University.

Barrows, H. S. (1992). *The tutorial process*. Springfield: Southern Illinois University.

Barrows, H. S. (1994). *Practice-based learning: Problem-based learning applied to medical education*. Springfield: Southern Illinois University, School of Medicine.

Barrows, H. S. (1996). Problem-based learning in medicine and beyond: A brief overview. *Bringing Problem-Based Learning*, 3-12.

Barrows, H. S., & Myers, A. C. (1993). *Problem-based learning in secondary schools*. Unpublished monograph. Springfield: Problem-Based Learning Institute, Lanphier High School and Southern Illinois University.

Barrows, H. S., & Tamblyn, R. N. (1980). *Problem-based learning: An approach to medical education*. New York: Springer.

Boud, D. J. (1985). Problem-based learning in perspective. In D. J. Boud (Ed.), *Problem-based learning in education for the professions* (pp. 13-18). Sydney: Higher Education Research and Development Society for Australia.

Boud, D. J., & Feletti, G. (1991). *Introduction*. In D. Boud, & G. Feletti (Eds.), *The challenge of problem-based learning* (pp 13-20). London: Kogan-Page.

Boud, D. J., & Feletti, G. (Eds.). (1991). *The challenge of problem-based learning*. New York: St. Martin's Press.

Boud, D. J., & Feletti, G. (Eds.). (1997). *The challenge of problem-based learning* (2nd ed.). New York: St. Martin's Press.

Braxton, J. M., Eimers, M. T., & Bayer, A. E. (1996). The implications of teaching norms for the improvement of undergraduate education. *Journal of Higher Education, 67*, 603-25.

Camp, G. P. (1996). Problem-based learning: A paradigm shift or a passing fad. *Medical Education Online, 1*(2). Retrieved March 30, 2005, from http://www.med-ed-online.org/f0000003.htm

Carnevale, A. P. (2000). *Community colleges and career qualifications*. Washington, DC: American Association of Community Colleges.

College Placement Council. (1994). *Developing the global workforce*. Institute for College and Corporations. Bethlehem, PA: College Placement Council.

Dewey, J. (1916). *Democracy and education*. New York: The Macmillan Company.

Duffy, T. M. (1994, August). *Problem-based learning*. NATO Advanced Study Institute Workshop on Supporting Learning in Computer Environments. Herriott-watt University, Edinburgh, Scotland.

Esch, C. (2000). *Project-based and problem-based: Same or different?* Retrieved March 30, 2005, from http://pblmm.k12.ca.us/PBLGuide/ PBL&PBL.htm

Finucane, P. M., Johnson, S. M., & Prideaux, D. J. (1998). Problem-based learning: Its rationale and efficacy. *Med J Aust, 168,* 445-448.

Knowles, M. E. (1980). *The Modern practice of adult education* (pp. 57-58). Cambridge: Prentice Hall.

Margetson, D. (1991). Why is problem-based learning a challenge? In D. Boud, & G. Feletti (Eds.), *The challenge of problem-based learning.* London: Kogan-Page.

Milter, R. G., & Stinson, J. E. (1993). Educating leaders for the new competitive environment. In G. Gijselaers, S. Tempelaar, & S. Keizer (Eds.), *Educatonal innovation in economics and business administration: The case of problem-based learning.* London: Kluwer Academic Publishers.

Prpic, K., & Hadgraft, R. (2002). *Problem solving objectives of problem-based learning.* Retrieved from http://www.dlsweb.rmit.edu.acc/eng/ beng0001/LEARNING/strategy/pblobjectives.html

Rao, M., & Sylvester, S. (2000). Business and education in transition: Why new partnerships are essential to student success in the new economy. *AAHE Bulletin, 52*(8), 11-13.

Samford. (2003). *Problem-based learning at Stamford University.* Retrieved from http://www.Samford.edu/pbl/definition.html

Schmidt, H. G. (1983). Problem-based learning: Rationale and description. *Medical Education, 17,* 11-16.

Toin, A. R. (1997). *Redesigning teacher education.* Albany, NY: Sunny Press.

Uden, L., & Dix, A. (2004). Lifelong learning for software engineers. *International Journal of Continuing Engineering Education and Lifelong learning, 14*(1-2), 101-110.

Vernon, D. T. A., & Blake, R. L. (1993). Does problem-based learning work? A meta-analysis of evaluative research. *Academic Medicine, 68*(7), 550-563.

White, H. B. (1996). Dan tries problem-based learning: A case study. In L. Richlin (Ed.), *To improve the academy* (Vol. 15, pp. 75-91). Stillwater, OK: New Forums Press and the Professional and Organisational Network in Higher Education.

Wilson, B., & Cole, P. (1992). An instructional design review of cognitive teaching models. *Educational Technology Research and Development, 39*(4), 47-64.

Chapter III

Why Problem-Based Learning?

Introduction

Since its adoption at McMaster University, Canada, in the 1960s for medical school teaching, PBL has gained popularity and has spread to many disciplines worldwide. Why has PBL become so popular? We will discuss the benefits of PBL for learning by students compared to traditional methods of teaching. Although PBL offers many benefits to students in their learning, it also has disadvantages. Some of these disadvantages are discussed in this chapter. The chapter concludes with personal testimonies from students describing their experiences using PBL in their studies as well as in their current jobs.

Benefits of PBL

Although PBL originated from the teaching of university students, it is increasingly being used in high schools, middle schools and elementary schools in many different countries. More and more tutors are taking on this method as a way of improving students' learning. It works well with educationally disadvantaged and minority students who, traditionally, have not done well in conventional educational settings. PBL provides an equal and exciting opportunity for learning to all students.

The PBL method is seen by many teachers as the answer to many of the problems of teaching in schools. It enables teachers to add many things to their traditional teaching, including problem-solving activities, critical-thinking exercises, collaborative learning, and independent study, and allows them to put these into context and give them meaning.

It is generally accepted by researchers that PBL offers many benefits to learning. Among these are:

- The PBL learning environment is more stimulating and human (Albanese & Mitchell, 1993; Norman & Schmidt, 1992).

- PBL promotes interdepartmental collaboration between basic and clinical scientists (Norman & Schmidt, 1992).

- Learning and teaching is more enjoyable for students and teachers in PBL (Albanese & Mitchell, 1993; Vernon & Blake, 1993; Norman & Schmidt, 1992).

- PBL promotes interaction between students and faculty (Finucane, Johnson, & Prideaux, 1998).

- PBL promotes deeper rather than superficial learning (Eagle, 1992; Newble & Clarke, 1986).

- Self-directed learning skills are enhanced and retained in PBL learning (Norman & Schmidt, 1992; Barrows & Tamblyn, 1980; Dolmans & Scmidt, 1996; Blumberg & Michael, 1992).

- PBL fosters self-directed learning skills (Barrows & Tamblyn, 1980; Norman & Schmidt, 1992; Blumberg & Michael, 1992; Dolmans & Schmidt, 1994).

- PBL promotes interaction between different disciplines (Finucane et al., 1998).

- PBL promotes collaboration between students (Banta, Black, & Kline, 2000).

- PBL enables reflection-in-action (Schön, 1983).

- PBL approach matches current efforts to involve students more actively in their education and it improves their learning (Norman & Schmidt, 1992).

- PBL enables students to spend more time on self-directed learning activities, using more information resources (Vernon & Blake, 1993).

- PBL enables staff to have more contact with students (Albanese & Mitchell, 1993).

There are also many studies conducted by researchers showing that PBL students performed better than traditional class students.

PBL Compared to Traditional Teaching

Research by Schmidt at Maastricht University found that medical students there had a much higher level of proficiency in the professional skills tested than those from another Dutch medical school with a conventional curriculum. There is some evidence that PBL contributes to the making of better doctors (Schmidt, 1998).

Students who acquire knowledge in the context of solving problems have been shown to be more likely to use it spontaneously to solve new problems than individuals who acquire the same information under traditional methods, learning facts and concepts through lectures (Bransford, Franks, Vye, & Sherwood, 1989).

Lieux (1996) conducted studies in a nutrition and dietetics course and found that PBL students perceived that they developed stronger thinking and problem solving skills, effective communication skills and sense of personal responsibility than students who received lectures.

Studies by Doucet, Purdy, Kaufman, and Langille, (1998) showed that Problem-Based Learning in continuing medical education in the area of headache management was associated with greater knowledge acquisition and with greater improvement in clinical reasoning skills than a lecture-based approach. PBL was also preferred by family physicians.

A study by Megendiller, Maxwell, and Bellisimo (2002), which examined the potential differences between PBL and traditional instructional approaches in building high school students' knowledge of macroeconomics, found that the PBL instructional approach was more effective than a traditional lecture/discussion approach in helping students to learn basic macroeconomics concepts.

Studies by Albanese and Mitchell (1993) show that learning was retained longer by PBL students than conventional students. The evidence comes from the fact that students' scores did not decline over time to the same degree as conventional students' scores.

Studies by Coulson, Eisenstaedt, and others, cited by Albanese and Mitchell (1993), show that PBL students have greater long-term retention than conventional students. The studies also showed that traditional students appear to have a broader grasp of content, whereas PBL students tend to retain their more narrowly focused knowledge longer.

It is obvious from the above discussion that PBL offers many learning benefits to students compared to traditional methods. Students who are taught using PBL have retained their learning better than non-PBL students. They also do as well in tests of content knowledge as students in traditional curricula (Banta et al., 2000).

Graduates of PBL found themselves to be better prepared than their peers in problem solving, self-directed learning skills, self evaluation, data gathering skills, and so forth (Albanese & Mitchell, 1993). Our own experience reflects that of these researchers (Uden & Dix, 2004).

Why PBL is a Useful Instructional Model

There is evidence from the various studies showing that PBL offers many benefits to students' learning. We will briefly review some of the reasons we believe PBL is a useful method of instruction.

PBL Promotes Deep Learning

The traditional method of teaching has been criticised for being devoid of cross-disciplinary integration, having insufficient interface with clinical problems, and exhibiting insufficient retention of basic knowledge and students' ability to apply to actual cases, as well as concern over accuracy of the knowledge base (Greening, 1998). This leads to shallow learning. To overcome this problem, students should be encouraged to develop deep learning. Deep learning promotes meaningful learning, where students can apply what they have learned to solve real life problems. There is strong evidence that PBL promotes deep learning in students (Coles, 1985; Newble & Clarke, 1986; Sobral, 1995).

PBL may be new to some people, but the strategies and materials used are not new. The materials used can be traced through case study methods (Christenen, 1987), experiential learning (Kolb, 1984), discovery learning (Bruner, 1961), and reflection in action (Schön, 1983).

Kolb (1984) suggests that learning is the process whereby knowledge is created through the transformation of experience. His theory provides a way of structuring and sequencing the curriculum and indicates how a session or whole course may be taught to improve student learning. Kolb's experiential learning structures a session or a whole course using a learning cycle. The different stages of learning are associated with the different learning styles. The core of Kolb's four stage model is a simple description of the learning cycle that shows how experience is translated through reflection into concepts, which, in turn, are used as guides for active experimentation and choice of new experiences. The four stages are concrete experience (CE), reflective observation (RO), abstract conceptualisation (AC), and active experimentation (AE). Because learners have to go through the cycles several times, it is best thought of as a spiral of cycles. The different stages are associated with distinct learning styles. Kolb believes that each student develops a preference for learning in a particular way. He identifies four learning styles, each of which is associated with a different way of solving problems:

- Divergers view situations from many perspectives and rely heavily upon brainstorming and generation of ideas.
- Assimilators use inductive reasoning and have the ability to create theoretical models.
- Convergers rely heavily on hypothetical-deductive reasoning.
- Accommodators carry out plans and experiments and adapt to immediate circumstances.

According to Kolb, learners learn better when the subject matter is presented in style consistent with their preferred learning styles.

Although advocates (Gibbs, 1992; Henry, 1989) of Kolb's theory believe that the theory provides a rationale for a variety of learning methods, including independent learning and learning by doing, there are a number of criticisms leveled at Kolb's method. First, the theory pays insufficient attention to the process of reflection (Greenway, 2004). Second, learning includes goals, purpose, intentions, choice, and decision making. It is not clear where exactly these items fit into the learning cycle (Rogers, 1996). Third, the model takes little account of the different cultural experiences and conditions. Fourth, the idea of stages or steps does not sit well with the reality of thinking (Smith, 1999). Fifth, Kolb's theory divorces people from the social, historical, and cultural aspects of self, thinking, and action (Reynolds, 1997). Finally, according to Miettinen (2000), Kolb's experience and reflections occur in isolation and there is the necessity for the individual to interact with other humans and the environment in order to enhance the reasoning and conclusions drawn.

According to Bruner (1965), the goals of education are to free society and assist students in developing to their full potential. Bruner believes that learning is an active, social process in which students construct new ideas or concepts based on their current knowledge. The student selects and transforms information, constructs a hypothesis, and makes decisions in the process of integrating experiences into their existing mental constructs (Flores, 2001). To Bruner, learning is a continual process that occurs in three stages. The first is enactive, in which children need to experience the concrete, such as manipulating objects in their hands or touching a cat, in order to understand. Iconic is the second stage when children are able to represent materials graphically or mentally. They can do basic additions in their heads. Finally, symbolic children are able to use logic, higher order thinking skills, and symbolic systems, such as using formula. Bruner believes that knowledge is best acquired through discovery (Bruner, 1961). Interaction between students and instructors is necessary for discovery learning. Tutors should try to encourage students to discover principles by themselves. The tutor and student should engage in active dialog. Bruner also believes that the curriculum should be organised in a spiral manner so that students continually build upon what they have already learned. To Bruner, there is no such thing as human nature, independent of culture. Culture moulds thinking and each culture enables individuals to make sense and prosper according to their culture. According to Bruner (1966), a theory of instruction should address the following major issues:

- Predisposition toward learning;
- The ways in which a body of knowledge can be structured so that it can be most readily grasped by the learner;
- The most effective sequence to present materials; and
- The nature and pacing of rewards and punishment.

Bruner also believes that good methods to structure knowledge should result in simplifying, generating new propositions, and increasing the manipulation of information.

Although Bruner's theory offers useful insights for learning, it is not without criticisms. According to Speaker (1999):

The immediate occasion for my concern with discovery—and I do not restrict to the act of finding out something that before was known to mankind, but rather include all forms of obtaining knowledge for oneself by the use of one's own mind ... It is rarely, on the frontier of knowledge or elsewhere, that new facts are discovered in the sense of being encountered as Newton suggested in the form of islands of truth in an uncharted sea of ignorance

In the course of cognitive growth, Bruner discusses three human information processing systems (enactive representation, iconic representation and symbolic representation) and what he calls " integration"—the building of higher order units, chunks or ensembles of the three. This poses the problem of the nature of internal representation systems and structure and their interactions as processes or structures. It also leaves open the possibility that there may be many other representational systems which a learner may use with any internal function or any external tool.

Finally, concerning a theory of instruction, Bruner is not able describe any of these in general details. The role of reflection in the professional practice has been inspired by the work of Donald Schön, "The Reflective Practitioner." Schön, in this work, makes references to two main processes of reflection in professional practice—reflection-*in* and reflection-*on* action. Reflection-*in*-action occurs in association with action and guides the process of action via knowledge in use, which is derived from theory in use, and makes limited contact with espoused theory. Espoused theories are those that are formally seen by the profession to guide action and encompass the formal philosophy of the profession. According to Schön (1983), reflection-in-action only occurs in situations where the action yields unexpected consequences and is not part of the actions that go according to plan. On the contrary, reflection-*on*-action is the form of reflection that occurs after action and relates, via verbalised or non-verbalised thought, to the action that a person has taken. It is a relatively narrow concept that is retrospective and has a role in learning, in informing action, and in theory building. Schön's work has inspired a great deal of other research, writing, and educational activity on the concept of the reflective practitioner. However, one of the main criticisms of Schön's work is that he is not very precise about the use of many of his terms, even though he tends to define them narrowly. In particular, he does not make a reliable case for the existence of reflection-in-action, which is the more contentious of the roles he gives reflection (Moon, 2002). However, the role of reflection-on-action does accord with the role of reflection in experiential learning and the common sense use of the term. Despite these limitations, reflection does have a role in learning and informing action and can be used in the building of theory to guide practice on action.

PBL Promotes Problem Solving Skills

Students will be faced with problems in real life that are ill-structured and complex. Information needs to be uncovered. As the information is uncovered, it dynamically changes the problem as it emerges. Decisions must be made, and actions taken, in the absence of complete information. Knowledge and techniques for acquiring information are changing at a phenomenal rate. This is particularly true for today's computing and engineering students. Computing and engineering students today must have the ability to identify formative evaluation and solve problems. Thus, problem solving skills are critical for these students. However, traditional teaching does not provide students with the development of relevant problem solving skills. The majority of the curricula emphasise facts, formulae and simple text book exercises that rarely reflect real life situations. There is little evidence in traditional approaches to develop deposition and competency necessary for students to become effective lifelong learners (Koschmann, Myers, Feltovisch, & Barrows, 1994). PBL can be used to help students develop the necessary problem solving skills needed by prospective engineers.

PBL Helps Students to Develop Metacognitive Skills

Very few problems in life or professional practice present themselves with all the information needed to understand them well enough to make valid decisions about their cause and their resolution. In almost all cases, more information is needed (Barrows, 1988). Some of the information needed to solve the problems has to come from knowledge stored in the memory of the learner; reflected facts, concepts, and prior experiences relevant to the problem. Some of this information may be recalled by the learner automatically, cued by memory associations with familiar factors of the problem encountered. To be able to recall the rest requires reflection, review, thought, and deliberation. In order to obtain some of the needed information, it is necessary for learners to obtain it by investigating the problem, making observations, asking questions, testing, and probing.

In addition to internal information, the problem solver needs external information in order to enlarge upon, correct, or sharpen the internal information in memory. This is particularly so in the case of new, unexpected, unusual or complex problems. There is a variety of external information, including records, books, technical reports, on-line information and journals, as well as various experts, and so on. Deliberation and reflection are again needed for learners to decide what external information resource is needed and where and how it might be found.

As the problem is being probed and examined through inquiry, new information is obtained. The new information may cause the perceived nature of the problem to change, as there may be new ramifications and twists to the problem, not anticipated at the outset. This, again, requires deliberation and reflection (Barrows, 1988).

At some point in the problem solving process, the learner is expected to make decisions and carry out actions on the basis of probability or intuition. As can be seen, the above steps, which are expected of a good problem solver, professional or expert, require deliberation, reflection, thinking, and review—generally referred to as metacognition. Barrows (1988) defines metacognition as the executive function in thinking; pondering, deliberating, or reflecting on the problem or situation; reviewing what is known and remembered about the kind of problem confronted; creating hypotheses; making decisions about what observations, questions, or probes need to be made; questioning the meaning of new information obtained from inquiry; pondering other sources of information; reflecting on and reviewing what has been learned, what it all means, and what needs to be done next,; and so on. In other words, metacognitive skills are "thinking about thinking." Metacognitive skills are required when we are confronted with a difficult, unexpected, or puzzling problem or situation. It is the conscious monitoring and direction of problem solving or reasoning activities (Barrows, 1988). This approach of metacognitive problem solving activities, used in many professions, is known as reflection in action (Schön, 1983).

PBL Embodies the Principles of Constructivist Learning

As a model used to implement constructivist learning, PBL encompasses many of the constructivist principles (Savery & Duffy, 1995). These include:

- Anchor all learning activities to a programme;
- Support the learner in developing ownership of the problem;
- Design an authentic task;
- Design the learning environment to reflect the complexity of real world problems;
- Design the learning environment to support and challenge the learner's thinking;
- Encourage the testing of ideas against alternative views and contexts; and
- Provide opportunity for, and support reflection on, both content learned and the learning process.

PBL Prepares Graduates for Jobs

Employers complain that graduates are not able to do the jobs they are given to do. There is mounting pressure from employers, government, and educational institutions, suggesting that a change is needed to address the problem. A driving force for this change is the realisation that successful employment and citizenship require different knowledge and skills than in the past (National Research

Council, 1996). It is no longer sufficient for future employees to possess only content knowledge that is traditionally taught in universities. Students who are the employees of tomorrow are expected to have the following abilities:

- To solve problems in real situations;
- To think critically;
- To work collaboratively in a team;
- To communicate effectively, verbally and in writing;
- To find, evaluate, and use appropriate learning resources; and
- To know how to learn effectively (lifelong learning).

There has been much criticism leveled at traditional lecture-based courses where there is a lack of attention to issues such as the relevance of subject, too little emphasis on encouraging team work, lack of attempts to develop problem-solving and critical thinking, and inadequate portrayal of the context of major issues. According to Boud and Feletti (1991), PBL addresses these criticisms head-on.

We believe that the aim of higher education is to assist students to develop their capabilities to benefit from, and cope with, modern life so that they can contribute productively to their society. This means that our role as teachers in higher education is to produce engineers, computer scientists, and so on. It is no longer adequate to help students acquire knowledge in the subject areas of study. Their learning must relate to their future professions. Students of today, who will become future employees, will expect massive changes related to their profession. This means that students of today will need to keep learning throughout their lives in order to cope with the rapid advances in society. This is particularly true in the engineering and computing fields. To be able to cope with lifelong learning requires not only domain knowledge, but also skills, such as communication, critical reasoning, a logical and analytical approach to problems, reasoned decision-making, and self-evaluation. We believe that PBL can help us to equip prospective employees with the necessary skills. PBL is perceived by tutors as an instructional practice that can help students acquire the necessary skills employers demand.

PBL Assists Students to Achieve Competencies

PBL is useful because it can be used as a method that will assist students in achieving a specific set of competencies. These include:

- Collaborating with others effectively in groups or teams;
- Coping with problems;
- Making reasoned decisions in unfamiliar situations;
- Thinking critically and creatively;
- Adopting a holistic approach to look at problems;
- Appreciating the views of other people;
- Identifying their own strengths and weaknesses and undertaking appropriate remediation, for example, through continuing self-directed learning;
- Adapting to and participating in changes within the organisation and the workplace; and
- Developing metacognitive skills for lifelong learning.

In addition to the competencies that can be acquired through PBL, it is also well suited to higher education learning. PBL allows the students to be involved in active learning by posing questions and seeking their respective answers. Learning through PBL integrates different subjects through the context of solving the real life problems students face. In PBL, learning is not merely the recall of isolated facts, but learning or understanding through appropriate opportunities to reflect on their experiences and feedback, linked with practices.

PBL Promotes Critical Thinking Skills in Students

Critical thinking skills are now recognised as important for those who will enter the twenty-first century workforce, where the information age requires individuals who are flexible, dynamic and resilient. Teaching students to become effective thinkers is increasingly recognised as the main aim of today's education. If students are to function effectively in a rapidly changing and highly technical society, they must be equipped with lifelong learning and thinking skills necessary to acquire and process information in an ever-changing world (Robinson, 1987).

The teaching of critical thinking is important because employers expect graduates not only to have skills to do their jobs well and learn, but also to think critically. To cope with the complexity and rapidly changing needs of technological advances, employers today need people who can examine assumptions, work through problems and evaluate different courses of action, consider the implications of situations, and look not only to first order consequences of actions, but to second and third order consequences as well (Eichhorn, 1994).

In order to help students to acquire critical thinking skills, students should be provided with an environment where thinking skills can be learned and then practised in realistic situations. It is our belief that critical thinking should be embedded in students' learning. To develop critical thinking skills, we have to teach about thinking, teach for thinking, and infuse thinking skills into content. Critical thinking must be modelled and facilitated throughout the educational process of students' learning (Eichhorn, 1994). Infusing critical thinking into students' learning requires courage and demands that we change the way we teach students. There are many times when it would be easier to give students the answers than to help them through the thinking they need to do to get the answers for themselves.

A strategy for teaching critical thinking skills includes: identifying the problem, deciphering the purpose, uncovering the assumptions, recognising and using different paradigms, demonstrating different methods of reasoning, examining data, creating alternative solutions, and evaluating one's thinking to improve it (Chubinski, 1996). PBL provides the ideal environment to help students to acquire much sought after thinking skills.

PBL Promotes Team Working Skills

Besides the acquisition of problem-solving, critical thinking, and self-directed learning skills, PBL also helps students to develop team working abilities. Traditional teaching assignment is typically individual. The ability to work collaboratively is one of the necessary skills in our modern society. The development of team working is not only important for a career in society; another benefit of collaborative working is that of bringing students from diverse backgrounds and traditions together. By getting students to work together with diverse groups, they can better understand one another and thus promote social interaction between different cultural groups. This enables the development of a community of learners.

In summary, PBL offers many benefits to engineering learning. It provides advantages, both for the acquisition of knowledge and the development of essential skills in problem solving. According to Barrows and Tamblyn (1980), information, concepts, and skills learned by the students are put into their memories in association with a problem. This enables the student to recall information more easily when faced with another problem in which the information is relevant. Recall is constantly reinforced and elaborated by subsequent work with other problems. In this approach, students are able to use the problem as a focus for the study of many different subjects, actively integrating this information into a system that can be applied to the problem at hand and to subsequent problems. Another advantage of this approach is that by working with an unknown problem, the student is forced to develop problem solving, decision making, diagnostic, and reasoning skills. The student needs to generate ideas, get information, look for cues, analyse and synthesise the data available, develop a hypothesis and apply reasoning skills to the problem to solve it. This is particularly challenging for students if the problem is a realistic one. Students will be motivated to work with the problem because they see it as a problem they will face in their professional field.

In PBL, students take on a problem as a stimulus for learning. In doing so, they exercise and develop problem-solving skills. This method of learning has two educational objectives: the acquisition of an integrated body of knowledge related to the problem and the development or application of problem solving skills (Barrows & Tamblyn, 1980).

Disadvantages

Despite the above benefits, there are several disadvantages expressed by educators. Central to this is the cost of implementing PBL compared to lecture-based courses. There are many factors to consider when implementing PBL. These include time commitment of faculty and students, requirements of support personnel, the need for rooms for the many small-group meetings, and resources such as library materials and others. The prime concern is the question of time. It is generally accepted that PBL takes more time to implement than lecture-based courses. Shahabadin (cited by Albanese & Mitchell 1993) estimated that it takes appropriately 22% more time to cover content in PBL (120 weeks by PBL compared to 98 weeks by lecture).

Another issue concerning PBL is that of learning content. When interviewed about learning, PBL students thought they had covered less material and were thus learning less than non-PBL students (Banta et al., 2000). This may be due to fact that PBL students have developed higher expectations of their learning. There is also concern that PBL students may not develop the cognitive structures necessary to assimilate new basic science information easily. However, there is no conclusive evidence that this is the case. On the contrary, there is mounting evidence from studies in science, engineering and business indicating that PBL students do as well in tests of content knowledge as do students in traditional curricula (Banta et al., 2000).

The success of the problem-based learning depends on students disciplining themselves to work with unknown problems in a way that will challenge the development of their problem-solving skills and stimulate relevant, self-directed learning. This means that the teacher who is doing PBL must have been well trained to do it. According to Barrows (1992), the success of PBL depends on the teacher who is conducting the PBL.

PBL is often perceived as an inefficient way to learn (Barrows & Tamblyn, 1980). Because there are many important and relevant areas that could be studied in any problem, it would appear that an enormous amount of time must be spent to complete the first problem in a new area. Some research suggests that PBL curricula cover about 80% of what might be acceptable in a conventional curriculum in the same period (Ablanses & Mitchell, 1993). PBL is not suitable for all students. Of the students who withdrew from the Medical program, (4.4%) more withdrew from the PBL curriculum than the conventional program (Albanese & Mitchell, 1993).

Finally, there is the question of assessment. To some, PBL does not facilitate the student's ability to pass certifying examinations that largely stress the recall of isolated facts and concepts. Despite this, we believe that the benefits outweigh the disadvantages. Our personal experiences testify to that.

Benefits of PBL for Our Students

For us, personally, our experience with PBL has been rewarding, challenging, and revealing. We observed many benefits in using PBL with our students. Among these are:

- Better retention of information and knowledge by students;
- Development of problem-solving, critical thinking, and communication skills;
- Development of an integrated knowledge base;
- Enjoyment of learning;
- Increased motivation;
- Better team working;
- Development of learn-to-learn strategies; and
- Improved communication skills.

Short-Term Benefits

Below is some of the feedback from our students, following the completion of the PBL course.

Student A. *I feel that the culture of PBL is very useful. I can now look at a problem and ideas more critically.*

Student B. *I am now able to define my goals and sub-goals of the task. I prompt myself to think about why and how to do each of the tasks. PBL taught me how to think, how to go about solving problems, and how to question myself on what and why I do certain things. It makes learning a very enjoyable process.*

Student C. *For me, group assignment was the most beneficial part of the course. It was more challenging and interesting for us to work as a group to accomplish our task with discussion and negotiation of knowledge toward our goals.*

Student D. *My main reason for writing to you is to highlight the importance of PBL. I am pleased that you took your time to teach your students about this method. I found this very useful as it guided me through the different stages of my final year project. PBL is a tool that helped me research and provided me with a step-by-step guide. By this I mean it is a tool, which made me question myself. I was critiquing my own work all the time, which means there is less pressure on the tutor. Every time I went to do my work, I am able to question myself as what to do next, if I have covered everything in this section, if someone not knowing my work would understand it and how I could improve it.*

Student E. *I believe the PBL is a very good tool for any kind of problems that need to be solved. I have used it to solve many of my problems. I have even applied PBL into my financial planning in my study at university. Thanks for the person who has developed PBL.*

Long-Term Benefits

Besides the short-term benefits expressed by the students following the PBL classes, what are the long-term benefits that students gained from PBL? We are very grateful that our students, who have graduated and are now in full employment in various jobs, have written and expressed their gratitude to us for their PBL studies. Students from different cohorts have written us letters and e-mails a year or two into their respective jobs to express the impact of PBL on their work. Below are some extracts from our graduates' letters since 1996.

From Doris and Wong (both working as software engineers at National Computer Systems):

As software engineers, ISD has equipped us to be better team players...to master new languages and software tools.

Jason, from a computer equipment firm in the UK writes:

I, personally, found the ISD module extremely useful, particularly the principles of problem-based learning, which I still use to day-to-day research problems.

David Grocott, Head of Infrastructure, Germany—BT Applications Hosting writes:

During my time at University, I found that I was able to absorb much more of the information in subjects, which were delivered using PBL. Having to negotiate and agree how to go about solving the problem in a group. This not only makes the subject more interesting, but is also good preparation for a work environment.

In the world of work, people must learn to be a team player something alien to most forms of University learning,, which, in my opinion, is individualistic and, to an extent, competitive.

Being able to critically examine a problem, and have a structured method for problem solving distinguishes those that can "hit-the-ground-running" from those who need hours of coaching from their managers.

From a business perspective, there are obvious time and, therefore, cost savings through staff efficiency to be gained by people who can get to the root of a problem quickly and propose viable solutions. Additionally, I have found that PBL can add value in the retention of on the job training and internally organised technical training.

I would, therefore, thoroughly recommend this approach to teaching and, as an employer, greatly value students who have studied in this way.

Of course, this is only anecdotal evidence. However, it is rare to find graduates who are able to point to specific elements in their courses and relate them to their job. This makes the above comments more substantial as an assessment of the course success. Even more important is the fact that the students felt able to make this assessment—that is, they are clearly demonstrating critical evaluation of their own learning, a meta-cognitive skill that goes beyond the content of the specific module.

In summary, there are several benefits that students of PBL have compared with traditional classroom teaching. PBL enables students to develop problem-solving skills on authentic situations. Students also develop critical thinking skills and independent learning skills. From our own experiences, we found PBL students have better retention of information and knowledge. Learning was also described as enjoyable by our PBL students. Besides short term benefits, we also observed long-term benefits for students. Many have written to us to express how PBL is helping them in their current jobs.

Conclusion

Although PBL offers many benefits to learning by students, it is not the silver bullet that will drastically increase the achievement of all students. Of course, the jury is still deliberating the verdict on the overall effectives of PBL. However, from our own studies and experiences, we have demonstrated that PBL did enable the majority of our students to learn more effectively than traditional teaching. Students not only learned more in their subject content, but they also developed problem solving and metacognitive skills. We hope our findings and experiences will encourage others to seek alternatives to traditional sage on stage pedagogy. It is our desire that our own experiences and evidences from students' testimonies will encourage other educators to embark on PBL to improve the learning of students. Despite the fact that PBL has some very positive outcomes in medical schools where evaluative studies have been undertaken, we believe that further studies should be directed towards more systematic evaluation.

References

Albanese, M. A., & Mitchell, S. (1993). Problem-based learning: A review of literature on its outcomes and implementation issues. *Academic Medicine, 68*(1), 52-81.

Banta, T. W., Black, K. E., & Kline, K. A. (2000). PBL 2000 plenary address offers evidence for and against problem based learning, PBL Insight to solve, to learn, together. *A newsletter for undergraduate Problem Based Learning from Stamford, 3*(3).

Barrows, H. S. (1988). *The tutorial process.* Springfield: Southern Illinois University.

Barrows, H. S. (1992). *The tutorial process.* Springfield: Southern Illinois University.

Barrows, H. S., & Tamblyn, R. N. (1980). *Problem-based learning: An approach to medical education.* New York: Springer.

Blumberg, P. (2000). Evaluating the evidence that problem-based learners are self-directed learners: A review of the literature. In D. H. Evensen & C. E. Hemelo (Eds.), *Problem-based learning: A research perspective on learning interaction* (pp. 199-226). Mahwah, NJ: Lawrence Erlbaum Associates.

Blumberg, P., & Michael, J. (1992). Development of self-directed learning behaviours in a partially teacher-directed problem-based learning curriculum.*Teach Learn Med, 4,* 3-8.

Boud, D. J., & Feletti, G. (1991). Introduction. In D. J. Boud & G. Feletti (Eds.), *The challenge of problem-based learning* (pp. 13-20). London: Kogan-Page Ltd.

Bransford, J. D., Franks, J. J., Vye, N. J. & Sherwood, R. D. (1989). New approaches to Instruction: Because wisdom can't be told. In S. Vosiadou & A. Ortony (Eds.), *Similarity and analogical reasoning.* New York: Cambridge University Press.

Bruner, J. S. (1961). The act of discovery. *Harvard Educational Review, 31*(1), 21-32.

Bruner, J. S. (1965). The growth of mind. *American Psychologist, 20.* 1007-1017.

Bruner, J. S. (1966). *Towards a theory of instruction.* Cambridge, MA: Harvard University.

Christenen, C. R. (1987). *Teaching and the case method.* Boston: Harvard Business School Publishing.

Chubinski, S. (1996). Creative critical thinking strategies. *Nurse Educator, 21*(6), 23-27.

Coles, C. R. (1985). Differences between conventional and problem-based curricula in students' approaches to studying, *Medical Education, 19,* 308-309.

Des Marchais, J. E. (1993). A student-centred, problem-based curriculum: Five years experience. *Can Med Assoc J., 148,* 1567-1572.

Dolmans, D. H. J. M., & Schmidt, H.G. (1994). What drives the student in problem-based Learning? *Med Edu, 28,* 372-380.

Dolmans, D. H. J. M., & Schmidt, H. (1996). The advantages of problem-based curricula. *Postgrad Med, 72,* 535-538.

Doucet, Purdy, Kaufman, & Langille. (1998). Comparison of problem-based learning and lecture format in continuing medical education of headache diagnosis and management. *Medical Education, 32*(6), 590-596.

Eagle, C. E. (1992). Problem-based learning. *Br J Hosp Med, 48,* 325-329.

Eichhorn, R. (1994). Developing thinking skills: Critical thinking at the Army Management State College. Fort Bevoir, VA: 22060-59334, USA: Army Management Staff College, Retrieved March 30, 2005, from http://www.armsc.belvoir.army.mil/roy.html

Finucane, P. M., Johnson, S. M., & Prideaux, D. J. (1998). Problem-based learning: Its rationale and efficacy. *Med J Aust. 168,* 445-448.

Flores, N. (2001). *Jerome Bruner's education theory. New foundations.* Retrieved March 30,2005, from http://www.newfoundations.com/GAL-LERY/Bruner.html

Fulop, T. (1984). Setting the stage: Problem-based Learning in the mirror of the great social target – health for all. In H. G. Schmidt & M. L. de Volder (Eds.), *Tutorials in problem-based learning: A new direction* (pp. 1-5). Assen, The Netherlands: van Gorcum,

Gibbs, G. (1988). *Learning by doing: A guide to teaching and learning methods.* London: Further Education unit.

Greening, T. (1998). Scaffolding for success in PBL. *Med Edu Online 3, 4.* Retrieved March 30, 2005, from http://www.Med-Ed-Online.org

Greenway, R. (2004). *Reviewing skills training, active learning.* Retrieved March 30, 2005, from http://reviewing.co.uk/research/experiential.learning.htm

Healey, M., & Jenkins, A. (2000). Kolb's experiential learning theory and its application in geography in higher education. *Journal of Geography, 99,* 185-195.

Henry, J. (1989). Meaning and practice in experiential learning. In S. Warner Weil & I. McGill (Eds.), *In making sense of experiential learning: Diversity in theory and practice* (pp. 25-37). Milton Keynes: The Society for Research into Higher Education & Open University Press.

Katzenbach, J. R., & Smith, D. K. (1993). *The wisdom of teams.* New York: Harper Collins.

Kolb, D. A. (1984). *Experiential learning: Experience as the source of learning and development.* Englewood Cliffs, NJ: Prentice Hall.

Koschmann, T. D., Myers, A. C., Feltovich, P. J. & Barrows, H. S. (1994). Using technology to assist in realising effective learning and instruction: A principal approach to the use of computers in collaborative learning. *Journal of the Learning Science, 3(2),* 227-264.

Lieux, E. M. (1996). A comparative study of learning in lectures versus problem-based format. *About Teaching, 50,* 25-27.

Megendiller, J. R., Maxwell, N. L., & Bellisimo, Y. (2002). *The effectiveness of problem-based instruction: A comparative study of instructional methods and student characteristics.* Retrieved March 30, 2005, from http://www.bie.org/pbss/pbe/index.php

Miettinen, R. (2000). The concept of experiencial learning and John Dewey's theory of reflective thought and action. *International journal of Lifelong Education, 19*(1), 54-72.

Moon, J. A. (2002). *Reflection in learning and professional development: Theory and practice.* London: Kogan-Page.

National Research Council (1996). *National Science Education Standards.* Washington, DC: National Academy Press.

Newble, D. I., & Clarke, R. M. (1986). The approaches to learning of students in a traditional and an innovative problem-based medical school. *Academic Medicine, 67,* 557-565.

Norman, G. R., & Schmidt, A. G. (1992). The psychological basis of problem-based learning: A review of the evidence. *Acad Med, 67,* 557-565.

Reynolds, M. (1997). Learning styles: A critique. *Management Learning, 28*(2), 115-33.

Robinson, I. S. (1987). *A program to incorporate higher-order thinking skills into teaching and learning for grade K-3* (p. 16). Fort Lauderdale, FL: Nova University.

Rogers, A. (1996). *Teaching adults* (2nd ed.). Buckingham: Open University Press.

Savery, J. R., & Duffy, T. M. (1995). Problem-based learning: An instructional model and its constructivist framework. *Educational Technology, 35*(5), 31-37.

Schmidt, H. G. (1998). Problem-based learning—Does it prepare medical students to become better doctors? Editorial. *The Medical Journal of Australia, 168,* 429-430.

Schön, D. A. (1983). *How professionals think in action.* New York: Basic Books Inc.

Schumm, J. S., & Post, S. A. (1997). *Executive Learning*, 282.

Smith, M. K. (1999). Critiques of David Kolb's theory from an informal education perspective. *Informal Education.* Retrieved March 30, 2005, from http:///www.infed.org/biblio/b-explrn.htm

Sobral, D. T. (1995). Peer tutoring and student outcomes in a problem-based course. *Medical Education, 27*, 284-289.

Speaker, R. B. (1999). *Reflections on Bruner.* Retrieved March 30, 2005, from http://ed.uno/Faculty/RSpeaker/Epistemologies/Bruner.html

Uden, L., & Dix, A. (2004). Lifelong learning for software engineers. *International Journal of Continuing Engineering Education and Lifelong Learning, 14*(12), 101-110.

Vernon, D. T. A., & Blake, R. L. (1993). Does problem-based learning work? A meta-analysis of evaluative research. *Academic Medicine, 68*(1), 550-563.

Chapter IV

The Tutor's Role

Introduction

Traditionally, learning has been dominated by explanation and by organisation of a body of knowledge. A typical mode of learning is that the teacher initiates the question, generally aimed at getting the student to display his or her knowledge. The student then responds and the teacher evaluates the response. The aim is often focused on having students learn facts. In PBL, learning is said to be student-centered, with students driving the discussion and teacher serving as guide on the side. Two essential factors that affect the success of a PBL curriculum are: the tutor's understanding of the educational theories underlying PBL and the group process in the tutorial. Understanding the role of teacher in student-centered learning is important in being able to implement PBL effectively. The facilitatory skills of the teacher are central to the success of PBL. This chapter describes the role of the tutor in PBL. It begins with a brief review of factors such as commitment, resources, design of a good problem or trigger, and assessment of learning. Subsequent sections of the chapter are devoted to the role of the tutorial. This includes skills that a good tutor should possess in order to implement PBL effectively.

Role of Tutor

We can sum up the skills of a good tutor into two sets of skills. The first set of skills consists of the step-by-step procedure of the tutorial process within a small group setting. A good tutor must have the skills to ensure that all students are involved in the discussion. He or she must keep the discussion focused on the problem, help students to avoid conflict, give time for students to think, and allow time to answer questions. Second, the tutor must have the necessary skills to foster thinking and metacognitive processes in students. Tutors should assist students to acquire problem solving or reasoning skills by encouraging them to hypothesise, justify, experiment, and question their reasoning processes (Mayo & Donnelly, 1995).

We believe that there are several important factors that should be considered for the role of the tutor. These include commitment, provision of resources, design of good problems or triggers, assessment of learning, and the tutorial role. Each of these will be discussed.

Commitment

The first issue concerns the commitment of the tutor. Tutors should first ensure that they have the commitment to devote the time to the tutorial process for each of the groups taking the PBL. Students have the tendency to work out whether or not the teacher is truly committed to PBL. If the teacher is motivated and committed, then he or she would take the students with him or her. Even the least motivated and skeptical students will be won over if the teacher can show that it is for their benefit that he or she undertakes the PBL tasks. Show your students that you are enjoying doing PBL. It is important to make your students know that you are keen for them to learn. The tutor should join in as part of the learning community with the students. To help students to know that you are not trying to intimidate them by challenging them with difficult and thought provoking questions, show your excitement with them as they begin to develop problem-solving and critical-thinking skills. A good tutor is interested in how the students study, wants to understand the problems students have, and tries to help the students to learn better.

Resources

It is important that there are resources available for students to conduct the PBL tutorial. This is particularly so when there are more than five groups in any one class. Students should be provided with facilities where they can sit round and conduct the PBL tutorial process. Tutors should make sure that there are the required resources available for students to use—resources such as books, journals, Web-based on-line information, and so on. It would be useful for the tutor to make sure that all necessary materials students need to refer to during their studies are available for them to access. The library should be informed of the journals, books, articles, CDs, or videos that students would be required to use for their studies. If possible, several rooms should be made available, especially set aside for the students to study. Besides physical resources, there is the human resource too. There should be enough tutors or facilitators available to take the group tutorial. Adequate time must be allocated for students to complete the problem.

Design Good Problems or Triggers

In PBL, the problem drives the learning, rather than acting as an example of the concepts and principles previously taught. Students learn domain content in order to solve the problem, rather than solving the problem as an application of learning (Jonassen, 1998). It is, therefore, important for tutors to design problems that are anchored in authentic contexts. This is to allow learners to manage complexity and behave like real practitioners. To engage students in meaningful learning requires that they take ownership of the problem or learning goal. Therefore, the tutor should provide relevant, engaging, and interesting problems for students to solve. The problems should not be over-simplified. They should be ill-structured or ill-defined and complex to reflect real-world cases.

Some theorists (Dick, 1991; Reigeluth, 1989) believe that the process of acquiring new knowledge and understanding is firmly embedded in the social and emotional context in which the learning takes place. This holistic approach can be reflected in the way that we set the problem. One of the principles of PBL is that of authentic activity. The problem given to the student should be carefully thought out, making sure that it reflects, as realistically as possible, the kinds of problems that students would encounter in real life. It is generally accepted that the whole is greater than the sum of its parts and that students learn best from experiences characterised by a high degree of personal relevance. It is important to provide a context for learning that supports both autonomy and relatedness (Lebow, 1993). Learning should not be the sequencing of instructional events, but the application of principles for responding to the needs of the situation. This means that there should be a shift to enhancing interest, engagement, and personal responsibility for the learning process.

Students often encounter learning in a discontextualised situation with little or no resemblance to a real-life problem. Problems given are often simple, discontextualised ones that involve little more than memorising some facts from the lecture. The problems given to students in PBL should be realistic, complex, and should reflect, as much as possible, the actual problems that students would encounter in real life. In this situation, students would have to learn to handle and work with the problem with the help and scaffolding that the teacher provides. There will be more on this topic in Chapter VI, "Developing Problems/Triggers."

Assessment of Learning

Assessment is a crucial part of all learning. It is important for tutors to make sure that assessment is consistent with learning objectives of the groups in PBL. Tutors should realise that students are constantly engaged in learning, therefore assessment of students should not be focused only on the final leaning product. PBL tutors need to understand meaningful ways of assessing students' work to motivate learning. For assessment to be implemented properly there should be well designed and clearly defined goals and objectives and well thought out strategies, techniques, criteria, and marking schemes (see Chapter VIII for details).

PBL Tutor

According to Zimitat, Hamtlton, DeJersey, Reilly, and Ward (1994), 70% of students in a PBL course found the tutor's role is essential to the success of PBL. Tutors play two important roles in PBL: facilitation of learning process via prompting and assisting in group processes to ensure that they maintain focus (Jones, Donnelly, Nash, Young, & Schwartz, 1993). Tutors should refrain from assuming the role of a "sage on stage," an authoritative source of knowledge. The question of whether a tutor should be a subject domain expert is a debatable one. Ambury (1995) believes that subject-based expertise is a disadvantage to student-centered learning and independence. On the contrary, Eagle, Harasym, and Mandin (1992) found that expertise to be favorable because it stimulates greater numbers of learning issues to be explored. The success of PBL depends on the ability of the tutor to use facilitating teaching skills in small group learning (Barrows 1992). Tutoring is a skill central to problem-based, self-directed learning (Barrows & Tamblyn, 1980).

Wood (1996) identified the following responsibilities of the tutor in PBL:

- Asking leading and open-ended questions to help the students to explore the richness of the situation and to help them develop critical thinking skills.
- Helping students to reflect on their experiences, because reflection improves problem solving.
- Monitoring progress to ensure students are still on track.
- Challenging students' thinking to help them develop critical thinking skills.
- Raising issues to be considered.
- Stimulating, encouraging, creating, and maintaining an environment where the students can share experiences.

There is no question that the ideal circumstance would be for the tutor to be both an expert tutor and a subject matter expert in the discipline being taught. According to Barrows (1988), the next best tutor is the one who is good at being a tutor, although not an expert in the subject matter. We concur with Barrows (1988) that since facilitation skills are crucial for students learning in PBL, a good tutor can be a successful tutor in any area.

Barrows (1988) recommends the following to help a non-expert tutor:

- Have well-stated curricular objectives so that the tutor and the students know what is to be accomplished.
- Provide the tutor with a set of learning issues that the faculty feels should be identified by the students with every problem.
- Orient the tutor about each problem, task, and situation to be used.
- Provide the tutor an expert with whom he or she can consult at any time and who might, on occasion, come to the tutorial group session to listen to the group's deliberations and give feedback about its understanding and progress.

To implement PBL effectively, the tutor should:

• Allow students to work on authentic problems (designing good problems or triggers).

• Provide an environment where there is integration of knowledge and skills from different disciplinary areas (designing good problems or triggers).

• Provide students with an environment to work as effective team group (group process).

• Help students to develop problem solving, critical thinking and metacognitive skills (role of tutor in the tutorial process).

We believe that the tutor plays a critical role in the students' learning in PBL. The tutor has a great impact on the conduct of the student. It is important to remember that the tutor's role in PBL is different from that of traditional lecture tutors. In traditional classroom teaching, the role of the tutor is that of an expert or "sage on the stage" who holds knowledge and directs students' thinking as well as evaluating them. In PBL, the tutor is no longer the expert, but a coach or facilitator who presents the problem to the students. He or she acts as coach initially, but fades away as students become more competent. The tutor is a co-investigator in the learning process with the students, as well as an assessor of the learning. Wood (1996) compares the tutor's role in PBL to that of a coach of a football team. Each member is very skilful, however, guidance by the coach is needed to develop trust, help each team member to see their contribution, to provide perspective, to encourage and to critique. The tutor guides the students through the learning process by ensuring that all students are actively involved in the group process (Barrows, 1988). This means that the tutor must have the skills in group dynamics where he or she is the catalyst.

Group Dynamics Skills

It is generally acknowledged that learning occurs through multiple interactions within the learning environment (Savery & Duffy, 1995). This means the ability of students to work together to identify and analyse problems and/or generate solutions.

Although tutor effectiveness is the crucial item in learning at the start of the curriculum, learning in the end is more a function of the small-group process (Kalain & Mullan, 1996). It is important for the tutor to realise that most students lack the necessary skills to work competently and effectively in groups (Jessup,

1995). This is no surprise, given that traditional lecture and textbook-generated learning is what students have been exposed to since elementary school through many graduate programmes. Students are often forced to learn to work in groups by trial and error. As a result, students often waste time, do not work productively, become confrontational, and/or feel left out. According to some researchers (Johnson & Johnson, 1997; Katzenbach & Smith, 1993), regardless of the problem posed to a group of students, learning is proportional to the ability of that group to work effectively together.

Students often find group/team work difficult because of their negative experiences. It is crucial for the tutor to devote time to helping them to learn to work effectively in teams/groups. Because students come from diverse backgrounds, it is hard for them to function well together initially. Issues related to group dynamics must be addressed in the first two weeks of PBL. Training and workshops should be conducted for students to participate in experiential and interactive learning activities, focused on the skills needed to be an effective team/group member. During these sessions, students gain insight related to their personal characteristics that can affect their ability to be effective group members. Students also have to learn to work with individuals who may have a different approach to the problem. These are valuable experiences that have effects on the team/group work later. Students must be allowed to evaluate the contributions of other group members. This enables the tutor to keep an eye on how the group is functioning. It also has a key role in assessment. To help the tutor keep a monitoring role on the groups, the tutor should regularly observe the groups as they work. This enables the tutor to know which member of the group is having problems and why. Immediate attention must be given to the group if it is not functioning appropriately. A non-functioning group must not be allowed to continue because it can jeopardise the learning of all members of the group and thus undermine the PBL approach to learning.

Students vary in their behaviour. Some are very confident, but others are hesitant to take risks in a group setting. This type of student may not learn much from their peers until they are comfortable with these peers. A few may be silent. This could be because they are shy or being polite, lacking in confidence, or having personal problems. The group consists of people with different personalities, abilities, and backgrounds. Some members of the group would tend to dominate the rest of the group, thus becoming leaders. It is important that the tutor avoids letting a dominant member of the group control it. It is the responsibility of the tutor to ensure that all members contribute constructively to the problem and no one is allowed to take control. Some members of the group will be weak, so the tutor should encourage other members of the group to administer support and encouragement. Besides academic learning, group working also provides opportunities for social interaction and the development of friendships.

There are always problems associated with group working of which tutors should be aware. From our experience, we found that students had very high ideals of group work after they had been shown how the group should function. Students initially may experience the first two weeks as a honeymoon period, where they begin to get to know each other and enjoy the social aspects of the group process. This can be problematic because no one wants to break the spell and get down to hard work. Tutors should be careful that this is not allowed to happen for too long. As students get into their learning they begin to experience frustration. Complaints of not knowing enough or not progressing fast enough will begin to surface. At this stage, students may feel overwhelmed by the vastness of the knowledge they have to know and have no idea as to where to start in obtaining it without the traditional support of lectures. The tutor needs to understand the frustration of the students and try to encourage and support them. Constant encouragement is a characteristic of a good tutor.

To function effectively, problems have to be solved within the group. Conflicts and differences of opinion are an inevitable and necessary consequence of group process. Arguments rarely provide resolution or satisfaction within a group—conflict and disagreement should allow an opportunity to deal with issues from various points of view.

Before the assignment of students to groups, the tutor should study the background and profile of each student, making sure that students of different backgrounds and experience are assigned in a group rather than assigning students to a group that share similar backgrounds. It is useful to group students of different abilities, gender, and nationalities together. This encourages discussion and a sharing of different cultures. Although the tutor may not have met the students and have a profile of them before the start of the course, a survey can be conducted prior to the commencement of the first session. This can be done by sending a questionnaire to each student asking for background information. Although this may take up some of the tutor's time to study the profiles of students, the effort pays off because students often find that they learned best when mixed with people of different background, expertise, and cultures.

Tutors should make sure that all members of the group take an active role. The group will depend on the contributions of each member by virtue of assignments directed to independent study time between the group sessions. Open discussion should take place if problems with individuals are identified. The tutor also needs to be aware that the group can be used to help students develop effective communication skills. Communication is an essential skill of all employees. Students, who are future employees, need to be able to communicate effectively. This entails communication not only of technical information, but also of feelings at a personal level. By practising communication in the group, between members, students can learn to improve their communication skills. In addition, it is also important that each member becomes an active participant in the group in order to contribute his or her unique knowledge and ideas to the learning process.

Forcing students to work in groups without proper training will not work. Without the interpersonal skills being taught to students, the only result will be frustration with their learning. Tutors should encourage more beneficial and meaningful group working by prompting students to pool their talents and resources. Students should also be guided to resolve conflicts whilst working together. We observed that the students who performed well in PBL were the ones who interacted well with other members and had team dynamics skills. It is our belief that students should be trained in interpersonal skills for group working. We will discuss how this can be achieved in Chapter V, "Preparing Students for PBL."

Although group process is important in PBL, students lack a model of group effectiveness. Tutors may realise the importance of group process, yet many do not facilitate reflection on group processes. It is our belief that greater emphasis should be placed on group processes training for PBL tutors. Failure in group process may be due to failure in the provision of appropriate scaffolding in both tutor facilitation of group processes and the establishment of a successful mental model of interaction within the group. Because the success of PBL relies heavily on group work, the tutor must lay the foundation for effective group functioning early.

To maintain the effectiveness of students learning in groups, the tutor should involve all students in the discussion. Keep the discussion focused on the problem. Students should also be given time to think and answer. In summary, the role of the tutor in group process includes:

- Establishing rapport and group interaction, reinforcements, and agreements;

- Intervening in conflict situations;

- Monitoring the group dynamics, making sure it is conducive to learning;

- Acting as a role model to encourage students to develop individual qualities within the group;

- Encouraging the students to promote good team spirit;

- Encouraging all members of the group to actively participate in group discussion;

- Helping the group to set goals and action plans that may be modified later; and

- Encouraging students to monitor the group's progress.

Besides group dynamics skills, a good PBL tutor should possess critical thinking skills.

Critical Thinking Skills

Besides the group process skills, the tutor as facilitator should have the skills to foster the reasoning or critical thinking and metacognitive process in students. What do we mean by critical thinking skills? According to Elder and Paul (1994), critical thinking is best understood as the ability of thinkers to take charge of their own thinking. This also requires that they develop sound criteria and standards for analysing and assessing their own thinking and routinely use the criteria and standards to improve its quality. Schumm and Post (1997) define a critical thinker as someone who is:

- Willing to spend time reflecting on his/her ideas;
- Able to think logically;
- Able to base his/her judgment on ideas and evidence;
- Willing to take a critical stance on issues;
- Able to ask penetrating and thought provoking questions to evaluate ideas;
- Able to identify arguments and issues; and
- Able to see connections between topics and use knowledge from other disciplines to enhance his or her reading and learning experiences.

Although there are different definitions given to critical thinking, almost all emphasise the ability and tendency to gather, evaluate, and use information effectively (Beyer, 1985). A critical thinker is one who is able to be in control of his or her thinking.

Potts (1994) identified several discrete skills related to an overall ability for critical thinking. These are:

- Finding analogies and other kinds of relationships between pieces of information;
- Determining the relevance and validity of information that could be used for structuring and solving problems; and
- Finding and evaluating solutions or alternate ways of treating problems.

According to Beyers (1985) and Costa (1985), the hallmarks of teaching critical thinking include:

- Promoting interaction among students as they learn;
- Using open-ended questions;
- Allowing time for students to reflect on the questions asked or problems posed; and
- Teaching for transfer.

Weaver (1997) believes that defining concepts and debating is the core of critical thinking. To Weaver, the internal and personal process of defining phenomena, establishing criteria, evaluating information, and choosing what is probably true and safe to believe, are essential to critical thinking. This involves the use of logic and inference. In order to teach critical thinking skills, there should be a shift in theories of how to teach. It is, therefore, imperative to teach students how to think so that they can find their own way through the problems and concerns they meet in life.

Metacognitive Skills

Because the role of the tutor is that of a facilitator or coach in the PBL lessons, many tutors who are used to traditional didactic teaching approaches would find the tutoring process difficult. Although the new tutors may know that they should facilitate or guide the learning by encouraging students to present and discuss their ideas and determine their own learning needs, many have no idea how to conduct effective tutoring. Barrows (1988) believes that the interaction at the metacognitive level is the basic function of the tutor. What do we mean by metacognitive skills? According to Barrows (1988), metacognitive skills are thinking about thinking. These are the skills that provide the key to the positive, active role of the tutor. Metacognitive skills are used when one is confronted with a difficult, unexpected, or puzzling problem or situation.

Problems in life are complex and few are presented with all the information needed to understand them well enough to make valid decisions about their cause and resolution. More information is generally required. The needed information can be obtained by investigating the problem, making observations, testing and probing. To do this requires reflection, thought, and deliberation. Barrows (1988) calls these metacognition. It regulates how we go about learning (Blakey & Spence, 1990).

Because metacognition plays such an important role for students in learning, students must acquire, through practice, well-developed metacognitive skills to monitor, critique, and direct the development of their reasoning skills as they work with life's ill-defined problems. Students need to critique the adequacy of their knowledge and to direct their own continued learning (Barrows, 1988).

Metacognitive thinking skills provide the key to the positive, active role of the tutor. What sort of strategies can be used to develop metacognitive skills? Blakey and Spence (1990) have identified the following:

1. Identify what you know and what you do not know. It is important for students to make conscious decisions about their knowledge.

2. Talk about thinking. It is important for tutors to think aloud so that students can follow demonstrated thinking processes. Paired problem-solving is useful: one student talks through a problem, describing his/her thinking processes. The partner listens and asks questions to help clarify thinking. Reciprocal teaching (Palincsar & Brown, 1984) is a good method where small groups of students take turns playing teacher, asking questions and clarifying and summarising the materials being studied.

3. Keep a "Thinking Journal". A thinking journal, or learning log, is a diary in which students reflect upon their thinking and make notes of their awareness of ambiguities and inconsistencies with comments about how they dealt with difficulties. The journal is a diary of process.

4. Planning and self-regulation—Students should be taught how to make plans for learning activities including estimating time requirements, organising materials, scheduling procedures necessary to complete an activity.

5. Debriefing the thinking process—Blakey and Spence (1990) recommend a three-step method. First, the tutor guides the students to review the activity, gathering data on thinking processes and feeling. Next, the group classifies related ideas, identifying thinking strategies used. Finally, they evaluate their success, discarding inappropriate strategies, identifying those valuable for future use, and seeking promising alternative approaches.

6. Self evaluation—Students should learn how to evaluate their own learning activities. When faced with different or unexpected problems or situations, their metacognitive skills enable them to ask and answer questions such as:

    •   What do I know about this topic, issue, or subject?

    •   How much time do I need to learn this?

    •   Do I know what I need to know?

    •   Do I know where I can get the necessary information or knowledge?

- How can I know when I have made a mistake?
- Do I understand what I have read?
- What strategies or tasks can I use to learn this?
- How can I refine my plan if it is not working as expected?
- Do I have the entire picture?
- Have I included all the possibilities?
- What is going on?
- Do I have all the relevant facts?
- What does this mean?
- What data do I need to use?
- What is the best way to manage this?
- Is this the best way for this, or is there another way of looking at it?
- Do I know enough about this type of thing? What facts do I know? Where can I find them?
- Is this really valid?

Barrows (1988) describes the tasks of tutor as one who enables students, with the help of other members of the group, to distinguish their difficulties in acquiring new information and help them to put forth directional activities to cope with those difficulties. This means that the tutor should be more concerned with the process of learning than the teaching of content. Instead of lecturing, the tutor should model the various methods of problem solving. Tutors should encourage students to explore their own knowledge and determine their own learning needs. Tutors are often told that they should not put students into a passive role by giving them facts they need or lecturing to them. Instead, students should be told to actively acquire the facts they need on their own. Tutors are told that they should not tell the students whether their ideas posited in discussions, or their answers to questions are right or wrong, but students should find out for themselves with the help of the tutor.

Tutors are told to facilitate or guide the learning by encouraging the students to determine their own learning (Barrows, 1988). Tutors new to PBL find this difficult and the result is that the tutor may mistakenly develop the belief that tutoring is nothing more than observing the tutorial process and student dynamics. Not understanding what to say or do, the tutor could inadvertently resort to the more comfortable didactic teaching method when students seem to be wandering off course.

According to Mayo and Donnelly (1995), the role of the tutor in PBL is similar to that of a symphony conductor. The performance of the symphony is based on a script, or score. It is the conductor's role to interpret the musical text to achieve a harmonious whole by balancing and blending the individual parts. The symphony conductor does not have to know how to play every orchestral instrument. Similarly, the PBL tutor does not have to be an expert in every field. The tutor should be a generalist or practitioner in the field. An effective tutor is more than a depositor of knowledge (Mayo & Donnelly, 1995).

According to Barrows (1988), an effective tutor is one who is competent in asking specific open-ended questions that are useful in guiding students through the reasoning process. Barrows (1988) calls this "Modulating the Challenge of Learning."

Because of the facilitatory role of the tutor in PBL, it is possible to talk about the role of the tutor in PBL as one of providing scaffolding. Scaffolding is described by Collins, Brown, and Newman (1989) as a means of coaching students to the extent that they can perform intellectual skills on their own. It is an important way of helping students to master the necessary skills. Tutors should devise effective scaffolding activities that help students to develop the right mindset, engage students with the problem, divide activities into manageable tasks, and direct student's attention to essential aspects of the learning goals (Ngeow & Kong, 2001).

Although PBL emphasises that students take ownership of, and responsibility for, their own learning, this does not preclude the use of scaffolding to assist in the development of these attributes and other skills to enable students to engage in meaningful learning. The control of the learning process essentially belongs to the students themselves. There is a well-defined curricular infrastructure undergirding the process (Koschmann et al., 1994; Greening, 1998).

Personal Attributes

We believe that a good tutor is enthusiastic about helping the students to learn more effectively. The tutor is interested in the student life and concerned for the learning of the students. A good tutor knows how students think and can cope with the different types of students in the groups. It is important that the tutor is patient with the students. Students must be allowed time to reflect and discover. A good tutor should be patient and not intervene too soon or too often when students get stuck in their thinking. It is important to remember not to push the students by being too authoritarian. The tutor should be passionate about PBL as an effective method for helping students to develop problem solving and metacognitive skills. A good tutor should act as a role model for the students and encourage students to take ownership of their learning. He or she should also be interested in PBL and have the time and energy to promote PBL.

Knowledge and Skills in Tutoring

We know the crucial role of the tutor in PBL, but what sort of knowledge and skills are required of a PBL tutor?

Knowledge

A good PBL tutor should have the following knowledge:

- An understanding of the principles of constructivist learning;
- A good understanding of the overall curriculum the students have to study;
- A good understanding of the principles of problems solving;
- A good understanding of critical thinking and metacognitive skills;
- A good understanding of the PBL tutorial process;
- An understanding of the learning objectives expected of the students;
- A good knowledge of the rationale and techniques of independent learning;
- A good knowledge of the basic principles and methods of evaluation;
- A good knowledge of the respective useful resources that are available; and
- A good knowledge and understanding of the importance of collaborative work.

Skills

Besides good knowledge, a good tutor should also possess the following skills:

- Skill in facilitatory teaching. This involves skills in:
    - Asking appropriate, stimulating questions to challenge students;
    - Indicating when external information is needed;
    - Directing students to appropriate resources;
    - Avoiding telling students what to do;

- Avoiding giving students the answers;
- Encouraging establishment of group dynamics conducive to learning;
- Monitoring, analyzing, and regulating the learners;
- Promoting multiple perspectives in learning; and
- Strengthening the learner's tendency to engage in intentional processes, especially by encouraging the strategic exploration of errors. (Lebow, 1993)

- Skills in promoting problem solving and critical thinking. These include:
  - Skills to design authentic problems that allow students to have opportunity to learn problem-solving and develop critical thinking skills;
  - Skills to be able to assess/appraise critically evaluate supporting hypotheses; and
  - Skills to identify hypotheses, generate ideas, formulate solutions, define, and synthesise information. (Queen's University, 2004)

In addition to these skills cited by Queens University (above), we strongly believe that a good tutor should also possess the following skills:

- Skills in promoting independent learning. These include:
  - Encouraging students to review and redefine explanation, making connections of concepts, processes, and principles;
  - Promoting deep learning;
  - Encouraging students to articulate their thinking;
  - Allowing students to think out loud to clarify their own conceptualisation;
  - Confronting student's misconceptions;
  - Helping students to identify gaps in their knowledge;
  - Encouraging students to summarise and help them to distinguish main points from minor issues;
  - Encouraging divergent thinking and creativity;
  - Helping students to generate a study plan;
  - Helping students to develop metacognitive skills;
  - Helping students to reflect on their learning;
  - Helping students to discover ways to correct mistakes;

- Helping students to identify the relevant learning resources needed for their studies;
- Helping students to define objectives;
- Reviewing and clarifying learning goals with students;
- Making the knowledge construction activities overt and raising their awareness about how they learn (Scardamalia, Bereiter, McClean, Swallow, & Woodruff, 1989);
- Supporting self-regulated learning by promoting skills and attitudes that enable the learner to assume increasing responsibility for the developmental restructuring process;
- Helping students to manage their learning activities;
- Helping Students develop project management skills and to estimate their own time requirements; and
- Helping students to select appropriate self-evaluation methods.

In addition to personal attributes, the tutor should also have questioning skills.

Questioning Skills

Since questioning is one of the most important skills used by tutors to facilitate learning in PBL, it is important that a good tutor knows what questions to ask, and when is the right time. The main objective in asking the right question is to help students to make explicit their implicit knowledge. Tutors should be sensitive to the questioning approach to students. It is the responsibility of the tutors to help students to bring their implicit knowledge to the surface. Tutors should not be satisfied too soon. Conversely, tutors should not bombard students with too many questions. This can make them frustrated and uncertain about their learning. Students may feel they are being criticised. Good questions do not require simple yes or no answers. Questions should ask for explanation, for comparison, or for differentiation between various ideas or points. Questioning is one of the most important ways to facilitate learning in PBL. It helps to keep the group focused and prevents it becoming bogged down. Appropriate use of questioning also helps group members by forcing them to present information and concepts more precisely. A good tutor knows when and how to ask appropriate questions. Useful questions to ask the students include:

- What are you hoping to find out?
- Why are you asking that question?

- How would knowing the answer make a difference in your understanding of the problem?
- Is there anything besides this that you may need to consider?
- Why do you consider that?
- What is the connection between analysis and design?
- How would the principles of software engineering relate to this application?
- Can you think of any more issues that need to be considered?
- What processes could have caused this problem?
- What are the mechanisms involved here?
- What is human-computer interaction?
- Why is it important?
- How do we decide what to do? (a higher-order question)
- Does everyone understand the information presented?

Besides questioning, it may be helpful to remember some useful hints, including:

- Do not dominate the group with your opinion, but rather facilitate the group dynamic.
- Encourage students to focus on their discussion.
- Remind students of previously discussed, but not fully understood topics.
- Always ask yourself the question, "Will my comment help the students to learn how to learn?" before considering intervention.
- Regularly remind students about how much they are learning.
- Remind students of available resources.
- Make sure students challenge assumptions.

How Do We Ensure the Success of Effective Tutors in PBL?

We believe tutors should be trained in the tutorial process of PBL in order to ensure its success. Because the tutor plays such an crucial role in the PBL process, tutors should recognise that students not only acquire knowledge and skills of their subject content, but they should also learn skills such as problem solving, critical thinking, metacognitive and communication skills in order to function as successful employees in society. It is essential for tutors to have the facilatory skills that recognise the value of each step of the tutorial process and be fully prepared, assimilated, and developed in the skills to take the students through each of the steps of PBL. By familiarising the necessary steps in the tutorial process, the tutor would be able to help students to develop and investigate a problem, access process, and apply information through a variety of resources to help students to formulate a solution; interpret the results of their solution that are appropriate for the problem, and to communicate their findings to others in a convincing way.

Conclusion

In summary, to implement PBL effectively, the tutor should:

- Provide an environment where there is integration of knowledge and skills from different disciplinary areas (designing good problems or triggers).
- Provide students with an environment to work as an effective team/group (group process),
- Allow students to work on authentic problems (designing good problems or triggers).
- Help students to develop problem solving, critical thinking, and metacognitive skills (role of tutor and the tutorial process).

It is now generally acknowledged by PBL users that the tutor plays a crucial role in the success of PBL. A good tutor in PBL is a coach who encourages students to attain a deep understanding of the knowledge acquired and ensures that students are actively involved in the group process. A good tutor observes, manages, and intervenes in student learning to ensure that the educational objectives are met, including the acquisition of relevant knowledge, development of problem-solving, critical thinking and self-directed learning, as well as team skills. To achieve this, a good tutor should be trained in the tutorial process and group dynamics skills to make PBL a success.

References

Ambury, G. (1995). *Beginning to tutor problem-based learning: A qualitative investigation of adragogy in medical curriculum innovation.* Retrieved March 30, 2005, from http://edu.queensu.ca/~amburyg/pbl-c.html

Barrows, H. S. (1988). *The tutorial process.* Springfield: Southern Illinois University.

Barrows, H. S. (1992). *The tutorial process.* Springfield: Southern Illinois University.

Barrows, H. S., & Tamblyn, R. N. (1980). *Problem-based learning: An approach to medical education.* New York: Springer.

Beyer, B. K. (1985). Critical thinking: What is it? *Social Education, 49,* 270-276.

Blakey, E., & Spence, S. (1990). Developing metacognition. *ERIC Digest.* Syracuse, NY: ERIC Clearing House on Information Resource.

Collins, A. S., Brown, J. S., & Newman, S. F. (1989). Cognitive apprenticeship teaching the craft of reading, writing and mathematics. In L. B. Resnick (Ed.), *Knowing, learning and instruction: Essays in honor of Robert Glaser* (pp. 453-494). Hillsdale, NJ: Lawrence Erlbaum Associates.

Costa, A. L. (Ed.). (1985). *Developing minds: A resource book for teaching thinking.* Alexandria, VA: Association for Supervision and Curriculum Development.

Dick, W. (1991). An instructional designer's view of constructivism. *Educational Technology, 5,* 41-44.

Eagle, C. J., Harasym, P. H., & Mandin, H. (1992). Effects of tutors with case expertise on problem-based learning issues. *Academic Medicine, 67*(7), 465-469.

Elder, L., & Paul, R. (1994). Critical thinking: Why we must transform our teaching. *Journal of Developmental Education, 18*(1), 34-35.

Greening, T. (1998). Scaffolding for success in PBL. *Med Edu Online, 3, 4.* Retrieved March 30, 2005, from http://www.Med-Ed-Online.org

Jessup, L. M. (1995). The senior experience: Applied, team problem solving in business education. *Journal of Education for Business, 71*(2), 82-86

Johnson, D. W., & Johnson, P. F. (1997). *Joining together: Group theory and group skills* (6th ed.). Boston: Allyn & Bacon.

Jonassen, D. H. (1998). Designing constructivist learning environments. In C. M. Reigeluth (Ed.), *Instructional theories and models* (2nd ed.). Mahwah, NJ: Lawrence Erlbaum Associates.

Jones, R. O., Donnelly, M. B., Nash, P. P., Young, B., & Schwartz, R. W. (1993). The ongoing development of a problem-based survey clerkship: Year three. *Medical Teacher, 15*(2/3), 207-215.

Kalain, H. A., & Mullan, P. B. (1996) Exploring factor analysis of students' ratings of a problem-based learning curriculum. *Academic Medicine, 71*(4), 390-392.

Koschmann, T. D., Myers, A. C., Feltovich, P. J., & Barrows, H. S. (1994). Using technology to assist in realising effective learning and instruction: A principal approach to the use of computers in collaborative learning. *Journal of the Learning Science, 3*(2), 227-264.

Lebow, D. (1993). Constructivist Value for Instructional System Design: Five principles toward a new mindset. *Educational Technology Research and Development, 41*(3), 4-16.

Mayo, W. P., & Donnelly, M. B. (1995). The characteristics of the ideal problem-based learning tutor in clinical medicine. *Evaluation and Health Profession, 18*(2), 124-136.

Ngeow, K., & Kong, Y. S. (2001). *Learning to learn: Preparing teachers and students for problem-based learning.* ERIC Digest D163: ERIC Clearinghouse on Reading, English and Communication, Indiana University, IN. Retrieved March 30, 2005, from http://eric.indiana.edu

Palincsar, A., & Brown, A. (1984). Reciprocal teaching of comprehension in fostering and monitoring activities. *Cognition and Instruction, 1,* 117-175.

Paul, R. (1993). Critical Thinking—What every person needs to survive in a rapidly changing world. In J. Willsen & A. J. A. Binker (Eds.), *Foundation for critical thinking* (3rd ed.).Santa Rosa, CA: Foundation for critical thinking.

Potts, B. (194). Strategies for teaching critical thinking. *ERIC/AE Digest.* Washington, DC: ERIC Clearing House on Assessment and Education. Retrieved March 30, 2005, http://www.ericfacility.net/databases/ERIC-Digests/ed385606.html

Queen's University. (2004). *Problem-based learning handbooks.* Retrieved March 30, 2005, from http://meds.queensu.ca/medicine/pbl/pblhome.htm

Reigeluth, C. M. (1989). Educational technology at the crossroads: New mindsets and new directions. *Educational Technology Research and Development, 37*(1), 1042.

Savery, J. R., & Duffy, T. M. (1995). Problem-based learning: An instructional model and its constructivist framework. *Educational Technology, 35*(5), 31-37.

Scardamalia, M., Bereiter, C., McClean, R. S., Swallow, J., & Woodruff, E. (1989). Computer-supported intentional learning environments. *Journal of Educational Computing Research, 5*(1), 51-68.

Weaver, B. (1997). *Critical thinking across the curriculum project.* Lee's Summit, Missouri: Longview Community College. Retrieved March 30, 2005, from http://www.kcmetro.cc.mo.us/longview/ctas/winners.htm

Woods, D. R. (1996). *Instructor's guide for problem-based learning: How to gain the most from PBL.* Hamilton, Ontario: Donald Woods.

Zimitat, C., Hamtlton S., DeJersey, J, Reilly, P., & Ward, L. (1994). *Problem-based learning in metabolic biochemistry.* Retrieved March 30, 2005, from http://florey.biosci.uq.edu.au/BiochemEd/PBLmetab.htm

Chapter V

Preparing Students for PBL

Introduction

Students working in PBL must be responsible for their own learning and for what they will actually do in their research. Throughout the PBL process, students have to define and analyse the problem, generate learning issues, and apply what they have learned to solve the problem. Instead of working as individuals in the class, students in PBL work as a team and they have to share their knowledge with others. This means that students who are used to traditional methods of learning do not necessarily have the required skills to cope with the different roles expected of them in PBL. This chapter begins with a brief review of the differences between conventional leaning and PBL. Subsequent sections of the chapter describe several important issues that are needed to prepare students for PBL.

Different Role of Students

We believe that it is important to prepare students for PBL so that they can approach PBL more effectively. Students in PBL are no longer passive agents in their learning, but they are actively involved in solving the problem, co-working with the tutor and other students. This means students have to shift from a research-for-solution to exploring-of-ideas approach to learning: "How do I perceive this problem?" "What type of information do I need to solve this problem?" "How can I best learn to become independent learner?"

Students must quickly learn how to manage their own learning in order to make good use of their tutorials and independent study time. The key emphasis in PBL is the changed role of the students in their learning. Instead of passively receiving instruction (objectivist learning), students in PBL are actively constructing their knowledge and understanding of the situation in groups. Students working in groups in PBL need to organise prior knowledge and identify the nature of the problem. They must also pose questions about what they do not understand, design a plan to solve the problem, and identify resources they need to do it.

Students not only have to concentrate on learning the relevant knowledge and skills to solve the problem, but they also have to develop problem solving and learning to learn skills. As students in PBL are expected to work in groups, they have to develop interpersonal and group process skills, such as effective listening or coping creatively with conflicts. In learning how to learn, students also have to measure their success. How do they know they are on the right track? Another problem facing students of PBL is that tasks they have to learn are not clearly defined for them by the tutors. On the contrary, problems students face are often messy, open-ended, real world problems that provide the stimulus for students' learning (Hmelo & Ferrari, 1997). This requires students to have metacognitive skills. It is obvious that students learning in PBL need a paradigm shift. These changes are not easy for students who are used to traditional learning methods, such as lecturing. So, how do we prepare students to cope with the change to PBL?

There are several important issues that need to be considered when preparing students for PBL. These include:

- Change of mindset;
- Commitment;
- Inquiry Learning;
- Making thinking visible;
- Information literacy;
- Team or group work;
- Interpersonal skills;
- Team leadership skills;
- Learning skills;
- Metacognitive skills; and
- Reflection skills.

Change of Mindset

To help students to better prepare for PBL, we found it useful to help them to change their attitudes about learning. As they are not used to the constructivist approach to learning, it is important that they are carefully told what to expect. Typically, students are used to being given lectures, told what to do in class, and then follow instructions, hoping that the knowledge from the teacher would be transmitted to them. In our experience, one of the hardest things for students was that they were no longer told what to do, but had to work it out for themselves. Initially, none of the students took kindly to this approach. It is, therefore, very important to help them understand the implications of learning with PBL.

As students are used to traditional methods of learning, it is important that they are told what the differences between PBL and traditional learning are. Unless the students understand the principles of PBL and what their roles are, they will find the PBL difficult. Students must be encouraged to change their role in learning. Instead of viewing the teacher as sage and guru, students should be told that they are now co-workers with the teachers in solving the problems. The teacher's role is now one of coach and no longer of one who is expected to tell students what to do. Students may not like the idea initially, but as they begin to learn the PBL tutorial process, they start to have more confidence in their own judgment and actually enjoy it.

We found that students were more responsive to PBL if we explained to them the principles involved. If students can see what the principles behind PBL are, they are better prepared to take on the new paradigm of learning that is often foreign to them and the opposite of what they are used to in the classroom. Among the principles that are relevant in PBL are authenticity, multiple perspectives, modelling, articulation, reflection, exploration, construction of knowledge, and so forth.

A useful way of helping students to see the benefits of PBL is to inform them of the lifelong learning skills they will gain from the study. It should be made clear that the skills not only help them in the learning of the domain knowledge of the subject, but also enable them to transfer what they have learned to other modules and their future working life. One of the most effective ways of introducing PBL to the students is to show them letters or e-mails received from past students at the university who are currently at work. The feedback from past students always generates enormous interest and stimulates discussion about their own longing to learn how to learn. The curiosity and discussion act as a stimulus to want to know more about PBL. They also generate enthusiasm among students for PBL.

Finally, students should understand that unlike traditional lecture-based teaching, where the goal is to teach content knowledge, PBL is broader than the acquisition and application of content. PBL is expected to influence the whole student in every aspect of the student's learning experience. PBL is about student-centered, problem-based, small-group learning where students, with the facilitation of the teacher, are able to acquire the skills that they need in real-life situations.

Commitment

Commitment is an essential issue that students should be aware of in PBL learning. Without commitment from the students to attend the tutorial and group work, there would not be much chance of them learning. Students should be told from the outset that PBL will only benefit them if they are prepared to commit themselves and take the tutorial process and group work seriously. Teachers must help students to take ownership of their problems. Once students have taken the step of owning the problem, they will want to take up the challenge of solving it and enjoy doing so. Each student should take full responsibility for his or her own learning. Taking ownership means there are certain responsibilities that each member should take. First, it concerns the issue of commitment and this should be emphasised regularly to remind students that the problem is theirs and it is their job to solve it. Commitment means turning up for all meetings and being punctual. As a team member, each student has a role to undertake, so it is the responsibility of each member to make sure the assigned tasks are completed before each meeting. The completed tasks must also be presented correctly and clearly to the rest of the team to maximise learning. We found that the team/group that worked well and benefited most was the one where the students took their responsibilities fully in their group work.

Inquiry Skills

According to Boud and Feletti (1997), success in PBL largely depends on whether students have sufficient skills as inquiry seekers and collaborative team players in the classroom. Students often find it hard to identify critical issues and to generate coherent research design. They often do not know how to relate what they are reading to what they already know. Students are usually unfamiliar with the different stages of the inquiry process such as generating hypotheses, identifying learning issues, transforming data into a product, and providing good, logical arguments. In order to help students acquire the necessary skills, they should be working in activities that involve inquiry learning, such as problem-framing, data gathering, divergent thinking, or idea generation. They should also be learning how to evaluate alternatives and apply a solution to the problem. In PBL, students need to take on the role of inquiry seekers (Boud & Feletti, 1997).

Inquiry is generally referred to as seeking for information or knowledge. It implies a need or a "want to know" premise. Effective inquiry is more than just getting the right answer. There may be more than one. On the contrary, the process of inquiry is seeking appropriate resolution to questions and issues. In education, inquiry implies the development of inquiry skills that enable students to continue the quest for knowledge throughout life. We believe that inquiry is very important in the generation and transmission of knowledge. This requires us to shift our focus from what we know to an emphasis on how we come to know.

The process of inquiry learning involves students investigating questions, obtaining factual information, and building knowledge that reflects their answer to the original question. Embedded within the inquiry process are numerous processes and thinking skills. Inquiry learning begins with asking or framing essential questions. These are questions that require students to make decisions or plan a course of action.

Students in PBL are expected to develop critical thinking abilities by constantly relating what they read to what they want to do with that information. They need to analyse information presented within the context of finding answers. To do this, students would have to answer, "What can I do with this information?" However, in reality, we found that students generally lack this type of skill. When faced with problems, students find it hard to identify critical issues to be learned and to generate learning issues. They are often not clear on how to relate what they already know to what they are currently reading. These students lack the skills to generate hypotheses, identify learning issues, provide logical arguments, and transfer data into solutions. We believe it is important to make the inquiry process visible to students.

To help students to develop learning to learn skills requires the explicit formulation of cognitive and meta-cognitive strategies and teaching centred on activities designed to convey these explicitly to the students. We believe that teaching methods should be designed to give students the opportunity to observe, engage in, invent, or discover expert strategies in context (Collins, Brown, & Newman, 1989). Doing so would help students to see how these strategies fit together with their factual and conceptual knowledge and how they cue off and make use of resources in the social and physical environment.

Making Thinking Visible by Modelling

Modelling involves an expert performing a task so that the students can observe and build a conceptual model of the processes that are required to accomplish it. This requires the externalisation of what are usually internal processes and activities—specifically the heuristics and control processes by which experts apply their basic conceptual and factual knowledge (Collins, Brown, & Holum, 1991).

One way of making thinking visible is to work, aloud, through a problem issue that is new to us and to the students. This gives students a more realistic picture of the mental efforts and processes we must put forth and go through when we approach a problem. We can point out the actual steps in our thinking process as we go along. In this way, we not only provide students with answers to the problems, but also valuable insights into our individual and discipline-related thinking processes. In addition, it is also important to show students how to critique and evaluate each other's work in both the formative and summative stage using questions such as:

- How effective is ....?
- How strong is the evidence for ....?
- How clear is ......?
- What are the justifications for thinking?
- Why is the method chosen?
- What is the evidence given to justify the solution?

Information Literacy

One of the main aims of PBL is the development of self-directed learning skills for students. We believe that information literacy is an integral part of self-directed learning. In today's information age, students are bombarded with vast amounts of information. The ability to make choices from the huge amount of information at hand is crucial for students to take responsibility for their leaning.

Information literacy involves the ability to:

- Know when there is a need for information;
- Identify the information needed to solve a given problem or issue;

- Be able to locate the needed information; and
- Use the information to solve the given problem effectively.

It is important for students to possess information literacy to scrutinise, judge, and assess relevance. During the tutorial process of PBL, students work in groups to generate learning issues. This means students are developing information literacy. The quality of students' formulation of common and individual needs is crucial to what their self-directed skills will generate (Silven & Uhlin, 2004). This is important because it is related to the kind of learning resources that are appropriate to the learning needs.

Students may encounter many different learning resources they should be able to use. However, they are often expected to know how to pick the relevant information and resources for their self studies. Whilst it is important to give students the freedom to search and make choices about what to read, we believe that students need challenges, support, and feedback to develop information literacy.

Our information society and the need to develop student centered learning have placed new demands on the roles of libraries and librarians in higher education (Silven & Uhlin, 2004). Gaining information literacy should be regarded as a learning process. It is useful to make sure that students are trained in information literacy by librarians. Skills required by students in information literacy include: how to prepare the search, how to carry out the research, and the sorting and assessing of information in general.

Team or Group Working

Collaborative learning is an important component of PBL. It is an educational approach to teaching and learning that involves groups of students working together to solve a problem or complete a project. It is a natural social act in which participants talk among themselves (Gerlach, 1994). Learning occurs through this talking. In collaborative learning, learners have the opportunity to talk with peers, exchange diverse beliefs, present and defend ideas, as well as questioning other ideas. Students working in the collaborative environment are provided with the challenge of actively engaging with their peers to process and synthesise information in their learning rather than simply memorise and regurgitate it. When students review and reflect on their learning process together, they pick up strategies and methods from one another.

In PBL, collaboration is necessary because it gives students opportunities to see and hear how other students approach and solve problems or make decisions. Students share ideas and perspectives by working together. Collaboration helps students to tackle complex problems that an individual student, working alone, would not be able to cope with. Students can go beyond their individual problem-solving abilities with the support of group members. This idea is reflected in Vygotsky's "Zone of Proximal Development (ZPD)". Vygotsky (1978) stated that students who are actively collaborating will be able to go beyond their current development levels. Collaboration can also encourage students to help each other grow as thinkers and problem solvers by providing constructive, individualised feedback to each member of the collaborative group.

Gijselaers and Schmidt (1990) found a causal relationship between tutor involvement in PBL and group processes that affect student motivation towards learning. Unlike traditional teaching, which is often conducted in lecture format, teaching in PBL typically occurs in small groups facilitated by a tutor. Consequently, group work is a crucial aspect of PBL. It encourages students to have an inquisitive and detailed look at all issues, concepts and principles contained in the problem. Working in groups promotes development of team working skills to prepare students for later life.

Because PBL promotes group processing of information rather than imparting of information by the tutor, students in PBL need to work well as a team. However, many students have had bad experiences in group work and view it negatively. One of the authors had a mature student, an ex-army man in his mid thirties, interested in taking a PBL module. On inquiry, this potential student was told that PBL would be used in teaching this module and it involved group work. When group work was mentioned, the student was very disappointed and insisted that he would have nothing to do with group work. As far as he was concerned, group work meant that he would have to do all the work whilst the others picked up the marks. As he really wanted to take the PBL module, he then asked if he could work on his own, and was told that he could not. Realising his frustration and disappointment, the author suggested that he come along and see for himself that group work in PBL is not like he envisaged, but that each person was a vital member of a team. Reluctantly, he accepted the challenge and later agreed that group work in PBL is very different from the kind of group work that he had been used to. We believe that the difference occurred because the students had been prepared for group working by the author.

It is important to devote time to helping students to learn to work effectively in groups. Groups frequently do not work well because of the diversity and different expectations and interests of the members. Some members are committed, whereas others are very "laid back." This creates tension and frustration between members.

The success of PBL depends heavily on group work. It is the duty of the teacher to lay the groundwork early for effective group functioning. One way to help dispel negative attitudes in group working is to initiate a discussion in which the students can describe their experiences working in groups. The students can then be asked to suggest behaviours to promote beneficial aspects of good group working and discourage unproductive ones. One of the lessons we have learned in PBL is that it is important to form groups and set them to work on the problem no later than the second week of the course. The groups formed should be permanent and selected by the tutor. Groups should be given an intentionally or randomly heterogeneous composition by the tutor. It is a good idea to choose students of different backgrounds in order to reflect on the diversity of experiences of the students. If the students are new to each other, the tutor should make efforts to introduce the members to the group to break the ice. Tutors can help students better understand the merits of group work by making sure that students know how to organise the work, distribute responsibility, break up complex tasks, and provide useful feedback on what is done.

Students should also be prepared to have listening and group skills in their group work. Workshops should be conducted to demonstrate to students how they could benefit in a group process before allowing them to get on with their group work away from the teacher. Besides listening skills, students should learn how to give constructive feedback and assessments within the group

Learning is proportional to the ability of the group to work together (Johnson & Johnson, 1997; Katzenbach & Smith, 1993). Group process and interaction skills are crucial for the success of PBL. Problems in a group will compromise the learning process. According to Hitchcock and Anderson (1997), there are five different small group dysfunctions, namely:

- Apathy or lack of meaningful interaction;
- Limited or focused discussion that ignores other aspects of an issue;
- Dysfunctional group members who do not participate or perform work equally with others in the group;
- The "scapegoat" student who becomes ignored by other student members; and
- The domineering student who disrupts or prevents others from learning through the process.

Interpersonal Skills

A group of talented individual learners will not necessarily produce a learning team; no more than a group of talented footballers will produce a winning team.

To be a learning team, learners must have interpersonal skills that will help them become an effective team (Peterson, 1997). We concur with Peterson that interpersonal skills relating to group process are essential for effective problem solving and learning. It is important that students are made aware of these interpersonal skills. Peterson lists the interpersonal skills that are necessary for successful team working as consensual decision making skills, dialogue and discussion skills, team maintenance skills, conflict management skills, and team leadership skills. According to Peterson (1997), students who have these skills have a better opportunity to learn than students who do not have these skills.

Consensual Decision Making Skills

Consensus means that every member of the team participates in the decision and everyone agrees with the decision. Reaching consensus requires that every participating student has an equal opportunity of being heard and for their ideas to become part of the team database. Consensual decision making involves contributions from all members. Reaching consensus requires patience, the ability to listen and learn from others, and a willingness to adjust one's needs with those of the team. This means that students must have the ability to effectively engage in dialogue and discussion.

Dialogue and Discussion Skills

Dialogue is a process that builds shared meanings and definitions of the problem between students within a group. Effective dialogue should be nurtured, not forced. It requires true facilitation, not manipulation, where value judgments are not allowed. Through dialogue, students learn how to think together. Brainstorming and clarification are two effective processes that enhance dialogue (Peterson, 1997).

Whilst brainstorming involves a random solicitation of information that favours the more verbose and quick-thinking individuals, brainstreaming allows all group members equal opportunity to participate in idea generation. Providing equal opportunity enables students to develop a sense of ownership and reduces the tendency to think without direction. Clarification is used to provide depth of meaning to the brainstormed items and to promote understanding between students about each item. Clarification requires skills that utilise effective, not arrogant, questioning to promote understanding. Questions should include "Help me understand what you mean by that statement," or "Please explain to me how your idea relates to our problem?" This allows students who brainstormed an item to clearly articulate what they mean. This, in turn, promotes critical thinking. All students in a group must be allowed to ask for clarification of an item.

Discussion is used for the purpose of making a decision or reaching closure on an issue or problem. Discussion is not a debate, but a skill that makes thought processes visible, allowing assumptions to surface and be challenged, and exposes the sources of disagreement. It is important to remind students that effective discussion focuses on issues not personalities. The student who is chairing the discussion must learn to monitor the discussion so that it allows others reach a decision, challenge assumptions, and involve all group members.

Maintenance Skills

The requirements of a team or group are to accomplish a task and to develop and maintain the team (Peterson, 1997). It is essential that team members follow methods and procedures that allow feedback. Feedback from others is necessary for both personal and team growth. Students should learn to self-manage their own groups by conducting ongoing evaluation. Debriefing is a useful telescope for promoting team maintenance. It is a technique used to discuss how the team is progressing. Debriefing should be done at the end of every class period.

Conflict Resolution Skills

Although conflict is healthy and necessary for team growth, it can be destructive to students' learning when it is personal or becomes an obstacle to task completion. It is important to mange and minimise conflicts. Peterson (1997) indicates that conflicts can be managed and minimised by:

- Focusing on the process not the people as the source of conflict;
- Providing a safe, non-threatening environment that allows conflicts to surface and be resolved;
- Developing common team purposes and goals;
- Building shared meanings and perspectives;
- Emphasising collaboration;
- Instituting a common approach to solving problems and accomplishing team tasks; and
- Understanding differences in thinking styles.

Ground rules should be established to govern student interaction and to promote the above objectives (Hitchcock & Anderson, 1997). Ground rules should be elicited from the group members, with some mandatory ones. Examples are rules such as punctuality in attending class, no value judgments during brain streaming/storming and clarification, and come to each session prepared.

Team Leadership Skills

The group or team should seek participation and input for all members. It is important for all team members to be able to lead the problem. This can be achieved through role sharing. Shared leadership leads to shared accountability and competencies. Students taking the role of the leader should focus on the process rather than the content of the problem solving process. He or she should take on the role of a facilitator, working to encourage and manage communication, participation, and consensus (Peterson 1997). It is important to emphasise to the student who takes the leader's role that the functions are to manage and implement dialogue and discussion appropriately as well as resolving conflicts.

The previously mentioned interpersonal skills are vital if students are to work effectively as a group. Students who come to PBL would not necessarily possess these skills. It is, therefore, important to teach students these skills before the start of PBL. Learning can be greatly enhanced by students who have these skills.

Students in PBL also need group process skills such as effective listening or coping creatively with conflicts in life. Working together requires students to show respect to others in the group.

Students should be reminded of the importance their behaviour towards members of the team. To work effectively, there should be respect shown to each member of the team. There must be respect shown concerning the use of words and non-verbal behaviour. No one should be rude, arrogant, or patronising to another member of the team. Each member should be allowed to express his or her opinions and give information without being humiliated or put down. It is important to stress that there should be every opportunity for everyone to express their views without any member being allowed to dominate. Some members have a tendency to talk more than others and tend to control the group. It should be stressed from the beginning that this is not acceptable. No matter how trivial the contribution made by another member, students should be told that all contributions should be acknowledged and open for discussion.

Another useful way of making sure that students work effectively as group is to establish a set of ground rules to which all members of the group agree in writing. This could be in the form of rules for working in groups as shown in Figure 5.1.

Figure 5.1. Example of rules for working in groups

Rules for Working in Groups	
Group Member:	
Name:	
E-mail:	
Contact number ---	

Rules	Consequences
1. Coming on time	
2. Prepared for class	
3. Respectful to others.	
4. Work commitment.	
5. Work done.	
6. .... etc.	
Signed: ....Date:.....................	

Learning Skills

Last, but not least, are the learning skills that students should be aware of when embarking on a PBL study. We find that making students aware of these knowledge and skills enables them to learn better. Although some of the skills are generic skills that can be used for all types of study, some of these are new to students. Each will now be briefly reviewed.

Time Management

Students often have very little knowledge or skill in managing their studies. Although assignments are handed out at the beginning of the semester, students typically leave the work until a few days before the hand-in date before starting on it. They are not very good at managing their time effectively in order to allow themselves plenty of time to complete the work. Project management is something students should be told they have to do in order to plan their workload and stagger the work rather than leaving everything until the last minute. This is particularly crucial in PBL for the problem to be solved. It can be achieved by insisting that students draw out an action plan in each tutorial. The action plan should include who is doing what, why, how long they should take, and when the work should be completed.

Resources

This is concerned with information literacy. Students have to be reminded that not all the resources used are sound. They need to have the ability to evaluate the resources used. They have to be able to evaluate the source of the resources used by asking the following questions:

- How current is it?
- Is there any reason to suspect bias in the source?
- How credible and accurate is it?

Students should constantly be reminded that they have to carefully appraise the worth of any resources used.

Metacognitive Skills

Flavell (1979) defines metacognition as the awareness and regulation of one's own cognitive processes. Metacognitive awareness means that learners are thinking about the effectiveness of the learning strategies they are using during learning. Each student needs to be engaged in activities that support the use of metacognitive skills

Metacognitive awareness is important because it is associated with successful learners. Successful learners are able to analyse what they are doing to determine what strategies they are employing, and to evaluate the value of these strategies (modelling or visualising the steps makes them overt). It is important to reflect on the process of learning as well as the resulting products. Students need to reflect on the processes they are using during the learning process, to compare one strategy with another, and to evaluate the effectiveness of the strategy used.

Reflection Skills

Reflection helps students refine and strengthen their high-level thinking skills and abilities through self-assessment. Reflection gives students opportunities to think about how they answered a question, made a decision, or solved a problem. What strategies were successful or unsuccessful? What issues need to be remembered for next time? What could or should be done differently in the future?

Although reflection is a crucial part of learning, students rarely conduct reflection. They are often caught up in completing a task and have no time to reflect. However, it is important to help students develop reflection skills. There are two types of reflection of which students should be aware (Ngeow & Kong, 2001). The first is on content. Students should ask questions such as, "What do I now know and how can I use this information to meet the problem goal?" The other type of reflection is on the learning process. Questions to ask follow. "How am I doing as a learner in this environment—as a self-directed learner, as a problem-solver, and a collaborator?" "What are my strengths and weaknesses?" "How can I improve?" "Is this reasonable or valid?" Students should be engaged in using knowledge and modelling problem-solving processes as well as being coached in self-questioning and other metacognitive skills (Collins, 1985).

Students should be encouraged to perform articulation and presentation of ideas, perspectives, strategies and tactics, procedures and approaches, solutions, creations, and product (Dunlop & Grabinger, 1994). Articulation is very important in knowledge construction. It requires students to do more than think or reflect on what they have learned via knowledge construction activities. According to Dunlop and Grabinger (1994), articulation means that students must make their ideas, perspectives, solutions, products, and so on, available to others to reflect, review, criticise, and/or use. They must reveal what they have learned, making their knowledge construction visible to others. It is only through articulation that students learn how to express their ideas, positions, and products in such a way that is understandable and usable to others.

Conclusion

Students in PBL have to become independent, self-directed learners who learn to manage learning effectively and develop an attitude of responsibility for life-long learning. Problem-solving requires the use of knowledge gained from a variety of resources such as experiential and personal knowledge. In addition, the self-directed learning process sets high expectations for students. The student's previous years of education are likely to have fostered dependency on directions from tutors and on studying a subject where content is presented, memorised, examined, and assumed learned. The change to PBL and student-centred learning can be very traumatic for many students. Letting go of old habits and developing new ones is not easy for them. Self-directed learning in PBL requires students to take initiatives, to participate in the acquisition of knowledge in the learning process. Students must learn how to learn: to assess what they know and the adequacy of that knowledge; to set learning goals and access learning resources; and to learn to evaluate the relevance of knowledge within the context of a given situation. This is a complex process.

The group in PBL, in contrast with other types of groups, is a working group with a mandate to learn. This basic premise must be understood by all participants of the group. The sharing of knowledge by each participant can be seen as the texture and resource for the learning process where students use and build knowledge by challenging one another's understanding (von Schilling, 1995).

The type of interaction and learning are influenced by group dynamics—how verbal and non-verbal messages are perceived and responded to from the perspectives of each member of the group. Individual personalities and established patterns of behaviour affect group work and learning. It is important to pay attention to these factors, otherwise learning will deteriorate and students become frustrated and demoralised and therefore reluctant to work in a group. Having good group dynamics will foster the development of communication and collaborative skills, essential in team work. The group process also provides the context for the other two processes of problem solving and self-directed learning. All in all, for problem-based learning to be successful, it is important that students are prepared for group working, problem-solving, and self-directed learning. This is worth the time and energy involved in equipping the students with the necessary skills before embarking on PBL.

References

Boud, D. J., & Feletti, G. (Eds.). (1997). *The challenge of problem-based learning* (2nd ed.). New York: St. Martin's Press

Collins, A. S. (1985). Teaching reasoning skills. In S. F. Chipman, J. W. Segal, & R. Glaser (Eds.), *Thinking and learning skills*: *Vol. 2, Research and open questions* (pp. 65-80). Hillsdale, NJ: Lawrence Erlbaum Associates.

Collins, A.S, Brown, J. S., & Holum, A. (1991). Cognitive apprenticeship: Making thinking visible. *American Educator Writer, 15*(3), 6-11, 38-46.

Collins, A. S., Brown, J. S., & Newman, S. F. (1989). Cognitive apprenticeship teaching the craft of reading, writing, and mathematics. In L. B. Resnick (Ed.), *Knowing, learning and instruction: Essays in honor of Robert Glaser* (pp. 453-494). Hillsdale, NJ: Lawrence Erlbaum Associates.

Dunlop, J. C., & Grabinger, R. S. (1994, August). *Rich environments for active learning in the higher education classroom.* NATO-ASI Workshop, Herriott-Watt University, Edinburgh, Scotland.

Flavell, J. H. (1979). Metacognition and cognitive monitoring: A new area of cognitive developmental inquiry. *American Psychologist, 34,* 906-911.

Gerlach, J. M. (1994). Is this collaboration: In K. Bosworth & S. J. Hamilton (Eds.), Collaborative learning: Underlying processes and effective techniques. *New directions for teaching and learning* (p. 59). San Francisco: Jossey-Bass.

Gijselaers, W. H., & Schmidt, H. G. (1990). Development and evaluation of a causal model of problem-based learning. In A. M. Nooman, H. G. Schmidt, & E. S. Essat (Eds.), *Innovation in medical rducation: An evaluation of its present status* (pp. 95-133). Berlin: Springer-Verlag.

Hitchcock, M. A., & Anderson, A. S. (1997). Dealing with dysfunctional tutorial groups. *Teaching and Learning in Medicine, 9*(1), 19-24.

Hmelo, C. E., & Fearrar, M. (1997). The problem-based learning tutorial: Cultivating higher order thinking skills. *Journal of Education of the Gifted, 20*(4), 402-422.

Johnson, D. W., & Johnson, F. P. (1997). *Joining together: Group theory and group skills* (6th ed.). Boston: Allyn & Bacon.

Johnson, D., & Johnson, R. (1990). Co-operative learning and achievement. In S. Sharon (Ed.), *Co-operative learning theory and research* (pp. 22-37). New York: Praeger.

Katzenbach, J. R., & Smith, D. K. (1993). *The wisdom of teams.* New York: Harper Collins.

Ngeow, K., & Kong, Y. S. (2001). Learning to learn: Preparing teachers and students for problem-based learning. *ERIC Digest D163.* Bloomington: ERIC Clearinghouse on Reading, English and Communication, Indiana University. Retrieved March 30, 2005, from http://eric.indiana.edu

Peterson, M. (1997). Skills to enhance problem-based learning. *Med Edu Online.* Retrieved March 30, 2005, from hppt://www.med-ed-online/

Silven, C., & Uhlin, L. (2004, June 14-18). Self-directed learning—A learning issue for student. *Proceedings of PBL 2004 International Conference,* Cancun, Mexico.

von Schilling, K. (1995). *The significance of the tutorial process.* Presentation at the International Conference on Problem-Based learning in Higher Education, Linkoping, Sweden

Vygotsky, L. (1978). *Mind in society: The development of higher psychological processes.* Cambridge, MA: Harvard University Press.

Chapter VI

Developing Problems / Triggers

Introduction

The starting point for problem-based learning is a problem statement, which is also often called a trigger since it starts the PBL case and prompts the development of learning issues. It is formulated as a problem, query or puzzle that the team has to investigate and may be presented in a number of ways, for example as a video or as a simple piece of text.

In many ways, the problem statement is the key to successful PBL. If it does not stimulate the students' interest or enable students to generate learning issues that relate closely to the desired learning outcomes, then there are likely to be difficulties with both team work and achieving cognitive learning outcomes.

In this chapter we will explore the issues around the development of problem statements and collect advice from a variety of experienced practitioners on what makes an effective problem statement as well as what to avoid. We will also describe a possible process for the development of problem statements (triggers) and discuss examples.

Fitness for Purpose

In many accounts of PBL, it is easy to pick up the impression that there are standard characteristics that all problem statements must have, in particular, they are ill-structured and real-world problems. Now we will freely admit that these terms are hardly precise in themselves, but there is a gaping hole in this generalisation and that is the issue of the context in which the problem is used. The constructivist approach to learning suggests that the context is very important.

The context for students includes many aspects: their experience of problem-based learning; their age and experience in education; their attitude to learning (Perry, 1970); the other activities and elements of the course; the resources and time available; and the facilitation, support, and guidance systems available to them.

A student's attitude to learning is often one of the first things to be displayed. Many students in technological disciplines start from the standpoint that there is a right or wrong answer and struggle with the transition to a pluralistic view.

It may seem like stating the obvious, but a problem for 18-year old students who are new to PBL is likely to need a greater amount of scaffolding, guidance, and support *designed into it* than one provided for their final year counterparts who have a couple of years of experience in PBL.

New undergraduate students in the United Kingdom arrive at university expecting to be told what to learn. They have many years of experience in this. It is not surprising that one of the aspects of PBL that they find very difficult is the creation of realistic, specific, and appropriate learning issues. However, like most skills, they improve with practice.

The term scaffolding is a very good metaphor, describing the temporary supports provided to learners, which are gradually withdrawn as students become more familiar and skilled with the PBL process. The right amount of scaffolding is particularly important. This is a point worth emphasising, since in certain contexts, it has been reported that ill-defined, real world problems may actually discourage students—leaving them feeling overwhelmed instead of motivating them. In cases like this, an initial structured problem (a complex problem broken down into sub-stages with clearly defined deliverables at each stage) has been found to ease them into the PBL setting. This "structuredness" can be reduced over time (Beaumont, Sackville, & Chew, 2004).

This context also includes the experience of the course designers and facilitators. Many tutors starting with PBL can be convinced of its benefits, but feel just as uncomfortable as students when it comes to running the sessions. Greening (1998) reports "some studies indicate that student reaction to PBL becomes more favorable in later incarnations of the course, and this may possibly be a result of incorporating pragmatism into, perhaps, an initially overly-idealized curriculum."

We think it is also worth stepping back at this stage and considering for what purpose the PBL is being used. Maggi Savin-Baden (2000, p. 127) provides five models of PBL. At one end of the spectrum, there is PBL for epistemological competence, in which the purpose is for students to learn, use, and manage a propositional body of knowledge within a discipline. In this model, Savin-Baden suggests that the problem scenario is likely to be relatively limited with well-known solutions.

A second model stresses professional performance and know-how. Problem scenarios for this model will be focussed on real-life situations that require a practical solution.

The third model she proposes (PBL for interdisciplinary understanding) is an extension of the second model by broadening the learning to include synthesis of knowledge and skills across disciplinary boundaries.

A further model sees knowledge as contextual and constructed, giving students opportunities to challenge and evaluate knowledge systems themselves; any propositional knowledge is merely a vehicle towards critical contestability. This model certainly empowers the students!

We would argue that there is in fact a continuum, rather than a number of discrete models, and that it can be difficult to classify models in this way, however, such a classification has a significant use: it makes explicit that which is often assumed by faculty.

Savin-Baden points out that the model used is often implicitly determined by the pedagogical orientation of the tutor, consequently students may take different approaches to the same problem statement depending on the beliefs of their tutor. This has particular significance for problem designers and implications for staff training to prepare tutors.

We have found that clearly identifying the purpose and model of the problem, together with the context and constraints in which you must operate provides some confidence that you are developing triggers that are fit for purpose. We return to the issue of tutor preparation when considering curriculum in Chapter X.

Other Principles of Good Trigger and Problem Design

Des Marchais (1999) provides a summary of criteria from the literature for Medical PBL problems and compares it with a prioritised list identified by faculty at Rouen. They identified "stimulating thinking, analysis, and reasoning" as the most important characteristic of good triggers.

Dolmans and others (1997) identified seven principles, based on findings on the nature of learning and cognition. The seven principles are consistent with those of Des Marchais, but provide rather more operational guidance. They are as follows:

1. "The contents of a case should adapt well to students' prior knowledge.
2. A case should contain several cues that stimulate students to elaborate.
3. Preferably present a case in a context that is relevant to the future profession.
4. Present relevant basic science concepts in the context of a clinical problem to encourage integration of knowledge.
5. A case should stimulate self-directed learning by encouraging students to generate learning issues and conduct literature searches.
6. A case should enhance students' interest in the subject-matter, by sustaining discussion about possible solutions and facilitating students to explore alternatives.
7. A case should match one or more of the faculty objectives." (Dolmans et al., 1997, p. 185)

Although these were developed in a medical context, they can be adapted readily to other disciplines. We will now discuss them in more detail.

- **Building on current knowledge and experience (principle 1)** is one of the principles of constructivist learning. Students need to be able to relate to the scenario, using and extending their knowledge. The scenario helps push them into their Zone of Proximal Development (Vygotsky, 1978). This needs careful consideration, since it is important both for subject or professional knowledge and also a student's experience of PBL. Students may be technically skilled but novices at PBL.
- **Stimulating the student to elaborate (principle 2)** Anderson (1990) suggests that new information is better understood and recalled if students elaborate on it. By elaboration, we mean that they are prompted to discuss, answer questions, ask critical questions and give explanations. These activities will help students build cognitive frameworks and develop connections between ideas. This requirement is met by providing cues for the students to pick up. The tutor can help novices analyse triggers and identify and elaborate on cues. More experienced students become skilled at spotting them.
- **Authenticity** is a word that is frequently associated with PBL. It is used to indicate that the problem occurs in a sufficiently real-world context so that it is true to life—(principle 3). This real-world nature can be motiva-

tional for the student. However, authenticity is a relative term that varies with student experience: what is authentic to a 15-year-old and relevant to their experience is likely to be very different to that of a post graduate student. Honebein, Duffy, and Fishman (1991), reported in Greening (1998), identify a number of elements, which lend authenticity to a task:

- Learner ownership—relating to the relevance of the problem to the student so that the student develops a sense of responsibility for managing the problem-solving tasks. We would regard this as linked to motivation.

- Project-based nature, which mirrors real-world practice. In some cases, traditional university courses have dissected the subject matter to such an extent that the project based nature is lost and students have particular difficulty in integrating learning. PBL offers the opportunity to provide the integration at the expense of requiring the collaboration of faculty across a number of disciplines.

- Multiple perspectives—the opportunity to consider multiple perspectives is important in developing expertise. This also gives the chance for different lines of research, alternative solutions, debate, and sometimes controversy! (Dolman's principle 2)

The above factors relate to the nature of the problem, but another factor is important in the authenticity of a problem—the presentation of the information and the resources that are available.

The presentation format may be simply a written narrative (low authenticity), or it may include video recordings or role-play simulations (high authenticity). We have found that role plays are particularly good for helping students develop communication skills (amongst others).

Not all the information for the problem needs to be presented at the start, there may be important information missing that students have to request when they discover that it is needed. Authentic problems often have irrelevant information and data included—reflecting the messy nature of real problems—which students must identify and discard.

Students adapt to this approach but we have found that they often require a high level of tutorial support at the start in order to identify cues and synthesise well-formed learning issues. Novices are also very unsure how much detail is required; they have been traditionally used to being told how much (and what) to learn, so the PBL approach is radically different.

However, this helps them develop analytical and critical reasoning right from the start. They have to make judgements and it provides a good opportunity for the facilitator (and other team members) to challenge them about those judgements.

It certainly avoids the "end of chapter" question approach where students look to see if they have used all the data provided as a check on whether they are on the right track or not!

- **The level of complexity** is important and is one of the most difficult aspects to judge. It is important that a simple "divide and conquer" approach does not work and that students have to combine their individual learning from their research. Without the integration of their learning, students only see (and understand) part of the solution. In such cases, there is little team collaboration and learning is actually reduced. This relates to Dolman's principles 2 and 5. Complexity can provide cues for discussion and questioning and can require students to elaborate on their current understanding to generate learning issues.

- **The possibility of alternate solutions** (principle 6) is a particularly powerful approach. Problems written in this way reinforce the transition from "right or wrong" answers. It stretches students to evaluate their alternatives and devise criteria for such evaluation.

- **Multi-disciplinary and trans-disciplinary problems** are cited by many as desirable features and relate to Dolman's principle 4. The benefits of integrating knowledge and thinking outside of the boundaries of a discipline are apparent. There are a whole range of possibilities here, ranging from introducing some business factors into a technical scenario to constructing student teams from different subject specialists. However, the degree to which this can be achieved is often a matter of course and programme design.

- **Promotes reflection & development of metacognitive skills**. Gijselaers (1995) emphasizes the importance of reflection in the process of learning. In particular, he believes that students should be challenged at a metacognitive level to review how they learn. He sees complexity, unfamiliarity, and novelty in the PBL scenario as the means of challenging them to re-evaluate their approach to problem-solving. This process corresponds closely to Schön's (1987) *Reflection-in-action* and is what we would look for in students who have gained some expertise in PBL. More novice students can be prompted towards a reflective approach by incorporating a distinct reflection (on action) stage at the end of the scenario.

If this long list of requirements seems off-putting, we would urge you not to be put off! Problems can be developed, reviewed, and usually amended after they have been presented. We also provide some ideas for problem sources and a process for developing triggers that we hope will help.

Possible Problem Sources

It can be a daunting task to find or create problems—particularly if they have to satisfy all the principles given above! The sources, duration, and styles of problem are likely to vary from discipline to discipline.

In technical subjects, such as computing, much professional practice is concerned with solving problems, so it is not too difficult to look for cases based on real projects that are aligned with the learning outcomes of the course. The trade press, newspapers, and sometimes academic journal papers, can provide a suitable source. Past assignments can often be a basis for problems.

An interesting example is provided by a Web site development course that is run by Rachel Harris at the University of Derby. The problems were set by local companies. The local chamber of commerce was contacted to identify companies that would be willing to collaborate in the module. Companies provide an information pack and brief for the Web site and are also involved in the final assessment, including the award of a small prize. This approach proved particularly motivational and was a rich source of effective triggers.

Another approach for converting a conventional course to PBL is explained by Don Woods (1996, ch. 4 p. 2):

Look at typical exams you have used in the past. Select a set of a dozen good questions. Analyze these and see which issues each question asks the student to demonstrate knowledge about. Cross compare these with your list of outcomes. Pose some trial questions and ask colleagues to list the issues that your question triggers. Check to see that all the key issues were included. If not, revise the problem statement. Example, for the 16 lectures, I listed about 27 issues or 'learning objectives.' I divided these into four different clusters, and these posed four different questions. The questions were short, similar to exam questions. Each 'problem' then becomes the focus for the sequence of goals, teach, feedback meetings. Thus, the 16 lectures became 5 weeks of PBL addressing four 'problems.'

An increasing number of resources are available on the Web, for example: University of Delaware http://www.udel.edu/pbl/, and Coventry http://www.hss.coventry.ac.uk/pbl/.

A Process for Developing Triggers

The following process is one that we have found useful in creating triggers.

Step 1: Start with the Learning Outcomes (or Learning Objectives)

These are what we want the students to achieve, so it makes sense to start here, though we have some sympathy with Rangachari (2004, p. 1) when he states:

Instructional objectives are the temptations of the devil and difficult to resist. Faculty often lay these on so thick that the poor student who gets buried beneath the weight of the Professor's erudition, surfaces periodically only to sink again.

Often this can be where the first issue appears—the subject learning outcomes for the course may have been developed with lecture-based delivery in mind and may be difficult to group them suitably for problems. There may well be too many for a PBL-based course. They may need to be revised and it is likely that the "content" will need to be reviewed. We would argue that one of the bonuses of PBL is that it quickly identifies out-of-date sacred cows in the content that have remained in the curriculum for years, even though its relevance to modern-day practice is highly questionable. However, at this point you need to be prepared to meet opposition and expect conflict with other faculty. There was probably a valid rationale for the much-cherished content of some courses and we have found that faculty often feel threatened when this is questioned.

It is also important to consider the process skills and the learning outcomes related to them at this stage. If we really believe these are important, then we need to state them explicitly, assess them and assign a weighting to them that shows to students that they are regarded as important.

Now this sounds fine in principle, but when you start to unpick the detail, the list can rapidly become very large. The following list is based on Woods (1994, 1996):

- Problem solving skills (e.g., awareness of problem solving processes, analysis of problems for issues, demonstrating a systematic approach, creativity, use of knowledge appropriately, generating & testing hypotheses, confidence in own ability);

- Team working skills (e.g., understanding of how groups and teams form and work, coping with and resolving conflict, showing respect, supporting others, challenging others, giving & receiving feedback constructively, chairperson skills, leadership, finding ideas, sharing ideas, evaluating ideas, meeting commitments, time management);

- Coping with change (e.g., familiarity with grieving process in change, apply change process, use stress management techniques);

- Self assessment (e.g., setting goals, criteria, identifying and evaluating evidence, providing feedback); and

- Self-directed learning (e.g., understand concepts of learning, identify & locate appropriate resources, frame questions, critically evaluate information, apply the learning to help synthesise problem solution, present information in a suitable form for others).

These skills can be taught in separate workshops, or within a module. If these skills are taught within the module, then it clearly reduces the time available for the PBL process. The degree to which each aspect of each skill is assessed and the method used also has an impact. These considerations affect the scope of the problem and time available.

Step 2: Look for Possible Problems that Involve the Subject Learning Outcomes

Past assignments, exam questions, press articles, and case studies can all form a suitable basis. Typically, these will need to be expanded, placed in a real-world professional context, and developed to make sure they conform to the principles outlined above

Step 3: What Learning Issues will the Students Generate?

This is the real test of the trigger. You can list what you think they are and check to see if they align with the planned learning outcomes. However, you already know the desired outcome, so it is useful at this stage to test out the trigger on colleagues and check that they would identify similar learning issues.

At this stage is also useful to check that the scale and scope of the problem is appropriate. The number of learning issues and depth of research required will affect the team size and duration of the problem. More detail of constraints may need to be added to tailor the problem for time available. It is worth checking that the learning issues can be researched independently, but there is sufficient synergy to ensure students cannot "just glue together" the results of their individual research to solve the problem.

Step 4: Thinking through the Process

This involves planning how the problem will be introduced, scheduled, and supported.

The first consideration is the student's experience—how much preparation for PBL will these students need? Will process skills be *taught* within this case or before or are students already skilled at PBL?

The amount of scaffolding can be considered at this point. For larger problems you can consider whether the problem should be staged. This can be particularly useful for novice PBL students who need more structure. The problem statement can be introduced with a series of questions to answer which helps guide their research (though this should be used with care—see section on pitfalls).

Clearly, some important issues are the amount of tutorial support that can be provided for students, the class size, and how much time is available. The environment also has a significant impact—if you are constrained to use a tiered lecture room, it certainly affects the approaches you can take to facilitation.

An approach known as "Guided Design" (Wales, C.E, A. Nardi and R.A. Stager, 1993) can be very helpful for novices. Here students are prompted through the decision-making process by a set of printed instructions. Students' answers are checked by the tutor and sample feedback answers are provided at appropriate times. Students are asked to reflect on any differences. This approach constrains the students, reduces their ownership, and also requires a large amount of preparation by the tutor. It can be a very good way to introduce aspects of PBL and the degree of guidance can be relaxed in later cases.

The next consideration is how the problem will be introduced and information provided. For example, will role play, video, or text be used? Will information be withheld to be released when students request it? There are alternative views about revealing learning outcomes to students: unless they are written in a very general manner, they may provide too many cues if revealed at the start of the problem. An approach that avoids this provides the outcomes at the end of the problem—students can then reflect on their own generated learning issues and compare them with the learning outcomes desired by the tutor.

Woods (1996) suggests visualising the types of meetings and suggests a minimum of two (goals meeting and teach meeting) and recommends starting with three meetings around 45 minutes long (goals, teach, feedback).

Next, it is worth identifying what deliverables students will produce. Staged milestones with deliverables can be very useful in keeping students on track with large PBL cases lasting several weeks. Deliverables can be reports, posters, presentations, software, or hardware artefacts.

Finally, it is essential to list and consider what assessment processes will be used and when will they be scheduled. It can be useful to create a grid showing the learning outcome, the assessment vehicle to be used, related deliverables, and deadline. This can throw up gaps, assessment bottlenecks, and instances of over-assessment. The issue of assessment is considered fully in Chapter VIII.

Step 5: Resources Review

Once the problem is set, the next stage is to identify suitable resources, to make sure students can achieve what is required. Students frequently head for a computer and Web search engine. Now, this can be a reasonable strategy in some cases, but often we want to try to make sure alternative resources such as books and journals are used. Providing a list of appropriate resources is important—as is ensuring the library has enough of them!

The virtual learning environment (such as WebCT, LearnWise, or Blackboard) has become almost pervasive in Universities these days and provides a useful repository for learning resources together with facilities for submitting work and communication tools. We discuss the use of information technology in the PBL environment in some detail in a later chapter.

Where there is a practical element, tutors need to decide whether students will be left to learn purely by themselves or whether to include short workshops (possibly on request). Such workshops can simulate real world training courses. For example, for one computer security scenario, students were required to install and configure networking software, including a firewall. Such software products are complex, and commercial training courses on the Firewall alone could be a week long. However, a two hour lab session proved useful and effective in helping students learn the basics so that they could practice and apply them to the PBL case.

Step 6: Write a Facilitator's Guide

A facilitator's guide replaces the traditional lesson plans and scheme of work. It is particularly necessary if there are a number of tutors running the course to help achieve a level of consistency, but we have found it invaluable even when we have designed and delivered the whole module! Useful contents can be:

- A schedule for the PBL case, identifying milestones, activities, deliverables;

- Sample questions to ask at each meeting;

- Assessment criteria;

- Details of what you expect students to achieve at each stage, for example, after the first session, the key learning issues, and appropriate resources; and

- If you are using guided design, then copies of the handouts and feedback sheets.

Stage 7: Final Review with Colleagues

Finally, the whole package needs to be checked and reviewed against the authenticity of the learning outcomes. This is a substantial process and we have provided a suggestion for a review checklist at the end of this chapter (Figure 6.2) in order to draw together the important considerations.

Pitfalls

The previous section discussed suggestions for creating successful triggers. However, it is often easier to analyse what constitutes an ineffective problem statement and identify what features of problem design may reduce the potential of problem-based learning. Gijselaers (1995) suggested the following, based on his experiences at the University of Limburg:

1. The titles of ineffective problems are similar to titles of textbook chapters.

2. An ineffective problem does not result in motivation for self-study.

3. Ineffective problem descriptions include questions that are substitutes for student-generated learning issues. It can be tempting at times to include questions to provide cues for students, but these can remove the need for analysis and drive inappropriate behaviour.

This advice would appear to conflict with the Guided Design approach outlined above and does hint at dangers if the guiding questions are not well formed. The following is an extract from a problem statement related to an example case study outlined in Chapter XI.

Figure 6.1. Example scenario

Ace Training, Ltd. now wants to host its own Web site in Liverpool (with a view to ultimately incorporating some forms of e-commerce & online course booking)

The Managing Director believes that this will attract both more customs (through advertising) and more security problems, since there will be more traffic.

He recently went to a vendors' seminar to try and understand more about this, but was confused by the jargon. Two particular phrases stick in his mind (which he may have misheard). These are:

"A security policy is the foundation stone of good security," and **"The Web server should be protected by using NAT in a DMZ (screened subnet) and that the DNS server should also be in the DMZ."**

He is concerned that little thought has been given to security and he has called you in to give him a report to help develop a secure networking environment at Ace Training, Ltd. He wants the report to address the following issues:

1. What do the technical terms in the statement mean?

2. Is the statement about NAT, DMZ, etc. correct? Justify your answer.

3. What is a security policy, and what should it contain?

4. What security threats are involved when there is an Internet connection?

5. What level of **risk** is there for each threat? To do this you will need to identify the company's main assets, any vulnerability in their infrastructure, and the threats you identified in question 4. You should also show how these risks could be minimised with your proposed solution.

6. Propose how you would create a secure LAN, with Internet access, and identify what access would be allowed (i.e. from particular sources to particular resources). Use a diagram. Show clearly where the new Web server (and any other networking equipment/servers) would be located on the network. Ace has also decided to host its own e-mail server, since all employees now want internal and external e-mail access.

7. Explain what IP addresses would be used (based on the given address shown below)

8. What additional issues are involved if the company decides to introduce a form of on-line booking (and payment)?

In the example above, the students had some experience of PBL, but the time available was limited so the inclusion of guiding questions was intended to speed up the process. It became very apparent soon after introducing the problem statement that students had stopped analysing the scenario and had adopted a "divide and conquer" approach based on the eight questions. One team had even gone so far as to allocate the questions in turn as their "learning issues". This showed virtually no analysis and students came unstuck very quickly, discovering that there were significant linkages between the questions.

Thus, the introduction of these questions was counterproductive. The students had no need to analyse the scenario thoroughly or make judgements about what was appropriate to go into the report for the Managing director.

A more effective approach would be to include questions requiring students to identify and suggest what would be appropriate contents of the report, to identify what constituted a secure environment, and devise criteria to do so.

Some other pitfalls that we have discovered (from bitter experience) are:

- Providing too much information with the trigger is worse than providing too little. It is tempting to provide copious contextual detail and data to go with a case. However, students can often drown in pages of text. There is no need to specify a problem completely and unambiguously, since the first part of PBL involves analysing the problem statement, posing questions, and identifying issues for learning and clarification. Much less information needs to be supplied initially compared to traditional assignments.

- Task focussed problems provide limited opportunities for analysis and making judgements. Traditional exercises are often task-focussed, but they can be adapted by adding a real-world context to increase their scope. This can provide additional opportunity for analysis.

- Underestimating time needed—Since the process is student driven, the time requirements can vary considerably, and it is difficult to estimate the time needed. When insufficient time is provided, it reduces the likelihood of students adopting a deep approach to learning. If students have insufficient time, they fall back on strategic approach to learning or even surface approach.

- Overemphasis on product rather than learning—There is a tension here: the purpose of the PBL case is to promote learning, however, students can perceive that it is to solve the problem. It is certainly much easier to focus on the product as it is often concrete and easier to assess. In our experience, changing the focus is highly dependent on the pedagogical stance of the tutor and can be manipulated by the assessment criteria (rewarding the learning, rather than the completion of the product). Students take a while to adapt to this, but it is understandable since many of us gain satisfaction from producing a high quality product.

Appendix 6 provides a number of extracts and examples from a variety of triggers, to illustrate these principles and the variety of approaches that can be used.

Conclusion

In this chapter, we have analysed the issues involved in constructing effective problem statements. We have also explained a process for creating problem statements that has worked for us, though we are not intending to be prescriptive.

Figure 6.2. Checklist for designing triggers

What is the purpose of the PBL?	For example, to learn and apply discipline-based knowledge, for professional action, or interdisciplinary understanding.
What is the prior Student Experience of PBL?	If students are novices they will need to learn the PBL process skills
Are you teaching process skills within the course?	Process skills can be taught in separate workshops or within the course.
What weighting are you attaching to the process skills relative to the subject knowledge and skills?	Which process skills are assessed in this Problem?
What Tutorial support model is being used?	For example, roving facilitator (tutor per class), tutor per team, or student facilitators.
How many students per team	The team size and time available affect the complexity and scope of the problem.
Problem statement issues	
Student's experience	How does it relate to students prior knowledge? Does it enable them to build on current understanding? Does the problem require knowledge integration??
Trans-disciplinary	Can trans-disciplinary or multi-disciplinary factors help students integrate learning effectively
Authenticity	How relevant is it to the students and the "real world"? How motivational would you regard it?
Complexity or ill-structured nature of problem.	Is there an appropriate level of complexity to require students to integrate their learning? Can students avoid analyzing the problem in detail? Are there appropriate cues that stimulate discussion and encourage students to search for explanations?
Learning Issues	What learning issues will students generate? How do these relate to the learning outcomes or objectives of the course?
Opportunity for reflection and self assessment.	Does it challenge student's existing approaches to learning? When will students have opportunity to reflect on the process?
Alternate solutions	Are there opportunities for critical evaluation and judgments of alternative "solutions"?
Minimum information provided	Is the trigger brief enough to avoid information overload?
Presentation and content of problem statement.	Does it identify context and task clearly and concisely?

The purpose of the trigger is to stimulate thinking and analysis and provide numerous avenues for research. Problems that have a high degree of authenticity with multiple perspectives have been found to be successful. Often these can be developed from trade press, journals, or even news broadcasts.

Some problem statements are more successful than others, but we do not believe there is a single recipe that is suitable for all situations. We see "fitness for purpose" as the key determinant and that depends on the individual context of the faculty and learners.

Figure 6.2. Checklist for designing triggers (cont.)

Process issues	
How will it be presented?	For example, text, role play, or video.
How will it be structured? How will information be revealed?	Will it be staged? Will information be withheld until requested?
Scaffolding provided.	Will Guided design or Relaxed guided design be used? What support will students receive in developing learning issues?
Resources available.	Can you ensure a range of resources are used and are available? Will short instructional sessions (e.g. labs) be available?
How much time is available? How long will the case last?	Do you expect students to meet outside of scheduled class time? If so, are there timetable issues?
What deliverables are there?	Will the deliverables be staged?
When will Learning outcomes be given to students?	Will students be asked to relate their learning issues with the PBL case Learning outcomes?
Facilitator's guide:	
Schedule/resources needed	How far do you expect students to get in a session? What will you/they need for resources at those sessions?
Sample questions for facilitators	Essential for novice facilitators.
Learning issues expected	A useful checklist, it is easy to forget these when dealing with multiple teams in one session.
Assessment criteria	Most important for assessors, but it helps facilitators understand what is being judged as important by the PBL designer.

One of the great strengths of PBL is that students have more control. The tutor makes fewer assumptions of a student's existing knowledge. This means that you learn a lot about the students very quickly. You find out how they interpret information, what they understand, and what phrases in problems statements *mean to them*. This can be very revealing—lines of thought that never occur to subject experts can crop up frequently, since students' cognitive framework is different. We think this has helped us become better teachers.

We believe that problems have a very important role in learning. A problem-based approach mirrors scientific research, as Popper (2002, p.222) puts it:

Science should be visualized as progressing from problem to problem—to problems of ever increasing depth. Problems crop up especially when we are disappointed in our expectations, or when our theories involve us in difficulties, in contradictions; and these may arise either within a theory, or between two different theories, or as the result of a clash between our theories and our observations. Thus, science starts from problems, and not from observations; though observations may give rise to a problem, especially if they are unexpected; that is to say, if they clash with our expectations or theories.

References

Anderson, J. R. (1990). *Cognitive psychology and its implications.* New York: Freeman.

Beaumont, C., & Fox, C. (2003). Learning programming: Enhancing quality through problem-based learning. *Proceedings of 4th Annual Conference for LTSN-ICS.* Retrieved April 16, 2005, from http://www.ics.ltsn.ac.uk/pub/conf2003/chris_beaumont.htm

Beaumont, C., Sackville, A., & Chew, S. C. (2004). Identifying good practice in the use of PBL to teach computing. *ITALICS, 3*(1). Retrieved March 30, 2005, from http://www.ics.ltsn.ac.uk/pub/italics/vol3iss1.htm

Des Marchais, J. E. (1999). A Delphi technique to identify and evaluate criteria for construction of PBL problems. *Medical Education, 3*, 504-508.

Dolmans, D. H. J. M., Snellen-Balendong, H., Wolfhagen, I. H. A. P., & Van der Vleuten, C. P. M. (1997). Seven principles of effective case design for a problem-based curriculum. *Med Teacher, 19*, 185-189.

Gijselaers, W. H. (1995). Perspectives on problem-based learning. In W. H. Gijselaers., D. T. Tempelaar, P. K. Keizer, J.M. Blommaert, E. M. Bernard, & H. Kasper (Eds.), *Educational innovation in economics and business administration: The case of problem-based learning* (pp. 39-52). Dordrecht; Boston; London: Kluwer Academic Publishers.

Greening, T. (1998). Scaffolding for success in PBL. *Med Educ Online, 3*, 4. Retrieved March 28, 2005, from http://www.Med-Ed-Online.org

Honebein, P. C., Duffy, T. M., & Fishman, B.J. (1991). Constructivism and the design of learning environments: Context and authentic activities for learning. In T. M. Duffy, J. Lowyck, & D. H. Jonassen (Eds.), *Designing environments for constructivist learning* (pp. 87-108). Berlin: Springer-Verlag.

Norton, L. (2004) *Psychology applied learning scenarios (PALS).* York: LTSN-Psychology. Retrieved April 16, 2005, from http://www.psychology.heacademy.ac.uk/docs/pdf/p20040422_pals.pdf

Perry, W. G. Jr. (1970). *Forms of intellectual and ethical development in the college years: A scheme.* New York: Hold Rinehart and Winston.

Popper, K. R. (2002). *Conjectures and refutations.* London: Routledge Classics Edition.

Rangachari, P.K. (2004). *Prolegomena to problem writing.* Retrieved October 1, 2005, from http://www.fp.ucalgary.ca/chari/pbls/writing/intro.htm

Sage® group plc. Retrieved August 16, 2004, from http://www.sage.com/

Savin-Baden, M. (2000). *Problem-based learning in higher education: Untold stories.* Buckingham: SRHE/ OUP.

Schön, D. A. (1987). Teaching artistry through reflection-in-action. In *Educating the reflective practitioner* (pp. 22-40). San Francisco: Jossey-Bass Publishers.

UK Problem-based learning Web site hosted at Coventry. Retrieved August 16, 2004, from http://www.hss.coventry.ac.uk/pbl/

University of Delaware problem based learning. Retrieved August 16, 2004, from http://www.udel.edu/pbl/

Vygotsky, L. S. (1978). *Mind in society: The development of higher psychological processes.* Cambridge, MA: Harvard University Press.

Wales, C. E., Nardi, A., & Stager, R. A. (1993). Emphasizing critical thinking and problem solving in L .Curry, & J. F. Wergin & Associates (Eds.), *Educating professionals: Responding to new expectations for competence and accountability.* San Francisco: Jossey Bass.

Woods, D. R. (1994). *Problem-based learning: How to gain the most from PBL.* Hamilton, Ontario: Donald R. Woods.

Woods, D. R. (1996). *Problem-based learning: Helping your students gain the most from PBL* (3rd ed.). Hamilton, Ontario: Donald R. Woods.

Appendix 6:
Examples of Problem Statements

Example 1: A Structured Multi-Part PBL Case – Ace Training, Ltd.

The following is an extract from a PBL case, which lasts the full semester of a second-year undergraduate degree module and is a quarter of the workload for a single semester. The full case and discussion are provided in Annex B.

Figure 6.3. Example problem statement for multi-stage case

Problem Statement

Ace Training, Ltd is a small company, which delivers technical computer-training courses at its training centre in Manchester and on customer premises throughout the UK. It employs a Sales manager, ten sales staff, two marketing people, and two accounts in its head office in Liverpool. The Managing Director (MD), his secretary and switchboard/receptionist are also located there.

At the training centre, there are the following employees: a manager, two administrators, one technician, and ten instructors.

The sales representatives make the vast majority of sales over the telephone. There is very little use of information technology in the head office. The marketing department has one Apple Macintosh ® computer, the accounts department uses one PC running *Sage®* accounting software, and the Sales department has one PC for preparing quotes. The MD's secretary also has a computer.

The Managing Director views the current system as inefficient. He has called in your team, as consultants, to advise him. He believes a network for the head office will improve sales performance significantly. Your terms of reference are:

♦ **To design and present a proposal for purchase, implementation, and support of a new network for Sales tracking, accounts, and general administration.**

This is a sizeable task, despite the small scale of the company. Clearly, factors such as cost of the solution, training, and support are required for a comprehensive solution.

There is insufficient information given above to specify the solution precisely. You will need to find out additional information by arranging interviews with appropriate people in the company. You are restricted to two twenty-minute interviews.

Deliverables:

1. At the end of the fist session (**week 1**): Submit a **plan** to your tutor, outlining Information you need to obtain from the interviews and learning issues you have generated.

2. Your team should produce an **User Requirements Specification in Week 3** of the module (end of PBL1). The information for this document should be obtained from the problem statement; together with information you obtained by interviews. A template for this specification is available (see module web site PBL1 information page).

3. Your team should produce a **final proposal in week 11**, according to the proposal template (see module web site PBL1 information page). This will comprise your requirements from PBL1 and solution from PBL2. Your team should present your solution to the board of Ace Training, Ltd. in week 12. A short **PowerPoint presentation** is expected as well as the written report. The presentation should last 15 minutes, with a further 5 minutes for questions.

4. Your team will demonstrate the network you have constructed after PBL3, in week 11.

The module was designed for problem-based learning, consequently, the subject learning outcomes relate clearly to the problem statement. They are phrased in a general way, which avoids revealing learning issues, and are as follows:

1. Critically analyse the requirements for a small-scale network.
2. Synthesise and evaluate a design for a solution to a network requirement.

Figure 6.3. Example problem statement for multi-stage case (cont.)

Further Information

Ace Training, Ltd. Business issues

1. The company has grown rapidly and a number of problems have arisen that cause serious inefficiencies in the sales processes. For example, all customer sales records are all kept on paper. Each sales rep keeps a diary and card index of the customers that they are responsible for. This means that the information on a particular customer is difficult to find—especially if a their sales rep is not in the office. This inefficiency has led to a number of lost sales opportunities. Since the sales people are largely paid on commission, this has caused low moral (and limited profits). The *ACT!*™ Contact management software from Sage® group plc. (http://www.sage.com/) has been selected as the preferred product.

2. A consequence of the new way of working is that maximum downtime of the system must be 2 hours.

---

3. The Training Centre manager often exchanges faxes with the Sales manager.

4. The Accounts department has an old version of Sage® Accounts, which does not cope with multiple currencies (in particular the Euro).

Scope

The Manchester training centre does not require networking, but the training centre manager will need access to e-mails (via the Internet).

Liverpool building

The Liverpool site is a single-storey building (internal dimensions 20m x 16m) with solid floor, suspended ceiling, and stud-partition walls. A layout plan can be found on the module Web site. The building was recently rewired and has more than adequate power supply with plenty of sockets located throughout the building. The company does not want any walls removed, though further partitions could be added if essential. The telephone system is not to be changed.

The module has additional learning outcomes related to the process skills.

The students' relevant prior experience consists of using the university network and studying the basic components and operation of a stand-alone computer system. It is easy to prompt students to elaborate on the features and facilities of the university network, which may be of use in this scenario.

This PBL case is sub-divided into three parts: requirements analysis, solution specification, and network construction. The distinct milestones help students plan their work to meet deadlines and receive formative feedback along the way.

There are some trans-disciplinary aspects to the case: there are many solutions possible; the choice depends on a trade-off of technical suitability and performance, cost, usability, and familiarity of the staff in the case study with certain technologies (for example Microsoft Windows ®). The case is presented as a competitive tender, and a small prize is awarded to the team whose solution is the winner.

The problem statement provides some detailed information for students to analyse, but equally has some missing critical facts. These omissions are used

Figure 6.4. Examples of learning issues

1.	What information is needed for a requirement specification?
2.	How do we interview in a professional way?
3.	What is a computer network?
4.	How can computers be connected together?
5.	What software is needed to connect computers together?
6.	How can a computer direct messages to another computer?

to stimulate requirements analysis and students have to firstly consider what information they will require from the client. They obtain this information by interviewing staff from the company (role played by tutors). The role play of interviews enables the tutor to provide immediate formative feedback on both the professionalism of their interviewing technique and also their success at knowledge elicitation.

The problem-statement provides an authentic scenario for a network designer, though the breadth of the experience in this case (sales interview, system design and specification, network construction, sales presentation, and sales proposal writing) go well beyond a single professional role. This may be a weakness in the case, but provides stimulating variety and enables students with very different strengths to demonstrate leadership in parts of the case.

There is a considerable complexity in the case. Students need to consider networking hardware, software, protocols, application software, issues of resilience, and elements of security. There are a range of possible solutions to all aspects of the case. Even the selection of an accounting package throws up a number of options. From a networking perspective, alternate technologies such as Ethernet (with a variety of connection media and data rate), Token ring and Wireless LAN need to be critically examined. Operating system software also poses options of (at least) Novell Netware®, Microsoft Windows ® and Linux.

When a small network is constructed, there is a need to understand IP addressing and domain names. Students may select wireless network adaptors or Ethernet adaptors depending on their solution design. In the network construction phase, students have access to technical handouts to help them perform such tasks as installation, configuration, creation of users and security groups, shared folders, and drive mappings. Students have some prior knowledge of similar tasks through the study of an operating systems module. Nevertheless, considerable lab support is required at this point and many students have not shown a systematic approach to planning and testing in this part of the case, though we acknowledge that there are time pressures in this final part of the module, which are undesirable from a learning perspective.

The PBL case can be run effectively with classes of 20 students, split into teams of 4 to 5 students, one roving tutor/facilitator, and technician support during lab sessions.

The PBL approach has led to attendances of over 90% throughout the semester, and a much higher degree of engagement than the prior course, which was based on lectures with lab sessions that illustrate certain features of computer networking.

Example 2: Triggers for an Instructional Software Design Module

The following problem statements are three alternative examples extracted from a final year module. We have included these to demonstrate a contrast with the previous structured PBL case. The trigger is considerably shorter, but requires more detailed and in-depth analysis. The level of analysis required means that the students need a considerable amount of active facilitator support in the early stages. This impacts the tutorial model that can be applied and the tutor spends the whole tutorial meeting with a single team in the early stages. The "roving facilitator" model would not be appropriate at that point.

Figure 6.5. Example problem statements for an Instructional Software Design module

---

Problem statement one

Mr John Hawkins, head of the IT department of a Stafford school, has recently installed a new network system in the school. He has been asked by the headmaster of the school to develop educational software to supplement the teaching of various subjects. One of the projects is to develop an interactive book for the learning of arithmetic for six and seven-year-olds. You are the new developer for the project. Your task is to investigate the problem and develop the interactive book for the school.

Problem statement two

Professor Brandt, working in the Information Science department, is trying to teach students how to use the Internet to search. He found that students have great difficulty searching for relevant information that they need. Students often get a vast amount of information that they do not want. Professor Brandt would like to have something that could help him to teach his students to search more effectively. He is particularly concerned with novice searchers who find the process daunting. You are an instructional software developer that has been assigned to help Professor Brandt to develop an application that will allow him to teach his students to search more effectively.

Problem statement three

The cognitive apprenticeship model is a constructivist model that can be used to develop learning environments. Miss Hacker is a teacher at Walton school, teaching Biology to 11- and 12-year-olds. She has been told that students would benefit from supplementing their learning with E-learning. As Miss Hacker has no experience of e-learning, she has asked the school to appoint an instructional consultant to help her. Your job is to help her develop the E-learning environment based on the cognitive apprenticeship model.

Learning Outcomes for this Module

- Develop knowledge and understanding of instructional design and learning theories and apply them to the design, development, and evaluation of learning technologies (application level).

- Make critical appraisal of the various design models for learning technology (problem solving level).

As we can see, both of the learning outcomes required students to be able to learn at Bloom's application and problem solving. That is the Evaluation level.

These are typical problems that were given to a group of students in the class. The students have no prior knowledge of the problem. It is the responsibility of the students to identify the problem and develop the required solution. There were no learning outcomes or objectives given to the students. We found that it is more beneficial for the students to identify the learning objectives of the problem. After all this is what they would be expected to do in real life. Students are expected to be given problems to solve in real life and get on with it.

Learning Issues for Problem One

These problem statements are ill-defined, complex, and have been crafted so that students cannot immediately identify a deliverable set of tasks that they can sub-divide.

The first requirement is for students to fully understand the trigger and determine the scope and context of the problem they had to solve. Students also needed to find out the time available and the type of artefact produced. In this case, students were told the four main requirements of the assignment: investigation, analysis and design, implementation, and evaluation.

The objective was to give the students an idea of the requirements we expected them to complete in line with the module descriptor. How and what they had to do was left to be determined by the students themselves as they worked through the problem in their tutorial groups. We felt that it was important that students had a good understanding of what was required of them. This is because each of the requirements constituted their assessments. The students found the whole concept of this daunting and expressed grave concerns. We had to constantly reassure them.

Figure 6.6. Examples of initial areas for investigation identified by students

Examples of learning issues

Educational software
Interactive book
Curriculum development
National curriculum
Learning theories
Instructional design theories
–   Gagne's conditions of learning
–   Elaboration Theory
–   Component display theory
Learning environment
Behavioural learning
Cognitive learning
Constructivist learning
–   Cognitive apprenticeship
–   Anchor instruction
–   Cognitive flexibility theory
Learning technology
Assessment
HCI
Multimedia
Web development
Design methodologies
Tools for implementation
Evaluation of instruction and interfaces
Learning objectives
Key stage one, two, and so on.

As time went by, students began to get on with their problem. Some of the areas for initial learning issues that students generated for problem one are shown in Figure 6.6. Many of these were further refined and developed in detail.

Example 3: Introductory Computer Programming Module

Learning computer programming is not found to be easy for many students studying Information Technology courses and it has long been a subject of debate for computing educators. Problem-based Learning is an approach that has been adopted (with some success) to try to address some of the difficulties (Beaumont & Fox, 2003). The following problem statement is the second encountered by students scheduled for a period of four weeks during their first semester at university.

The subject-specific learning outcomes were as follows:

1.   Demonstrate competence at simple procedural programming.

2.   Demonstrate awareness of HCI issues and apply HCI heuristics in a restricted domain.

Figure 6.7. Example PBL case for introductory computer programming

Problem Statement

EdgeWise Games, Plc. is developing a simple animation game for children. The basics of the game involve a small animated figure moving backwards and forwards across the screen. The figure is controlled by the mouse by clicking on various objects on the screen.

Unfortunately, the prototype is not fully working. It has been provided for you on the college network in the folder: R:\CC\CW01.

EdgeWise Games, Plc. has called in your team to advise them. They require your team to:

a)   Evaluate the interface of the prototype from an HCI (Human Computer Interaction) perspective (and fix any bugs).

b)   Design an improved version.

c)   Implement a number of your suggested improvements.

d)   Present your results to EdgeWise Games, Plc., both orally and as a report.

EdgeWise Games, Plc., has asked a number of other teams to advise them. It is a competitive situation and the best solution will be awarded a (small) prize.

Outline Specification for the Game

The game is intended for young children, to develop co-ordination, especially with a mouse.

Functional Requirements

1.   An animated image of a small character moves across the screen and back, controlled by a mouse. The image should change to simulate movement (e.g., 3 images minimum should be used to show movement).

2.   The speed of movement should be adjustable.

3.   The image should automatically turn when it reaches the edge of the screen.

4.   The user should be able to control the image in the following ways, by means of the mouse:

    a)   Stop the image moving and change it to a standing position.

    b)   Start the image moving.

    c)   Reset the image to the start position.

    d)   Change direction of the image.

    e)   Make the image jump.

5.   There should be an obstacle for the image to jump over. Unsuccessful attempts should stop the image, while successful attempts should increase the score.

Non-Functional Requirements

1.   The interface should be intuitive, employing good HCI design principles, for example, good visibility and feedback.

2.   EdgeWise Games, Plc., quality standards for software documentation must be adhered to.

Prototype Screen Dump

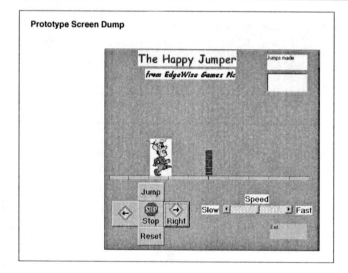

Figure 6.8. Examples of learning issues

1. What criteria make a good interface?
2. What are EdgeWise Documentation standards? [These are provided on request, but not before!]
3. What should the report contain?
4. How does the prototype work? (moving the animated image, changing the image)
5. How do you trace any faults? (e.g., Debugger)

As usual, process learning outcomes were assessed, including communication, problem-solving, team working, and improving own performance. We have not found programming the most obvious candidate for PBL. Programming requires detailed knowledge of code and a "messy" or ill-defined problem is contrary to all the tenets of software engineering and computing science. The provision of scaffolding and resources, such as self-paced texts is important for success.

There are a number of cues provided in the problem statement and students are expected to identify learning issues such as those in Figure 6.8.

The logic required for detecting a collision between the animated image and the wall, with a successful "jump" over the wall, provides an excellent opportunity for some detailed thinking and some simple algebra. Students devise a variety of algorithms.

The case builds on prior experience, extending and consolidating knowledge of events, variables, assignment statements, and selection statements. It also introduces new features such as the Visual Basic Timer control. By providing students with some code to analyse, fix, and extend, they are not faced with a blank sheet of paper and they can discuss and elaborate on their understanding of how it works. The application chosen (a simple graphical game) provides immediate feedback if the solution is correct (or not) and has proved motivational as a context. Assessment criteria are chosen to reward creativity and extension of the game for higher grades, another factor that increased motivation.

Example 4: Developing Managerial Skills Module[1]

This example presents three triggers, which provided the basis for a second year undergraduate module in management, which had duration of one semester. The subject-specific learning outcomes were as follows:

1.   The student will demonstrate conceptual knowledge in managerial skills. These could include, but are not limited to:

1.1   Problem analysis

    1.2   Communication

    1.3   Conflict management

    1.4   Empowerment and delegation

    1.5   Information management

2.   The student will be able to evaluate critically and recognise how these skills can be better applied within a practical context.

3.   The student will be able to gather and interpret information to support inquiry into, and make informed judgement about, management and organisational behaviour.

Each of the PBL cases in Figure 6.9 lasted three to four weeks.

These examples show how triggers can be introduced as very short, focused statements linked to a realistic real-world scenario. These statements require much less analysis than the examples for computer based learning (Example 2), but students need to research the general principles of the topic in detail, finally applying it to the specific scenario.

In situations where learning issues are clearly apparent, it makes it possible for a facilitator to manage more teams simultaneously.

The nature of these triggers makes it almost impossible for students to employ the "divide and conquer" approach. Indeed, it is appropriate for all students to research the same learning issues in these cases and then share their findings, discussing and elaborating on knowledge.

In these cases, a substantial list of references was provided for resources. This illustrates an alternative manner of subdividing work: students research the same learning issues using different resources.

Example 5: Counselling Psychology[2]

This example shows a trigger together with an approach to analyzing it. The example has been provided by Lin Norton from a mini-project funded by the UK Learning & Teaching Support Network for Psychology, (Norton, 2004, p. 7)

Students present their results as an oral presentation, identifying a therapeutic approach to the case and providing a reasoned justification.

Teams can produce different recommendations depending on the theoretical approach that they decide to take.

Figure 6.9. Example triggers for managerial skills module

Task 1: Communication

You have taken over as the new manager of *The Business*, a Recruitment Agency, with 36 staff members. You need to get to know all staff speedily and put communication systems in place.

Clearly explain what you would need to consider in developing communication systems and procedures.

Present your answer in a formal business report and address this to your tutor. This is a group assignment and must be 2,800□ 3,200 words. Your report must be correctly referenced, with a complete reference list.

Task 2: Conflict Management

After your first month in post, you are trying to review *The Business*'s mission statement and operational procedures. You are facing opposition from the Deputy Manager, who was the Acting Manager before you were appointed, and some other members of the staff team.

Clearly identify the issues of potential conflict and explain how these might be overcome.

Present your answer in a formal business report and address this to your tutor. This is a group assignment and must be 2,800□ 3,200 words. Your report must be correctly referenced, with a complete □Reference List□.

Task 3: Managers and Leaders

To make the staff more effective at *The Business*, you are reorganising the present structure that is very hierarchical and had staff responsibility aligned to specialist areas. You feel that this has encouraged □cliquish□ behaviour and want to introduce a team structure.

Clearly identify the benefits and disadvantages of team-based organisation. You must also clearly explain how the change will affect management and leadership opportunities and styles.

Present your answer in a formal business report and address this to your tutor. This is a group assignment and must be 2,300□ 2,800 words. Your report must be correctly referenced, with a complete reference list..

Rachel is a very attractive woman in her mid thirties who has come for counselling because although she is never without a boyfriend and frequently has more than one pursuing her. She finds that she cannot sustain a meaningful and lasting relationship with any of them. The men she gets involved with only seem to be after a sexual relationship and nothing else. Rachel always obliges, but despises herself for sometimes sleeping with men she does not even like in a, sometimes desperate, search to be loved. This self-hatred got so strong a couple of years ago that she took an overdose, but was found in time and taken to hospital. The psychiatrist who saw her suggested that her inability to sustain love

Figure 6.10. Example of Psychology Applied Learning Scenarios (PALS) (Norton, 2004, p. 7)

Rachel is a very attractive woman in her mid thirties who has come for counselling because although she is never without a boyfriend and frequently has more than one pursuing her. She finds that she cannot sustain a meaningful and lasting relationship with any of them. The men she gets involved with only seem to be after a sexual relationship and nothing else. Rachel always obliges, but despises herself for sometimes sleeping with men she does not even like in a, sometimes desperate, search to be loved. This self-hatred got so strong a couple of years ago that she took an overdose, but was found in time and taken to hospital. The psychiatrist who saw her suggested that her inability to sustain love in others might be connected to the fact that, as a child, she was severely deprived of love since her mother, a single parent, resented having to give up a promising career as an actress to look after her. Rachel does not accept this interpretation:

"*I don't believe in psychiatrists, I'm not mad. I don't believe in all the rubbish about my mum, I don't need her. I just want someone to help me find out what I'm doing wrong, so that I can find someone nice and settle down.*"

in others might be connected to the fact that, as a child, she was severely deprived of love since her mother, a single parent, resented having to give up a promising career as an actress to look after her. Rachel does not accept this interpretation:

I don't believe in psychiatrists, I'm not mad. I don't believe in all the rubbish about my mum, I don't need her. I just want someone to help me find out what I'm doing wrong, so that I can find someone nice and settle down.

Norton (p. 9) provides an example of deconstructing the case into six elements: *facts about the client; the presenting problem; the client's self-evaluation; the counsellor's assumptions; the client's assumptions and identifiable themes.*

She stresses, however, that this model is not prescriptive and students should be encouraged to generate their own understandings of the case. The model she provides is, therefore, an example of scaffolding to assist problem-statement analysis.

The case is reproduced below, showing how this analysis can be performed by highlighting key information in the problem statement for four examples out of the six elements. We have <u>underlined</u> parts of the case that can be categorised as facts, *shaded with italics* those sections that provide identifiable themes, displayed in `courier type` the problem presentation, and highlighted in a box the client's self evaluation.

Norton then links these to Dolmans (1997) criteria as follows:

Figure 6.11. Annotated PALS (Norton, 2004, p. 7)

Rachel is a very attractive woman in her mid thirties, who has <u>come for counselling</u> because, although she is never without a boyfriend and frequently has more than one pursuing her, she finds that she cannot sustain a meaningful and lasting relationship with any of them. The men she gets involved with only seem to be after a sexual relationship and nothing else. ***Rachel always obliges***, but despises herself for sometimes sleeping with men she doesn't even like in a, sometimes desperate, search to be loved. <u>This self-hatred got so strong a couple of years ago that she took an overdose, but was found in time and taken to hospital.</u> The psychiatrist who saw her suggested that her inability to sustain love in others might be connected to the fact that, ***as a child, she was severely deprived of love*** since her mother, a single parent, resented having to give up a promising career as an actress to look after her. ***Rachel does not accept this interpretation***:

'I don't believe in psychiatrists, I'm not mad. I don't believe in all the rubbish about my mum, I don't need her. I just want someone to help me find out what I'm doing wrong, so that I can find someone nice and settle down.'

Facts about the Client

Rachel has come for counselling, she sleeps with men she does not like, she has taken an overdose in the past, but she was found in time and taken to hospital. These stark facts illustrate a number of PALS objectives:

- *Meeting specified learning outcomes of the counselling psychology course: The fact that Rachel has come voluntarily raises issues about the nature of therapy, what it can offer, and the implications of taking different approaches.*
- *Building on what students already know in Psychology: Rachel's self-destructive behaviour would encourage students to reflect on what they have already learned in other psychology course, such as self–esteem, as well as link to different theoretical interpretations from the counselling psychology literature.*

- *Authentic learning, which links to the work of the professional counselling psychologist: Rachel poses a real-world problem that students could readily see as linking to the work of a counselling psychologist. The fact that she took an soverdose might stimulate students to consider the "risk" that Rachel might harm herself in the future and bring in a discussion of ethical issues related to counselling, a fundamental principle of being a professional counselling psychologist.*

Problem Presented

- *Stimulating interest in the psychological aspects of the case: Rachel is presenting a paradoxical problem—she has many boyfriends but cannot sustain a close stable relationship. Students may be encouraged to think behind the presenting problem to psychological explanations as to why this should be.*
- *Facilitating self-directed and independent learning: There is a certain amount of ambiguity here to persuade students to search for additional factors and explanations for Rachel's problems.*

Client's Self-Evaluation

- *Enabling students to understand basic psychological concepts: Self-esteem, rejection, and the need to be loved can encourage students to draw on their psychological knowledge of development and look at issues such as attachment, bonding, and so on.*

Counsellor's Assumptions

- *Authentic learning, which links to the work of the professional counselling psychologist: By describing Rachel as very attractive, students may explore the difficulties of attempting to be non-judgmental, setting aside prejudices and one's own values, which are promoted as essential attributes of the professional counsellor.*
- *Complementing objectives of psychology overall and counselling psychology in particular: The fact that the case study refers to another professional's interpretation could encourage a wider understanding of the contributions that psychology makes*

to understanding emotional distress. It also enables students to step back and look at how different theoretical approaches can determine what issues a therapist might "see" in a client. This is one of the key learning objectives of the Counselling Psychology course.

Client's Assumptions

- *Authentic learning, which links to the work of the professional counselling psychologist: Rachel has been written to challenge students' understandings of what counselling is. By describing her as wanting an easy solution, students will be stimulated to consider a common problem that professional counsellors face.*
- *Self-directed and independent learning: Rachel's assumptions about herself and about what counselling can offer will give students opportunities to discuss how they would interact with her and what part their own theoretical assumptions would play in this interaction.*

Identifiable Themes

The themes designed into Rachel's case study have, for the purpose of this illustration, been defined in terms of Freudian psychoanalytical theory, that is, the concept of denial and resistance. Similarly, the detail about her mother might be picked up by students who were taking a theoretical approach, which emphasised the importance of past childhood experiences.

These particular themes have been construed to help students build on what they know in psychology and to consider the fundamental objective of the counselling psychology course, which is not only to be able to apply a specific theoretical approach to a given case, but to understand how taking different approaches determines the issues that the counsellor will see and the therapy that will be offered. By doing this, it is hoped that students will appreciate that a theory offers but one lens with which to view the client. (Norton, 2004, p. 9)

This is a good illustration of the detailed analysis that can be performed on a short problem-statement. It demonstrates two important points: First, that a short, well-crafted scenario can meet all the requirements of a good trigger, as identified by Dolmans. Second, it illustrates the power of detailed analysis of the problem-statement to derive learning issues.

We would expect that students are likely to require guidance (at least initially) to be able to perform such detailed analysis.

Example 6: Textual Analysis Applied to a Computer Network Scenario

This example is provided by courtesy of Seah Chong Poh and Chew Swee Cheng of Temasek Polytechnic, Singapore. The PBL case is used within a Systems and Network security module within a diploma programme. It was used over a six-week period, the second half of a semester. Students had been introduced to some security concepts and techniques and the PBL case extended that knowledge, requiring them to apply it in a specific scenario, including practical lab sessions, building and configuring a secure network.

Appropriate, relevant learning outcomes to which this scenario relates are:

- Critically and systematically analyse the exposure to security threats of a networked computer system.

- Formulate a reasoned and appropriate plan to address the risks in a networked computer system.

Figure 6.12. An example Security Problem statement[3]

Problem Statement

Your company is a pharmaceutical manufacturer located in Japan. The Research Department of the company managed to produce a vaccine to effectively immunise humans against the SARs virus.

The Research Department is a small office with about 15 personal computers connected through a LAN. The SARs vaccine data collected is documented and stored electronically. The vaccine must be tested before being released to the health and government organisations.

The Norwegian HQ would need high availability access/exchange of information and to store data in Japan so as to replicate the vaccine and conduct a full quality test. It was revealed in the initial investigations that rival companies may have engaged notorious hacker group(s) in Japan to obtain the vaccine data. Thus far, there is no concrete evidence on the exploits.

Your department (Japan), Information Systems Security, is asked to review the current security concerns of the Research Department. The Research Department will need to use the local ISP to connect to the Norwegian HQ.

Your team is to submit recommendation(s) to improve on various security issues on the WAN, bearing in mind that rival companies may have huge resources to conduct electronic espionage or disrupt your company's operations, which may, in turn, delay the release of the vaccine.

You are required to mock-up WAN security for presentation to the senior management and document the risk and prevention policies.

You are to recommend means to detect possible exploits to your systems and network. Your CEO will be present at this presentation and he is interested in how it is going to be managed.

Figure 6.13. Annotated example of a network security problem statement

---

Problem Statement

Your company is a pharmaceutical manufacturer located in Japan. The Research Department of the company managed to produce a vaccine to effectively immunise humans against the SARs virus.

The Research Department is a small office with about 15 personal computers connected through a LAN. The **_SARs vaccine data collected is documented and stored electronically_**[1]. The vaccine must be tested before being released to the health and government organisations.

The Norwegian HQ would **_need high availability access/exchange of information and to store data in Japan_**[2] so as to replicate the vaccine and conduct a full quality test. It was revealed in the initial investigations, that **_rival companies may have engaged notorious hacker group(s) in Japan_**[3] to obtain the vaccine data. **_Thus far there is no concrete evidence on the exploits_**[4].

Your department (Japan), Information Systems Security, is asked to **_review the current security concerns_**[6] of the Research Department. The Research Department will need to **_use the local ISP to connect to the Norwegian HQ_**[5].

Your team is to **_submit recommendation(s) to improve on various security issues_**[6] on the WAN, bearing in mind that rival companies may have huge resources to **_conduct electronic espionage or disrupt your company's operations_**[3] which may in turn delay the release of the vaccine.

You are required **_to mock-up WAN security for presentation to the senior management and document the risk and prevention policies_**[6].

You are to recommend means to detect possible exploits to your systems and network. Your CEO will be present at this presentation and he is interested in how it is going to be managed.

- Use appropriate tools to implement aspects of security in a networked computer system.

The scenario is presented to students as follows in Figure 6.12.

There are a number of cues within this statement; some related to the fundamental themes of network security (maintaining availability, integrity and confidentiality of information), the systematic methods of analysis (assets, threats, vulnerabilities, risks and controls/ prevention measures), and also the roles of security professionals (Analysis, planning, implementation of controls and auditing).

Students are provided with a template as a scaffolding measure to assist them in analysing the scenario. This is provided in the form of a table and requires them to identify each particular phrase or sentence in the problem statement and state the corresponding learning issues that have been generated from it.

Some examples are provided below, expanded from the facilitator guide and analysis provided by the case author. We have underlined key phrases and explained the learning issue generated.

1. "...SARs vaccine data collected is documented and stored electronically." In the context of information security management, this is a cue to identify:

   a. an information asset (the stored data) that is critical to the company, thus Integrity and confidentiality are vital.

b.   Learning issues: How can data be stored to maintain integrity, confidentiality, and availability to the appropriate users? What threats are there to the system? This will lead to investigation of encryption methods, secure storage methods, and backup procedures.

2.   "...need high availability access/exchange of information and to store data in Japan." This is a cue to identify:

a.   High availability of information and the related issue of how can this be provided. Later in the scenario, the Internet is identified as the communication channel.

b.   Remote access methods that may be used to access the data that is stored in Japan from the Norwegian HQ. There are a number of remote access methods that could be investigated.

c.   Confidential transport of information over the Internet, leading to the issue of how this may be provided and related issues of Authentication and authorisation. There is opportunity to investigate alternative, secure transport mechanisms, such as Virtual Private Networks (VPN) using IPSec protocol or SSL. This affords critical evaluation of the suitability of alternatives.

3.   "...rival companies may have engaged notorious hacker group(s) in Japan "..."to conduct electronic espionage or disrupt your company's operations." This is a cue to identify:

a.   What methods hackers could use to obtain or disrupt access to the data stored on the systems or while being transmitted.

b.   What response methods can be employed, such as hardening of critical servers and database management system and tools or hardware/software to prevent intrusion.

4.   "Thus far there is no concrete evidence on the exploits." This is a cue to investigate:

a.   What tools and techniques can be used to detect intruders or attempts to damage the integrity of data?

5.   "...use the local ISP to connect to the Norwegian HQ." This relates particularly to items 2 and 3 above, since it sets the context for the communications over an insecure public network, rather than a dedicated connection. High availability takes on a new significance on the Internet in the light of possible Denial of Service (DoS) and Distributed DoS attacks. This is a cue for:

a.   Investigation of malware and related responses/controls.

b.   Investigation of Dos, Ddos, and so on, and methods to ensure availability.

6. "review the current security concerns"…"submit recommendation(s) to improve on various security issues"…"to mock-up WAN security for presentation to the senior management and document the risk and prevention policies." These statements provide clear cues about the role of the students in this scenario. It is a cue for students to:

   a. Identify a systematic methodology for reviewing and documenting the information security management system. Students are provided with a resource template for such an approach.

   b. Design a secure architecture for the network and remote access.

   c. Construct, implement, test, and document a small network with appropriate defence technology. Students have prior experience in configuring a firewall, provided in a lab session (emulating an industrial training course).

This problem statement, once again, clearly demonstrates desirable characteristics of triggers that are relevant to a real-world scenario with authentic activities. Development of an Information Security Management system is a very large task and this scenario focuses on a restricted aspect of the technical security measures. However, it is expressed in a way that provides cues to link the technical to the managerial aspects of security management—in particular, the link to assets and policies. It manages this without overwhelming the students with details of company data and assets. There are alternative solutions to the scenario and this encourages students to debate, discuss, and elaborate on their research findings. It would also be possible to analyse the scenario from a managerial perspective, rather than technical, though students would be expected to generate many more requests for clarification of information held by the organisation.

A further interesting aspect of this scenario concerns missing information. The most common breach of security of an information system is through employees. This scenario deliberately provides no direct cues for this threat, and students are expected to uncover this in their research.

Endnotes

[1]   Example provided by Tessa Owens, Liverpool Hope University.

[2]   With thanks to Professor Lin Norton, Liverpool Hope University.

[3]   With thanks to Seah Chong Poh and Chew Swee Cheng, Temasek Polytechnic, Singapore.

Chapter VII

The Tutorial Process

Introduction

The tutorial process is at the heart of PBL. In addition to the acquisition of knowledge and conceptual understanding relevant to the given problem, we believe the tutorial group also has positive cognitive and motivational effects on students' learning. There are variations of the PBL tutorial process, based on the Barrows' model. This chapter describes the tutorial process we used for our students.

Traditional vs. PBL Tutorial

The tutorial process in PBL is often confused with the case method of teaching (Barrows, 1992). It is important to distinguish between the two. Although the case method teacher does not directly give information to students, but challenges them to present their own thinking, he or she does provide students with information and direction. This is done by responding to students' ideas with counter examples, absurdities that would result from their ideas, or by providing new facts that will shape their thinking at a critical point. On the other hand, in the PBL tutorial, the case or situation generates the analytical process in which the students have to discover what they know and what they need to know in order to deal with a given situation. Students in the study have to take responsibility to acquire and test the applicability of knowledge for understanding issues and determinants from a potential practice perspective (von Schilling, 1995). The tutorial process is a regular meeting of students and tutors to discuss a topic. In PBL, the tutorial process structures the discussion and it provides students with a framework for working through their tutorial topic, presented as a problem (Clarke, 2002).

According to Bertola and Murphy (1994), successful tutorials contain the following features:

- Clarifying the role of tutor;
- Clarifying expectations;
- Planning session;
- Providing clear tasks;
- Modelling the kind of behaviour that the tutor wants to encourage and observe in students;
- Providing a conducive environment;
- Keeping students' attention on the topic and its relation to the "big picture" of the unit;
- Listening effectively; and
- Focusing on the process as well as content.

However, the tutorial in PBL is different from that described by Bertola and Murphy (1994). The main difference is that in PBL there are no clear tasks. The tasks in PBL are typically open-ended and "messy" in order to provide suitable stimulus for higher-order learning. Although there are different versions of Barrows' tutorial process, the basic concept is the same. During the tutorial process, the students actively engage with a problem, formulate hypotheses, identify learning issues, evaluate, reformulate, and revise them.

Students work through the same phases of the PBL process for each problem. The tutorial process provides a framework for working on the problem and allows the tutor and students to independently and collectively monitor and manage student progress in working through the problem. All PBL processes involve a sequence of working steps. The PBL process at Maastricht University consists of the following seven steps:

1. Group clarifies the text of problem.
2. Students define the problem.

3.   Group brainstorms to identify explanations of the phenomena observed in the problem scenario.

4.   The group reaches an interim conclusion of the problem.

5.   Group formulates the learning issues.

6.   Group conducts independent study to achieve learning outcomes.

7.   Group discusses the knowledge acquired.

Step 7 is generally a second tutorial where students re-examine the problem in the light of the new knowledge. Students can also critique the resources used and summarise and integrate the knowledge acquired. Students also evaluate their performance in problem solving, self-directed learning, and tutorial performance at the end of the session.

It is generally acknowledged by PBL practitioners that the role of the tutor in the tutorial process is to help students acquire the knowledge and skills to solve the problem, develop reasoning skills, team skills, and self-directed learning skills. We concur with Hmelo and Ferrari (1997) that the key benefits of the PBL tutorial are:

- Development of professional reasoning or higher-order learning skills; and

- The practice of reflection or self and peer assessment of the attainment of knowledge, the value of resources and the performance of professional skills.

Small Group Tutorial

In PBL learning, the group consists of five or six students with a tutor as a facilitator. The tutorial session begins with a problem given to the group by the tutor. The problem serves as a stimulus for learning. Rather than teaching the results of the investigation of others, so that the students learn passively, the tutor assists students in learning and mastering through the process of active investigation. The process involves the ability to formulate good questions, identify and collect evidence, present results systematically, analyse and interpret results, formulate conclusions and evaluate the worth and importance of those conclusions (Lee, 2004). The process also includes the ability to identify and examine the problems, generate possible solutions, and select the best solution with appropriate justification.

This approach to learning fosters intellectual development and maturity, and the recognition that ambiguity and uncertainty are inevitable. Students must learn to make reasoned judgements and act in ways consistent with those judgements. In the PBL tutorial, the tutor guides students in reasoning their way through the problem. Significant findings, hypotheses, and learning issues—knowledge needed to better understand and further pursue the problem—are recorded by the group. In the small group process, the tutor facilitates students' access to their prior knowledge and the identification of the limitations of their knowledge. During the tutorial process, the tutor also guides students to articulate their knowledge of the relevant disciplines as it relates to the given problem.

The need for information to solve the problem generates learning issues for further studies. Students working individually or in small groups identify and use a variety of resources to study the learning issues. They then return to the group to discuss and share what they have learned and apply their new knowledge to the problem. They are then able to confirm or reject their hypothesis. The tutorial process allows integration of learning, as students study different aspects of the problem. Members of the group also access the resources used by each of the other members of the group.

Despite the different variations on the tutorial process, it typically consists of:

- Identifying the facts in the problem;
- Generating ideas about the problem;
- Identifying things that they have to learn—learning issues—so that they can test their ideas or hypotheses; and
- Evaluating the ideas to see if these are valid solutions to the problem.

The above inquiry-organising steps help students become familiar with reasoning processes, to fill in what they do not know in their knowledge base, and to use the newly acquired knowledge to refine or discard their ideas, thus generating a whole new set of learning issues.

The PBL Tutorial Process

The purpose of the tutorial process is to guide students, through inquiry, to answer their own questions, search out answers to problems, and relate their knowledge to real-life applications (Ward & Lee, 2002). It encourages students to look for new solutions to relevant problems, using available knowledge and resources. According to Ward and Lee (2002), the tutorial process expands students' critical thinking and problem-solving skills whilst enhancing their creative capabilities.

It is important for tutors to understand the flow of activity during the PBL stages. This includes beginning the problem, inquiry, investigation, problem solution, and debriefing in order to coach students effectively (Stepien & Pyke, 1997). PBL begins when students understand the problem statement, build hypotheses that launch investigation, and list what they already know, what they do not know, and what they need to know to solve the problem. Listing what they know, what they do not know, and what they need to know is an important step in the group tutorial process. During the tutorial session, as students gather and share information, the "what they need to know" column is updated. The "needed to know" information is updated to "what they know" as new information is acquired. Other needed information will be identified by the students as the problem evolves. This is then added to the "what they need to know" list. We have adopted a slight variation of the Barrows model. Our tutorial process consists of four main phases as shown in Figure 7.1.

The four stages represent steps in the group's reasoning through a task or problem. More than one session is often required for the tutorial process. During the first stage, students begin the problem. They then define their objectives, reasoning their way through the problem and identifying what they need to learn. Students then go off and carry out self-directed learning to achieve the identified learning needs. In the third phase, students return from their self-directed study to apply what has been learned during the self-directed study. There may be more sessions held for the problem or task if students find there are more needs to be learned during the application of their newly acquired knowledge. In stage four, the group presents and reports the findings of the problem, following its completion, to the tutor and their peers. Students also conduct self-evaluation of their learning and performance of the problem.

During the tutorial session, students should identify the problem, identify what is already known by activating their prior knowledge, suggest possible causes,

Figure 7.1. The four phases of PBL

	Activity	By Whom
Phase 1	• set the scene • present problem • set hypothesis • identify learning • assign tasks	• group (with tutor) • group (with tutor) • group (with tutor) • group (with tutor) • group (with tutor)
Phase 2	• self-directed learning • group sharing without tutor	• individual • individual and group
Phase 3	• evaluate resources • re-examine the problem • revise hypothesis and learning issues	• group (with tutor) • group (with tutor) • group (with tutor)
Phase 4	• present findings • metacognitive critique • self evaluation	• group to peers and tutor • tutor and peers • group (with tutor)

explain their reasoning in terms of evidence presented, explore the limits of their understanding, ask questions, and formulate learning issues, discover and incorporate new learned information, and revise thinking.

For each tutorial session, students should come prepared to discuss the problem and the learning issues that have been researched since the last tutorial. Each student should actively participate in the group discussion and contribute to learning by debating evidence related to the case, based on the learning issue developed.

Phase 1

Step 1. Setting the Scene

Before the tutorial process, the roles of the team should be determined. A scribe should be chosen to write down all the discussion. Each member of the team should take turns as the scribe or reporter. In addition to the scribe, a chair person should be appointed by the group. The role of the chair person is to ensure that the group process functions properly. Before the first tutorial session, there should be group process training for students, as mentioned in Chapter V. The students should have known each other and the tutor before Phase 1 of the tutorial process commences.

Ground rules should be established before Step 1 of the tutorial process. It is very important to establish the general rules, outlining how each member of the group will interact with one another and honour the PBL tutorial process. Ground rules are written down and students are reminded of them before each tutorial process. They are necessary because they establish common expectations of each member's role in the group. Conflicts can be avoided by having some ground rules—they help smooth group interaction. If conflicts do arise, ground rules can be used for diagnosing problems and deciding what to do to resolve the conflict. Two types of ground rules are necessary: programmatic and group interaction (University of New Mexico, 2002). Programmatic ground rules are those considered to be essential for PBL learning to take place. These rules must be made explicit to the students. They include:

- Roles of tutor and students;
- Punctuality and regular attendance;
- All steps of tutorial process must be followed;
- All students must research major learning issues;
- Conduct individual, self-directed learning;

- Teach others what you have learned;
- Conduct regular reflection and assessment; and
- Complete assigned tasks.

Group interaction ground rules concern with how group members will treat each other in their interpersonal interaction. Issues to be addressed include:

- Being courteous and respectful to each other;
- Providing constructive feedback;
- Acknowledging others' contributions;
- Attempting to resolve conflicts;
- Helping to maintain group dynamics; and
- Negotiating alternatives if unable to complete assigned tasks.

Step 2. Present the Problem

During this session, the tutor distributes the problem to the students in the group. Each member of the group reads the problem. In the first tutorial session, it is very important to make sure that students really understand what they have to solve. The tutor should fully conceptualise the problem by brainstorming possible linkages to course content. Although the process is meant to be student-centred, the tutor needs to anticipate certain paths that students may take in order to steer them in helpful directions that could support the learning of problem-solving and critical-thinking skills.

The PBL process starts with students understanding the problem statement. Students then have to build hypotheses and launch the investigation. To help students to better understand the problem, the tutors should make sure students know what assumptions are made about the problems, the context of the problems, and what is expected from them. The role of the tutor in the tutorial process is that of a coach, to assist students by developing questions about the issues under investigation; determine activities that help to answer the questions, and produce a solution that is viable for the problem.

Issues in the Problem

It is important for students to understand the problem before they start to solve it. There are facts already given in the problem, but there are also many that are

Figure 7.2. PBL tutorial chart (adapted from Duffy, 1994)

Idea (Hypothesis)	Facts	Learning issues	Action Plan
Students' conjectures regarding the problem may involve causation, effect, possible resolution, and so on.	A growing synthesis of information abstracted through inquiry is important to the hypothesis to be generated	Students' lists of what they need to know or understand in order to complete the problem task.	Things that need to be done in order to complete the problem task.

missing. It is important that students understand the context of the problem to be solved. Students need a deep understanding of the issues in the problem before they can solve it. Questions that are helpful to find out the issues of the problem include:

- Where did the problem occur?
- What physical resources surround the problem?
- Who has the opinion about the problem?
- What is the nature of the business, agency, or institution?
- What do they produce?
- What are the values, beliefs, and socio-cultural expectations of the people involved?
- What is the science in the problem?
- What are the skills and backgrounds of the people involved?

To help students to structure their thought processes, a four-column chart (as shown in Figure 7.2) can be used (adapted from Duffy, 1994).

To help solve the problem, students first have to identify the facts they already know or are available to them. This can be written down in Column 2 of the PBL Chart. Here, students share their own knowledge and experience.

Step 3. Generating Hypotheses

Although some of the facts may already be known by the students, there are many more facts that are not provided when the problem is first given. Typically, in most ill-defined problems, the information needed to solve the problem is not readily available at the outset. An inquiry has to be undertaken to obtain the information needed to determine the nature of the problem, what may be the cause, and then to effectively manage the problem. A number of possible causes for the problem (hypotheses) must be generated to serve as a guide to the inquiry. Inquiry involves asking questions. It is important to generate appropriate questions to help solve the problem.

It is important for students to identify what they do not know. To do this, students need to generate ideas or hypotheses. That is, to brainstorm for ideas. This is a crucial step in the problem-solving process. With brainstorming, each member of the group makes suitable suggestions until no more ideas are forthcoming. To help students to generate hypotheses, it is useful to ask questions about what is interesting, puzzling, or important to find out, in relation to the problem. We believe that by asking students open-ended questions, a discussion environment can be created for considering what needs to be learned to solve the problem. Students should be asked to generate broad hypotheses and rationales of the problems, individually and/or as a group, using the first column of the PBL chart in Figure 7.2.

The tutor should discourage students from going into too much detail during this brainstorming step. This is essential as it encourages students to come up with different solutions to the same problem. All ideas or hypotheses generated by students are written down in the first column of the chart. At this stage, all ideas are feasible solutions and must not be discarded. Students are then asked to rank the hypotheses on the chart, either as individuals or as a group. There should be discussion among the group as to why hypothesis one, two, three, and so on, are so ranked.

There are various problem-finding strategies that can be used to identify and clarify problems. Inquiry-guided questions can be used to help students strategise and plan their investigations. Questions that help probe hypotheses include:

- What assumptions are you making about the problem?
- What could we assume instead?
- What sort of ideas or concepts do we need to investigate here?
- Does any idea come to mind that we can investigate?
- How can we proceed to solve this problem?
- What do you think is missing from the information given?
- What sort of skills do you need to help solve this problem?
- What knowledge do you need to help solve this problem?
- What issues do you need to consider here?

Step 4. Testing Hypotheses

Here, the group examines, in more detail, the ideas or hypotheses raised in the brainstorming and compares their ideas against the problem outline to see how well they match, which solutions are linked, and where further explanation is needed. It may be useful for students to write hypotheses on one side of the board and problems on the other, and then connect the two by explaining how one leads to another. The emphasis here should be on how. It may be necessary to facilitate the reworking of hypotheses at any time, using new information or rationales. The tutor can help students to discover what they know, explore the group's current knowledge, and lead them to discover what they need to know to understand and address the problem.

Step 5: Identifying the Learning Issues

Questions needed to explain a hypothesis that cannot be answered by the group during the time of the tutorial session are known as learning issues. Learning issues are topics that are deemed by the group members to be of potential relevance to the problem that they do not understand as they should. Learning issues can be identified at any step and at any time as the tutorial process unfolds (UNM, 2002). For each idea generated, students are then asked to identify learning issues that are relevant to the ideas, that is, the learning outcomes or objectives that they will need to know for the solution to the problem. All relevant learning issues, identified for each of the ideas generated, are written down in the third (learning issues) column of the chart. Learning issues should be written as complete sentences that generate higher levels of thinking and focus on the problem. They should not be "yes" or "no" answers, or solely "what" questions. Instead, they should involve "how" and "why" questions. The identification of learning issues reflects on the biases and individual characteristics of the group. The tutor assists in the processes of identification and discussion. He or she monitors group progress and interaction, intervening where necessary, to help maintain the direction of the group. It is important to remember that the problem is a springboard to learning. The problem acts as a stimulus for discussing and asking questions and as a framework for organising the knowledge. It allows for the acquisition of essential information, encourages the development of sound concepts, and leads to the establishment of principles that are essential to the students. There are no pre-specified objectives presented to the students beforehand. Students have to generate the learning issues (objectives) based on the analysis of the problem. In order to identify learning issues, students have to ask basic questions such as:

- What do I need to know in order to address this problem or question?
- What are the main points to be addressed?
- How does this ..... relate to .....?
- How does this relate to our problem/discussion/issue?
- What method/approach can be used to solve this?
- Is there any method we know that can be used to help us in solving this?
- How does that apply to this case?

It is important that every member of the group agrees on the group's learning issues; that is, what the group wants to achieve? What knowledge and skills do they want to acquire in their activities with the problem or task?

Step 6. Plan Action: Assign Tasks

Having identified all of the important learning issues, the next step is to write an action plan, consisting of the tasks to do for each of the learning issues for the next session. Next, the group must decide which issues everyone will tackle and which issues will be divided up for individuals to tackle. The identified learning issues are ranked in order of priority. Each student is assigned certain learning issues to study. Some fundamental learning issues will be studied by all students. Others will be divided up among the members of the group. Details regarding the learning issues and actions to be taken are written down in Column 4 of the PBL chart. An elaborate planning sheet, such as the one in Figure 7.4 at the end of Appendix 7B, can be used to help students to assign tasks and plan work. Besides the assignment of learning issues to group members, the type of resources expected to be used are included, for example, looking up notes, books, conducting a literature search, searching the Internet, asking an expert, and so on.

In summary, the steps for this phase consist of:

1. Writing down a list of tasks to do.
2. Deciding on what issues everyone will tackle.
3. Deciding on specific issues each individual will tackle.
4. Deciding on what resources to use.

A session is not complete until each student is fully aware of the responsibility that he or she will take as well as particular learning issues that have been identified. Since all this is taking place in front of the tutor, he or she is able to keep a close eye on the progress of each member of the group. This also helps the tutor to monitor the learning outcomes of the students to ascertain that their hypotheses generated are not completely off target. The tutor would also learn which student is doing what, thus ensuring that all are contributing. Once this has been agreed, students would go away to do their self-directed or independent work. Before the tutorial ends, the schedule for the next tutorial is drawn up and agreed.

Phase 2

Self-Directed Learning

After the tutorial session, students all engage in self-directed learning. Self-directed learning happens when the learner initiates the learning and makes decisions about what to learn and how to learn. The learner selects his or her own learning goals, objectives, strategies, and means of evaluating whether the goals were met.

According to Hiemstra (1994), educators can facilitate self-directed learning by:

- Making sure that learners are aware of the objectives, learning strategies, resources, and evaluation criteria once they are decided upon.
- Teaching inquiry skills, decision making, personal development, and self evaluation of work.
- Helping learners to develop positive attitudes and feelings of independence relative to learning.
- Helping to match resources to the needs of learners.
- Helping learners to locate resources.

Self-directed learning is a core component of PBL. We concur with Silen and Uhlian (2004) on two issues that are important in improving students' self-directed learning. These are student's inquiry into their learning process in the tutorial process and information literacy during self-directed learning. Students should be helped to develop both inquiry process and information literacy for the tutorial process. Information literacy is an integral part of learning. Students must be able to search and make choices from the huge amount of information available. They must have the ability to scrutinise, judge, and assess relevance.

The learning issues identified during Step 5 of the tutorial session are crucial to what students' self-directed learning will generate. It is also important to consider the kind of learning resources that they need to use to research their learning issues. When students are working alone, outside of their group session, they will inevitably encounter many different resources that they could use. There are many questions that need to be addressed, such as, "How do I prepare for the search?" (How to carry out the search, the sorting, and assessment of information), "How do I know I have the right information?" and so forth. Many students lack information-literacy skills and are often confused as to how to proceed. We believe that students need challenges, support, and feedback to develop information-literacy skills. Gaining information-literacy skills is now regarded as an important learning process (Limberg, 2000; Silen & Uhlin, 2004).

Step 7. Individual Learning

During this step, students will individually seek out any available resources to obtain the information that will contribute to understanding, explaining, and solving the problems for the different learning issues they need to learn. After each group meeting, the next stage of the self-study work is developed. This is the time in which students conduct their own studies. The time spent outside the group facilitates the development of skills such as literature retrieval, critical appraisal of available information, and the seeking of opinions of peers and specialists. Students are expected to research and elaborate on new information and concepts that each of them is allocated from the learning issues/objectives defined during the tutorial session. As they return to their small groups, they will bring this new knowledge and information to the group.

During the individual study, each student should research the learning issues identified during the tutorial group session using various resources. Having researched for new information, students should critically evaluate the credibility of the sources and the validity of the information obtained from the research. Once the student has done this, he or she should integrate what has been learned through research, lectures, or other means into what is discussed in the tutorial sessions. Besides integration, students should also synthesise what they have learned. This is to prepare them for discussion—without reading from their materials as much as possible—and applying it to the problem at the next tutorial session.

Step 8. Group Sharing without the Tutor

This is not a typical step in traditional PBL. However, we believe it is a very useful extra step to have in the tutorial process. Before students return to their tutorial session with their tutor, the group meets together. This meeting serves two purposes. First, it is to ensure that each member of the group has completed his or her assigned work. Second, each of the members of the group has to teach and explain to the others what he or she has researched and learned. This enables the student who is doing the explaining or teaching to articulate his or her learning. We found this helpful to students because they tend to have a better understanding of the learning when required to teach or explain it to others.

To help students to prepare for this, we explain to them the characteristics of the strategies that can help them better process information and regulate learning, how these are used, what skills are involved in them, when, how, and why to use one strategy or another, and what they are used for. To do this effectively, students are expected to assume responsibility for their own learning as well as their group's progress. The quality of the learning in the group is dependent on the quality of the input by the members of the group taking an active role in helping one another to learn.

Phase 3

Step 9. Group Reassembles to Report on Self Study

In this second meeting with the tutor, the group returns to discuss what they have learned in their self-study. Each student reports on the output of their study, shares information about the sources they used, helps each other student understand the problem, and identifies problem areas that need further study or that require help. During this session, students must apply, through their interactive discussion in the tutorial, what they have learned. They must do this in a manner that will provide a deeper understanding of the problem and make sure of the recall of that information when they encounter similar problems in the future. In this step, the tutor asks the students to start over with the problem or situation from the very beginning and describe what they now realise they should have thought and done with the problem (hypothesis, inquiry strategy, synthesis, decision, and so on), based on their new learning. Students should be made to compare their new thinking with what they had thought and done previously. Information obtained by each student's self-directed learning is then brought into the picture at the point the issue was raised in the prior discussion so that the new knowledge can be applied to the problem and integrated into what is already known (Barrows, 1988). By doing this, students critique prior knowledge and reasoning and apply new knowledge as they reason, linking reasoning skills and knowledge in the long-term memory.

During this step, students analyse and evaluate information for relevance. They will review the hypotheses that were generated prior to the self-directed study. Students discuss and share what they have learned and apply their new knowledge to the problem by either confirming or rejecting their hypothesis. Any suggested changes in the hypothesis will reflect what was learned during self-study and open an interactive discussion of what was learned. This tutorial process enables the integration of learning as students study all facets of the problem. Information from all relevant disciplines is studied and applied to the problem, since integration of knowledge is essential to the problem-solving process.

Information gained through inquiry during the self study is assembled into a growing representation of the problem (problem synthesis). To help students to analyse its relevance to the hypothesis generated or to decide whether a new hypothesis needs to be considered (analysis), the tutor can help students by asking relevant metacognitive questions such as:

- What do you mean by .....?
- Can you give an example of this?
- Can you elaborate on this?
- Why do you say that?
- What do you imply by that?
- How can we know we are right?
- How can we find out?
- Can we break this down further?
- Is the evidence sound?
- Can someone else give evidence to support that?
- How did you come to that conclusion?
- How do we find out if it is true?
- Can you explain your reason to us?
- Is there a reason to doubt the evidence?
- Why is this issue important?

When students have gained new information from their studies, they should then use this information to refine their hypothesis. As the problem unfolds and the students evaluate their hypothesis, they should consider what information is needed to help make the hypothesis more—or less—likely. If their hypothesis is correct, what predictions would they make? (UNM, 2000).

When blind alleys are encountered, or inquiry reveals new aspects of the problem, the process becomes cyclical; new hypotheses are developed and new inquiry strategies are undertaken. Steps 7 to 9 of the tutorial process are repeated

Figure 7.3. Problem follow-up chart

IDEAS (Hypothesis)	FACTS	LEARNING ISSUES	ACTION PLAN
Revise	Apply new knowledge and re-synthesise the problem	Identify new issues (if necessary)	Redesign decisions

until the group feels they have completed the problem. During this step, it is important to have a critical look at the resources the students have used. Students evaluate what was useful and what was not so useful. Students should also evaluate how current their resources are. How credible and how accurate are they? Is there any reason to suspect bias in the source? The tutor should ask each student to describe what resources they actually used during self-study and to criticise them. It is important to make sure that students do not describe what they have learned from the resource, but rather to critique it as a resource.

Students work on the problem with the new information learned from their self-studies. They do not simply tell what they have learned. Instead, they use the learning to re-examine the problem. The cycle is repeated if new learning issues arise—typical of many problems in life. In summary, this step of the tutorial process is used to reassess the problem. The columns of the PBL chart in Figure 7.2 are now altered to those of Figure 7.3 (adapted from Duffy, 1994).

Phase 4

Step 10. Present Findings and Communicate Results

When students have completed their problem, they should present and communicate their results to their peers and tutor. Following the completion of their presentation, students should reflect upon what has been learned and determine if there are any things that they have missed out in their overall understanding of the problem. They should also reflect on how their new learning relates to prior problems and prepares them for future problems. By doing so, students can determine and discuss what important overall concepts or principles have been learned. This is important because it helps to convert procedural knowledge, gained through problem solving, into declarative knowledge for recall and use with other problems in the future (PBLI, 2004). If this step is not taken, those things that have been learned may not be consciously recalled by students for transfer to other problem contexts in the future. The tutor can help students by asking them questions such as, "What have you learned from the problem? What new facts or concepts have you learned?"

During the evaluate-and-report step of the tutorial process, the types of questions to be considered should include:

- How are we doing?
- What is working?
- What is not working?
- How do we know we are progressing?

Step 11. Self Reflection

Self and peer assessment should be conducted after the completion of each problem. It is important for students to become proficient in assessing their individual learning progress and that of their peers. If the students are to assume responsibility for their own learning, they have to be able to accurately assess the ability to work with a problem or task. If students have the self-assessment skills, they can conduct their own performance assessments at the end of their course of study.

It is important for the tutorial group to undergo a formal evaluation session after completion of the problem. Each member of the group should be asked to describe what they thought of how they had reasoned through the problem (problem solving), self-directed learning strategies used, and support of the group process. Following the evaluation by each individual member of the group, the tutor should ask the other students to comment on that evaluation and add their own opinions about the student's performance. The ability to accurately monitor the adequacy of their own personal performance is essential for students in developing life-long, self-directed learning skills. Students should be helped to reflect upon individual and group performance based on the following criteria: knowledge base, communication, assessment skills, and reasoning processes. The tutor should:

- Provide constructive feedback to students.
- Include feedback from each person about him or herself and the group process.
- Model the processes (UNM, 2000).
- Provide reflection: A good coach encourages learners to reflect on (monitor and analyse) their performance. This can be achieved by inserting provoking questions that:
  - Ask the learners to reflect on what they have done.
  - Ask the learners to reflect on what assumptions they have made.

- Ask the learners to reflect on what strategies they have used.
- Ask the learners to explain why they have made a particular response.
- Ask the learners to confirm an intended response.
- Ask the learners to state how certain they are in a response.
- Require learners to argue with the coach.
- Provide puzzles that learners need to solve that will lead to appropriate performance.

Appendix 7A is a typical example of how Phase 1 of the tutorial process is conducted from a problem given to students. Appendix 7B shows the facilitator's notes, given to help him or her during the tutorial process.

Factors Affecting the Tutorial Process

We believe that several factors affect the success of the tutorial process, among them are the following:

- According to Barrows (1992), it is important for tutors to make sure that each phase of the tutorial process is taken in the right sequence. The tutorial process must be kept moving to make sure that no phase of the learning process is passed over or neglected.

- There must be a deeper probe of students' knowledge during the tutorial session. It is important for the tutor to continually ask, "Why?" "What do you mean?" "How do you know it is true?" "What does that mean?" until the students reach a deeper understanding of the knowledge expected of them. Students must not be allowed to get away with a superficial understanding of the ideas and terms used.

- All students should be involved in the group process. Tutors should make sure that all students' opinions or points of view are heard.

- Each student's progress should be monitored by the tutor to ensure that no one is falling behind or having difficulty learning. The tutor must watch all students, all of the time, and make sure everything is progressing well with their studies.

- The tutorial process should be modulated to the challenge of the problem or task at hand. The tutorial session should not be too slow or easy, nor should it be too complex and overwhelming.

- It is important for the tutor to realise that his or her role in the group tutorial process is at the metacognitive level, dealing with the reasoning or problem solving process required for the task, situation, or problem confronting the students in the group (Barrows, 1988).

- At this stage, it is important to ensure that students explore all possible hypotheses for the cause of the problem before they start conducting inquiry to gain more information about the problem, that is, they should be seeking learning issues. It is important, during this step, that the tutor never allows terms, ideas, explanations, or comments to go unchallenged or undefined. Questions such as these should be used to challenge students:

  - Can you tell me more about that?
  - What do you mean by that?
  - Why do you say that?
  - How do you know that it is true?
  - Can you define the term used?
  - Why do you want to know that?

During the tutorial session, the tutor must apply these metacognitive challenges constantly, making sure that students carefully consider each step in their reasoning process, their learning needs, and the identification of learning resources. The tutor should model the thinking process for the students, demonstrating the questions that should be asked to deal with the problem or task (Barrows, 1988).

It is important that the tutor makes sure that students go through each stage of the group tutorial process and consider their thinking as they work through the problem. Students must be able to generate hypotheses, develop inquiry strategies to solve the problems, analyse new date in the light of generated hypotheses, synthesise and give a problem description or formulation from the significant new data obtained, and make evaluative (diagnostic) and management (treatment) decisions (Barrows 1988). Tutors must not give students information, but stimulate them to determine what they need to learn and how to learn it on their own.

Conclusion

PBL provides a well-described method for constructivist learning, modelled on the example of cognitive apprenticeship (Brown, Collins, & Duguid, 1989). The role of the tutor is to make expertise visible and the tacit thinking processes explicit. In addition, the tutor must guide students through the learning process, pushing them to think deeply and modelling the questions that students need to ask themselves. The tutorial process is the hub of learning in PBL. It is significant for developing students' critical thinking and metacognitive skills in dealing with relevant professional problems. Through the tutorial process, students become independent, self-directed learners who learn how to manage learning effectively and develop an attitude of responsibility for life-long learning. Developing group skills is also a prerequisite for tutorial learning. Faculty development and support for tutors in the tutorial process is essential for the success of PBL. Tutors must be properly trained in the tutorial process. Adequate time must be given to help tutors acquire this important skill before allowing them to take on the tutorial role. The tutorial process is very labour intensive. Novice facilitators often find the process very difficult. As the novices struggle with the facilitation, they may be overly directive as they try to guide the group's agenda. One method to address this is to have the questions that the expert asks by incorporating them as procedure facilitations for the novice tutors in different stages of learning (Hmelo-Silver, 2000). These types of hints can be incorporated into an on-line tutor tool kit. Another solution would be using a distributed PBL system (Steinkuehler, Derry, Hmelo-Silver, & DelMarcelle, 2002).

References

Barrows, H. S. (1988). *The tutorial process.* Springfield: Southern Illinois University, School of Medicine.

Barrows, H. S. (1992). *The tutorial process.* Springfield: Southern Illinois University School of Medicine.

Bertola, P., & Murphy, E. (1994). *Tutoring at university: A beginner's practical guide* (A CAUT National Teaching Development Fund Project). Curtin University, Western Australia: Paradigm Books.

Brown, J. S., Collins, A., & Duguid, P. (1989). Situated cognition and the culture of learning. *Educational Researcher, 8*(1), 32-42.

Clarke, S. (2002). *Developing quality participation in tutorial.* Sydney: HERDSA.

Duffy, T. M. (1994, August). *Problem-based learning.* NATO Advanced Studies Institute Workshop on Supporting Learning in Computer Environments. Herriott-Watt University, Edinburgh, Scotland.

Hiemstra, R. (1994). Self-directed learning. In T. Husen & T. N. Postlethwaite (Eds.), *The International Encyclopedia of Education* (2nd ed.). Oxford: Pergamon Press.

Hmelo-Silver, C. (2000). Knowledge recycling: Crisscrossing the landscape of educational psychology in a problem-based learning course for preservice teachers. *Journal on Excellence in College Teaching, 11*, 41-56.

Hmelo, C. E., & Ferrari, M. (1997). The problem-based learning tutorial: Cultivating higher-order thinking skills. *Journal for the Education of the Gifted, 20*, 267-273.

Lee, V. S. (2004). Promoting learning through inquiry. *Teaching excellence: Towards the best in the academy, 15*(3), 203-204.

Limberg, L. (2000). Is there a relationship between information literacy and learning outcomes? In C. Bruce & P. Candy (Eds.), *Information literacy around the world: Advances in programs and research*. Wagga Wagga NSW: Centre for Information Studies, Charles Sturt University.

Problem-Based Learning Initiative (PBLI) (2004). *The minimal essentials for problem-based learning in medical education*. Retrieved March 30, 2005, from http://www.pbli.org/pbl/medical_pbl.htm

Silen, C., & Uhlian, L. (2004, June 14-18). *Self-directed learning—A learning issue for the student*. Paper presented at *PBL 2004 International Conference*, Cancun, Mexico.

Steinkuehler, C. A., Derry, S. J., Hmelo-silver, C. E., & DelMarcelle, M. (2002). Crackling the resource nut with distributed problem-based learning in secondary teacher education. *Journal of Distance Education, 23*, 23-39.

Stepien, W., & Pyke, S. L. (1997, April). Designing problem-based learning units. *Journal for the Education Leadership*, 25-28.

University of New Mexico (2002). *Faculty and student guide: To problem-based learning (PBL) Tutorial in Phase I curriculum of the University of New Mexico, School of Medicine*. Retrieved March 30, 2005, from http://hsc.unm.edu/som/TED/tutorialprocessoverview.pdf

Von Schilling, K. (1995). *The significance of the tutorial process*. Presentation at the International Conference on Problem-Based Learning in Higher Education, Linkoping, Sweden.

Ward, J. D., & Lee, C. L. (2002). A review of problem-based learning. *Journal of Family and Consumer Sciences Education, 20*(1).

Appendix 7A. PBL Case:
Requirements Analysis

Appendix 7B is an example of the facilitator notes given to the tutor for this PBL case.

Phase 1

Step 1: Setting the Scene

Initial Formalities

Choose a chairperson for this first PBL case. The task of the person is to ensure that steps 1 to 5 of the PBL method have been completed and documented by the end of the meeting.

1. Choose a scribe for this case. The task of the scribe is to produce minutes, detailing the main points and actions, and distribute copies to each member of the team.
2. Decide on a team name.
3. Remember that the last event of any meeting should be to check the actions to be taken deadlines and individual responsibilities.

Step 2: Present the Problem

Students are given the following problem.

Scenario

Ace Training, Ltd., is a small company, which delivers technical computer-training courses at its training centre in Manchester and on customer premises throughout the UK. It employs a Sales manager, ten sales staff, two marketing people, and two accounts staff in its head office in Liverpool. The managing director (MD), his secretary, and switchboard/receptionist are also located there.

At the training centre there are the following employees: a manager, two administrators, one technician and 10 instructors.

The sales representatives make the vast majority of sales over the telephone. There is very little use of information technology in the head office. The Marketing Department has one Apple Macintosh® computer, the Accounts Department uses one PC, running *Sage*® accounting software, and the Sales Department has one PC for preparing quotes. The MD's secretary also has a computer.

The managing director views the current system as inefficient. He has called in your team, as consultants, to advise him. He believes a network for the head office will improve sales performance significantly. Your terms of reference are:

> ♦   To design and present a proposal for purchase, implementation, and support of a new network for Sales tracking, accounts, and general administration.

This is a sizeable task, despite the small scale of the company. Clearly, factors such as cost of the solution, training, and support are required for a comprehensive solution.

There is insufficient information given above to specify the solution precisely. You will need to find additional information by arranging interviews with appropriate people in the company. You are restricted to two twenty-minute interviews.

To assist you in solving this problem, I have structured it as a series of smaller problems, which will be referred to as PBLs 1, 2, and 3. They are:

1.   PBL1. Perform a Requirements Analysis: The output is a requirements spec in Week 3.

2.   PBL2. Draft System Specification: You need to decide on the software and hardware for your system before you can build a demo system. This should be handed in at the end of Week 6.

3.   PBL3. Build and install a system (3x PCs) to demonstrate your solution. Configure the application software, users, printer, and so on, to demonstrate your solution. Lab notes for practical tasks are available on module Web site.

> **Make sure you involve everyone in this activity. At this stage, it will be worth going round in turn to identify any parts of the question that you are unsure about.**

Activity 1. Now read the information given to you about the Ace Training scenario.

Activity 2. Make a list of issues that need to be clarified. Are there any parts of the problem statement that are unclear or incomplete? Are there any terms used that you do not understand? If so, list them in your learning log.

Activity 3. Define the problem—in this case it is to identify the requirements of Ace Training.

Activity 4. Identify what you know about this already. That is, identify the requirements that you can find from the information provided. The requirements can be broken into a number of headings, such as functional requirements (what the system must do) and non-functional (e.g., Support, training, constraints on hardware, software or location). The scribe should make a list of all that have been suggested.

Step 3: Generating Hypothesis

Activity 1. Brainstorm ideas or hypotheses for things that you do not know. The hypotheses generated should be written down in column 1 of the PBL chart in Figure 7.2. No ideas should be discounted and all participants must be included. Use inquiry-guided questions to help with hypotheses generation.

Step 4: Testing Hypotheses

Hypotheses raised during brainstorming should be compared with the problem outline to see how they match.

Step 5: Identify Learning Issues

Do not rule out any suggestions at this stage. The purpose is to generate ideas.

Activity 1. For each hypothesis generated, identify learning issues or objectives to be learned. This should be written down in column three of the PBL chart in Figure 7.2.

Activity 2. Make a systematic list. Examine the learning issues your team has produced. Organise the connections between them, group ideas into categories and value, and sort out what is irrelevant.

Activity 3. Rank the learning issues in the order of their importance.

Activity 4. Make a list of the learning issues to be investigated by the group.

1.   Generate a list of things you need to investigate/find out/get answers to. These are called learning issues.

| Identify what you do not know and what you need to learn or understand to solve the problem. |

Important!

For example, what information do you need from Ace Training? You should have a long list here. Categorise it.

Do you know what should be included in a requirements specification? If not, how are you going to find out?

How are you going to find the information and the processes used? Are you confident about tackling this? If not, what can you do?

Do you need to do any preliminary research for background information? If so, related to what?

Step 6: Plan Action—Assign Tasks

Activity 1. Create a plan to solve the learning issues.

After identifying what you do not know or what you need to know, you will create a study or work plan that will include all or part of the following steps. Use the planning sheet—you need to hand one copy to your tutor.

Activity 2. Prioritise learning needs.

Activity 3. Set learning goals and objectives.

Activity 4. Decide who will do what, by when.

Activity 5. Decide how and when the individual learning will be shared with the rest of the group. Give a copy of your plan to your tutor before you leave.

Phase 2

Step 7: Individual Work

You are now ready to complete your study plan.

Each member of the group should decide his or her knowledge and learning needs. He or she should organise his or her own way to the new knowledge. Members can work individually or within groups.

Remember that the timescale is very tight—realistically so—for this part of the case study. You will not have a lot of time available to interview your clients next week, so you must be well-prepared.

Resources

There are a number of resources available to you:

1. For information about networking technology and terminology, see the course text and resources available on the module Web site.
2. For resources about interviewing skills and information about Ace Training, consult the module Web site.
3. Template for requirement specification—see module Web site.

Deliverables

You must produce a draft requirement specification and submit it via your team user id to LearnWise. You will receive feedback on this.

Appendix 7B: ACE Requirements—for PBL Case 1 Facilitator Notes

Trigger: See Students' Guide to PBL1

Schedule:

	Class activities	Independent study/submissions
Week 1	**Intro to course (plenary lecture)** **Intro to PBL1: Requirements analysis** Explore scenario, generate list of questions/information required for interviews next week. Create plan.	Plan interview and locate resources.
Week 2	**Role play interviews.** View, analyse and evaluate Video interviews (for technique and information content). Interview Managing Director (20 minutes) and receive oral feedback. Interview Sales Manager (20 minutes) and receive oral feedback.	Review findings and construct requirements specification.
Week 3	**Sharing/meeting** Review progress, identify any other information required, and request information from tutor. Finalize requirement specification. Review team performance to date.	Submit draft requirement specification.

Resources

The Module Web site identifies a long list of suitable resources linked to the PBL case. These are:

- PBL process documentation in the module guide;
- Notes on interviewing techniques;
- An example template for a Requirements Specification;
- Ace Training's software and hardware inventory;
- Ace Training's organizational chart;
- Layout of Liverpool office and details of construction;
- Some sample forms (invoices or orders), which were once requested by a team (these are irrelevant); and
- Video of interviews (good and bad techniques) with the Accounts department manager.

Background

Following is summary of requirements as an aide memoir for the role plays. Students should work from their own requirements, generated at the end of PBL1. Assessment criteria are in the module guide and Web site.

Role play information is included for faculty in *Guide for Sales Manager* and *Guide for Managing Director*. Note, there is a conflict: MD does not want internal email, but the Sales Manager and Accounts Manager do. Students need to acknowledge and discuss approach to resolve this. Different client views are realistic.

Requirements

Sales Dept	
1. Contact management software, enabling all sales representatives to access all client details from their own PC.	2. PC per sales person including manager
3. E-mail to Manchester via ISP.	4. Web site with email inquiry (not e-commerce).
5. High speed printer.	6. Facility for sales representatives to produce own quotes and letters.
Accounts Dept	
1. Update Sage to latest Line50 Accounts (Euro & performance issues).	2. 2 x new PC
3. Replace Printer.	
Marketing Dept	
1. Keep iMac/printer off the network	2. Create in-house mailing list (use contact mgt software to generate it).

Contineud on following page

Requirements

General Admin	
1. Provide PC for all staff except Marketing.	2. Secure –personnel, data, Sales and Accounts by separating. Provide Internet security needed.
3. All PCs are to be networked, including current ones if possible.	4. Budget - within GBP40k
Training Requirements	
1. Provide on-site training for sales in small groups. Can not release more than half at a time.	2. Provide general PC training in-house.
3. Training schedule and plan are required.	
Installation requirements	
1. Installation must take place outside working hours	
Support requirements	
1. Develop specifications for a technician/Web developer. Include qualifications and salary.	2. Maximum down time is half an hour during working day

Week 1

Aim: Today, the aim is to ensure they have explored the problem statement and have:

1. Elected team leader and scribe for PBL1;
2. Analyzed the problems statement and background to produce an outline list of requirements;
3. Identified a list of information that they will need to get from the interview;
4. Explored the Module Web site for resources; and
5. Created a plan specifying who will do what, by when.

This is the first time they have done this. You need to make sure:

- You give them lots of encouragement;
- They follow the PBL stages systematically (see module guide);
- Everyone is involved;
- They discuss feelings as well as task (at start or end);
- A plan is produced; and
- Times are arranged for interviews next week.

Prompt them towards considering the following without directly giving them the topics. If they cannot get there, they need to investigate what is needed in a network.

Possible questions to ask:

1.   What do they need to know about the company and why?

 •   For example, company processes, communication, decision making, services and product lifecycles, organisational structures, future plans and acquisitions, as well as customer, partner, and vendor relation-ships.

2.   What sort of things will they have to specify, eventually and do they affect questions they will ask?

 •   What are the system software, choice of O/S and required facilities?

 •   What applications are needed?

 •   What does resilience mean?

 •   What are the security issues?

 •   Networking: Cabling compatibility;

 •   Hardware to support software. Server (see notes on WebCT under resources), printers and, clients;

 •   Training—Application;

 •   Installation—costs, cable runs, time, and so on;

 •   Support—after identified O/S.

3.   Interviewing—how to do it well. They need to think about interviewing.

 •   Is the purpose just to get information? (E.g., impress with your professionalism)

 •   Who should they interview? (Should they identify a number of people for different perspectives? It is limited to two. Who would be most appropriate?)

 •   What is a good or bad interview?

 •   What sort of questions will you ask? Do you ask the same questions of all clients? Would you ask the MD what operating system he wants to use, Linux or Windows? Why not?

 •   What structure should there be to the interview?

 •   How will you record answers?

We would expect them to plan a meeting to finalize interview questions prior to the interviews. Emphasize that all students must participate in the interview.

Week 2

Aim: Today the aim is for students to practice interview technique, collect useful information, and receive formative (oral) feedback on their interview performance.

Video of accounts manager interviews (lecture theatre):

1. Play bad interview and ask students to identify poor technique.
2. Play good interview and ask students to identify improvements, in particular the structure (general situation to client problems, the impact of those problems, and the value of resolving them).
3. Students can borrow copies of the video to extract information about the Accounts department requirements.

Role play interviews:

1. Collect role play advice as a guide for your role as managing director or sales manager.
2. Use the interview checklist during the interview to determine if they have elicited the appropriate (complete) information, have all taken part, followed a systematic structure, and behaved professionally.
3. Ask them to self-assess (briefly) their impression of their performance.
4. Provide oral feedback at end of interview based on your notes.

Grading Criteria:	Pass	Good Pass	Excellent
Communication: C2 Collect appropriate information in a structured manner during an interview.	Asks clear questions in a logical manner, mostly open questions.	Clear structure to interview follows up answers with more detailed exploration.	Includes checkpoint summaries and uses suitable interview model.

Week 3

Aim: Today the aim is for students to review and finalize their requirements specification and to conduct a preliminary team reflection on performance.

Resources:

• Group work checklist for reflection.

During facilitated PBL team meeting:

1. Ask them to explain their requirements and to identify any weaknesses and corresponding actions.

2. Conduct discussion about group performance, using the group work feedback sheet.

3. Team to provide constructive feedback to team leader.

4. Elect leader for next PBL case.

5. Ask them to identify and document points for improvement.

6. Refer them to the assessment criteria for the requirement specification.

Grading Criteria:	Pass (threshold)	Good Pass (GP)	Excellent
LO2 Critically analyse the requirements for a small-scale network.	Key appropriate functional and non-functional requirements correctly identified and in an appropriate format.	Most requirements are identified correctly and in appropriate format and are prioritised appropriately.	Comprehensive list of functional and non-functional requirements unambiguously and correctly identified and in appropriate format as well prioritised appropriately.

Figure 7.4. Example planning sheet

Planning Sheet—Week 1	Team Name:		

Learning issues/tasks:

Issue/Task	Who	Target Date
1.		
2.		
3.		
4.		
5.		
6.		
7.		
8.		
9.		

Chapter VIII

Assessment

Introduction

Assessment probably has a more important effect on student learning than anything else. For the student, high grades and good qualifications signify success and open better opportunities in life. The converse is also true; so it is no wonder assessment drives student behaviour. Ramsden (1992, p. 187) expresses it succinctly: "From our students' point of view, assessment always defines the actual curriculum."

When you add to this the consideration that assessment results are not only important to students, but also to teachers, departments, and whole institutions that are also judged on the results of their students, assessment becomes a hot topic.

Thus, whatever we say we value, however well we design PBL cases and facilitate tutorials, at the end of the day the assessment is the key driver for student learning. What we value must be reflected in what we assess. In this chapter we explore a number of issues connected with assessment of PBL. PBL raises some particular difficulties, but in many ways it can quite naturally provide a constructively aligned system for teaching, learning, and assessment (Biggs, 1999).

There are five fundamental questions we need to answer when considering assessment. *Why* are we assessing? What is the purpose of the assessment? *What* are we going to assess? How do we decide which learning outcomes will be assessed? *How* do we assess them? How do we develop the assessment tasks and grading criteria? *When* are we going to perform the assessment and, finally, *who* will do the assessing? In this chapter we will consider these in turn.

Why Assess?
What Are We Trying to Do?

Assessment is a multi-headed monster; the results are used to judge and rate students, teachers, departments, and institutions. It is charged with emotion and is closely coupled to the labels *failure* and *success*. In higher education, we often compound this by adding strict rules about the number of resubmissions and the maximum scores that a student can achieve on resubmission.

Within a course itself we can use assessment for a variety of purposes: to measure student performance, competence, or mastery through reliable tests; to provide feedback to students and teachers about how learning is improving; and even to control and motivate students. For example, in some UK institutions, attendance is included within the assessment criteria to pass a module.

Assessment can be categorized in a number of ways, but two fundamental and important classes are *summative* and *formative* assessment.

Summative assessment, designed to provide a grade, which counts towards the module result, is regarded as "high stakes" assessment (Knight, 2000) and requires considerable effort to ensure validity and reliability.

Formative assessment, on the other hand, which is designed for feedback to students to aid their learning, can be regarded as "low stakes." This means that the accuracy, reliability, and validity are not so important, but the turnaround time of the assessment is vital.

Since it is the summative assessment that counts towards a grade, it is the most powerful motivator and needs to be aligned clearly with the learning outcomes of the module and the activities the student undertakes during the learning in the module (Biggs, 1999).

The classic model, therefore, is to start with the learning outcomes, then identify suitable (valid) summative assessment tasks that test if the learning outcomes have been met, and, finally, identify appropriate grading criteria that can be applied reliably.

What Do We Assess?
What is Different with PBL?

In some models of problem-based learning, students devise their own learning outcomes, for example the open discovery model (Swanson, 1997). However, it is more common for the learning outcomes to be predefined during the validation of the programme. We will confine the discussion to this situation.

In most respects, assessing for PBL is no different from the classical model outlined above. However, the first difference is usually in the learning outcomes themselves.

We would expect to include specific learning outcomes, which are related to the subject knowledge and any subject specific skills as in traditional programmes, but in PBL we would also seek to examine the level of *integration* of that knowledge.

We have pointed out earlier that if we value the process skills involved in PBL, then we must include them in the learning outcomes and consequently devise ways of assessing them. So we would expect to include assessment of some (if not all) of the skills listed in Chapter VI (Woods, 1996).

- Problem solving
- Team working skills
- Coping with change
- Self assessment
- Self-directed learning

The skills listed above are stated in a generic way, though it is worth pointing out that some authors suggest that the skills should be refined for the particular discipline rather than simply taken off the shelf. For example, Yip and Ghafarian (2000) identify nine skills in the context of a systems analysis problem case within the discipline of information systems. These are: problem understanding, use of resources, teamwork, critical thinking, project management, writing, oral presentation, team communication, and self-assessment. They also provide a set of indicators for each of these skill objectives. However, with the exception of project management, they can all be reclassified easily into Woods' (1996) categories.

We think it is worth raising the danger of over assessment at this point. One of the consequences of the "assessment for motivation" culture has been a gradual increase in the amount of summative assessment to the point where the workload for students and teachers has grown rapidly. If it is not assessed, students will not do it. Now if PBL is to be integrated fully into the curriculum, there will be several opportunities to assess the process skills. Assessing the same skills summatively and repeatedly in several modules certainly is not motivational for the students—or the teacher for that matter. One way around this is to conduct a programme-wide audit of skills assessment and decide how to distribute it throughout the programme. This reduces workload and still maintains the overall validity of the programme. Use summative assessment sparingly!

How Do We Assess?

The next stage is to consider how we go about assessing the learning outcomes that we have devised. We think it is worth briefly discussing the terms peer and self assessment, since their meanings can differ from author to author.

Self assessment, in its purest form, can be assessment by a student against learning outcomes and *criteria also devised by that student.* However, this presupposes that students have developed the skill to create the criteria. Where students have not reached this stage, it is still useful for them to assess themselves against outcomes and criteria devised by the tutor. We will use the term self-assessment for both of these situations in this chapter.

We will use the term peer assessment to denote any situation where students use criteria, which may be devised by other students or the tutor, to assess a student.

We will discuss this in two parts: first, the assessment of the subject knowledge and skills and second, the process skills.

Assessing Subject Knowledge and Skills

If our model of PBL is to help induct students into a community of professional practice, then we will be looking to develop criteria that assess both a student's performance—what the student can do—and their underpinning knowledge that is relevant to competent performance in the defined context. Conway, Chen, and Jefferies (1999) calls this assessment of "professional competencies."

Biggs states that in PBL, the "crucial assessments should be performance-based, holistic, allowing plenty of scope for students to input their own decisions and solutions" (Kingsland, 1995), quoted in Biggs (1999, p. 210). A holistic assessment recognizes overall performance on the task, rather than analyzing and giving marks for each component part. In the latter, it could be possible to achieve a pass by knowing very thoroughly several components of the solution, but being incapable of evaluating it in context and synthesizing a viable solution. This holistic approach corresponds to a qualitative view rather than a quantitative view, judging how well the knowledge and skills are integrated rather than how much the student knows.

So what methods can we use to test this? Ideally, we should continue the theme of authenticity so that the outcome of the PBL case matches the expected outcomes of a real-world scenario. Typically, these can be a report, presentation, or the construction of some artifact, such as a computer program. In the case of the example at the end of Chapter VI, we chose methods that correspond to professional tasks of sales support and technical support staff: A written sales proposal and presentation as well as the construction and demonstration of a Local Area Network.

This raises an important issue: Does this mean that we should never test subject knowledge that is taken out of a real world context? There is some variation of opinion here! Norman (1997, p. 264) states, "Since knowledge and problem solving are closely related, then we may unapologetically ask that our students know something and we may, and should, test for knowledge." Norman strongly recommends multiple choice questions (MCQs), which can be used efficiently, reliably, and effectively to test understanding and application of knowledge. Further support for this view is provided by some professional certification programmes, for example Microsoft® Certification qualifications use multiple-choice tests, so it could even be argued that the use of MCQs within a PBL programme is authentic.

However, this needs to be used with care as traditional summative methods, such as MCQs and examinations, can be seen to undermine the aims of PBL. MCQs can encourage rote learning and often assess a "canon" of knowledge. At some stage students take a strategic view and direct their learning towards the problem of passing the exam. This can also reveal itself when students worry if they have *learned something in sufficient detail for the exam.*

Despite the above criticism, our survey (Beaumont, Sackville, & Chew, 2004) found that examinations were often used to test declarative knowledge.

If examinations are being used, then there are methods that can be used to help align them with PBL and reduce the impact on behaviour noted above. One approach is to use a "seen" examination—where the examination paper is distributed to students several days or weeks prior to the examination itself. The questions can be simpler scenarios that relate to the knowledge learned in the PBL cases and the analysis and integration of knowledge that has already been assessed in the team. A second approach is to use an unseen examination, which asks students to discuss aspects of the PBL cases that they have studied in their team. The purpose of such examinations is principally to assess the *individual's* learning from the team PBL cases.

Further issues of assessment have been raised by Ellis, Carswell, Bernat, Deveaux, Frison, Meisalo et al. (1998), including the tension between creativity and assessment. For example, some first year Bachelor of Science (BSc) Information Systems students were concerned about whether it was better to be ambitious and creative in implementing enhancements to a computer program— with risk of failure—or to take a safe, easy option.

Grading and Criteria

This last point takes us to the thorny topic of grades and criteria. It is considered good practice to share assessment criteria with students.

Indeed, we think it is unfair not to do so. Students are keenly interested in their grades and the vast majority want to know what they need to do to pass, or excel if they are keen. One of the difficulties in any classroom is helping students interpret criteria accurately. Simply stating criteria in terms that are understood by teachers does not always mean that students share the same understanding!

However, here lies the dilemma: if we provide very explicit criteria, linked to a problem solution, then we can risk providing too many cues towards the solution. If we provide more vague criteria we can make it difficult to mark reliably and risk being unfair to students.

In some cases it may be appropriate to negotiate the criteria with students. This has the great advantage of promoting a shared understanding and ownership of them. It forces students to think in terms of what constitutes appropriate professional competence in this context. The tutor's job is to moderate and ensure the standards are appropriate, fair, and practical. However, it can be time-consuming.

Maggi Savin-Baden sums it up as follows:

It is vital to demystify assessment criteria and help students become stakeholders in the assessment process. One way to do this is to have students develop their own marking criteria, because they will then understand what the process of grading involves. This may seem time-consuming and difficult, but it may lessen plagiarism, and encourage honesty and personal responsibility in the team, while also helping students perform better on other forms of assessment. Savin-Baden (2003a)

Figure 8.1 is an example, set by tutors, that we have used successfully that relates to the Ace Training scenario in Chapter VI.

Figure 8.1. Example of assessment grading criteria for subject knowledge

Learning Outcome/Weight	Pass (Threshold)	Good Pass (B)	Excellent (A)
Subject knowledge & skills: Quality of solution	Proposal accurately specifies appropriate software and hardware to meet the key requirements.	Pass Most of solution has a suitable level of detail Solution is clearly justified Solution is linked to most of the requirements	As B All solution is detailed Some critical evaluation of alternate solutions is provided.
Self-Assessment			
Evidence	(outline justification)		

When students encounter this table, we expect them to question what the key requirements are and, of course, we bounce it back to them immediately. They have to identify and justify their thoughts. This provides students with the opportunity to explore the meaning of the criteria and elaborate on their knowledge. Essentially, the bare pass threshold constitutes a workable solution; we are assessing the team's ability to integrate their learning and apply it to synthesise a viable, holistic solution. The assessor's guide provides a more detailed list of what we would expect to be in the solution at each grade point to provide more objectivity and reliability in the marking process. It is perhaps also worth pointing out that multiple choice questions are used in addition to this to assess individual fundamental knowledge.

Formative assessment is particularly valuable in this process. In the example above, students identify a list of requirements as the first stage of the PBL case. This is marked formatively so they gain confidence and are not left wondering whether they have identified appropriate requirements.

An area where we have found that students are weak is in linking their solution explicitly to the requirements. This is the principle focus of grade B. Finally, to excel, we expect them to demonstrate critical evaluation of alternatives.

Assessing Process Skills and Behaviours

Before discussing how we might assess the process skills, it is worth emphasizing that *"the opportunity to develop skills does not guarantee that students will develop them."* The reason for stating this here is that we have encountered a number of modules, traditional as well as PBL, where students are assessed on something they have not been taught. For example, it was somehow assumed that students would become better problem solvers by providing them with lots of problems to solve. Woods (1995) shows that this is not the case.

*Just setting up a small group, self-directed, PBL group does **not** develop these skills.* (Norman & Schmidt, 1992, 1993; Woods, 1993)

You provide an opportunity; but you do not develop skill. To develop skill requires that you explicitly take the skill apart, ask them to try it, figuratively hold up a mirror so that they can see how they did the skill, describe potential target skills, and then give them practice + feedback, practice + feedback until they know they have the skill. Continually ask them to reflect on the processes they are using. Writing a reflective journal about those processes has a very positive impact. This all takes time. Woods (1996, ch. 3, p. 1)

In PBL, we provide triggers and subject **resources** to assist students to learn the subject matter. We must do the same for the process skills and must provide explicit criteria and learning outcomes associated with each one. However, as Woods points out, skills development requires repeated analysis of the skill, practice, and feedback. This means:

- Frequent formative feedback;
- Reflection by individuals; and
- Setting new performance goals.

This suggests that formative assessment is essential for developing skills and frequency, rather than accuracy of feedback, is most important. However, as we pointed out earlier, summative assessment of skills is also necessary to show that it is valued.

One of the most difficult tasks is to identify learning outcomes and criteria associated with process skills.

Learning outcomes for a skill can be divided into two aspects:

- Knowledge and understanding of the skill; and
- Degree of expertise displayed at exercising it.

Woods (1995, section D3) provides one of the most comprehensive treatments, listing possible objectives and assessments for skills in the areas of: *Stress & time*

Figure 8.2. Example objectives for processing skills (Woods, 1995, Section D)

MPS 2 Problem-Solving

1.1 Given a term listed under "concepts introduced", you should be able to give a word definition, list pertinent characteristics, and cite an example.

1.2 You will be able to describe the cognitive and behavioral understanding of "problem-solving," contrast this with "exercise-solving," and understand the role of "pattern recognition."

2.1 You will be able to explain why successful problem-solvers are active, methodical, and accurate.

5.1 Given situations encountered in other courses, at work, or in your everyday life, you will be able to reflect on how you solve problems in these contexts.

5.2 Given a personal goal, you will be able to write that in observable terms, create measurable criteria, select evidence, and write a reflective journal such that an independent assessor will agree that you have achieved your personal goals.

6.1 Given a checklist of characteristics of successful problem solvers, you will be able to self-rate your approach to solving problems. From this rating you will create goals for improvement.

Concepts introduced

Problem, exercise, problem solving, exercise solving, pattern recognition, internal representation, successive approximation, optimum sloppiness, Pareto's principle, LTM, STM, chunks, OPV, knowledge and knowledge structure, relationship between knowledge structure and problem solving, and working backwards versus working forwards.

MPS27 Group Skills

1.1 Given a term listed under "concepts introduced", you should be able to give a word definition, list pertinent characteristics, and cite an example.

2.2 Given a problem, as a member of a group, you will participate in the task and morale components of the process such that your participation will be judged by an observer to be "active" and to have more positive than negative contributions.

2.3 Given a problem, the group will complete the assigned task by the designated time and over 60% of the group members will choose to work together again.

2.4 Given a group solving a problem, you will be able to observe the group, record positive or negative contributions towards both task and morale components. You will be able to do this by observing an individual client or the group as a whole. Your records will agree within 80% of the average records made by four other observers or with those of the tutor.

[Omitted 2.1, 2.5-2.7]

Concepts introduced

Concepts introduced include task and positive and negative contributions towards task; morale and the positive and negative contributions towards morale; and FIRO-B ®, stages in group evolution, and feed back form.

---

management; problem-solving; self-directed learning; group process and personal contributions; change management; managing own learning; chair person skills.

Figure 8.2 provides extracts taken from Woods (1995, section D) as illustrations of the detail that can be applied. These illustrate particularly clearly the requirement for students to understand the knowledge components of the skills (e.g., MPS2: 1.1, 1.2, and 2.1), and perform them (e.g., MPS27: 2.2, and 2.3). The importance of being able to self assess and also reflect on the skill development is emphasized (e.g., MPS 2: 5.1 and 6.1).

Once the outcomes and criteria are defined, we need to identify the forms of evidence, consistent with the criteria, that will demonstrate achievement of the outcome and, finally, how that evidence will be collected (the assessment process).

Assessment of the knowledge and understanding components can be achieved through traditional methods, for example, written answers to questions. Students can also be asked to analyze scenarios. Examples could be to discuss conflict resolution strategies in a particular scenario or problem solving techniques.

Assessment of performance can be provided by peers, tutor, and self. Since the performance of a skill has many facets and changes with the context of the performance of the skill, if students are to receive useful feedback, the multi-dimensional nature of evidence is particularly important.

Students often object to peer and self assessment, frequently justifying this by saying it is the tutor's job, not their own. This often betrays underlying anxiety about the task, especially if they have not encountered it before. Self and peer assessment are difficult skills and need to be taught and developed like any of the others. Students usually accept the justifications that professionals should be able to demonstrate the ability to provide colleagues with accurate feedback and also should be able to monitor the adequacy of their own performance.

Tutors can develop suitable feedback forms to help students focus on the particular learning outcome, criteria, and evidence. Figure 8.3 shows an example from Woods (1995), which relates to the group skills objectives listed in Figure 8.2. (MPS27 objective 2.4). To use this form, a group is observed and ticks are recorded in the +/- rows for individuals exhibiting the behaviour.

A further, more simple feedback form that we have used is shown in Figure 8.4. This requires students to self-assess against a set of behaviours. In this example, we have identified behaviours in grading bands. Team work is a many-faceted skill and we have found it useful to focus on a few aspects at any one time. An important, but difficult, part is to require students to identify evidence to support their judgments.

Reflective journals or logs can be extremely useful vehicles for monitoring skill development and metacognitive development and much has been written about using them. They can also provide the evidence base for demonstrating skill development.

There is debate about how or if such journals should be summatively assessed, who should assess them, and, indeed, the rigor of the concept of reflection (Clegg, Tan, & Saeidi, 2002), although Mezirow (1981) suggests seven hierarchical levels of reflection.

The nature of the journal entries and the structure that is imposed will depend on the purpose of the journal, the stage of the course, and the experience of the student at reflecting. Early attempts at reflection by students are usually

Figure 8.3. (Woods, 1995, pp. 5-9)

Task			Group Members			
Observer—Task process	Orients group, monitors, summarises, seeks direction, and, identifies phrases.	+				
	Ignores phrases, asks whatever he or she wants, blocks, unaware of contributions.	-				
Giver—Information Opinion	Assertively gives information and makes suggestions.	+				
	Withholds information, is silent, or is aggressive or passive.	-				
Seeker—Information Opinion	Asks questions for opinions of others and checks comprehension	+				
	Refuses to ask for information, is silent.	-				
Energiser—Risk taker	Is enthusiastic, introduces spark and novel ideas.	+				
	Is follower, agrees, is silent, or is unsure.	-				
Morale						
Observer—Interpersonal Process	Sensitive to interpersonal dynamics, comments..	+				
	Ignores conflicts and tension and hopes it disappears.	-				
Giver: Praise, Support	Warm, responsive, gives help, and regards.	+				
	Puts down, is aggressive, is self-centred and is defensive.	-				
Seeker—Interpersonal Problem-solver	Mediates, harmonises and helps resolve conflicts.	+				
	Causes problems and seeks personal goals.	-				
Energiser—Tension relief	Jokes, laughs, and shows satisfaction.	+				
	Is withdrawn and causes tension.	-				

Figure 8.4. Example assessment grading criteria for team working

Learning Outcome	1. Pass (Threshold)	2. Good Pass (B)	3. Excellent (A)
Team working - a) Takes responsibility. b) Meets deadlines c) Shows sensitivity, respect, and support.	*Meets commitments to team.* Indicators: • Is punctual • Is prepared for meetings. • Completes assigned tasks. • Contributes positively during team meetings. • Keeps others informed of progress.	As pass and *Assists team development.* Indicators: • Demonstrates sensitivity. • Listens and responds empathetically. • Acknowledges contributions. • Helps organise team • Provides constructive criticism.	As grade B and *Shows leadership.* Indicators: • Takes initiative in task. • Helps resolve conflicts. • Encourages others. • Recognises and assists in difficulties. • Proactively works towards consensus.
Self Assessment			
Evidence to support judgement	(e.g., From peer assessment feedback forms, minutes, and agendas of meetings, reflective journals, and attendance records.)		

Figure 8.5. Example of peer assessment form assessing teams and individual contributions

Team member's Name:				
Taking responsibility for team success				
Worked co-operatively and shared information.	1 2 3 4	1 2 3 4	1 2 3 4	1 2 3 4
Was productive (prepared, met commitments, reliable).	1 2 3 4	1 2 3 4	1 2 3 4	1 2 3 4
Kept team members informed about progress of work.	1 2 3 4	1 2 3 4	1 2 3 4	1 2 3 4
Took Initiative, was proactive.	1 2 3 4	1 2 3 4	1 2 3 4	1 2 3 4
Contributed regularly and usefully to team discussions.	1 2 3 4	1 2 3 4	1 2 3 4	1 2 3 4
Found new ideas.	1 2 3 4	1 2 3 4	1 2 3 4	1 2 3 4
Willing to ask for help when needed.	1 2 3 4	1 2 3 4	1 2 3 4	1 2 3 4
Sensitivity, respect, and support				
Listened actively.	1 2 3 4	1 2 3 4	1 2 3 4	1 2 3 4
Showed respect by not interrupting.	1 2 3 4	1 2 3 4	1 2 3 4	1 2 3 4
Supported and gave help to others.	1 2 3 4	1 2 3 4	1 2 3 4	1 2 3 4
Evaluated ideas presented by others.	1 2 3 4	1 2 3 4	1 2 3 4	1 2 3 4
Challenged others.	1 2 3 4	1 2 3 4	1 2 3 4	1 2 3 4
Helped resolve conflict.	1 2 3 4	1 2 3 4	1 2 3 4	1 2 3 4
Encouraged/Motivated others.	1 2 3 4	1 2 3 4	1 2 3 4	1 2 3 4
Responded well to criticism/advice.	1 2 3 4	1 2 3 4	1 2 3 4	1 2 3 4

Comments on overall team performance, strengths, and weaknesses. Did you achieve the team aim you identified at the start of the PBL case?

Who was the team leader?
Provide some constructive comments to help him or her improve. How well did the leader ensure a plan was produced, tasks were completed, and members worked together (e.g., all involved, ensure absentees were contacted/involved).

descriptive, with little demonstration of skills of critical inquiry (Richardson & Maltby, 1995).

We have found that it is useful to structure students' reflections in some way, either requiring them to follow a model (Boud, Keogh, & Walker, 1995) or to use specific forms containing questions to focus their attention on particular aspects. Reflection could be focused at a micro level, an activity, or on a macro level, a PBL case or whole course (Basile, Olson, & Nathenson-Mejia, 2003).

For example, a student can be asked to reflect on team working or problem solving skills for a particular session or case, to relate it to understanding of the processes, the approach they took, learning that occurred, and actions for improvement. The student can be assessed later to examine how successful they were in achieving their actions.

Students often meet outside of class time and tutors seldom obtain a full picture of student activities in PBL. Therefore, some form of peer assessment is useful. An example of the assessment of particular aspects of team working is shown in Figure 8.5. In this form, students list the name of the other students in their team and rate their contribution. The scores are rolled up and fed back anonymously. The student is then asked to reflect on the feedback. It is, however, vital that students are prepared and trained to use such tools. On one occasion a student read anonymous feedback at 1 a.m. via a virtual learning environment (VLE) and was very upset.

Assessing Teams and Individual Contributions

The age-old problem that is raised when discussing PBL assessment is the difficulty of accurately assessing the contribution of an individual to a team. This manifests itself most strongly in assessing subject skills and knowledge learning outcomes for a team product. How do you know each individual has attained the learning outcome and met the criteria?

Very often, students who have excelled at individual assessment are the most vociferous in their objections. They complain that others "drag their marks down" and that those who have contributed less also obtain disproportionately high marks.

Since PBL is a team-based activity, the deliverables are generally team products. There are two fundamental approaches to identifying individual contributions.

The first is to try and unpick the individual's work and contribution within the team's assessed result. One approach requires the team to identify an individual's contribution to a team product and the tutor to grade that contribution. However, this has very significant drawbacks since it promotes the "divide and conquer" approach and actively discourages collaboration. It contradicts the principle of holistic assessment identified earlier. An alternative that is frequently used is to require students to assess their peer contribution, for example, to divide up 100% among the team members. This can prove successful, but can lack validity either because of dominant individuals or a desire to avoid conflict.

There is a second approach, which decouples the team product that attracts a single team mark from individual assessment. In this strategy we include additional individual assessment to verify the criteria. The crucial aspect of this approach is to make sure that the individual and team components are aligned and not seen as completely separate assignments. This can be done in a number of ways.

One example is *Tripartite assessment* (Savin-Baden, 2003). This has three components:

a.   A team component (report) for which they receive a mark;

b.   An individual piece of work they researched; and

c.   An individual account of the group process that is linked to the theory of group work.

The three components are complementary, yet they are still clearly integrated within the PBL case. This is important since an individual component that does not support the team component can encourage the wrong behaviour. Students will concentrate more on their own individual work at the expense of the team work.

A similar approach we have used requires students to prepare handouts for their team members as part of their individual research. These handouts are also submitted for marking and can be used to assess individual contribution. An example template is shown in Figure 8.6.

Another approach requires individual students to answer questions about their solution, either as a viva or as written work, possibly under examination conditions. One advantage of this approach is that it promotes holistic under-standing: students are keen to ensure they have not "missed anything" in the teach/share PBL sessions. An extension of this is the use of case-based individual essays or case-based seen examination papers.

There are a number of other alternatives: Portfolios and a variation known as "Patchwork text" (Winter, Buck. & Sobiechowska, 1999) can be used for students to collect evidence. Students accumulate written text from various sources and use different styles (such as an article review, interview transcript, or personal account) in their course work over a number of weeks. These pieces of work are shared with other students in discussions.

An extension to Viva, an individual PBL case, known as the "Triple jump" (Painvin, Neufeld, Norman, & Walker, 1979) is time-consuming but can be effective with small numbers of students.

Figure 8.6. Example of template for individual research handout

Individual Research Handout

The purpose of the handout that you will prepare is fourfold:

a) To provide information for other members of your team;

b) To demonstrate your understanding of the topic;

c) To develop your skills of critical analysis, selection, précis, and referencing; and

d) As resources for your explanation of your research to your team members.

Expected Content

1. **The research question:**

   This is a brief statement of the subject of your research.

2. **Summary of findings**

   a. Key points (with outline explanation)

   b. Recommendations: How relevant are your findings to this PBL problem?

3. **Details and explanation of findings**

   Explain the main points from your research in your own words. You can include quotes where strictly relevant. You must not cut and paste whole chunks of articles from the Web. By explaining in your own words, you are demonstrating understanding. This is hard work, but it is where the real benefit lies. Remember you need to write it so your team members can follow and learn from it and you need to critically evaluate any alternatives for a high grade.

4. **References**

   What did you consult for this research? (Use Harvard Referencing System)

5. **Time taken (approx hours for research and write-up)**

Assessment Criteria

The following criteria will be used to assess the individual handouts

Learning Outcome/Weight	Pass (Threshold)	Good Pass (B)	Excellent (A)
Explain and Demonstrate understanding of the underpinning knowledge and concepts of computer networks.	Handouts produced provided key points and accurate summaries of topics researched.. Correctly referenced.	As Pass and Handout is thorough. Relevant application of findings to PBL case is clearly demonstrated.	As B and critical evaluation of alternatives are provided.

What About Freeloaders?

The assessment methods discussed above help to identify the relative work done by students, but there will still be cases when some individuals simply do not pull their weight. Dealing with this situation has always been difficult, particularly since tutors see only part of the evidence. This last point means that it is important to empower the students to deal with the situation themselves. However, the tutor needs to provide a framework, which is shared right at the start.

Approaches we have used include:

Figure 8.7. Examples of team ground rules

- We treat each other with respect at all times.
- We arrive on time for meetings.
- We do not have any side conversations during meetings.
- We will give positive feedback regularly and tell members they have done a great job.
- We will give negative feedback constructively.
- We will encourage full participation by inviting quieter members into the discussion
- We will ask for help when we need it; doing so is not a sign of weakness.
- We will be honest and say what is on our minds—It is all right to push back and disagree.
- We will stay focused on the task at hand.
- We will celebrate successes.
- We will honour your commitments; if we have committed to do something and a problem arises that will prevent us from finishing on time we will let the team know *in advance*.
- If my work is completed and another team member is overloaded, I will offer to help.
- We will resolve conflicts with other team members without delay and without discussing it with others.

1. Teams identify and negotiate ground rules and penalties. Some examples are shown in Figure 8.7. This must also be negotiated with the Tutor, especially for inexperienced students. Sample ground rules may be needed. Students can often specify unachievable standards at the beginning, which causes them to disregard the ground rules later on.

2. The tutor can be called in as a mediator and an official warning letter, or "yellow card," can be sent to non-contributors.

3. Students can ultimately expel the student from the team, at which point the student can be deemed to have failed the team learning outcomes. The student may have to undertake the entire PBL case individually.

An excellent resource for developing the interpersonal skills needed for managing teams is provided by David Johnson (2003). A particularly useful feature of the book is the large number of exercises and tests that it contains. These exercises can usefully be included in PBL skills workshops, for example exercises in resolving interpersonal conflicts, helpful listening and responding, building relationships, and developing trust.

When Should We Assess?

The timing of assessment is largely governed by the purpose of the assessment and the nature and duration of the PBL case. If PBL cases are short, then the end of the case is a natural place for assessment, particularly the summative assessment of products relating to subject matter. If PBL cases last several weeks, then we have found it beneficial to have a number of staged deliverables which helps focus students and assists them in planning their workload. Such stages can provide good opportunities for formative assessment, which can be turned around rapidly since the emphasis is on feedback for learning rather than accuracy and precision of measurement.

While it may be appropriate to assess subject knowledge after a number of weeks and at the end of a PBL case, assessment of process skills can be much more frequent and can focus on improvement rather than absolute standard. For example, a team of students can be asked to reflect on and assess their own and their peers' performance at the end of a team meeting. They can be required to identify areas of improvement, which in turn can be criteria used to assess them in a subsequent meeting. This kind of approach moves assessment from the success or failure purpose towards the healthier developmental purpose.

The key point about any formative assessment is timely feedback, so students can apply the feedback as quickly as possible.

One further principle that we have found useful is to insist that students always have an opportunity to be formatively assessed against any learning outcomes before they are summatively assessed against that outcome. By using this approach and focusing on assessment for learning, we have been able to reduce the student culture's attitude that "if it doesn't count for the grade, we won't do it."

Who Should Assess?

Typically, in traditional classes, the tutor is the assessor who judges the students' work. This aligns clearly with the concept of the tutor as the subject matter expert who evaluates the extent to which the students have leaned and can apply the knowledge in this domain. However, in PBL, Maggi Savin–Baden (2003) argues, if the facilitator is also the assessor, the power dynamics of the team are affected as the facilitator is seen as both the co-learner and gatekeeper. She therefore recommends that such assessment is done anonymously by someone else. This is certainly the ideal situation, though resource constraints often preclude this approach.

We have argued that we want to develop self-assessment skills and self-directed learning. It is therefore consistent that there are plenty of opportunities provided for self and peer assessment. In the case of team working skills, the tutor often has a very limited view and therefore it is most appropriate to put the most weight on students' assessments. As Don Woods (1996) points out, opportunity for practice is not sufficient to develop competency; students need *training* as well as practice and feedback on their performance to develop confidence and accuracy in self-assessment.

However, even in the subject knowledge domain, since we are trying to help students to progress towards professional competence, we would expect them to increasingly develop self-assessment skills and, thus, we start building this in at an early stage (see Figure 8.1), even if the grading for that outcome is purely dependent on the tutor's mark.

While we can justify self and peer assessment for learning, we acknowledge that many Universities limit the weight that such assessment can carry in an individual module. Clearly, in high stakes summative assessment, validity and reliability are essential. In any situation where peer or self-assessment are used, students need to be able to interpret criteria consistently according to the appropriate standards. The use of multiple forms of evidence can be helpful here.

Conclusion

In this chapter, we have explored the issues associated with assessment in problem-based learning courses. PBL is an effective way for students to learn subject knowledge and skills. However, since we argue that the process skills are important within PBL, it follows that they should be specified as learning outcomes and should also be assessed. Thus, PBL has an extra dimension—the assessment of process skills.

PBL seeks to give students more responsibility in learning and consequently self and peer-assessment methods are consistent with this approach. They are also suitable methods for assessing some of the process skills.

We have provided a number of examples of tools that can be used formatively or summatively to assess skills and knowledge. An important point is the need for formative feedback to be given quickly, especially in the case of skills assessment. However, since formative assessment does not count towards a student's overall grade, the feedback need not be so accurate. Tutors need not spend time ensuring high validity and reliability. Peer assessment can also reduce assessment demands on faculty.

Since most PBL implementers use team work, the perennial, thorny issue of freeloaders will arise. We believe that two strategies are useful here: Incorporating elements of individual assessment that is, the Tri-partite system described previously; and empowering and training the teams to deal with this themselves.

Finally, as co-learners in PBL we need to constantly reflect on and review the effectiveness of the PBL case, student learning, and its assessment. The following checklist provides a set of questions that can help the tutor consider issues in the design of a PBL assessment task. We have also drawn together all the criteria used for the case study in chapters six to eight and included them in

Figure 8.8. Checklist of considerations for assessment

1. What is being assessed?	Are you assessing Subject Knowledge? Process skills? Attitudes? Behaviours? Is everything that is assessed clearly related to learning outcomes?
2. Subject knowledge and skills	Are you assessing just the component parts, or is there also some holistic assessment? Holistic assessment is recommended as important by Biggs (1999).
3. Authenticity	How authentic is the **assessed task** to the students and to professional practice?
4. Alignment with PBL case	Does the assessment strategy drive students towards deep approaches to learning or surface approaches?
5. Process skills	Which of the process skills (Problem Solving, Team working, Coping with change, self assessment, self-directed learning) are you assessing? How are you assessing them?
6. Formative assessment	Which outcomes are being formatively assessed? When and how will the assessment take place? When and how will feedback be given?
7. Summative assessment	Which outcomes are summatively assessed? When will the assessment take place? When and how will feedback be given?
8. Criteria	Who has set the criteria? Students or staff or is it negotiated? Are the assessment criteria for all learning outcomes (subject knowledge and process skills) clear and explicit to staff and students? How do you ensure students understand the criteria? How will achievement of criteria be measured? What evidence will be used? Is the evidence multi-dimensional?
9. Who assesses?	Where will self-assessment be used? If so, how will students be prepared for self-assessment? Where will Peer assessment be used? If so, how will students be prepared (e.g., to give balanced, objective, specific, and supportive (BOSS) feedback?) Does the facilitator or other faculty member assess the students?
10. Preparation for assessment	How will students and faculty be prepared to assess?
11. Fair and reasonable	Is the volume of assessment practicable (for staff and students)? How will team and individual components be weighted? How will you deal with freeloaders? This needs to be made explicit to students at the start. What ground rules are set? What influence can students have on ground rules? Can they set penalties for non-compliance?
12. Relation to other modules	How does the assessment (deadlines, learning outcomes) relate to other modules the students study? Is there over assessment? Are learning outcomes being summatively assessed in many modules? For example, process skills may be assessed simultaneously in several modules if you are not careful. Is there progression?

Figure 8.9. Complete table of assessment criteria for case study used in Chapters VI to VIII

Computer Networks Assessment Criteria (PBL 1, 2, 3)

Learning Outcome	Evidence	Pass (threshold)	Good Pass (GP)	Excellent	Weight
LO2 Critically analyse the requirements for a small-scale network.	1. Team final proposal	Key appropriate functional and non-functional requirements correctly identified and in appropriate format.	Most requirements identified correctly, are in appropriate format, and prioritised appropriately.	Comprehensive list of functional and non-functional requirements unambiguously and correctly identified, in appropriate format, and prioritised appropriately.	10%
LO3 Synthesise and evaluate a design for a solution to a network requirement.	2. Team final proposal	Proposal accurately specifies appropriate software and hardware to meet the key requirements in suitable format.	As Pass and most of solution has suitable level of detail and clearly justified and linked to most requirements. Some benefits of solution identified.	As GP and all solution detailed and some critical evaluation of alternate solutions provided.	25%
	3. Individual research handout	Handouts produced providing correct summaries of topics researched	As Pass and relevance to PBL case is clearly demonstrated.	As GP and critical evaluation of alternate solutions provided.	10%
	4. Presentation	Presentation is consistent with, and relates to, report.	Presentation is balanced and discusses key points.	Presentation is persuasive and clearly links features and benefits of solution with client needs and problems.	5%
LO4 Construct, install, and use a range of administration tools for a small LAN.	1. Demonstration	Shows evidence of planning, all team involved, shared or restricted access, user login and applications demonstrated. Questions answered showing some correct knowledge. Likely to need significant prompting.	As Pass and evidence of thorough organisation of the demonstration, relates to client requirements. Questions answered correctly, may be some prompting.	As GP and all aspects of demonstration systematically related to client requirements. Questions answered confidently, correctly and comprehensively	10%
Problem Solving:					
P1 Solve problems in a systematic manner, using appropriate tools.	5. Reflection	Describes problems and approach to solving	Demonstrates a systematic approach	As GP and identifies learning.	15%
Communication:					
C1 Perform written communication for a purpose: (business proposal, personal reflection and research handout)	6. Proposal 7. Individual handouts	Structured with headings. Acceptable spelling and grammar.	As Pass and structured according to advice provided. Written in clear appropriate style of English.	As GP and demonstrates appropriate level of detail (critical judgement).	5%
	8. Interview skills (formative)	Asks clear questions in logical manner, mostly open questions.	Clear structure to interview, follows up answers with more detailed exploration.	Includes checkpoint summaries, uses suitable interview model.	0%
C2 Collect appropriate information in a structured manner during an interview.	9. Presentation	Presentation within 5 minutes of agreed time & Logical structure. Clear speech, some eye contact. Co-ordinates with other team members. PowerPoint uses appropriate text and graphics.	As Pass and clear introductions, summary, and signposting. Answers questions knowledgeably. Explains slides.	As GP and confident, enthusiastic, persuasive, does not read from a script, and relates to clients	10%
C3 Deliver a sales presentation in a professional manner.					
Working with Others:					
W1 Participate constructively in team by	10. Peer assessment (with tutor moderation)	*Meets commitments to team* Indicators: • Punctual. • Is prepared for meetings. • Completes assigned tasks. • Contributes positively during team meetings. • Keeps others informed of progress	As pass and *Assists team development* Indicators: • Demonstrates sensitivity. • Listens and responds empathetically. • Acknowledges contributions. • Helps organise team. • Provides constructive criticism.	As *grade B and shows leadership* Indicators: • Takes initiative in task. • Helps resolve conflicts. • Encourages others. • Recognises and assists in difficulties. • Proactively works towards consensus.	10%
1. Taking responsibility for aspects.					
2. Showing sensitivity and providing supportive feedback to others.					
3. Meeting deadlines					

Figure 8.9. This shows how a wide variety of criteria have been combined in this particular module and linked to the module learning outcomes.

References

Basile, C., Olson, F., & Nathenson-Mejia, S. (2003). Problem-based learning: Reflective coaching for teacher educators. *Reflective Practice, 4*(3), 291-302.

Beaumont, C., Sackville, A., & Chew, S. C. (2004). Identifying Good Practice in the use of PBL to teach computing. *ITALICS, 3*(1). Retrieved March 30, 2005, from http://www.ics.ltsn.ac.uk/pub/italics/vol3iss1.htm

Biggs, J. (1999). *Teaching for quality learning at university*. Buckingham: SRHE & OUP.

Boud, D., Keogh, R., & Walker, D. (1995). Promoting reflection in learning: A model. In D. Boud, R. Keogh, & D. Walker (Eds.), *Reflection: Turning experience into learning*. London: Kogan Page.

Clegg, S., Tan, J., & Saeidi, S. (2002). Reflecting or acting? Reflective practice and continuing professional development in higher education. *Reflective Practice, 3*(1), 144-146.

Conway, J., Chen, S. E. & Jefferies, M. C. (1999). Assessment of professional competence in problem-based learning settings: Two case studies. *Proceedings of 1st Asia Pacific Conference on Problem-Based Learning*, Hong Kong.

Ellis, A., Carswell, L., Bernat, A., Deveaux, D., Frison, P., Meisalo, V., Meyer, J., Nulden, U., Rugelj, J., & Tarhio, J. (1998). Resources, tools, and techniques for problem-based learning in computing. *ITiCSE '98,3rd Annual Conference on Integrating Technology into Computer Science Education*. ACM/SIGCSE.

Johnson, D. W. (2003). *Reaching out* (8th ed.). Boston: Pearson Education.

Kingsland, A. J. (1995). Integrated assessment: The rhetoric and the students' view. In P. Little, M. Ostwald, & G. Ryan (Eds.), *Research and development in problem-based learning* (Vol. 3, pp. 309-324). Sydney: PROBLARC.

Knight, P. T. (2000). The value of a programme wide approach to assessment. *Assessment and Evaluation in Higher Education, 25*(3), 237-251.

Mezirow, J. (1981). A critical theory of adult learning and education. *Adult Education, 32*(1), 3-24.

Norman, G. R. (1997) Assessment in problem-based learning. In D. Boud & G. Feletti (Eds.), *The challenge of problem-based learning* (2nd ed.) (pp. 263-266). London: Kogan Page.

Norman, G. R., & Schmidt, H. G. (1992). The psychological basis of problem-based learning: A review of the evidence, *Academic Medicine, 67,* 557-65.

Norman, G.R., & Schmidt, H.G. (1993). Where is the learning in problem-based learning? *PEDAGOGUE, 4*(2), 4-6.

Painvin, C., Neufeld, V. R., Norman, G. R., & Walker, L. (1979). The triple jump exercise—A structured measure of problem solving and self-directed learning. *Proceedings of the 18th Conference on Research in Medical Education,* Washington, DC.

Ramsden, P. (1992). *Learning to teach in higher education.* London: Routledge

Richardson, G., & Maltby, H. (1995). Reflection-on-practice: Enhancing student learning. *Journal of advanced nursing, 22,* 235-242.

Savin-Baden, M. (2003). *Facilitating problem-based learning in higher education: Illuminating perspectives.* Buckingham: SRHE/Open University Press.

Savin-Baden M. (2003a). Assessment, the last great problem in higher education? *PBL Insight, 6*(1). Retrieved August 23, 2004, from http://www.samford.edu/pbl/PBLInsight6/SavinBaden.html

Swanson, D., Case, S., & van der Vlueten, C. (1997). Strategies for student assessment. In D. Boud & G. Feletti (Eds.), *The challenge of problem-based learning* (2nd ed.) (pp 269-282). London: Kogan Page.

Winter, R., Buck, A., & Sobiechowska, P. (1999). *Professional experience and the investigative imagination.* London: Routledge.

Woods, D. R. (1993). On the learning in problem-based learning? *PEDAGOGUE, 4*(2), 2-3.

Woods, D. R. (1995). *Problem-based learning: Resources to gain the most from PBL.* Hamilton, Ontario: Donald Woods.

Woods, D. R. (1996). *Problem-based learning: Helping your students gain the most from PBL* (3rd ed.). Hamilton, Ontario: Donald R Woods.

Yip, W., & Ghafarian, A. (2000*).* Problem-based learning assessment for information systems courses. *Proceedings of the 15th International Conference on Informatics Education Research .* Retrieved August 23, 2004, from http://www.iaim.org/IAIM2000/iaim00.htm

Chapter IX

Integrating
E-Learning Technology

Introduction

Information technology has been used in teaching, learning, and assessment for many years, from programmed learning and on-line tutorials, which are teaching-centred, at one end of the spectrum, to computer-supported collaborative environments, which are learning-centred.

The term e-learning has developed over recent years to subsume these and related terms. The UK Joint Information Systems Committee (JISC) provides the following useful explanation:

E-Learning can cover a spectrum of activities from supporting learning, to blended learning (the combination of traditional and e-learning practices), to learning that is delivered entirely online. Whatever the technology, however, learning is the vital element. (JISC, n.d.)

A number of specifications and standards are starting to emerge around e-learning. For example, relating to the Communication Interface: how resources communicate with other systems or meta-data; how to describe e-learning resources in a consistent manner and packaging; and how to gather resources into useful bundles. Organisations such as the IMS Global Learning Consortium 1 help contribute specifications in this area.

In this chapter we will focus on the pedagogy and identify relevant aspects of e-learning technology that we believe are particularly relevant to problem-based learning.

Ron Oliver (2001, p. 407) points out that "e-learning, when done well, can improve learning and deliver enhanced learning outcomes," which is certainly encouraging, but the qualifier "when done well," requires rather more explanation to avoid the pitfalls along the way.

Oliver provides a useful model to describe on-line learning designs and help analyse the balance of a particular learning design. The model is summarised in Table 9.1.

These critical elements are interrelated, but the real benefit of this model is that it helps the learning designer to identify any particular emphasis in a learning design. For example, teacher-centred learning places most emphasis on learning supports. As we would expect, resource-based learning (RBL) places most emphasis on learning resources—particularly the content. Oliver argues that designers of on-line courses spend far too much of their time on the production of "content."

So, what is the right balance? Where should we place the emphasis? Peter Goodyear, following Oliver, emphasises the importance of learning *tasks*:

We are committed to the view that educational outcomes are unlikely to be enhanced through networked learning unless careful attention is paid to the design of learning tasks, the learning environment, and the social dynamics of learning. In particular, we believe that designers need to have their eyes firmly on what the learner will be doing. (Goodyear, 2001, p. 97)

Table 9.1. Framework describing critical elements of online learning settings (Oliver, 1999)

Learning design elements	Description
Learning tasks	The activities, problems, and interactions, used to engage the learners, on which learning is based
Learning resources	The content, information, and resources with which the learners interact, upon which learning is based.
Learning supports	The scaffolds, structures, encouragements, motivations, assistances, and connections used to support learning

The tasks that Oliver refers to are learning activities, such as inquiries, problems, projects that require access to resources, and support. He believes it is important that these tasks are aligned with constructivist principles, citing PBL as an example.

Having briefly identified critical elements and emphasis needed for successful e-learning, we now consider specifically how this relates to PBL.

Problem-based learning is consistent with a social constructivist learning pedagogy. One of the challenges we face is to integrate e-learning technologies into PBL *where it is appropriate*—that is where it supports the learner. We feel strongly that the pedagogy should come first, and that the technology should support, rather than conflict with, the pedagogy.

Within the PBL learning system, Ronteltap and Eurelings (1997) classified student-related PBL activities into two sets. The first is *information-related learning activities*. These are largely related to individual research and comprise resource-based search, selection, collection, analysis, synthesis, and presentation activities. The second set is comprised of *communication and collaboration activities*. These include peer, tutor, and expert communications that question, challenge, and co-construct knowledge. A third set of PBL activities is associated with assessment and reflection. These three activities are, of course, closely interrelated as indicated in Figure 9.1. This can be a useful framework to identify how technology can support PBL.

This classification also emphasises the close alignment between PBL and information and communication technologies (ICT).

In this chapter we will use this framework to explore how information and communications technology can be used within PBL programs. There is a wide range of possibilities; some are easier to use than others, ranging from simple provision of resources via a Web page and on-line assessment to the provision

Figure 9.1. A classification of activities

of a rich environment of synchronous and asynchronous tools needed for distributed (virtual) PBL.

Supporting Information-Related Activities

PBL requires students to perform research. This presupposes access to appropriate resources and the ability to search, select, collect, analyse, evaluate, and present the results of their research. information technology can provide good support for all of these tasks.

Resources

A critical factor in the success of PBL is the provision of appropriate resources for students, so that they can perform active research and locate information to solve the problem posed. Many students head straight for the Web as the first port of call. George Watson (2002) claims that the Web is "an excellent proving ground for engaging and developing critical thinking skills." Since selection and evaluation of information for relevance and accuracy is important in PBL, the Web provides students with ample opportunity to develop these skills. When students have researched problems in the subject of computer networking, they have sometimes discovered data and information, which is more up-to-the-minute than we had known!

One of the difficulties of using search engines on the Web is the issue of formulating effective queries and filtering the huge volume of results returned. To help students who are starting with PBL[2], we have found it useful to provide links to some suitable resources on a Web page for the module or PBL case. However, to make these effective, such resources must be structured in an easy-to-access way. It helps if they are well organised and include short descriptions of the contents of each resource. Links can be made to on-line journals and newspaper articles as well as specific Web sites. If the resources are substantial, it is desirable to provide search facilities within the site.

Structuring a PBL Case

A related area is the provision of organisational resources. Online resources accessible via a Web site or even a CD-ROM can be very useful to support a PBL case. One of the difficulties students experience in PBL is often the lack of structure, especially where a PBL case lasts several weeks.

Web pages are now commonly used to provide organisational information about the module. In the PBL context this can also include:

- Explanation of PBL and links to some of the many PBL sites;
- Roles and responsibilities of participants, including students, facilitators, tutors, and the team leader;
- Expectation of time to be spent individually and in meetings;
- Milestones, deliverables, and deadlines for PBL cases;
- Suggested team ground rules;
- Frequently asked questions; and
- Links to tutorials and advice regarding process skills such as problem-solving, inter-personal communications, conflict resolution, coping with change, self and peer assessment, and research strategies.

It is also useful to indicate team composition on the Web site.

Figure 9.2. Example Web page

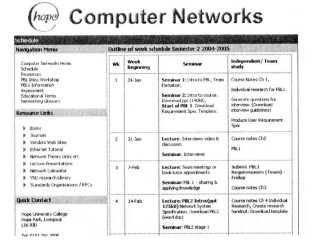

A sample section of a schedule is shown in Figure 9.2. This provides an outline guide of activities, links to resources, and links to downloadable documents.

The next stage in developing information resources using ICT is to change the Web site from static to dynamic. In a face-to-face situation in a classroom, the resources, format, and activities change from week to week. To be most effective, an on-line environment should also adapt to the student experience and progression.

One aspect of this is to incorporate dynamic content to the site, for example, the progressive revealing of information for a PBL case. This is easily achieved either on a Web site or virtual learning environment (VLE) such as WebCT®.

A further extension of this approach to increase the reality of the PBL case is to develop it from Web pages providing details of the case to include simulations, Flash animations, streaming media — for example, an interview with one of the players in the case — and the use of computer gaming technology to build virtual reality environments that allow students to explore aspects of the case. Clearly these require considerable investment in resources to create and they are currently one of the subjects of our research. Many students are familiar with computer gaming and the application of the technology in a PBL setting appears to have great potential.

Wireless and Mobile Technology

Wireless laptops can also have a beneficial effect on the environment for PBL. The flexibility enables students to move from one phase of PBL to the next seamlessly and perform real time research where it is critical. Similarly, teams can integrate contributions, finalise presentations and reports, and perform data analysis much more conveniently. We expect this to be the norm before long.

Resources for PBL Tutors

George Watson (2003) suggests that on-line resources can support PBL courses by providing information and inspiration for both problem design and problem-solving.

He suggests that the plethora of on-line newspapers and on-line databases are good sources of inspiration for developing problem scenarios and regional perspectives. Extreme positions can be found easily. Additionally, film and television Web sites can provide supporting character material and ideas for scripts. This can add interest, reality, and authenticity to a PBL case.

At this point, it is also worth highlighting that there are Web sites that provide sample PBL cases as resources for tutors. Probably the best known is the University of Delaware Clearinghouse, which is an on-line database of PBL articles and problems. All material is peer-reviewed by PBL practitioners for content and pedagogy. The database is searchable by author, discipline, key-words, or full text. It has controlled access using free user subscription at https://chico.nss.udel.edu/Pbl/.

A smaller collection of cases is also available via the UK PBL Web site, hosted by Coventry University at http://www.hss.coventry.ac.uk/pbl/.

Supporting Communication and Collaboration Activities

The second major set of activities in PBL involves team working and associated communication. Problem-based learning is dependent on student collaboration for its success. This is traditionally achieved in face-to-face meetings, which raises a question: Why should we be concerned with using technology in this area?

Setting aside the issue of distributed or virtual PBL, it is interesting to note that a review conducted among all students and staff at the University of Maastricht prioritised the use of communication tools because planned face-to-face meetings "appeared to be insufficiently supportive of the learning process" (Ronteltap, Goodyear, & Bartoluzzi, 2004, p. 4274).

One of the most challenging tasks is to design and manage an effective communication space for on-line learning. The facilities have been expanding year by year and there are a variety of asynchronous and synchronous tools available.

A considerable amount of research has been conducted, particularly around the use of computer supported collaborative learning (CSCL). Much of this is based on the use of asynchronous forums, conferences, and bulletin boards. More recent work has included blended learning, a term used to describe a learning solution that combines several delivery methods, typically on-line learning via the Internet, with a traditional classroom environment (Miller, Jones, Packham, & Thomas, 2004). Some useful general design principles for on-line communities have been collected together by Kollock (1997), which draw on studies of communities acting together and the analysis of social dilemmas. They are summarised in Table 9.2.

We do not have space to consider these in detail and we will restrict ourselves to discussion of specific technologies that we have found relate closely to PBL.

Table 9.2. Principles for the "design" of effective online communities (Kollock, 1997)

- Requirements for the possibility of cooperation:
    - Arrange for individuals to meet each other again.
    - They must be able to recognise each other.
    - They must have information about how the other has behaved until now.
- Ostrom's design principles of successful communities:
    - Group boundaries are clearly defined.
    - Rules governing the use of collective goods are well matched to local needs and conditions.
    - Most individuals affected by these rules can participate in modifying the rules.
    - The right of community members to devise their own rules is respected by external authorities.
    - A system for monitoring members' behavior exists; this monitoring is undertaken by the community members themselves.
    - A graduated system of sanctions is used.
    - Community members have access to low-cost conflict resolution mechanisms.
- Godwin's principles for making virtual communities work:
    - Use software that promotes good discussion.
    - Do not impose a length limitation on postings.
    - Front-load your system with talkative, diverse people.
    - Let the users resolve their own disputes.
    - Provide institutional memory.
    - Promote continuity.
    - Be host to a particular interest group.
    - Confront the users with a crisis.
- The Doblin Group's elements of community:
    - Effort: obligation, participation, responsibility, collaboration, consequence
    - Purpose: focus, influence, shared activity, progress, shared vision
    - Identity: character, bounded, coherent, authentic, shared history, emergent
    - Organic: decentralised, richness, co-constructed, interdependent, balanced
    - Adaptive: flexible, scaleable, responsive, resilient, feedback
    - Freedom: rights, access, choice, empowering, fit

Asynchronous Forums and Conferences

Clearly there appears to be a great opportunity in PBL for the use of asynchronous forums. They can be used for the sharing of research by posting handouts and findings in a team conference. Threaded discussion postings can ideally be used to pose questions, argue, and challenge statements that have been made, achieve consensus, and co-construct meaning. The team can also use them for socialisation and organisation of meetings.

Although it is possible to use the tools in this way to operate at the higher levels of Salmon's (2002) 5-step model (knowledge construction and development), there are also considerable obstacles. Cox, Clark, Heath, and Plumpton (2000) analysed over 3,000 messages from students on an on-line Open University technology course. Despite the inclusion of activities to train and involve students, their findings showed:

"Most students did not actively contribute in either their own tutor conference or the national conference.

- There were an average of 2.3 messages per thread, which must have affected the development of substantive discussion.
- Queries and requests for help were often repeats of previous messages...little use made of the ability to search through messages for key words or phrases.
- Similar or linked messages or threads seldom drawn together by students or tutor.
- Little use of ability to quote text from other messages in order to build dialogue. Key messages, advice, summaries etc. often missed.
- Students became selective about which messages they read (e.g., only tutor or certain other students).
- Students who did not log on (to the national conference) very often were faced with a sea of red flags [unread messages] and began to feel intimidated.
- In a complex (conference) structure...the total volume of messages gets spread more thinly so it looks like there is not much interest.
- Organisational structure broke the conversations down into too many categories."

These are significant issues, which need to be managed. Cox suggests that a very important role of the tutor is to "weave." "Student messages come in all over the conference, at any time and anywhere. It is a continuous stream of data, ideas, questions, communications, and information, synchronous and asynchronous—one and the same, yet different—like a piece of elastic. A "weave" is an open ended pulling of things together and then encouraging further discussion into another strand, a seamless pattern, illustrating the group's development and thinking. Messages need rearrangement, renaming, summarising or linking with each other. Even the simple act of rearranging or renaming can be important in helping students structure thinking and reading" (Mason, 1998).

However, this approach clearly identifies a power relationship, with the tutor responsible to perform this task. One of the reasons for the issues could be lack of ownership by the students. In PBL, we want the students to perform this task as part of the team collaboration to co-construct knowledge. How can this be developed?

One interesting approach in dealing with the issue of overcrowding of messages, naming, and categorisation has been developed by the Learning Lab at the University of Maastricht. (POLARIS, 2004). In many conferencing systems, the conference moderator is the only user with the power to edit, remove, and otherwise manage the messages. This power imbalance forbids students from restructuring the knowledge base. In POLARIS, students can classify content (question/answer, discussion, and addition) and can also add personal markings in the collective environment and a consent-function that clarifies which documents have a central function in the collaboration.

The aims of POLARIS, as explained by Ronteltap and Eurelings (1997), are to support both the individual information-related activities and provide a collaborative environment.

The individual learning environment will hold an integrated set of tools:

- *To give access to information resources: e-mail, campus information systems, library catalogues, navigation tools for WWW-searches, computer assisted instruction, formative testing, etc.;*
- *For information processing: text, graphics, statistics, presentations;*
- *A study information manager: database services for storage and retrieval of study documents.*

The collaborative work environment will be the tool for communication between peers and with the tutor in preparation for the discussion in the next meeting of the tutorial group. In this environment individual learning fades into collaborative learning. The collaborative learning environment must enable learners:

- *To present the results of the learning process in different formats;*
- *To ask questions to peers, tutor, or experts;*
- *To attach reactions, comments, or answers to submitted documents;*
- *To connect related documents by the user as well as by the system;*
- *To access information in the shared environment in individual adapted selections."*

POLARIS can be integrated with the BlackBoard® Virtual Learning Environment.

Figure 9.3. Example of ideas map

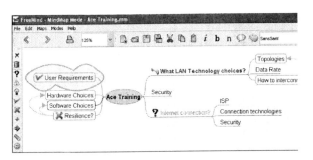

Construction of Meaning

In social constructivism, we believe that learning consists of the construction of meaning by integrating knowledge and experience into a learner's own mental model.

The points identified by Cox also highlight interaction, but limited engagement—mainly at the level of exchanging information. There could be many reasons for this, but it demonstrates that current asynchronous media, such as threaded discussion forums, do not easily assist students in demonstrating connections and integrating the information easily and clearly.

POLARIS shows one approach to enhance the facilities available to students. Another approach, which bears some similarities, and seems to be increasing in popularity, is the development of *wikis*.

A *wiki* (pronounced "wicky" or "weeky") or *WikiWiki* as defined by the Wikipedia[3] is a Web site (or other hypertext document collection) that gives users the ability to add content, as on an Internet forum, but also allows that content to be edited by other users.

The pages are written in "wikitext," a form of hypertext that is much simpler than HTML. This simplicity, together with the facility for users to edit the content, adds an extra dimension to the facilities offered by the familiar single-dimensional threaded discussion forum. There are a number of wiki engines, which provide facilities such as searching, change logs and some control of users.

Thus, students could use a wiki relatively easily to integrate information and represent links between ideas, concepts, and research findings.

Another way to represent connections is to use Buzan and Buzan's (1996) mind mapping techniques with software to support it. The student team builds up the map and integrates its research into a Web site that demonstrates the links. This enables any student (or tutor) to browse the site and follow the semantic links.

A benefit of this approach is that it represents information more visually and also uses more than one dimension. Figure 9.3 shows part of a map created with FreeMind[4]. Nodes can hold references to documents as well as text and the map can be exported to HTML.

Synchronous Communications

Asynchronous tools offer the advantage of enabling reflection before contribution to a discussion and reducing the time constraint, but they form just one element of a communications space. Synchronous communication is also a vital requirement for collaborative learning. It is usually provided by face-to-face meetings, but technology can help, particularly where distance is an issue. In our research (Chew & Beaumont, 2004) we found that an integrated set of synchronous and asynchronous tools were important within a distributed PBL environment.

In recent years the range and effectiveness of synchronous tools has expanded dramatically. Mobile phones are now ubiquitous and students use them as a prime means to organise and schedule meetings. Instant messaging, with tools such as MSN Messenger® and AOL Instant Messenger®, are regularly used by students in their social lives. Virtual Learning Environments, such as LearnWise® and WebCT®, now incorporate synchronous chat. Web cams are developing to the point where Broadband availability makes them useful tools rather than simply fun toys. Video conferencing, using ISDN, can also provide a high-quality medium.

We recently finished analysing the use of communication tools by PBL teams where half the team was in the UK and the other half was in Singapore (Chew & Beaumont, 2004). The UK students and Singapore students held their own face-to-face meetings and communicated with each other using a rich set of synchronous and asynchronous tools.

The importance of the rich environment of communication tools became clear in this project, particularly given the global distribution of the teams. This rich set of tools enabled the students to overcome a number of difficulties. For example, students regarded synchronous discussion as essential for decision-making. However, Web cam video and audio proved ineffective because of bandwidth, latency, and language difficulties, though we may expect the technology to improve in the future (Knutson, Knutson, & Slazinski, 2003).

The students overcame these issues by using instant messaging software, such as Microsoft Messenger® or NetMeeting®, to chat. They also demonstrated flexibility in arranging meetings to overcome the seven-hour time difference.

The asynchronous tools (file dropbox and threaded discussion forum) were widely used for complementary tasks, such as exchange of information and product delivery (dropbox), and challenging contributions and constructing shared understanding (threaded discussion forum).

Our analysis shows that the semantic threads incorporated both synchronous and asynchronous tools in a rational way. This emphasises the need for an integrated set of such tools to encourage the development of high-performing teams.

It is more difficult to draw conclusions regarding the ISDN Video conference. It provided good quality audio and video, but technical difficulties restricted its use to one conference at the end of the first phase. It was also the only tool that was not available "on-demand."

Results also suggested that prior experience—and hence, preparation—of students is significant in the way they select communication tools.

Blended Learning

The introduction of technology provides alternatives to the traditional PBL approaches to information-related activities, communication, and collaboration. ICT can be used to replace the traditional methods or to integrate them to enhance the learning experience. It is at this point that the course designer must bite the bullet and decide which tools should be used and how they should be used. This is where the pedagogy must come before the technology. If students see the technology as an extra imposition, rather than being useful in their learning, then it will be unsuccessful. Integrating, rather than supplementing ICT, is perhaps one of the keys to blended learning.

Interestingly, Kiser reported on a two-year study by Thomson Learning of 128 respondents investigating the effectiveness of blended learning in comparison with a pure on-line course. It identified five core elements contributing to the success of a blended e-learning programme, namely:

- *Use of scenario based exercises to teach a subject;*
- *Integration of learning objects with realistic scenarios;*
- *Early use of the knowledge or skills;*
- *Access to live mentors during the online portion of the training; and*
- *Assessments designed to mimic real world tasks.* (Kiser, 2002, p. 10)

These are core characteristics of PBL, which reinforce our argument that PBL and technology can indeed be integrated successfully to the benefit of students.

Intelligent Learning Guide (Learning Companion)

The tools discussed so far have assisted human communication. A further development that we are exploring is the concept of an intelligent learning guide (ILG), built on intelligent agent technology. This guide is a type of learning companion system (LCS) (Chou, Chan, & Lin, 2002) applied to problem-based learning. An LCS is a development of an intelligent tutoring system (ITS), but, whereas an ITS is built around a pedagogical model of instruction, educational software agents within an LCS can have a variety of roles, for example: a competitor, collaborator, troublemaker or critic.

The learning guide is conceived as taking the role of a reactive facilitator, in which a student consults for advice. The ILG will respond by suggesting courses of action that the student can take by prompting with questions. Ideally, such agents should adapt depending on the experience of the user.

One particular benefit of such a guide for researchers is the ability of the ILG to collect the dialogue and analyse the student's development.

Supporting Assessment-Related Activities

The third and final bubble in Figure 9.1 concerns assessment-related activities. We incorporate reflection in this set, since it is a form of self-assessment, with peer, formative, and summative assessment.

Reflection is one of the skills that help students construct meaning and traditionally the use of learning journals and paper-based feedback forms have been used. Recent developments, such as Web logs (blogging) and Wikis, may possibly provide a role facilitating reflection, though their very public nature is likely to influence the nature of the contributions. Perhaps they constitute more of a team reflection.

In the previous chapter, we discussed assessment in some detail. ICT can be particularly supportive in many aspects:

First, students can use applications to analyse data (e.g., spreadsheets) and present their conclusions to a case, either as a word-processed report or as a presentation using a tool, such as PowerPoint®. These products can be assessed. Many virtual learning environments now include facilities for students to submit such deliverables electronically. These are time-stamped by the system and automatically archived, saving staff time. Some VLEs provide the facility for tutor feedback, but usually as a summarised set of comments. A further enhancement is provided by the Electronic Tutor Marked Assignment (ETMA) system developed by the Open University in the UK, which also enables tutors to electronically annotate student work and return it with a summary of comments, using Microsoft Word®.

Subject knowledge and application have been easily and reliably tested for many years using multiple choice questions (MCQ). Virtual learning environments usually provide for a range of different types and formats of questions. Small scenarios and associated MCQs that require students to analyse and apply knowledge relate well to the PBL approach.

Perhaps one of the most effective and time-saving applications of IT is in the implementation and summarising of self and peer-assessment questionnaires. Self-assessment questionnaires that measure a student's confidence in skills such as problem solving using Likert scales can be constructed relatively easily to be delivered via the Web. This can be summarised automatically for tutors and students and can provide a profile at an instant in time. Since the IT facilitates repeated application of such an instrument, the student's profile can be monitored over a period of time.

A good example of a peer assessment instrument is provided by Chew (2002) at Temasek Polytechnic, Singapore. Each student provides feedback about his or her team members via on-line forms. The forms consist of a number of Likert scale responses to statements with a text box for open comments. The system collates the feedback for an individual that has been submitted by all their team members and presents the (anonymous) feedback to the student at a certain point. Checks can be built in to ensure that a student does not receive feedback before a tutor monitors it.

Conclusion

In this chapter, we have identified a number of ways in which ICT can effectively support PBL. Indeed, we would assert that the student-centred, task-focused, research-based, collaborative learning characteristics of PBL make it a particularly suitable environment in which to blend technology.

Figure 9.4. Checklist for integrating e-learning components

Checklist

Supporting Information related activities	
Resources for the PBL case	How will resources for the case be provided? That is, a list of references (on line/off-line), library catalogues, links to Web pages of organisations that might provide contextual information. Are there search facilities to help students locate information? Can simulations or multi-media resources be included? Are the resources adaptive? For example, a dynamic Web site can provide different information over time, such as progressively revealing information about the case.
Organisational resources	How are deadlines, deliverables, contact information, time expectations, locations, and possible ground rules communicated?
PBL resources:	Is there information to help students understand PBL, the roles and responsibilities of students and facilitators, and so on.
Process Skills Resources	Are there links to guidelines or tutorials on skills, such as problem solving, conflict resolution, peer assessment, and self-assessment?
Access to ICT resources	How can students access the resources? Will mobile technologies be used (e.g., wireless laptop, PDA, mobile phone)
Supporting communication/collaboration activities	
Asynchronous communication/collaboration	Will asynchronous collaboration be provided? For example, VLE threaded forum, wiki, or POLARIS? If so, what is their role in relation to face-to-face meetings? How often are students expected to access/contribute? Will these be private for the team or public (or both)? Will students be able to/expected to summarise, annotate, delete, and search contributions? What is the role of the tutor? Are tutors expected to monitor or moderate forums?
Synchronous tools	Is there a place for synchronous tools such as Web cam, instant messaging, ISDN videoconference? If so, what is their role in relation to face-to-face meetings? Will tutors be included?
Tutor/student communication	How are students and tutors expected to communicate (e.g., e-mail, conferencing, or face to face appointments)?
Co-construction of knowledge	Are there any facilities for students to represent the process and product? For example, Web site, wikki, or mind map.
Assessment and reflection	
Self assessment/reflection	Use of on-line questionnaires for self assessment, on-line journals, or Web logs
Peer assessment	On-line questionnaires, processed and summarised.

Figure 9.4. Checklist for integrating e-learning components (cont.)

Knowledge assessment	Formative/summative/MCQs can be used where appropriate.
Submission of deliverables	Many VLEs provide facilities for submission and storage, and enable tutors to provide feedback to students.
Feedback	Can feedback be generated automatically (e.g., from on-line quizzes)?
Training and preparation	How will students and tutors be trained and prepared to use the technology selected?
Blended learning	What is the rationale for including the particular technology? How will it be integrated with traditional approaches? How does it enhance student learning?

One important factor we have not touched on in this chapter is students' (and tutors') skills at using the technology. Students must be taught and prepared for the use of any technology before we can expect them to use it effectively.

Finally, David Boud (2004) suggests that technology can be used in a number of ways. He contrasts the *"Logic of control with the logic of affordances."* In the former, the technology can be used to determine student activities. In the latter, the technology provides opportunities for students to explore and learn, but the control is with the student. The inclusion of ICT enables us to provide a richer learning environment, with more opportunities. The challenge is to get the blend right.

The following checklist highlights and summarises issues the tutor needs to consider when integrating PBL and e-learning technologies.

References

Beaumont, C., Sackville, A., & Chew, S. C. (2004). Identifying good practice in the use of PBL to teach computing. *ITALICS, 3*(1). Retrieved August 24, 2004, from http://www.ics.ltsn.ac.uk/pub/italics/vol3iss1.htm.

Boud, D. (2004, April 5-7). Control, influence and beyond: The logics of learning networks, *Proceedings of 4th International Networked Learning Conference*, Lancaster. Retrieved August 25, 2004, from http://www.shef.ac.uk/nlc2004/home.htm

Buzan, T., & Buzan, B. (1996). *The mind map book: How to use radiant thinking to maximize your brain's untapped potential* (reprint ed.). New York: Plume Books.

Chew, S. C. (2002). Personal Communication.

Chew, S. C., & Beaumont, C. (2004, June 28-30). Evaluating the effectiveness of ICT to support globally distributed PBL teams. *Proceedings of ITiCSE Conference, ACM/SIGCSE* (pp. 47-51).

Chou, C. Y., Chan, T. W., & Lin, C. J. (2002). Redefining the learning companion: The past, present, and future of educational agents. *Computers & Education, 40*, 255-269.

Cox, E. S., Clark, W. P., Heath, H., & Plumpton, B. (2000). *Herding cats through piccadilly circus. The critical role of the tutor in the student's online conferencing experience.* Retrieved August 12, 2004, from http://iet.open.ac.uk/pp/r.goodfellow/Lessons/cats/catsAUG00.htm

Goodyear, P. (2001). *Effective networked learning in higher education: Notes and guidelines.* Networked Learning in Higher Education Project (JISC/CALT). Retrieved April 23, 2004, from http://csalt.lancs.ac.uk/jisc

JISC (n.d.). *Starting point.* Definition. Retrieved April 18, 2005, from http://blackboard.sihe.ac.uk/support/jisc/html/start_defin.htm

Kiser, K. (2002, June 1). Is blended best? *E-Learning Magazine.* Retrieved March 29, 2005, from http://www.elearningmag.com/elearning/article/articleDetail.jsp?id=21259

Knutsen, D., Knutson, E., & Slazinski, E. (2003). Employing new advances in IP videoconferencing to enhance teaching and learning through the use of a hybrid distance-learning course. *Proceedings of the 4th Conference on Information Technology Curriculum on Information Technology Education* (pp. 72-75). Lafayette, IN.

Kollock. P. (1997). Design principles for online communities. *The Internet and Society: Harvard Conference Proceedings.* Cambridge, MA: O'Reilly & Associates.

Mason, R. (1998, October). Models of online courses. *ALN magazine, 2*(2). Retrieved August 24, 2004, from http://www.aln.org/alnWeb/magazine/vol2_issue2/Masonfinal.htm

Miller, C., Jones, P., Packham, G., & Thomas, B. (2004, April 5-7). A Viable Solution: The case for blended delivery on an online learning programme. *Proceedings of 4th International Networked Learning Conference,* Lancaster (pp. 497-502). Retrieved August 24, 2004, from http://www.shef.ac.uk/nlc2004/home.htm

Oliver, R. (1999). Exploring strategies for on-line teaching and learning. *Distance Education, 20*(2), 240-254.

Oliver, R. (2001). Developing e-learning environments that support knowledge construction in higher education. In S. Stoney & J. Burn (Eds.), *Working for excellence in the e-conomy* (pp. 407-416). Churchlands, Australia: We-B Centre.

POLARIS (2004). Retrieved July 12, 2004, from http://www.ll.unimaas.nl/ polaris/index2_english.htm

Problem Based Learning Clearinghouse (n.d.). Retrieved February 27, 2005 from, https://chico.nss.udel.edu/Pbl/

Rapanotti, L., Blake, C. T., & Griffiths, R. (2002). E-tutorials with voice groupware: Real-time conferencing to support computing students at a distance. *Proceedings of the 7th Annual Conference on Innovation and Technology in Computer Science Education* (pp. 116-120). New York: ACM/ SIGCSE Press.

Ronteltap, C. F. M., & Eurelings, A. M. C. (1997). POLARIS: The functional design of an electronic learning environment to support problem-based learning. In T. Müldner & T.C. Reeves (Eds.), *Educational multimedia and hypermedia* (pp. 1802-1807). Charlottesville: Association for the Advancement of Computing in Education.

Ronteltap, C. F. M., Goodyear, P., & Bartoluzzi, S. (2004). A pattern language as an instrument in designing for productive learning conversations. *World Conference on Educational Multimedia, Hypermedia, and Telecommunications, 1*, 4271-4276.

Salmon, G. (2002). *E-tivities: The key to active online learning.* London: Kogan Page.

UK Problem-Based Learning Web Site. Retrieved August 23, 2004, from http://www.hss.coventry.ac.uk/pbl/

Watson, G. (2002, May/June). *Technology to promote success in PBL courses.* Retrieved August 23, 2004, from http://ts.mivu.org/

Watson, G. (2003, June 3). *Shifting sand: Integrating problem-based learning and technology in education.* Asia Pacific Conference on Education, NIE Singapore.

Endnotes

[1]   http://www.imsglobal.org/

[2]   This needs to be used with care—providing many detailed references can also discourage active learning and research (Ronteltap & Eurelings, 1997).

[3]   http://en.wikipedia.org/wiki/Main_Page

[4]   FreeMind is free software distributed under the GNU Public License© Joerg Mueller http://freemind.sourceforge.net/

Chapter X

Curriculum and Organisational Issues

Introduction

The subject of problem-based learning can raise some surprisingly strong emotions, both in terms of the right process to use and the right curriculum model.

For example, on the PBL Initiative Web site (director, Howard Barrows, n.d.), the minimum essentials for PBL are stated, and include: "Problem-based learning should not occur within a single discipline or subject." Specifically for medical education, the recommendations are further specified:

Problem-based learning must be the pedagogical base in the curriculum and not part of a didactic curriculum. Problem-based learning should not be episodic, added on to or mixed in with more traditional, didactic, teacher-directed, passive, memorization-based and lecture-based educational methods. (PBL Initiative)

This requires a large-scale intervention, obtaining commitment, collaboration, and consensus from staff in multiple subject areas, followed by much planning and training. It can be quite discouraging for a teacher who can see many benefits in the PBL approach and would like to try out PBL "in the small."

While there are numerous benefits for implementing PBL throughout a curriculum—we will discuss in more depth later in the chapter—there is an alternative view of PBL as a pedagogical approach, one that can be applied at several levels, from a single session to a fully integrated curriculum. Ranald Macdonald (2001) puts it like this:

So, what is the big deal with PBL? For me it's nothing more nor less than the fact that problems, tasks, queries (Boud, 1995), or the every day necessity to learn to meet unexpected situations, form the starting point for learning. The real motivation for using it, whatever 'it' is, is a desire to improve the quality of student learning and to prepare students for future learning needs by giving them greater responsibility for their own learning now. As such, it doesn't matter whether we adopt PBL across a whole programme, within a single subject, or as the basis for a single learning experience. It is the intention to provide a need to acquire knowledge, develop skills, or demonstrate applied understanding that is the starting point for PBL.

In this chapter, we will explore some of the curriculum and organizational issues of implementing PBL, both "in the small," that is at a module level, and "in the large," throughout the curriculum.

PBL in the Small

Forms of problem-based learning have often been introduced at a module level, especially outside of Medicine. Many of the published case studies are from individuals or small teams who have decided to introduce aspects of PBL into an otherwise traditional programme.

There are a number of issues that need to be addressed in such a situation. We have discussed some of these in detail in previous chapters. We will provide a brief summary here.

Learning Outcomes and Assessment

Introducing PBL at a module level can require review of the learning outcomes, as discussed previously. The content-related outcomes may need t be reduced to make way for outcomes related to PBL team and process outcomes. Adding PBL methods while maintaining the "volume of content" can have an adverse effect as we need to provide sufficient time for students to explore a case. Lack of time is likely to drive a surface approach to learning. Once learning outcomes have been revised, the assessment methods and strategy also needs to be re-examined as discussed in Chapter VIII.

Preparing Students

Don Woods (1996) discusses the details of student preparation in some detail and provides an excellent student text (Woods, 1994). The level of preparation needed clearly depends on a students' previous experience of PBL. If this is the first module they have encountered, then a considerable amount of time is needed to help students adapt and develop the process skills required. We have found that, initially, students can be quite hostile to PBL, particularly those that learn well from traditional methods and can see team working as a possible threat to their grades. Many students also have poor experiences in group working, where typical issues are dominant individuals, poor attendance by some members, and freeloaders who do not complete their share of the work. It is vital to decide in advance who will deal with these issues and how they will be managed, since they will always occur to some extent.

When students have previous experience of PBL, the benefits become evident very quickly. We have found that they perform at a high standard from the start; they are very aware of the team issues and how to deal with them and they have become familiar with the PBL process.

Team Size and Facilitation

In the classical medical model, students may work in teams of eight to ten students and are facilitated throughout by a faculty member. This is resource intensive and most undergraduate programmes cannot provide this level of tutor contact. If the PBL initiative is working within a traditional framework, it is usual that the norms of that framework cannot be varied significantly. We have found it necessary to devise a model to enable a single tutor to manage a class of 20 students. There are essentially three approaches we have used:

a.   *The (very) dedicated tutor model.* In this model, the tutor increases his or her contact time workload voluntarily to facilitate each team on the medical school model. Fortunately, as students become more familiar with PBL, the contact can be reduced. This approach can double or even triple the workload at the start of the module and does not scale well! However, it can be an effective method of inducting students into PBL for relatively small classes and it ensures that the tutor is available to deal with the start-up issues of PBL as soon as they arise.

b. *Roving facilitator model.* In the roving facilitator model, a number of teams meet at the same time, often in the same classroom. The tutor rotates through the teams, checking understanding and progress (for example the learning issues generated). This works particularly well where students are already familiar with PBL and it can allow tutors to pick up common issues and provide mini-plenary sessions within the class. However, this is much more difficult for tutors to understand fully how a team is operating. We have found it possible to facilitate a maximum of four five-student teams simultaneously for Computing PBL cases.

c. *Peer/student facilitator model.* In order to increase the facilitation contact with each team, it is possible to use students as facilitators. In a first year undergraduate programming course (Beaumont & Fox, 2003), we used final year undergraduate students as facilitators (called learning team coaches [LTC]). These LTCs had prior experience of PBL and had undertaken a one-day training course for the role. They also received some pay for the task and met with the tutors for support sessions on a weekly basis. We found this system effective and the first-year students accepted them as facilitators. However, there were additional, unforeseen benefits. Students regarded LTCs as peers and they were prepared to confide in them much more than they did with tutors. The LTCs relayed the "real" progress, problems, and issues to the tutors to provide additional insight. The system was subsequently extended, by enabling LTCs to obtain academic credit for the work and by formally validating a module to include teaching and learning theory in addition to the LTC practice.

Classroom Facilities

The facilities in most universities are designed to support lectures, seminars, or laboratory sessions rather than small-group PBL. Where a PBL module is incorporated into a traditional structure, usually these resources must suffice. Rearranging furniture, together with several (or mobile) whiteboards and screens, can go a long way to providing a workable environment. The provision of wireless-LAN enabled laptop computers can further enhance the facilities.

On occasion, with the roving facilitator model, we have allowed some teams to meet in separate rooms, though this was not always satisfactory. In some cases, we discovered that the rooms were empty as teams had decided to finish early without reporting progress to the tutor.

Although lectures are not generally regarded as being part of the problem-based learning model, they can still serve a useful function within the module framework. Rather than being the main vehicle for transmitting knowledge, they can take on a supportive function. For example, we have found them useful to introduce a PBL case or to communicate organizational details at the start of a course. They can also be scheduled as resource sessions, focusing on specific issues that students find difficult. The topic of a lecture can be suggested by students and the scheduling, duration, and content negotiated with the tutor. Such lectures can be optional. Students attending are actively applying the knowledge to their PBL case. Laboratory sessions can be scheduled in a similar way and students can book particular sessions. These approaches mimic aspects of *real-world* training courses.

Fitting PBL Modules into Traditional Structures

Although PBL can be incorporated into individual modules, if the programme is to be coherent, it is important to consider how this will fit into the entire programme. A single module in the programme is burdened with the PBL start up costs of preparing the students and quite often the real benefits cannot be gained in isolation. Students often say that more is demanded of them in PBL classes and that they spend more time on those modules. They often see this imbalance as unfair, especially in the academic credit awarded.

If there are several PBL modules, the students have more time to practice and improve the skills needed, but if PBL modules are electives there can be real difficulties because of the varied prior PBL experience of students.

A further issue of PBL adoption by a single faculty member for a module is the sustainability of the innovation. Very often, innovations by a single member of staff do not endure when the member of staff leaves or changes responsibilities. Thus, for maximum benefit and sustainability, PBL needs to be designed into the curriculum of the entire programme.

PBL in the Large

Embedding problem-based learning within the curriculum means that it should be one of the core requirements that are considered by whatever committee designs the curriculum. It means explicit support from the organization and commitment to the model and resources required to implement it.

Now that sounds fine in principle, but it begs a number of questions.

First, how much PBL should be incorporated? While integration is beneficial for student development and progression and sustainability of the innovation, it does not necessarily mean that 100% of the curriculum should be PBL.

This may sound strange in a book advocating the benefits of PBL, but there are costs alongside the benefits. For a student, PBL is stressful. Moffat, McConnachie, Ross, and Morrison (2004) identified particular stress areas for problem-based learning students. These were: individual study behavior; progress and aptitude; and specific concerns about assessment and availability of learning materials. The study was conducted among medical students at Glasgow. Other issues students have raised with us include uncertainly about whether they have "learned enough," team working difficulties, and, particularly at the early stages, "whether they are correct."

Students can also benefit from a *variety* of teaching and learning strategies (so long as they promote active learning). A course that is 100% PBL runs the risk of boredom with the repetition of the same learning process.

For the institution, PBL is also resource-intensive and expensive.

A hybrid approach, with a PBL theme running through the core of the programme and other more traditional courses running in parallel, can help overcome some of these issues by providing variety of learning experiences and making resourcing more manageable for the institution.

One interesting approach is described by Polanco, Calderón, and Delgado (2004) in two years of an Engineering programme. Courses in computer science, math, and physics were combined into one integrated PBL course. This model is particularly interesting in the team organization and the three-stage learning system adopted. Students were assigned to permanent teams for the duration of the course. In the first stage, the team is confronted with a typical real-world problem, learning issues are generated and areas of specialization are identified in the normal PBL manner. In the next stage, students are redistributed into temporary teams that specialize in mathematics, computing, or physics. The purpose of these teams is to develop competence in the area by solving small-scale problems. Once this is achieved, the permanent teams are re-formed and the specialists share the knowledge gained while in the temporary specialist team. Finally, each permanent team applies the knowledge to produce a solution to the original problem, which is presented and discussed with the others. The authors evaluated various aspects of student performance and judged the approach to be successful.

A second question concerns organisational support. PBL can be driven by senior management in a top-down manner or can be the result of a dedicated group of faculty pushing from the bottom-up. John Cavanagh (2001) suggests that a mixture of both strategies are needed: faculty need to be convinced and committed to the change for it to work, but support of senior management is essential if barriers to innovation are to be removed and resources (including development time) are to be made available. In particular, rewards for pedagogical reform and innovation need to be recognised as being as valuable as research.

There will inevitably be a range of views about adoption (and the extent of adoption) of PBL. Where implementation is trans-disciplinary and spans more than one department, the role of senior management to facilitate the development is essential. In an integrated curriculum, there is much greater interdependence of study units than in conventional courses and the communication and planning between faculty in different disciplines and departments raises the complexity and difficulty of the task considerably.

Similarly, if the programme is to be sustainable, there needs to be an on-going staff-development programme and support for staff as they change role from lecturer to facilitator. Some institutions provide dedicated staff developers to assist.

Wiers, van de Wiel, Sá, Mamede, Tomaz, and Schmidt (2002, p. 46) proposes a ten-step model shown in Table 10.1 for the design of a problem-based curriculum, adapting the general literature on curriculum design.

They stress that the process is iterative rather than truly linear as appears from the table.

The rationale can be based on many factors, such as market demand, graduates' needs, and professional bodies' stipulations. The curriculum planning requires a different approach to the traditional subject-based approach, since the curriculum is integrated. Two types of integration are often identified: vertical and horizontal integration. Vertical integration consists of themes throughout the programme; horizontal integration consists of inter-disciplinary integration within

Table 10.1. Ten-stage model of PBL curriculum development (Wiers et al., 2002, p. 46)

1.	Give the rationale for the curriculum and form a curriculum planning group
2.	Generate general educational objectives of the curriculum.
3.	Assess the educational needs of future students.
4.	Apply the educational principles of PBL to the curriculum.
5.	Structure the curriculum and generate a curriculum blueprint.
6.	Elaborate the unit blueprints.
7.	Construct the units.
8.	Decide on student assessment methods.
9.	Consider the educational organization and curriculum management.
10.	Evaluate the curriculum and revise it (when necessary).

PBL units. Thus, curriculum planning requires a multi-disciplinary team to co-ordinate development.

In a PBL curriculum, educational objectives are likely to be derived from competencies of current and future professionals, since one of the aims is to move toward inducting students into a community of professional practice. Thus, interviews with experts and task analysis of those working in the field will contribute to this. The educational needs of future students determine the starting point, the prior knowledge expected by the entrants to the programme. This can identify both lack of knowledge and misconceptions.

Lloyd-Jones, Ellershaw, Wilkinson, and Bligh (1998) point out that it is "sometimes difficult for individual disciplines to identify their own subjects within a PBL curriculum," and they recommend that all contributing disciplines explicitly identify their own departmental core content at the start of the planning process. This process can give complementary input to the planning process and can help build multi-disciplinary ownership of the course.

Stages four and five involve the identification of the model of PBL to be employed and how the themes of the programme are constructed from units. The core of the unit is the PBL tutorial, but other activities such as lectures and lab sessions can compliment it. Wiers identifies two other key issues to define at this stage: the unit specification (multi-disciplinary contents and theme) and the sequence of units within the programme. He suggests a concept map of core concepts in the curriculum is useful at this point.

Stages six through eight have been considered in some detail in earlier chapters. Stage nine, educational organization and curriculum management, is critical to a full PBL curriculum, since it is multi-disciplinary and, therefore, not owned by one department or subject area. Wiers et al. (p. 50) states:

Taking the final responsibility for the curriculum from the departments to a central level of decision-making is thought to be crucial for the success of problem-based curriculum development.

Evaluation of a PBL curriculum can occur on a number of levels. The first might be called fine-tuning, consisting of annual review, collecting feedback from stakeholders (students, tutors, external examiners). The second level of evaluation occurs when a more major review is required and this poses particular problems because of the tight integration and multi-disciplinary nature of the programme. Solomon and Geddes (2001) describe such a review process that involves the participation of stakeholders and external consultants, which mirrors many of the steps in the initial curriculum development outlined above.

A further level of evaluation, which we must mention, is the question of the relative effectiveness of PBL versus a traditional curriculum. Such an evaluation is inherently problematic.

When such an evaluation is performed, it is very important to clearly identify the criteria to be used to judge success. If we restrict the evaluation purely to the cognitive domain, then "PBL does not result in dramatic differences in cognitive outcomes" (Norman & Schmidt, 2000, p. 721).

However, such a comparison ignores much of the motivation for PBL. It is performing a comparison on one dimension when PBL is multi-dimensional.

To illustrate this, we will consider one example of an evaluation of a pilot implementation for a computer programming module. Barg et al. (2000) describe a number of success criteria based on factors such as student performance, additional skills gained, cost of delivery, student opinion, fair assessment, and staff willingness to tutor the course.

Even in this relatively restricted evaluation of "PBL in the Small," there are many dimensions to be considered. At the end of the day, the result depends on the values and beliefs of those setting the success criteria: what is most important?

The University of Manchester1 has considerable experience in implementing various models of enquiry-based and problem-based learning in subject areas as diverse as English, engineering and dentistry. Evaluations of the student experience highlighted the importance of induction and preparation of students for PBL. Facilitator enthusiasm and skills were also identified as critical. However, even where students had some negative experiences, they were very positive regarding PBL, which suggests students may be easier to convince of the benefits than many of the faculty.

Conclusion

In this chapter, we have considered organisational and curriculum design issues. In our view, problem-based learning principles can be applied at any level of the curriculum and many examples exist of incorporation at a module level within a subject area. However, we accept that for students to gain the most benefit, PBL needs to be integrated into the curriculum. This also improves sustainability of PBL within the course.

PBL can be incorporated in a variety of models in the curriculum, as an integrating theme alongside traditional subject-based courses or as a fully integrated course. When PBL is fully integrated, there are often supporting activities including lectures, lab sessions, and skill sessions. It is recommended that the design of such a programme is co-ordinated and driven by a multi-

Figure 10.1. A checklist for developing problem-based learning in the curriculum

Checklist (Based on Wiers' Model)

How extensive is PBL implementation?	Within a module or throughout the curriculum? Where will the process skills be developed?
Identify rationale for the curriculum and form a curriculum planning group.	Where PBL is integrated throughout the curriculum. Planning group should be multi-disciplinary.
Generate general educational objectives of the curriculum	Derived from task analyses of practitioners with input of departmental objectives.
Assess the educational needs of future students.	What prerequisite knowledge, skills, and misconceptions are they likely to have?
Apply the educational principles of PBL to the curriculum.	Identify curriculum themes—vertical integration. How much PBL will be incorporated?
Structure the curriculum and generate a curriculum blueprint.	Refine and identify units and horizontal integration.
Elaborate the unit blueprints.	Generate detailed learning outcomes for each unit. (See Chapter 6)
Construct the units.	Plan PBL cases in detail and other supporting activities.
Decide on student assessment methods.	See Chapter VIII
Consider the educational organization and curriculum management.	
Evaluate the curriculum and revise it (when necessary).	

disciplinary team. Wiers' 10-step model for implementation was discussed and the following checklist is based on the model. It is provided as a summary and "aide memoir" for curriculum designers.

References

Barg, M., Fekete, A., Greening, T., Hollands, O., Kay, J., & Kingston, J. H. (2000). Problem-based learning for foundation computer science courses. *Computer Science Education, 10*(2), 109-128.

Barrows, H. (n.d.). *The minimal essentials for problem-based learning in medical education.* Retrieved October 3, 2005, from http://www.pbli.org/pbl/generic_pbl.htm

Beaumont, C., & Fox, C. (2003, August 26-28). Learning programming: Enhancing quality through problem-based learning. *Proceedings of 4th Annual Conference of LTSN-ICS,* Galway. Retrieved August 25, 2004, from http://www.ics.ltsn.ac.uk/pub/conf2003/index.htm

Cavanagh, J. C. (2001). Make it so: Administrative support for problem-based learning. In B. J. Duch, S. E. Groh, & D. E. Allen (Eds.), *The power of problem-based learning*. Sterling, VA: Stylus.

Lloyd-Jones, G., Ellershaw, J., Wilkinson, S., & Bligh, J. G. (1998). The use of multi-disciplinary consensus groups in the planning phase of an integrated problem-based curriculum. *Medical Education, 32*, 278-282.

Macdonald, R. (2001, January 16-17). What's the big deal with PBL? *Implementing Problem-Based Learning in Higher Education* (Endnote to conference proceedings). Retrieved August 25, 2004, from http://www.ics.ltsn.ac.uk/pub/pbl/macdonald_end_note.pdf

Moffat, K. J., McConnachie, A., Ross, S., & Morrison, J. M. (2004). First year medical students stress and coping in a problem-based medical curriculum. *Medical Education, 38*, 482-491.

Norman, R., & Schmidt, H.G. (2000). Effectiveness of problem-based learning curricula: Theory, practice and paper darts. *Medical Education, 34*, 721-728.

Polanco, R., Calderón, P., & Delgado, F. (2004) Effects of problem-based learning program on engineering students' academic achievements in a mexican university. *Innovations in Education and Teaching International, 41*(2), 145-155.

Savin-Baden, M. (2000). *Problem-based learning in higher education: Untold stories* Buckingham: SRHE/OUP.

Solomon, P., & Geddes, E. L. (2001). A systematic process for content review in a problem-based learning curriculum. *Medical Teacher, 23*(6), 556-560.

Wiers, R. W., van de Wiel, M. W. J., Sá, H. L. C., Mamede, S., Tomaz, J. B., & Schmidt, H. G. (2002). Design of a problem-based curriculum: A general approach and a case study in the domain of public health. *Medical Teacher, 24*(1), 45-51.

Woods, D. R. (1994). *Problem-based learning: How to gain the most from PBL*. Hamilton, Ontario: Donald R Woods.

Woods, D. R. (1996). *Problem-based learning: Helping your students gain the most from PBL* (3rd ed.). Hamilton, Ontario: Donald R Woods. Retrieved August 24, 2004, from http://www.chemeng.mcmaster.ca/pbl/pbl.htm

Endnote

[1]   Personal communication, September 2004

Chapter XI

Lessons Learned and Tips

Introduction

We have been applying PBL to learning by our students since 1996. Although many lessons have been learned, we are still continually learning and discovering new insights each year in our PBL process. Our desire is to find out and learn as much as we can about how students learn and how we can make the PBL process more effective for our students. We are very thankful to our students for their continuing support of our endeavors to make learning interesting, effective, and fun for them. Students continue to give us feedback and their input has shed much light on our PBL process. As a result of their feedback and honest discussion, we are continually striving to improve on our tutorial process.

We must confess that our experiences with PBL were not easy ones to start with. There were times of encouragement and frustration, especially early in the course when students were facing a major change in their educational mindset, when motivation and encouragement were important. Above all, we have learned that implementing PBL is not easy! We have learned many insights during our experiences with PBL. It is our belief that some of these insights would help others to better understand the implementation of PBL. In this chapter, we share with readers some of the issues that we have learned are important to PBL implementation. For each of the issues discussed, we have also incorporated guidelines to help readers.

Insights Learned from PBL

There are many books and articles written about PBL and its benefits. Occasionally there have been articles describing experiences of authors implementing PBL. We hope that by sharing our experiences, we can encourage others to take on PBL. We have identified many issues that we feel are useful tips that can help readers to understand the process of PBL and how these issues are useful when implementing PBL. Some of these are concerned with what we have learned from our experiences. Others are insights that we gained from interaction with our students and their studies.

Domain Analysis

In designing a PBL curriculum, we have to analyse what must be learned. In doing this we have to combine identification of key concepts, procedures, and so on, with analysis of the professional use of those concepts. Identification of key concepts is a matter of what is most important for students to "know." This must include the learning outcomes of the module as stated in the degree scheme. The identification of key concepts is defined through the professional activity that calls for their use: that is, it is defined in the activity of the learner. In our case, the activity was to design instructional software to solve user's problems.

There are two things that must be emphasised. First, our analysis must not preclude any type of learning activity—memorization of a list or extensive practice of a skill may be necessary—but it should arise out of the need to use the information in authentic tasks. Second, what must be learned includes not only information in the content domain, but also metacognitive, collaborative, and other skills that are necessary for participating in authentic activity. In particular, a crucial issue is how to ensure that the problems designed are educationally rich enough that in seeking answers, students must gain understanding of significant subject matter concepts. Problems also need to be feasible and manageable, given the time and resources available to the students. However, artefacts should be rich enough to promote both depth and breadth of knowledge in their creation as well as demonstrate student mastery of the content. Artifacts must require students to integrate information and use complex thought.

Problems must be designed to sustain student motivation and thoughtfulness. A number of factors should be considered in problem design that affect students' motivation to tackle the problem in a manner that fosters understanding. These factors include whether students find the problems to be interesting and valuable, whether they perceive that they have the competence to engage in and complete the problem, and whether they focus on learning rather than outcomes and grades. Initially, the students found PBL very difficult and frustrating as they were so used to passive learning. They frequently asked for answers, which we were tempted to give, but our role was as facilitator of thought in the students, not as answer provider. Patience was required on both sides as we attempted to make students think for themselves. Students initially lack proficiency in cognitive and metacognitive skills to generate plans, systematically make test predictions, interpret evidence in the light of those predictions, and determine solutions. One of the techniques which they found particularly helpful was "thinking aloud," that is verbalising their thought processes as they attempted to think through a problem. This required us to explain and demonstrate the technique quite early in the PBL sessions. We found that the interest and value students attributed to the problem affected how motivated they would be to engage in learning. Students' interest and perceived value are enhanced when:

- The tasks are varied and included novel elements;
- The problem is authentic and has value;
- The problem is challenging;
- There is closure, so that an artifact is created;
- There is choice about what and/or how work is done; and
- There is the opportunity to work with others.

Tutor Change of Perspective

An important issue that we learned from our experience as tutors was that corrective feedback during the preliminary problem solving was important. We found it useful to facilitate learning by stepping in to correct basic misconceptions that might lead individuals or groups astray. However, it does not mean that we become self-promoted expositors of all the basic conceptual issues in tutorial. Instead we should remain alert to the discussion, able to step in and steer the discussion appropriately. This epitomises the facilitation role (Neville, 1999). It means that the tutor needs to know when to step in. This can only happen if he or she has knowledge of the content under discussion. Is content expertise of tutors necessary? We believe that it is useful for tutors to have both subject matter knowledge and process facilitation skills if students have little prior content knowledge and are unfamiliar with the PBL process. An ideal tutor is someone who is flexible and sensitive to the learning needs of the students. With novice students, with little experience of PBL or prior knowledge, it would be useful to be directive and content knowledgeable in order to provide the necessary foundation upon which to build their learning. As students mature in knowledge as well as familiarity with PBL, it is important that students take on more self-directed learning roles.

Students in PBL are expected to carry out self-directed learning during individual studies. What sorts of competencies are needed for self-directed learning? Appendix 11a contains some self-directed learning competencies for interested readers. Tutors should have understanding of the learning process of self-directed learning. According to Neville (1999), andragogical self-directed learning in a PBL environment stresses a student-centred approach to learning where students determine their learning objectives, how to learn them and to evaluate what they have learned. In order to help PBL tutors to prepare for the role of learning facilitator, Malcolm Knowles (1975) has identified seven elements for an andragogical learning process design. These are listed in Appendix 11b.

PBL literature stresses the importance of the tutor in the success of any PBL program. PBL requires changes in the way tutors plan instruction, direct learning, transmit knowledge, supervise instruction, and assess learning (Gordon, Rogers, & Comfort, 2001). A major change is required in the tutor's perspective. The tutor's traditional views of problem solving are influenced by their areas of content specialisation. There has been much debate surrounding the optimal role of the tutor in facilitating a PBL tutorial group, including level of participation, content knowledge, and involvement in student evaluation. There is a clear divergence in the literature as to the benefit or disruptiveness of tutor as the content expert on the facilitation of student learning and tutorial functioning (Gilkison, 2003). We believe that there is still inconclusive debate going on concerning the benefit or detriment of PBL tutor expertise. The debate does little to help tutors in determining effective ways of stimulating critical thinking and student-directed learning (Gilkison, 2003). Instead, it would be more useful to focus on how tutors ought to function to promote optimum student-directed learning.

Successful learning in PBL depends on the interactions of its sessions and effective group facilitation (Hendry, Frommer, & Walker, 1999; Neville, 1999). According to Wilkerson, Hafler, and Liu (1991), guiding the work of the group involves the tutors being in student-directed mode, allowing students to initiate and sustain discussion, using infrequent questions to guide the group process. The tutor should probe for understanding, encourage students to listen to one another, tolerate silence, and collaborate by postponing their own suggestions, acceding to the students' selection of objectives, fostering a feeling of cooperation rather than competition.

We found it difficult initially to change from a teacher to a facilitator of learning. We had to extricate ourselves from the compulsion to pose as an expert and become a continuing co-learner. The debate over what constitutes effective facilitation of students' learning in PBL is a tricky one. Evidence cited in the literature favours role dichotomy between process facilitator and content resource. It is our belief that a balanced interaction of those functions is an optimal one. The proposed approach should be based on a natural desire to be directive and teach with the desired goal of enhancing student-centred, self-directed learning. We concur with Wilkerson (1992) that two important skills for effective facilitation are (a) the skills to guide the work of the group, that is the roles of probing, questioning, achieving a balance of problem-solving and subject knowledge acquisition, and (b) promoting interaction, describing issues relating to successful tutorial dynamics. According to Margeston (1994), the tutor facilitates the tutorial by questioning, probing, encouraging critical reflection, suggesting, and challenging in helpful ways, but only "where necessary." Tutors new to PBL are challenged by the "where necessary" (deciding when and how) part of intervention as we were in our early tutoring experiences.

An effective facilitator knows where it is necessary to intervene in the tutorial group. Woods (1994) suggests two question-based ways for tutors to intervene during tutorials. First, to ensure that students approach the problem appropriately and second to challenge students' assumptions, to ensure that they reflect on and justify their assertion. A third intervention is suggested by Maudsley (1999), namely to close each session by enabling reflection of the dynamics of the group and what has been learned.

As part of the facilitation involves intervention of the tutor in the PBL group process, we found it useful to know some of the techniques that can be used in PBL, including elicitation, re-elicitation, prompting, refocusing, facilitating, in-forming, and direct learning. Appendix 11c provides a list of techniques that can be used by PBL tutors for their intervention (Gilkison, 2003).

We found that questions that elicited more information from students seemed to raise their awareness. It is our belief that as tutors we should always aim to raise students' levels of thinking to a metacognitive level. Tutors should provoke students' problem solving and critical thinking by using open-ended questions.

Tutors in PBL are the custodians of the group process. They must guide for discovery rather than act as an information-dispensing model of perfection or as an over-enthusiastic subject matter expert. For effective tutoring, we have found the need to change from our traditional stance to learn about our students and how best to be of use to them. We need to reorient our approach from the traditional to the problem-based philosophy. For effective tutoring, we found that our relationship with the students became more one of colleagues instead of tutor to student. This was very difficult initially for the students to adopt this new mindset. Our attitude toward them had to be one of a senior colleague to a novice colleague, guiding them and supporting them where necessary. This was not easy, as we had to keep reminding ourselves that we were coach and not teacher.

We had to relearn teaching in order to empathise better with the students' emotional struggles, sensitive to their self-esteem while challenging them to justify assumptions exposed by group discussions. It is useful for tutors to understand group facilitation and what a facilitator does during the group process. Guidelines for Facilitators can be found in Appendix 11d.

Principles of PBL for Tutors

The philosophical and theoretical underpinnings of PBL are not explicit in the early PBL literature (Rideout, 2001). Those like Barrows and others, who developed PBL, had no background in educational psychology or cognitive science. It is generally acknowledged that PBL shares many of the principles of cognitive and constructivist learning theories. We found that we coped much better and improved our PBL tutorial process when we understood the instructional principles deriving from constructivism. These principles provided us with insights of how PBL environments should be carried out. Savery and Duffy (1995) have listed the eight instructional principles for the design of a constructivist learning environment for PBL:

1.   Anchor all learning activities to a larger task or problem.
2.   Support the learner in developing ownership for the overall problem or task
3.   Design an authentic task.
4.   Design the task and the learning environment to reflect the complexity of the environment they should be able to function in at the end of learning.
5.   Give the learner ownership of the process used to develop a solution.
6.   Design the learning environment to support and challenge the learner's thinking.
7.   Encourage testing ideas against alternative views and alternative contexts.
8.   Provide opportunity for and support reflection on both the content learned and the learning process.

Categories of Learning Outcomes

In order to help us to be more effective in our role as tutors, we found it useful to have an understanding of learning outcomes. This is because different types of learning require different kinds of learning strategies. In 1948, following the Convention of the American Psychological Association, Bloom formulated a classification of the goals of the educational process (Bloom, 1956; Bloom, Mesia, & Krathwohl, 1964). Bloom established a hierarchy of educational objectives known as "Bloom's Taxonomy." The taxonomy of learning objectives is an attempt, within the behavioural paradigm, to classify forms of learning. There are three domains identified. These are the cognitive domain; the affective domain; and the psychomotor domain. The cognitive objectives are subdivided, ranging from the simplest behaviour to the most complex. These are knowledge, comprehension, application, analysis, synthesis and evaluation. A brief review of the cognitive domain of Bloom's Taxonomy can be found in Appendix 11e.

Besides Bloom's taxonomy, there is Gagné's conditions of learning. According to Gagné (1985), there are different types of learning; each requires different instructional strategies to learn. Gagne has identified several types of learning (verbal learning, attitude, motor skills, problem solving, rule learning, concept learning and cognitive strategies). One good way of identifying the types of learning is to ask, "what is it that students are learning to do?"

For someone to possess verbal learning, the student should be able to state information. Attitudes are demonstrated by students being able to choose to do something. Rule learning is demonstrated by students being able to apply rules and demonstrate principles. Concept learning is demonstrated by students being able to label or classify items as members or non members of a class. Problem solving is represented by students generating solutions or procedures to find solutions. Appendix 11f presents a brief review of Gagné's Conditions of Learning.

Another instructional theory, like Gagné's Conditions of Learning, is that of component display theory (CDT) by Merrill (1983). CDT integrates knowledge about learning and instruction from three major theoretical perspectives: behavioural, cognitive and humanistic (Merrill, 1983). Unlike Gagné's approach, CDT only deals with the cognitive domain and within the cognitive domain it only deals with the micro level, (e.g., instruction that relates to teaching a single idea, such as a single concept or principle). Instead of a single dimension for classifying objectives, CDT classifies objectives into two dimensions: types of content (facts, concepts, principles and procedures) and desired level of performance with that content (remember, use and find). A brief review of the different types learning in CDT is in Appendix 11g.

In addition to the above categories, Reigeluth (1999) has categorised cognitive learning into different types: memorisation, understanding and applying. A brief review of the different levels of cognitive learning can be found in Appendix 11h.

We have found that not only tutors benefited from having an understanding of the different categories of learning, students also benefited from having an awareness of them. It may seem strange that students' learning could be enhanced by having an understanding of the different types of learning. We have interviewed students to find out what caused them to make such a claim. The feedback from the students was that:

- They were able to distinguish between the different levels of learning starting from the lowest, such as memorisation to understanding, application and higher-order thinking skills.

- Having this understanding enabled them to ask the right type of questions in their identification of learning issues at the appropriate stage.

- From their understanding of higher-order thinking skills, they know what they need to look for in solving a problem, as well as the need to critically appraise their solution.

Central to the different categories of learning is that of higher order thinking skills. The concept of higher order thinking skills became a major educational agenda item with the publication of Bloom's Taxonomy of educational objectives. Bloom's taxonomy serves as the basis for what are now called higher order thinking skills. The cognitive domain of Bloom helps to create a standard which deals with the concepts of higher and lower order thinking. The taxonomy has six levels from lowest thinking to higher. These are: knowledge, comprehension, application, analysis, synthesis and evaluation. The collection provides educators with a structure which can be used to build curriculum materials that take learners more deeply into any area of study. The taxonomy takes on renewed importance in the information age. For example, without the ability to recall all inter-related range of basic information such as terms or words, it is impossible to effectively use a search engine. That is, without skills at the knowledge level the user does not know what item to type in when needing information on the Web design methodology nor what synonyms might be helpful if nothing is retrieved from use of the first term. At the other end of this thinking continuum, effectively evaluation collected data in the ethnography study to determine the best choice of competing methods require skills with each of the earlier levels.

Higher order thinking or critical thinking skills means thinking that takes place in the higher levels of the hierarchy of cognitive processing of Bloom's taxonomy. It can be viewed as a continuum of thinking skills starting with knowledge level thinking and moving eventually to evaluation level of thinking. Higher order thinking skills are closely related to critical/creative/constructive thinking. They are inseparable. Having an understanding of the different types of learning objectives enables us to know what type of questions are appropriate to ask at the different levels of the problem solving process. Some of the questions that we used, derived from the different categories of Bloom's Taxonomy, are shown in Appendix 11i. Many of the questions derived from the different levels of the cognitive objectives can be used to help students develop higher order thinking skills or critical thinking skills.

A Clear Non-Competitive Criteria-Referenced Grading Scheme

Students must take account of their own learning and not expect to get good grades for work not done. They cannot be "hitchhikers" and accept grades. A common misconception among students was that group work automatically entailed group grades. It is important to point out at the start of the course that this far from the truth. Unless students are made aware of this, some would try to take advantage of this assumption. Tutors should make sure that they have established clear criteria for success. Students who contribute little should not be awarded the same grade as those who contribute more.

Group Dynamics Skills

It is very important that a graduate has the ability to work effectively as a member of a team. Although students had to work in groups, most of them preferred to work as individuals. Working with others requires that students are able to discuss ideas, communicate clearly, consider alternatives systematically, monitor their own understanding, compare their points of view with those of others, ask clear questions, and share the workload fairly.

According to Spaulding (1991), some tutors made a naïve assumption about a successful tutorial group. They believed that the only necessary ingredients for a successful tutorial group were a small number of students and a faculty member. There was little consideration given to group dynamics. These people did not foresee the difficulties that can arise when a group of people of diverse personalities, age, and background mix in an intensive learning environment. It was taken for granted that students and tutor would be considerate of each other's learning needs and try to help each other to find solutions to the topics under discussion (Neville, 1999). This assumption is not true.

It is our belief that knowledge of why groups behave in particular ways is crucial to understanding facilitation in PBL. Group dynamics and skills in group facilitation are important for an effective learning in PBL. We know that working in groups is an essential part of nearly all professional work. Successful group learning depends on a high level of group functioning. The tutor plays a crucial role in helping students establish group set norms for group functions, maintaining trust, and attending to the dynamics and characteristics of the group. What goes wrong in human relationships in teams and organisations can be predicted and is preventable if we have some knowledge of group dynamics. Group dynamics is concerned with the study of the interaction of the behaviour of individuals as members of a group and of the behaviour of groups generally. There is a clear correlation between positive group dynamics and team productivity (Wheelen, Murphy, Tsumura, & Kline, 1998). Knowing how to draw together a team and how to provide them with the skills and supports necessary is the most important part of PBL. We believe that tutors should have an understanding of group dynamics to create an effective learning environment.

Group dynamics typically includes group development and group process. We believe that having an understanding of group development process is crucial for tutors in PBL. Tuckman (1965) developed a four stage model of group development: forming, storming, norming, and performing. The forming phase involves the introduction of group members at the start of the meeting. As the group members get to know each other, the group enters to the storming phase. The storming phase is characterised by competition and conflicts in the group as members attempt to express their different opinions and interests. A good group will understand the conflict, actively listen to each other and negotiate a way forward. In order to move to the next phase, members must move from a testing and proving mentality to a problem solving mentality (Tuckman, 1965). Tutors must help the group to navigate through this phase. As the group emerges with an agreed way of working, they enter the norming phase. During this phase, members are able to reconcile their own opinions within the greater needs of the group. Collaboration and cooperation replace mistrust and conflicts. The final phase is the performing. This phase may not be reached by all groups. Relationships are settled and group members are likely to build loyalty towards each other. We found it useful to have an understanding of group development or group formation theory. This process can be subconscious. Having an understanding of the stages can help the group reach effectiveness more quickly and less painfully. Understanding the development stages is useful so that when the group appears to go nowhere or members are arguing a lot that no work is done. We know that this is normal. When we understand this pattern, it empowers us to work towards moving the group onto the next stage. A brief review of group development can be found in Appendix 11j.

Besides group development, understanding group process and what constitutes effective group process was useful to help us in dealing with the students during the tutorial group work. Guidelines for group process and features of an effective group process can be found in Appendix 11k. We found that students need to know how to function in the group in order to be productive and accomplish their tasks effectively. An effective process requires students to have various skills. Firstly, members must know which roles they are filling (e.g., researcher, scribe or facilitator). Secondly, members must know how to plan and manage a task, how to manage their time and how to conduct a tutorial session. Thirdly, all group members must take on responsibility and accountability. Each student should determine what he or she needs to do and take on responsibility to accomplish the task(s). Each should be held accountable to their tasks. Fourthly, each member of the group must help to develop and use strategies central to their group goals. Last, but not least, group members should give and receive feedback about group ideas. Constructive feedback should be given that requires focusing on ideas and behaviours instead of individuals.

As it was a requirement that the students work collaboratively, we had to instill into these students the concept of a team that operated as one unit rather than "group work" where one or two people do all the work and the rest observe. This was not easy for students or for ourselves and required us to have regular sessions with the students to ensure true teamwork resulted. They soon learned how to discuss issues, share, and plan work within the group. Their attitudes toward collaborative work changed as the PBL session progressed. Students began to see the benefits of sharing work and working as a team to solve complex tasks. They also began to enjoy each other's company and fostered social as well as academic relationships.

The evidence of team work made such an impact that they sought to work with other students outside of the university. In the main, this was achieved by e-mail and computer-mediated conferencing facilities. A CMC discussion group was set up via the Internet between postgraduate students in computer-based instructional design at a university in the USA and our own students. The discussion centred on current issues, strategies, and methodologies for computer-based design and development, forming into teams and designing computer-based instructional products, and making designs available to other teams for comment and critique. The unique part of this discussion framework was that the students would be discussing issues with everyone, including members of the class in the USA, and would be receiving comment and criticism from the other class as well. The CMC discussion was remarkably successful and both groups of students enjoyed learning from each other.

Formation of Groups

Group work is part of our everyday life. Employees are expected by their bosses to work in groups and it is impossible for them to choose with whom they would like to work. This perspective should be reflected in our PBL groups. We decided from the outset that students should be allocated to groups and not allowed to choose their own members. Forming students into groups who were not initially friends assists them to develop collaboration and negotiation skills and more accurately reflect the work place experience. By deciding on the formation of the group ourselves, we were able to mix nationalities and thereby increase the possibility of bringing a wider range of perspectives to the task. The students did to take kindly to this idea and there was considerable resistance to it at the start of group formation. It was necessary to explain to the students why we have made this choice. Reluctantly they accepted the rationale and agreed to join the group to which we had allocated them. Although we understand their reluctance to work with people they did not know, it was important that students be working in as authentic an environment as possible to reflect real life.

There was one particular student, D, who was adamant that he was not going to join the group to which we had allocated him at the start. D wanted to be with his friends that he knew well. Although he was strongly determined to change groups, we did our best to convince him of the benefits of reflecting the work situation. Reluctantly he agreed to stay in the group allocated. When asked later about his reactions to his group, D told us that he was very glad we had refused to let him join the group he wanted. With hindsight, he was glad he was allocated into this particular group with its diversity of abilities, gender, and cultural background. D not only learned a lot academically from the group, he also learned a lot about the other members' cultures. He is now a good friend of the other members and is still in constant touch with them. D told us that he really appreciated and valued the time he spent with the group. For interested readers, Appendix 111 gives a brief procedure of how we form groups.

Social Support Helps Groups Grow

For groups to be effective there must be social support. Social support is a natural way to enhance personal growth for members of the group. It comes from the tutor and the group members. Social support helps to create a dynamic climate for positive growth in groups. What we have learned from our experiences is that it is crucial for tutors to demonstrate a caring attitude towards each individual in the group. Tutors can provide social support in the group process by paying particular attention to taking a personal interest in monitoring the progress of each member of the group and encouraging activities outside of the tutorial sessions for the groups. Activities could be getting together for a meal, a drink, and sharing life stories in a social environment. This helps members to develop trust for the tutor as well as trust among members of the groups. This is particularly useful when the groups are first formed. A list of suggested ways to improve social supports in a group, adapted from Neil and Dias (2002), can be found in Appendix 11m.

Groups function well when members of the group can accept the others socially. We tried to encourage social interaction among students besides their tutorial groups. This was achieved by having students getting to know members of the group outside of tutorial sessions. Occasionally we would arrange social evenings where the members of the groups could get together for a meal at one of the students' house. We found it helpful for students to get to know members of their group socially. It was important because our students came from different cultures and from different countries. Initially it was hard for the members to mix and get on with each other. Our group members came from different social, ethnic and cultural backgrounds. They also came from different countries. In traditional classroom environments, the local students seldom mix with the overseas students. If there was any group work, students tended to work and choose groups among their friends. It was virtually impossible to have overseas students working with local students. In order to promote integration, each of our groups was typically comprised of students from different cultures and nationalities. There was much resistance when we initially formed the groups. Students knew that to work effectively as a group, they had to accept and transcend the differences. Many expressed fears of not knowing how to react to other cultures and nationalities for fear of being accused of discrimination.

It was important for us to help students to remove their fears by pointing out to the benefits of a multicultural environment with a rich diversity of experiences and backgrounds. When the ice was broken within the group, students began to share their experiences. With constant monitoring and engagement from us, they began to realise that there was really little difference between them concerning their aspirations and goals. The students began to appreciate each other as they could identify that each shared a common goal—to learn well. As time went by, the group came to communicate openly while working toward common goals. In time, the group learned how to drop their pretences, overcome obstacles and reach out to one another in help and emotional support. They began to share about their cultures, food, and languages. They found surprising strength and support among the members. There was a growing collective spirit among the group as the tutorial group progressed. Members became so fond of one another that they regularly arranged social meetings among themselves for meals. It was a joy to us to witness that a community had been built as a result of students being willing to take risks and encouragement from us. Members witnessed commitment, support, and mutual care for one another. This has great impact on the group because each member was motivated and committed to work for the benefit of the community instead of merely a tutorial group organised by the tutor.

One of the students told us that in normal group work, he would be a loafer because he disliked hard work and his lack of effort would not be noticed. He felt he could never do this in the PBL group because the other group members had become his friends and he could not let them down. He was motivated to work, attending the tutorial and contributing because he cared for his friends and knew that they cared for him in return. The social activities did not cease when the students left university, but have continued way beyond it into employment. Many of our former PBL students are still in contact with one another because of their meeting at PBL tutorials many years ago. One can observe that PBL has enabled our students to form social interactions and lifelong friendships. In our experience we found that our students acquired not only academic skills, but also social skills.

The Importance of Communication Skills

Group dynamics is the attitude, exchanges, and interaction of group members. It is possible see these forces at work. The success of the group process depends on small group decision making, which in turn is influenced by communication and interpersonal skills of group members. In Chapter V we have discussed the importance of interpersonal skills that students need for successful PBL. Feedback from discussions with past PBL students also revealed that communication skill was crucial to the success of the group and brought benefits to the individual. It is our belief that strong communication skills are crucial to effective group process.

To function successfully in small groups, students need to be able to communicate clearly on intellectual and emotional levels. Effective communicators can explain their ideas clearly, listen carefully to others, have the ability to ask questions to clarify other ideas and emotions, and can reflect on activities and interactions of their group and encourage other members of the group to do so.

There are two types of communication in group process: interpersonal and intra-team communication. Interpersonal communication is the process that we use to communicate ideas, thoughts, and feelings to another person. Conversely, intra-team communication is a process through which team members communicate with one another (The Foundation Coalition, 2004). Communication, listening, and speaking is the core of the abilities required to function as a team. Faulty communication is the cause of conflict that may lead to ineffective communication. According to Algert and Watson (2002), over 90% of conflicts are attributed to faulty communication between sender and receiver.

We believe that it is important for students to have an understanding of how the communication process works and what are the skills that are required in order to communicate effectively with others in the group. Having an understanding of this enables students to work better and also improve their communication skills. A brief review of the communication process and effective skills for communication is briefly reviewed in Appendix 11n.

Trust

It is our belief that trust plays an important role in relationships. Trust is the glue that holds the group together. There are two kinds of trust that we found necessary for successful PBL: trust in the tutor and trust among members of the group. When the level of trust in increased, there is a higher level of cooperation and performance. When trust is decreased there is lower performance and inferior group processes. According to Mayer, Davis, and Schoorman (1995), trust is a willingness of a party to be vulnerable to the actions of another party, based on the expectation that the other will perform a particular action important to them, irrespective of the ability to monitor or control that party. Interpersonal trust can be defined as the dependability of the partner and the extent to which that partner cares about the group's interest. For our study, we focus on trust in group members (interpersonal), as opposed to another group. Our experience with students working in groups has indicated that interpersonal trust played a crucial role for the success of PBL. Since group work plays such a critical role in PBL, it requires that individuals work together. Trust is expected to increase the performance of the group (Dirks, 1999), both in terms of effectiveness and efficiency.

The most important step after establishing ground rules is to develop group trust and teamwork. This requires that we begin by modeling the students' behaviour. We found that it is important for students to share their experiences of group work during the first meeting after the introduction. Students should be reminded by the tutor why they are there as a group and the purpose of their studies

For group process to function effectively, it is necessary that each member of the group is willing to share and exchange knowledge with others. Trust plays a critical role in exchange and sharing of knowledge during the tutorial process. It is also an important facilitator in communication. Trust facilitates transactions and collaboration (Fukuyama, 1995). It involves willingness to make oneself vulnerable to others and involves various facets of another party, therefore: trust in their competence; trust in their openness and honesty; trust in their intention and concerns and trust in their reliability (Mishra, 1996). Where relationships are high in trust, people are more willing to engage in cooperative interaction (Nahapiet & Ghoshal, 1998).

According to Sharratt and Usoro (2003), trust can be conceptualised across three dimensions: integrity, benevolence and competence. Integrity-based trust is the perception that another party is honest and reliable. Benevolence-based trust is related to the perception that another party would keep the best interests of the trustor at heart. Competence-based trust is rooted in the perception that another party is knowledgeable or possesses a certain level of competence.

For PBL groups to be successful and effective, trust must be ingrained in the culture of this group process. We believe that building trust begins with creating a shared sense of commitment across the group. For each member of the group to have a shared sense of commitment requires that there is a sense of community (SOC) within the group. That is, a feeling that members belong to the group and matter to one another, and a shared faith that members needs will be met through their commitment to be together (McMillan & Chavis, 1986). According to Sharratt and Usoro (2003), where SOC is stronger, participation in sharing will be greater. Our experiences showed that several types of trust affected the performance of the knowledge sharing in the groups. For members to share and work effectively, there must be trust in their openness and honesty. Initially members of the group were reluctant to exchange or share knowledge because of lack of benevolence-based trust. As the members were new to each other, there was little confidence that one could trust the other to keep the best interests of the trustor at heart. This required constant encouragement and reminders from us that they ought to give each other the benefit of the doubt and begin to trust one another.

Besides benevolence-based trust, integrity-based trust is also important. It plays a crucial role in motivating group working and knowledge sharing. One is not likely to be motivated to share one's knowledge with another if one perceives them to be dishonest or unreliable. Students have to be confident and convinced that the team is upholding trustworthy values such as honesty, reliability, mutual reciprocity, and commitment before they can work effectively together. We have found that the greater one's perceived trust in a group, the greater the engagement of the group.

One of the problems we found with sharing of knowledge was that of competence. Some of the group members found it difficult to trust the other members' contributions of knowledge because of fear that what they have delivered was not sound. It is important that the tutor is aware of this fear and tries to build competence-based trust in the group. Students should be monitoring constantly to make sure that their progress in learning is not being hindered by lack of competence-based trust in the group.

Some of the students in the groups were very shy and they found it difficult to contribute for fear of giving incorrect or misleading contributions, or they believed that their contribution might not be relevant or important. This made them unwilling to share or contribute because of fear of "losing face." The higher the perceived benevolence of the group, the more likely one is to feel less threatened by making mistakes or making less relevant contributions. A benevolent group is more likely to encourage the participation and development of its members.

It is not only that there should be trust among the team members, but students should have complete trust in the tutor too. We found that unless the students can trust in the openness and honesty of the tutor, they would become de-motivated and lose interest in attending the tutorial group process. From our personal experiences, we found that trust in the tutor by the students has a great impact on students work. Students need to feel that the tutor cares for them and what he/she says is reliable. Honesty is important to the students. As students were generally used to being taught in the traditional manner, through lectures, they would not find PBL easy. This has to be made clear to them at the outset. We have found that students like to be told the truth, even though they may not like it.

Feedback from students told us that they kept coming because they perceived us to be honest and had their welfare and interests in mind. It is important for students to know that we care and have their interests and studies in mind. When students perceived that we cared, they began to respond and work collaboratively as a group. We have found that where the relationships are high in trust, students are more active in their work and there is a greater degree of cooperation and exchange of knowledge sharing.

Ritual Behaviour

Although we had positive outcomes for our PBL groups, it was not without problems. Discussion in the tutorial groups should have positive effects on student learning (Dolmans, Wolfagen, Van der Vleuten, & Wijnen, 2001). According to these authors, in the tutorial group, elaboration takes place through discussion, note taking or answering questions. These cognitive activities stimulate learners to actively construct explanatory models, which in turn facilitate the processing of new information.

Although students in the group would appear to work well initially, there were occasions that led to ritual behaviour (Dolmans et al., 2001). Ritual behaviour in the tutorial group is a situation in which students maintain an appearance in the tutorial group of being actively involved. Dolmans et al. (2001) identified three types of ritual behaviours. First, new ideas are brought into the discussion without connections being made to other ideas. Second, students generate learning issues that do not clearly demarcate what should be studied. Third, students have not really studied in depth during individual investigation.

During the first few tutorial sessions we found that students generated learning issues that did not clearly demarcate what should be learned. Students would come into the tutorial session not really knowing the subject they were supposed to have investigated. They would read aloud from the notes they had made, but when we tried to probe deeper, they simply had no idea how to apply the knowledge to the problem under investigation. This was frustrating for us. Our initial response was to insist that students must study the subject matter in depth for the next tutorial. There was not much change by the time of the next tutorial session, however. When challenged as to why they have not mastered the subject matter well, their response was that they had no idea how to do it. They told us that they needed help.

As the problem was very complex and students were not used to working out solutions for themselves, we decided to help them to acquire the meta-cognitive skills they needed to solve the problem. During subsequent tutorial sessions we decided to challenge student's thinking by asking stimulating questions in order to activate their prior knowledge. Questions were asked that prompted students to make connections between the issues explored in the tutorial sessions. We also helped and prompted students to formulate learning issues that clearly demarcated the literature involved. Instead of reading aloud from their notes, we insisted that students repeated or explained in their own words to each other. We also challenged the students to apply newly acquired knowledge to their problem, which at first they found very difficult. We encouraged them to persevere and were delighted that our persistent encouragement and perseverance paid off. Students began to take on a more responsible attitude and interest in their own learning. Many told us that they actually began to find learning exciting, interesting, and challenging.

The Uncommitted Group Member

It is argued by many PBL tutors that groups develop team spirit that encourages the members of the group to work together. Members care about the group because they want to succeed and do well. Although this may generally be the case, there were many occasions when one or two members of the group refused to pull their weight and let the group down by not attending all of the tutorial sessions. These students let the others do all of the work. Some of the students who were initially motivated began to contribute less when they discovered that some of the members were not doing any of the work. This led to social loafing (Slavin, 1996).

Our initial reaction was to enforce compulsory attendance so that those who failed to turn up would be penalised in their final assessment. Although the students concerned were coerced to attend, we had not achieved the main principle of constructivism that students should take responsibility for their own learning. While students were attending the tutorial sessions, they lacked motivation and were often reluctant to contribute. This forced us to change our approach, because other students were complaining about the lack of contribution from these students. We decided to take a three-pronged approach. First, we called in the students concerned individually and explained to them the importance of attendance and how we cared very much for their studies and were concerned that they work hard to achieve what they had come to university for. This often led to revelations that they had not taken the tutorial sessions seriously.

From this meeting we were able to identify the reasons behind the failure to attend. These ranged from lack of motivation to problems with the group process. If the problem was concerned with motivation, we pointed out to the students concerned that we expected them to be active participants in the tutorial process as part of their responsibility. At the same time, we tried our best to show them that we really want them to succeed and do well. We also told them that we have confidence and believed that they could do well. When the problem concerned the group process, we called in the whole group to discover what was going wrong. Very often the student concerned did not attend because he or she felt that the rest of the group did not value his/her contributions or as a result of shyness on the part of this student. The group was then reminded of the importance of group work in real life and the need to work as a team to be successful. Using the analogy of a football team, we stressed the importance of team spirit and how the game would not be won if one member of the team suffered. This analogy appeared to work well with the students and it often led to members of the group taking extra efforts to help the shy student.

For our part, we also made sure we facilitated the learning process by regular evaluation and by establishing a personal interest in each of the students in the group. The formative evaluation of the students' performance in the group helped to improve the students' behaviour in group work. Besides this formative evaluation by us, we also used self and peer evaluation by students by helping the groups to evaluate on a regular basis and developing self-reflection in students. Based on self-reflection, students were able to assess how their own learning was progressing and this helped them to better manage their performance. We found that this approach helped us to shift the responsibility of learning to the students.

Motivation

We have found that motivation was a key to our students learning in PBL. Students learn best when they see themselves engaged in learning for their own intrinsic reasons (i.e., learning because they want to rather than because the have to). It is important as tutors that we maintain the interest of the students in their learning throughout PBL. There has been much written in the literature concerning strategies to enhance motivation. Many of these are very useful as guidelines for tutors to promote motivation. A list, consisting of ways to motivate students, suggested by researchers, can be found in Appendix 11o.

To help us establish what motivated our students and how we could help them to enjoy their learning, we have been receiving regular feedback from our past PBL cohorts. Student feedback confirmed our studies that the following factors affected the motivational behaviour of our students:

1. Tutor's care: Students told us that they knew and could sense that we cared for them, so they responded with interest and motivation. We took great interest in their studies and personal interests. They saw us as approachable human beings and not aloof authorities. Because they knew that we care, they responded to our concern for their work. Students trusted us when we told them of the benefits of acquiring problem solving and critical thinking skills. We have also been very honest with them by stating at the beginning that studying using PBL was not easy and demanded a lot of time and commitment. Despite the hardship they had to persevere to learn. They accepted the challenge because they believed that in the long term they would be rewarded by becoming better learners.

2. High expectations of the students: We told our students at the outset that we had high expectations of them and expected them to do well in their studies. Although some students found it hard to believe in their own abilities to achieve our expectations, we constantly reminded them that with determination and motivation they could achieve high standards. All we wanted from them was that they should do their very best. Students' performance typically indicated that the majority of students responded to our expectations and achieved more than they ever dreamed possible.

3. Enthusiastic about the subject: We found that enthusiasm played a crucial part in student motivation. Students lost interest and became bored if they perceived that we had become apathetic. When the students saw that we were confident, excited about PBL and enjoyed the facilitation process in the tutorial sessions, they became interested and motivated. Our enthusi-

asm for their learning spurred them into active participation of the learning process.

4.   Emphasise learning rather than grades: Instead of emphasising grades, we kept stressing the importance of students mastering problem solving, creative thinking and learning to learn skills that they would need in their professional lives. Initially the students found the idea strange, but as we progressed through the tutorial sessions, they came to see the importance of these skills as they got deeper into the problems set. By the end of the course, all students would have their mindset changed from grades-seeking to that of satisfaction and enjoyment in their learning.

5.   Make learning realistic and fun: Students need to realise that what they are learning is relevant for them in their jobs later on. It is important that we give them problems that reflect real world applications. Our problems were developed so as to reflect what they will have to do in their professional lives. Some of the problems given were actual real work cases that they worked on as projects. Because the students were involved in real world problems, they could see the relevance of the learning and this motivated them in their learning.

Information Literacy

There is some confusion between computer literacy and information literacy. Computer literacy requires a technological know-how to use computer hardware or software. Information-literacy requires knowing more than that. It requires knowing how to clearly define a subject area of investigation; select the appropriate terminology that expresses the concept or subject under investigation; formulate a search strategy that takes into consideration different sources of information and the variable ways in which that information is organised; analyse the data collected for value, relevancy, quality, and suitability; and subsequently turn that information into knowledge (ALA, 1989).

Although information literacy is related to computer literacy, or information technology skills, it has broader implications for individuals, the educational system, and society (ACRL, 2000). It is our belief that students should be aware of the differences between information literacy and computer literacy. Until recently, most learners would expect to deal with carefully selected collations of reference materials from libraries in the form of published books, journals, and periodicals. Nowadays, students can access masses of information using the internet. Since anyone can make a Web page, it is important for students to make sure that the information they obtain is sound and comes from reliable sources.

That is, information that has passed through traditional editorial constraints or undergone some kind of fact-checking required in conventional published printed media. We found that most students simply take for granted that anything that appears on the www must be fine. We had to constantly challenge them about the validity and credibility of the materials they obtained. Students found this annoying at first, yet it is important for students to evaluate the credibility of the information obtained. Our students were often lured to the easy and accessible materials that came off the computer, rather than trying to find true sources such as well indexed books. They also needed reminding of the increasing quantity of information from all sources and the need to seek out knowledge from multiple sources rather than passively receiving and repeating back facts.

We believe that a successful way to help students to develop information-literacy skills is through resource-based learning, which involves having students take more responsibility for locating the materials from which to learn. This approach helps students to develop lifelong learning skills. The advantage of resource-based learning is that it enables students to choose materials that match their academic levels and preferred learning styles, making it possible for them to individualise the learning process.

Generally students were unaware of the range of sources of information that they could use to identify relevant information. They also found it hard to locate the materials in the library. Many students were unaware of the role of the Online Public Access Catalogue (OPAC). Students were also unaware of the fact that indexes to articles could be found on CD ROM related to their disciplines. They also had little idea of the relative merits of different sources of information. From our experience, we found it useful to remind students that they should consult the libraries to seek guidance and training. This had an impact on the students as they began to realise the benefits of resource-based learning.

Another important part of resource-based learning is the need to search for information. Students might be aware of Boolean logic, but might have great difficulty creating search strategies. Many had no idea of how information is structured in systems, nor did they realise that different systems wok in very different ways. Effective searches rely entirely on the searcher him/herself. A computer only retrieves what it has been asked to find, and if the terms it is searching for are not useful or relevant to the task at hand, the results of the search would be useless.

To search effectively requires certain skills. We found that it is important for students to have an understanding of the various formats for information-finding purposes. Students also need to have searching skills to help them use the most appropriate searching strategies to obtain the relevant information they need by constructing effective search queries. It is useful to have staff from the library to provide appropriate training to help students to learn how to obtain information effectively.

Students in an information-literate environment should be able to engage in active, self-directed activities. The role of the tutor is to facilitate students' learning by providing them with resources that will enrich their learning.

Changing Attitudes to Learning

Another frustration experienced by the students was their initial inability to integrate the diverse ideas generated by the nature of the problems they were investigating. It was necessary to constantly reassure and motivate them without actually providing the answers. By challenging their guesses and assumptions we were gradually able to focus their minds on relevant factors and enable them to reject ideas which lead only into blind alleys." All of this was very labour intensive, but after a few weeks perseverance the students began to realise what a powerful tool we were putting into their hands. Once the light dawned, the students began to use PBL on other areas of their study, and reported back how much the concept had enabled and empowered their critical thinking skills, not only on the initial problem set, but in all aspects of their study. Students often came with different attitudes from ours towards their learning. Many perceived learning as a means to external ends such as grades and status among their peers and tutor, and above all obtaining good examination grades. Because of this, they tended to focus on low level learning without having the need to be involved in higher order cognitive processing. We had to work hard to change these attitudes. Appendix 11p contains extracts of testimonies from our PBL showing their change of attitude to learning.

Learning Can Be Great Fun

We feel strongly that students should value learning as an end in itself. To achieve this we want them to see learning as fun in order to benefit from assignments and demonstrate greater levels of cognitive engagement in their work, be able to apply critical thinking, metacognitive, and self-directed learning skills to the development of understanding of subject content. This was perhaps one of the hardest tasks we faced. However, as we continued the PBL sessions, the students began to see the benefits of being cognitively engaged in their work.

As they became more and more involved with the problems, they began to really enjoy the higher level of processing demanded of them. Many had a change of mindset. These students found learning so interesting that one of them actually openly expressed that he did not realise learning is such fun.

Conclusion

There have been many articles written about the benefits of PBL in students learning. It is our experience that PBL provided many benefits for our students in their learning. We have been implementing PBL for many years. Despite our experiences, we are continuing to research into how to effectively improve the PBL process so that we can help our students to be better learners. Feedback from students and our interaction with the tutorial process provided us many insights to our work. We have learned that implementing PBL is not easy. As tutors we have to remind ourselves our roles as tutors and not fall back to our traditional didactic approach of teaching. Having a greater understanding of the tutorial process, in particular the facilitation process and group dynamics gave us the necessary knowledge and skills needed to implement PBL. Our goal is to help students to equip them with the professional skills that they need to function in real life. Besides our tutorial skills, we also found that students responded better and became motivated when we showed we cared. Students responded positively when they could trust that we have their well-being in mind.

References

ACRL (Association of College & Research Libraries) (2000). *Information Literacy Competency Standards for Higher Education.* Retrieved from http://www.ala.org/ACRLPrinterTemplate.cfm?Section=acrlstandards &Template=/C

ALA (American Library Association Presidential Committee on Information Literacy) (1989). Final Report. Washington, DC.

Algert, N. E., & Watson, K. (2002). *An introduction to conflict management for individuals and groups.* Bryan, TX: The Center for Change and Conflict Resolution.

Bloom, B. S. (Ed.). (1956). *Taxonomy of educational objectives: The classification of education goals: Handbook I, cognitive domain.* New York; Toronto: Longmans, Green.

Bloom, B. S., Mesia, B. B., & Krathwohl, D. R. (1964). *Taxonomy of educational objectives* (two vols: The affective domain & The cognitive domain). New York. David McKay.

Dirks, K. T. (1999). The Effects of interpersonal trust on work group performance. *Journal of Applied Psychology, 84,* 445-455.

Dolmans, D. H. J. M., Wolfagen, I. H. A. P., Van der Vleuten, C. P. M., & Wijnen, W. H. F. W. (2001). Solving problems with group work in problem-based learning: Hold onto the philosophy. *Medical Education, 35,* 884-889.

The Foundation Coalition (2004). *Effective interpersonal/intrateam communication.* Retrieved from http://www.foundation.org

Fukuyama, F. (1995). *The social value and the creation of prosperity.* New York: The Free Press.

Gagné, R. M. (1985). *The conditions of learning and theory of instruction* (4th ed.). New York: Holt, Rinehard and Winston.

Gilkison, A. (2003). Techniques used by expert and non-expert tutors to facilitate problem-based learning tutorials in an undergraduate medical curriculum. *Medical Educator, 37,* 6-14.

Gordon, P., Rogers, A., & Comfort, M. (2001). A taste of problem-based learning increases achievement of urban minority middle-school students. *Educational Horizons, 79(4),* 171-175.

Hendry, G. D., Frommer, M., & Walker, R. (1999). Constructivism and problem-based learning. *Journal of Further and Higher Education, 23,* 359-371.

Knowles, M. (1975). *Self-directed learning. Guide for learners and teachers.* Toronto: Prentice-Hall

Neville, A. J. (1999). The problem-based learning tutor: Teacher; Facilitator; Evaluator. *Medical Teacher, 21*(4), 393-401.

Manzo, A. V., & Manzo, U. C. (1994). *Teaching children to be literate: A reflective approach.* Harcourt College Publishers.

Margeston, D. (1994). Current educational reform and the significance of problem-based learning. *Student Higher Education, 19,* 5-19

Maudsley, G. (1999). Roles and responsibilities of the problem-based learning tutor in the undergraduate medical curriculum. *British Medical Journal, 318*(6), 657-661.

Mayer, R. C., Davis, J. H., & Schoorman, F. D. (1995). An integrative model of organisational trust. *Academy of Management Review, 20,* 709-734.

McMillan, D. W., & Chavis, D. M. (1986). Sense of community: A definition and theory. *Journal of Community Psychology, 14*(1), 6-23.

Merrill, M. D. (1983). Component display theory. In C. M. Reigeluth (Ed.), *Instructional design theories and models: An overview of their current status* (pp. 282-333). Englewood Cliffs, NJ: Laurence Erlbaum Associates.

Mishra, A. K. (1996). Organisation responds to crisis: The centrality of trust. In R. M. T. R. Tyler (Ed.), *Trust in organisations* (pp. 261-287). Thousand Oak, CA: Sage

Nahapiet, J., & Ghoshal, S. (1998). Social capital, intellectual capital and the organisational advantage. *Academy of Management Review, 23*(2), 242-266.

Neil, J. T., & Dias, K. L. (2002). *Social support helps people grow.* University of New Hampshire and Northern Territory University.

Neville, A. J. (1999). The problem-based learning tutor: Teacher, facilitator, evaluator. *Medical Teacher, 21*(4), 393-401.

Reigeluth, C. M. (n.d.). *Levels of cognitive learning.* Retrieved from http://www.indiana.edu/~idtheory/methods/m1d.html

Rideout, E. (2001). Evaluating student learning. In E. Rideout (Ed.), *Transforming nursing education through problem-based learning* (pp. 215-239). Sudbury, Jones, & Bartlett.

Risdon, C., Braley, D., & Gordon, N. (2002). *Facilitating small groups: PBL learning. Desired tutor competencie*s. Retrieved from http://www.fhs.mcmaster.ca/facdev/Small%20group%20tutoring%20competencies.pdf

Savery, J. A., &. Duffy, T. M. (1995). Problem-based learning: An instructional model and its constructivist framework. *Educational Technology, 35,* 31-38.

Sharratt, M., & Usoro, A. (2003). *Understanding knowledge sharing in online communities of practice.* Academic Conferences Limited. Retrieved from www.ejkm.com

Slavin, R. E. (1996). Research on cooperative learning and achievement: What we know, what we need to know. *Contemporary Educational Psychology, 21,* 43-69.

Spaulding, W. B. (1991). *Revisiting Medical Education, McMaster Medical School. The early years 1965-1974.* Philadelphia; Hamilton, Canada: Becker.

Tsai, W., & Ghoshal, S. (1998). Social capital and value creation: The role of intrafirm networks. *Academy of Management Journal, 41*(4), 464-476.

Tuckman, B. (1965). Development sequence in small groups. *Psychological Bulletin, 63,* 384-300.

Wheelen, S. A, Murphy, D., Tsumura, E., & Kline, S. F. (1998). Member perceptions of Internal group dynamics and productivity. *Small Group Research (FSGR), 29*(3), 371-393.

Wiederhold, C. (1997). *The q-matrix/cooperative learning & higher-level thinking.* San Clemente, CA: Kagan Cooperative Learning.

Wilkerson, L. (1992, April). *Identification of skills for the problem-based tutor: Student and faculty perspective.* Paper presented at the Annual Meeting of the American Educational Research Association, San Francisco.

Wilkerson, L., Hafler, J. P., & Liu P. 1991). A case study of student directed discussion in four problem-based tutorial groups. In R*esearch in Medical Education, Academic Medicine, 66,* S79-S81

Woods, D. R. (1994). *Problem-based learning: How to gain the most from PBL.* Waterdown, ON: Donald Woods.

Appendix 11

Appendix 11a: Self-Directed Learning Competencies

According to Simons (1991), self-regulating processes in learning consist of monitoring, testing, and questioning, revision and evaluation. Monitoring refers to the constant observation and interpretation of the learning processes in the light of the goals. Learners must observe and interpret their own behaviour and thinking, and control whether they are still on their way to the goals and whether the information is recalled, understood, integrated or applied. Testing is concerned with the explicit attempt to check if one is still progressing towards the learning goals through paraphrasing, trying to think of new examples, schematising, searching an analogy, etc. Answering self-made or supplied questions, self-regulated learners can test their state of knowledge and understanding. Revision refers to the decisions one has to take when problems occur. There is growing evidence that reflection plays an important aspect of self-regulated learning.

We agree with Simons (1991) concerning self-directed learning. Self-regulated learning is the ability to prepare one's own learning, take the necessary steps to learn, regulate the learning and provide for one's own feedback and judgement, keeping one's concentration and motivation high. A self-regulated learner has the ability to execute learning activities that lead to knowledge, to comprehension, to integration and to problem solving.

According to Knowles (1975), self-directed learning involves the following competencies:

- The ability to develop and be in touch with curiosities; i.e. ability to engage in divergent thinking.
- The ability to formulate questions, based on personal curiosities that are answerable through inquiry.
- The ability to perceive one's self objectively and accept, non-defensively, feedback, from others about personal performance.
- The ability to diagnose one's own learning needs in the light of models of competence required for performing life roles.
- The ability to identify human, material, and experiential resources for accomplishing various kinds of learning objectives.
- The ability to identify data required to answer various kinds of questions.
- The ability to select and use the most efficient means for collecting any required data from various sources.
- The ability to organise, analyse, and evaluate the data so as to get valid answers to questions.
- The ability to design a plan of strategies for making use of appropriate learning resources in answering questions or meeting learning needs. The ability to carry out a learning plan systematically and sequentially.
- The ability to collect evidence of the accomplishment of learning objectives and have it validated through subsequent performance.

References

Knowles, M. S. (1975). *Self-directed learning.* New York: Associated Press.

Simons, P. R. J. (1991). Constructive learning: The role of the learner. In T. M. Duffey, J. Lowyck & D. H. jonassen (Eds.), *Designing environments for constructivist learning.* NATO-ASI series. Berlin: Springer-Verlag.

Appendix 11b: Knowles' Seven Elements of Facilitation

(From Neville, 1999)

1. Climate setting: helping learners become acquainted with each other as persons and as mutual learning resources, developing the skills of self-directed learning and understanding the role of the tutor.

2. Planning: deciding on how tutorial will run and how tutorial process and function decisions are made.

3. Designing needs for learning: consideration of how the tutor can frame content objectives so that students can take ownership of the learning process and compare their knowledge with the required objectives.

4. Setting goals: helping the students translate the diagnosed needs into clear, feasible learning objectives.

5. Designing a learning plan: helping the students design their learning plans, develop strategies for accessing resources.

6. Engaging in learning activities: whereby the tutor considers what part of the learning should be his/her responsibility and what the students should be responsible for, individually or collectively.

7. Evaluating learning outcomes: how to give constructive feedback to the students so as to enhance the self-directed learning process.

Reference

Neville, A. J. (1999). The problem-based learning tutor: Teacher, facilitator, evaluator. *Medical Teacher, 21*(4), 393-401.

Appendix 11c: Techniques Used to Intervene in PBL Tutorial

(From Gilkison, 2003)

- Elicitation: This always involves the tutor asking a question of the group or an individual that requires a verbal response from students.

- Re-elicitation: Where the tutor repeats the same elicitation or rephrases it. A response is required from the students. This results from an inadequate response given previously.

- Refocusing: When the students wander off the subject, the tutor uses refocusing to bring the students back to the topic or case scenario.

- Prompting: A technique used to gather more information, or to get the students to expand on something they had not fully explained.

- Facilitating: Occurs when the tutor guides the students in a certain direction, suggests what they do next, or attends to group dynamics.

- Evaluating: Refers to comments made by the tutor to evaluate the group process, or to evaluate individual students.

- **Summarising:** Refers to the tutor summarising a section of discussion. This usually signals the closing of the topic before the group moves to the next.

- **Giving Feedback:** Occurs when the tutor confirms that he or she has heard or seen an appropriate response.

Reference

Gilkison, A. (2003). Techniques used by expert and non-expert tutors to facilitate problem-based learning tutorials in undergraduate medical curriculum. *Medical Education, 37,* 6-14.

Appendix 11d: Guidelines for Facilitators

The role of the facilitator is crucial to the PBL tutorial process. Effective facilitators should have the following skills and traits.

- Knowing the dynamics of group processes and being skilled in using techniques for keeping the group task focused, encouraging creative thinking, building consensus and keeping all group members involved (Hawkins, 2004).

- A critical skill is the ability to create and maintain a safe, open, and supportive environment for all group members (Hawkins, 2004).

- Being able to recognise and deal with disruptive behaviour (Hawkins, 2004).

- Should always be issue-neutral during the tutorial session. Facilitators should never advocate a point of view (Hawkins, 2004).

- Must have listening and observation skills.

- Must be aware of what is being discussed or decided (content) and how the group is functioning (process).

- Needs to know how to effectively intervene when discussion is veering off the subject (Hawkins, 2004).

- Making sure that the group works as a constructive and cohesive unit.

- Making sure that the learning objectives are met and members know what to do at the end of the session.

- Encouraging constructive debate between group members.

- Promoting new discussion if the group is interacting poorly or going in the wrong direction.
- Making sure no-one dominates the group.
- Ensuring contributions to the discussion are treated equally.
- Controlling problem-members within the group to allow everyone to join in the discussion.
- Forging a team from a group of individuals through motivation an empowerment of the individual.
- Acting as a guide and timekeeper.
- Acting as a role model.
- Creating a safe motivating environment for students to learn.
- Using questions effectively.
- Helping students to articulate their learning.
- Helping students to develop learning issues.
- Helping students to explore existing knowledge and test hypotheses.
- Helping students to discuss learning issues and application to the problem at hand.
- Monitoring the tutorial process to maintain active participation by students.
- Encouraging students to reflect on their learning.
- Observing, making behavioural notes and providing constructive feedback.
- Facilitating the tutorial process.
- Encouraging establishment of group dynamics conducive to learning.
- Taking charge of the tutorial process without imposing oneself.
- Intervening in conflict situations.
- Assisting students in identifying resource, and materials.
- Encouraging students to act as agents of change within the group.
- Encouraging students to develop professional behaviour in group.
- Establishing rapport and encouraging group interactions, reinforcements, and agreement.
- Encouraging students to develop their individual qualities within the group, encouraging positive qualities, and discouraging negative ones.
- Encouraging active participation, focusing attention and reinforcing group discussions.
- Encouraging students to review and redefine explanations by making connections or links of concepts, principles, processes, etc.

- Encouraging deep probing, referring back questions, comments, and suggestions to the group and stimulating thinking by encouraging hypothesizing.

- Assisting students to realize their full potential and to appreciate their own limitations.

- Encouraging analysis, synthesis, and evaluation of the problem or data and summarizing of discussions.

- Encouraging students to continuously evaluate their achievements.

- Modelling the meta-cognitive process to the students.

Problems Facilitators Face

Individuals differ from one another. In group working, there would be different people from different backgrounds with different behaviours. Some may be shy; others may be loud-mouthed and difficult. How do we deal with group members of different dispositions? Some possible suggestions are:

Shy, Quiet Members: A member is very quiet and not participating as he or she should. This could be because the member is shy, insecure or timid, bored, feeling superior, having trouble understanding the topic, etc. Possible solutions are:

- Ask privately why that student is so quiet.
- Suggest that everyone in the group take a turn to speak.
- Ask the student some questions.
- Recognise his/her contribution and encourage more.
- Try to bring this student into the conversation whenever there is an opportunity.

Talkative Students: The talkative student has the tendency to dominate the talking. Reasons for this could be (a) seeking attention, (b) wanting to be dominating, (c) knowing a lot and wanting to share, or (d) wanting to show off his/her knowledge. Possible solutions are:

- Remind him/her of the ground rules of group behaviour.
- Stress the importance of sticking to relevant points and time limits.
- Ask the student to explain how his/her comments add value to the discussion.

- Remind this student privately about his/her need to allow equality of contributions from each member.

Disagreeable Student: This member is generally antagonistic and highly argumentative. This may be caused by the student (a) feels he or she is being ignored, (b) has a need to show off, (c) has an aggressive personality, (d) is not able to make suggestions constructively, (e) is upset by some of the other members' suggestions, or (f) is trying to score points. Some possible solutions are:

- Remind student of his/her ground rules of group behaviour.
- Tell student that due to time constraints, his/her comments will be dealt with at the next meeting.
- Open the discussion of the student's comments to the group.
- Comment on his/her suggestions and move on.
- Find out privately from the student why his/her behaviour was so aggressive.

Side Conversations: The student may be talking to another group member without paying attention to the tutorial group. This may be due to the student (a) being bored with the meeting, (b) wanting to be the centre of attention, (c) feeling the need to introduce an item not on the agenda, (d) having a point to raise that the group ignores, or (e) feeling that his/her point is better than what is being discussed. Some possible solutions are:

- Asking the student to share his/her comments with the group.
- Reminding the group of their code of conduct in group working.
- Restating a discussed topic and asking the student to express his/her opinions.
- Calling the student by name and asking if he or she wishes to add their topic to the group discussion.

Reference

Hawkins, C. (2004). *Effective meeting com.: Your meeting resource centre.* Retrieved from http://www.effectivemeetings.com/teams/difficult/hawkins.asp

Appendix 11e: Bloom's Taxonomy

There is more than one type of learning. Benjamin Bloom (1956) developed a taxonomy for categorizing levels of abstraction of questions that commonly occur in educational settings of intellectual behaviour in learning. This taxonomy contains three overlapping domains: the cognitive, psychomotor, and affective. Domains are generally known as categories. Cognitive is for mental skills (knowledge), affective is for growth in feelings or emotional areas (attitude), while psychomotor is for manual or physical skills (skills). Within the cognitive domain, he identified six levels: knowledge, comprehension, application, analysis, synthesis, and evaluation. These domains and levels are very useful to help the development of critical thinking skills of students. Critical thinking involves logical thinking and reasoning including skills such as comparison, classification, sequencing, cause/effect, patterning, analogies, deductive, and inductive reasoning, forecasting, planning, hypothesizing, and critiquing.

Bloom's Taxonomy attempts to divide cognitive objectives into subdivisions ranging from the simplest behaviour to the most complex. An example adopted from Weiderhold (1997) is used to illustrate the application of the six categories of Bloom's Taxonomy to the Pledge of Allegiance. The six levels from lowest to highest are:

- Knowledge: Knowledge is defined as the remembering of previously learned material. This typically involves the recall of a wide range of material, from specific facts to complete theories. It represents the lowest level of learning outcomes in the cognitive domain. Example: "Say the Pledge."

- Comprehension: Comprehension is defined as the ability to grasp the meaning of material. These learning outcomes go one step beyond the simple remembering of material, and represent the lowest level of understanding. Examples of learning objectives at this level are: understand facts and principles, justify methods and procedures etc. Example: "Explain what individualistic, liberty, and justice mean."

- Application: Application refers to the ability to use learned material in new and concrete situations. This may include application of rules, methods, concepts, principles, laws, and theories. Learning outcomes in this area require a higher level of understanding than those under comprehension. Examples of learning objectives include applying concepts and principles to new situations, applying laws and theories to practical situations, solving mathematical problems, and demonstrating the correct usage of a method or procedure. Example: "Create your own pledge to something you believe in."

- Analysis: Analysis refers to the ability to break down material into its component parts so that its organizational structure may be understood. This includes identification of parts, analysis of the relationship between parts, and recognition of the organizational principles involved. Learning outcomes in analysis category represent a higher intellectual level than comprehension and application because they require an understanding of both the content and the structural form of the material. Examples of learning objectives at this level include: recognising logical fallacies in reasoning, recognising un-stated assumptions, distinguishing between facts and inferences, analysing the organizational structure of a work (e.g., writing). Example: "Discuss the meaning of "and to the Republic for which it stands" in terms of its importance to the Pledge."

- Synthesis: Synthesis refers to the ability to put parts together to form a new whole. Learning outcomes in this area stress creative behaviours, with major emphasis on the formulation of new patterns or structure. Examples of learning objectives at this level are: write a creative short story (or poem or music), propose a plan for an experiment, integrate learning from different areas into a plan for solving a problem, and formulate a new scheme for classifying objects (or events, or ideas). Example: "Write a contract between yourself and a friend that includes an allegiance to a symbol that stands for something you both believe in."

- Evaluation: Evaluation is concerned with the ability to judge the value of material (statement, novel, poem, research report) for a given purpose. Learning outcomes in this area are highest in the cognitive hierarchy because they contain elements of all the other categories, as well as conscious value judgments based on clearly defined criteria. Examples of learning objectives at this level are: judge the adequacy with which conclusions are supported by data, judge the value of a work (art, music, writing) by use of external standards of excellence. Example: "Describe the purpose of the Pledge and assess how well it achieves that purpose. Suggest improvements."

References

Bloom, B. S. (Ed.). (1956). *Taxonomy of educational objectives: The classification of education goals: Handbook I, cognitive domain.* New York; Toronto: Longmans, Green.

Bloom, B. S., Mesia, B. B., & Krathwohl, D. R. (1964). *Taxonomy of educational objectives* (two vols: *The affective domain & The cognitive domain*). New York: David McKay.

Wiederhold, C. (1997). *The q-matrix/cooperative learning & higher-level thinking.* San Clemente, CA: Kagan Cooperative Learning.

Appendix 11f: Gagné's Conditions of Learning

Gagné's system for classifying objectives according to the different types of learning outcomes and the conditions that are required for the various learning to occur prescribes instruction for all three of Bloom's domains of knowledge: cognitive, affective, and psychomotor. Within the cognitive domain it prescribes methods for teaching verbal information, (remember-level knowledge), intellectual skills (application of general knowledge) and cognitive strategies (the higher thought processes) (Petry et al., 1987).

- Verbal Information: Students have learned verbal information when they are able to recall it. They may write, list, state or recite information such as names, labels, sentences, single propositions, etc. It is similar to Merrill's .remember-instance" and "remember-generality" Verbal information is sometimes called declarative knowledge.

- Intellectual Skills: Individuals use intellectual skills when they show competence, or interact with the environment using symbols or language. They demonstrate that they know how to do something of an intellectual nature. Intellectual skills are subdivided into five sub-categories. These are: discriminations, concrete concepts, defined concepts, rules, and higher order rules (problem solving) as shown in Table 11.1.

- Discriminations: Learners discriminate when they state whether things are the same or different. They may distinguish, for example, colour, shape, sizes, and sound. This is the lowest form of intellectual skills and is very basic.

- Concrete Concepts: Learners have acquired concrete concepts when they can identify previously unencountered instances of a class of object, class of object properties, or class of events by instant recognition. Concepts of

Table 11.1. Sub-categories of intellectual skills

Type of intellectual skill	Performance
Discrimination	Discriminate between stimuli that differ along one or more physical dimensions.
Concrete concept	Identify instances of concept by pointing to examples.
Defined concept	Classify objects, events, or states using verbal descriptions or definitions.
Rule	Demonstrate application of a rule.
Higher-order rule	Generate new rule for solving the problem.

this type are identified by pointing at them or marking them in some way—they usually cannot be identified by means of a definition. Examples of concrete concepts are ball, wheel, penny, triangle, and rectangle, etc.

- Defined Concepts: Learners have acquired a defined concept when they can use a definition to put something they have not previously encountered into a class (or some things into classes). Their behaviour shows that they know the parameters of the class or classes. Examples of defined concepts include family, electrical resistance, cousin, alien, etc.

- Rules: Learners have acquired a rule when they can demonstrate its application to previously un-encountered instances. A rule is a relation between two or more concepts. An example is the use of Ohm's law represented by $V = IR$ to solve electrical circuit problems.

- Higher-Order Rules (Problem Solving): When learners use two or more previously learned rules to answer a question about an unfamiliar situation, they are attaining a higher-order rule by problem solving. To be successful at problem solving involves mastering a set of concepts and rules that must then be combined to solve the problem. In addition, because the situation itself is unfamiliar, the learners must search out and choose which rules to use.

- Cognitive Strategies: Learners have acquired cognitive strategies when they have developed ways to improve the effectiveness and efficiency of their own intellectual and learning processes; when they can learn independently; when they can propose and solve original problems. This is the highest form of learning.

- Attitudes: Attitudes are complex mental states of human beings that affect their choices of personal action toward people, things, and events. Learners have an attitude when they make consistent choices in repeated situations.

- Motor Skills: Learners have developed motor skills when they perform physical tasks utilising equipment or materials according to a routine procedure. Driving a car, throwing a ball, and typing a letter are all examples of motor skills.

- Conditions for Learning: Another way of classifying learning outcomes is according to types of learner capability (Aronson & Briggs, 1983). According to Gagné (1985), different sets of conditions must be established or provided for the different types of outcomes to occur. There are two types of conditions: internal and external. Internal conditions refer to the acquisition and storage of prior capabilities that the learner has acquired that are either essential to or supportive of subsequent learning. External conditions refer to various ways that instructional events, outside the learner, function to activate and support the internal processes of learning. For an intellectual skill to be learned, it is necessary that certain previously learned prerequisites be recalled. For example, to be able to solve the area of a triangle, it is necessary that the person be able to recognise a triangle and use rules. The most widely used of the conditions of learning is for the teaching of intellectual skills.

References

Aronson, D. T., & Briggs, L. J. (1983). *Contributions* of Gagné's and Briggs' to a prescriptive model of instruction. In C. M. Reigeluth (Ed.), *Instructional design theories and models: An overview of their current status.* NJ: LEA

Gagne, R. M. (1985). *The conditions of learning and theory of instruction* (4th ed.). New York: Holt, Rinehard, and Winston.

Petry, B., Moulton, H., & Reigeluth, C. M. (1987). A lesson based on the Gagné-Briggs theory of instruction. In C. M. Reigeluth (Ed.), *Instructional theories in Action: Lessons illustrating selected theories and models.* Hillsdale, NJ: Lawrence Erlbaum Associates.

Appendix 11g: Component Display Theory (CDT)

(From Merrill, 1983)

CDT developed by Merrill (1983), deals only with the cognitive domain. It defines several categories of objectives using a two-dimensional classification system with performance level as one dimension and content type as the other. According to Merrill (1983), for each type of objective there is a unique combination of primary and secondary presentation forms that will most effectively promote acquisition of that type of objective.

Like Gagné's work, CDT assumes that learned capabilities can be categorised into a limited number of categories. CDT assumes that the most useful classification should have two dimensions: performance and content type. For each performance-content category there is a combination of primary and secondary presentation forms that will result in more effective, efficient and appealing acquisition than will any other combination of displays. The heart of CDT is the performance-content classification system as shown in Figure 11.1.

Figure 11.1. Performance-context matrix (Merrill, 1983)

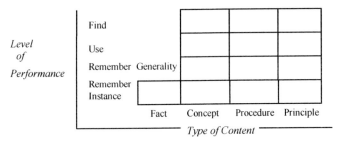

The intersection of the content and performance dimensions defines the various outcomes of learning as illustrated in Figure 11.1. Three performance levels are remember, use, and find. There are four content types: facts, concepts, procedures, and principles.

Performance Categories

Remember is that performance that requires the student to search memory in order to reproduce or recognise some item of information that was previously stored. An example of remember would be, "The symbol for a resistor would be ...?" Use is the performance that requires the student to apply some abstraction to a specific case. "What would happen in the circuit shown below if the load resistor were shorted?" (Circuit diagram shown) is an example of a use category. Find is that performance that requires the student to derive or invent a new abstraction. An example of the find performance is, "Invent a simple circuit that will gradually slow a direct current motor until it stops."

Content Categories

Merrill views contents as consisting of facts, concepts, procedures, and principles:

- *Facts* are arbitrarily associated pieces such as proper name, a date or an event, the name of a place or the symbol used to name particular objects or events.

- *Concepts* are sets of objects, events or symbols that all share some common characteristics and that are identified by the same name.

- *Procedures* are an ordered sequence of steps necessary to accomplish some goals, solve a particular problem, or produce some product.

- *Principles* are explanations or predictions of why things happen in the world. Principles are those cause-and-effect, or correlated relationships that are used to interpret events or circumstances. A principle explains what will be the result of a given action and why—how it works. A procedure merely explains how to do something.

Performance-Content Classification

CDT classifies objects into one or more cells of the performance-content matrix of Figure 11.1. The following examples illustrate this two-dimensional classification:

- Remember-fact: The value of pi is ... Facts have no general or abstract representation, so there is no use-fact or find-fact level in the matrix.

- Remember-concept: Define positive reinforcement.

  Use-concept: Read the story and identify the paragraph that best represents the climax of the story.

- Find-concept: Figure a way to group students in a classroom that assumes a range of ability, a range of sex, and a mix of ethnic background in each group.

- Remember-procedure: Describe the steps to solve a quadratic equation.

- Use-procedure: Demonstrate how to clean a clarinet.

- Find-procedure: Write a computer program that will allow users to search and retrieve recipes.

- Remember-principle: Explain what happens when water evaporates in terms of molecule movement and heat.

- Use-principle: There are two ocean-vessel pictures. Explain and give three different reasons why these pictures are different.

- Find-principle: Set up an experiment to show how water gets into a well.

Merrill's system is, in fact, quite compatible with Gagné's. The three levels of performance correspond to Gagné's three cognitive domains: verbal information, intellectual skills, and cognitive strategies; and within the intellectual skill domains, Gagné distinguishes between what are, in effect, content types, including concepts, and rules.

Reference

Merrill, M. D. (1983). Component display theory. In C. M. Reigeluth (Ed.), *Instructional design theories and models: An overview of their current status* (pp. 282-333). Englewood Cliffs, NJ: Laurence Erlbaum Associates.

Appendix 11h: Different Levels of Cognitive Learning by Reigeluth (1999)

According to Reigeluth (1999), cognitive learning can be classified into different levels: memorisation, understanding and applying. Most content can be learned at any of these three levels. Memorisation is the lowest and simplest form of cognitive learning. This is rote learning. Learners can memorise the value of pi when they are able to re-state or recall it. Understanding involves meaningful learning. It entails relating a new idea to relevant prior knowledge, such as understanding what causes the "greenhouse effect." The behaviours that indicate this kind of learning has occurred include comparing and contrasting, making analogies, making inferences, elaborating, and analysing. Application is when learning is generalised to new situations, or transfer learning. This means when, for example, students can use quadratic equations to solve construction projects. Application learning entails identifying critical commonalities across situations, such as predicting the effects of price increase. The behaviour that exhibits this type of learning is when the learner can successfully apply a generality to a diversity of previously unencountered situations.

Reference

Reigeluth, C. M. (n.d.). *Levels of cognitive learning.* Retrieved from http://www.indiana.edu/~idtheory/methods/m1d.html

Appendix 11i: Questions Based on Bloom's Taxonomy of Learning

Knowledge Level

- Describe what happened at:
- Can you tell me what is ... ?
- What is the meaning of ...?

- When did this happen?
- What is a ...?
- Who did...?

Comprehension Level

- Tell me in your own words...
- What was the main idea?
- What is the difference between..?
- Can you give me an example of ...?
- Compare this ... with ...
- What do you think happened next?
- Can you give a brief outline of..?

Application Level

- What would you change if....?
- Can you develop a set of instructions or material from the information given?
- Can you apply the material to some other task?
- Do you know of another instance where...?
- What questions would you ask of...?

Analysis Level

- How was this similar to..?
- Can you distinguish between..?
- What would happen if...?
- What was the underlying theme of ...?
- Why did the change occur?
- What is the possible cause of ...?
- What are some of the problems of..?
- What was the problem with..?
- What are other possible outcomes?
- Is the information relevant?
- What were the motives behind..?
- How does ... work?
- What information is needed?
- What kind of a ... is this?

Synthesis Level

- What generalisation can you make from this information?
- How would you develop a method for..?
- What is the overall theme of ...?
- Can you find a new method or technique to address this?
- How would you devise your own way to..?
- What is a possible solution to..?
- What would happen if...?
- If you had all of the data, how would you deal with it?

Evaluation Level

- What would you have done in this situation?
- How effective are...?
- What do you think about..?
- What changes would you recommend to ...? Why?
- Is there a better solution to ...?
- What does this mean to you and how does it affect others?
- Do you think ... is a good thing or a bad thing.
- Is there anything that would need attention?
- How would you feel if ...?
- How do know you are right?
- Give an opinion on ... and justify it.
- How are the conclusions supported by the data/facts/evidence? Explain.
- Which ... is the best and why do you think so?
- Was the argument convincing? Why?
- Was this experiment well designed? Justify.
- Is there anything wrong with this solution? If so, how would this be solved?
- What more needs to be known or done to understand or do this better?
- How is this different from what you have read or done?

Appendix 11j: Group Development

(Adapted from Tuckman & Jensen, 1997 and Risdon and others 2002)

To be called a group, the members of the group must interact with one another, share goals or objectives, be socially attracted to one another and share an identity that is different from the other groups. The benefit of working in groups is that each member of the group can combine their talents and provide solutions that would be better than one single solution. There is also the possibility of delegating responsibilities to group members. Brace Tuckman (1965) developed a simple four stage model of team development that has been accepted as part of thinking about how teams develop. His model has become the staple of group dynamics. Tuckman has identified the four stages of team development as: Forming, storming, norming, and performing. He later added a fifth stage to it (Tuckman & Jensen, 1977), the adjourning phase. The phases are not to be perceived as sequential, because groups are messy, and cycle through the phases throughout their process. Risdon and others (2002) have adapted the four stages in their facilitation of small groups for PBL.

1. Forming

This is the stage when the group comes together. Personal relations are characterised by dependence. Group members at this stage have a desire for acceptance by the group and also a need to know that the group is safe. Members look to group leader for guidance and direction. They set about gathering impressions and data about the similarities and differences among them and forming preferences for future sub-grouping. Everyone is very polite and conflict is seldom voiced directly. Rules of behaviour are to keep things simple and avoid controversy. During this stage formalities are preserved and members are treated as strangers. Students at this stage are normally pretending to get on or get along with others. Individuals at this stage are gathering information and impressions about each other and the scope of the task and how to approach it. Members take a wait and see approach. Leaders may be allowed to lead, but that does not guarantee support. The process is driven by the leader. Individuals are not clear about their contributions. It is a mainly get to know you stage. Trust may start to be built. The avoidance of conflicts and threats means that not much gets done.

The major task functions concern orientation. This is an important stage because it serves to clarify the team's mission and bond team members in the group. Groups that pay attention to building relationships as well as focusing on the task tend to do better than those that skip over relationship building. Members attempt to become oriented to the tasks as well as to one another. Discussion centres around deficiency in the scope of the task, how to approach it. In order to progress to the next stage, members must relinquish the comfort of non-threatening topics and risk the possibility of conflict.

During this stage, tutors must provide a lot of direction to students. Students would expect guidance from the tutor. It is important for tutor to be clear, pointing out when things go right, helping students understand how their behaviour fits in with the tasks of the group, All of these are essential to building the trust necessary to function smoothly further down the line.

Questions Members Often Ask Themselves

There are many questions, concerns, and fears that the members will be experiencing during this stage. Among these are some of the following:

- Am I considered to be important in the group?
- What will I achieve here?
- Will the group accept or reject me?
- What will the group session like?
- Am I different from the other people?
- Will I be pressured to do things?
- Will I have to take risks?
- How will the group be different from other groups?

Concerns and Fears

- Will the other members of the group like me?
- Do I appear stupid to them?
- What will happen if I open out to these people?
- Will I appear nervous and frightened to the others?
- Will I embarrass and make a fool of myself?
- What will happen if they find out what I am really like?
- I am frightened that I will become passive and withdrawn.
- What will I do if I am asked to do things I do not want?
- Will the group attack me?

According to Risdon and others (2002), characteristics of initial stage are:

- Impatience to get the ball rolling.
- Silence and awkwardness.

- Having a tendency to talk about others and things outside of group.
- Confusion about what everybody is supposed to be doing.
- Central issue is trust versus mistrust.
- Testing of each other and of the leaders.
- Request for greater leader involvement.
- Safe talking.
- Having high anxiety.
- Competing for informal leadership.

Tutor's Role

The tutor's role during this stage is to review individual conflicts in terms of task if there is any. There may initially be a lack of structure and purpose in the deliberations. Impose both in terms of the task. There may be disputes between alternative courses of action, negotiate in terms of tasks.

We concur with Risdon and others (2002) that trust is a key issue in a newly formed group. It is important for the tutor to help build trust by:

- Reminding students of the importance of group working.
- Remaining neutral—not displaying any vested interest in one person or another or one solution over another.
- Being clear about the ground rules for the group.
- Making task expectations clear to the students.
- Stressing the importance of active participation by each member of the group.
- Modelling warm personal regard and respect for all group members.
- Providing positive feedback when things go well.
- Listening carefully.
- Alleviating fears and anxiety among members
- Showing patience and care.

2. Storming

This is the stage when members are letting down the politeness barrier and trying to get down to the issues even if tempers flare up The storming stage is characterised by competition and conflict in the personal-relations dimension and organisation in the task-functions dimension. Conflicts will result as the group members attempt to organise tasks. Individuals have to bend and mould their feelings, ideas, attitudes, and beliefs to suit the group organisation. Because of fear of exposure or fear of failure, there will be an increased desire for structural clarification and commitment.

Although conflicts may not surface as group issues, they do exist. Questions may arise as to who is going to be responsible for what, what the rules are, what the reward system is, and what criteria for evaluation. These conflicts reflect our leadership, structure, power, and authority. Some members may remain completely silent, while others attempt to dominate because of the discomfort generated at this stage. Members also compete for position as they try to establish themselves in relation to others in group. Members will try to seek for clarification of purposes. There will be plenty of uncertainties. Cliques and factions form. There may be a power struggle. The process is likely to break down until conflicts are resolved. Decisions are hard to make. Members are not willing to give way. Compromise is the likely outcome. It is important for members to focus on goals in order avoid distraction from relationship and emotional issues.

Tutor's Role in Storming

Recognising and naming conflicts as they arise is a vital role of the tutors. According to Risdon and others (2002), the evaluation time of the tutorial group is the ideal time to surface conflicts, normalise them as necessary to groups ongoing evolution, and help the group to find ways to meet everyone's needs. The recommended solution will be a win-win one because it helps the group to continue deepening trust and learning.

During this stage, the tutor may need to provide clarification or support to individual members if they are unsure or insecure about their own role within the group. It is important for tutors to make sure that no member is treated unfairly or harshly. Group members must move from a testing and proving mentality to a problem solving mentality in order to progress to the next stage. Tutor must have the ability to listen in order to help groups move on to the next stage.

3. Norming

Norming happens when the team agrees on a method of operating. Interpersonal relations are characterised by cohesion. Group members are engaged in active acknowledgment of all members' contributions, community building and maintenance, and solving of group issues. Members are willing to change their preconceived ideas or opinions on the basis of facts presented by other members, and they actively ask questions of one another. Leadership is shared, and cliques dissolve. When members begin to know and identify with-one another, the level of trust in their personal relations contributes to the development of group cohesion. It is during this stage of development that people feel part of the team and realise that they can achieve work if they accept other members and are willing to reconcile their opinions with greater need of the team. Conflicts and mistrust are replaced by co-operation and collaboration. Roles and responsibilities are clear and accepted. Major decisions are made by group agreement. Commitments and unity are strong. The team may engage in fun and social activities.

The major task function of stage three is the data flow between group members: They share feelings and ideas, solicit and give feedback to one another, and explore actions related to the task. Creativity is high. If this stage of data flow and cohesion is attained by the group members, their interactions are characterized by openness and sharing of information on both a personal and task level. They feel good about being part of an effective group. The major drawback of the norming stage is that members may begin to fear the inevitable future break up of the group; they may resist change of any sort.

Tutor's Role in Norming

The group is functioning independently at this point. However, the tutor should stay engaged, tracking group function and offering corrective feedback when necessary. Because there are fewer active facilitation demands by the students, the expert tutor may be tempted to direct the content of the group's learning. Resist the temptation to do it.

4. Performing

The performing stage is not reached by all groups. If group members are able to evolve to stage four, their capacity, range, and depth of personal relations expand to true interdependence. In this stage, people can work independently, in subgroups, or as a total unit with equal facility. Their roles and authorities dynamically adjust to the changing needs of the group and individuals. Stage four is marked by interdependence in personal relations and problem solving in the realm of task functions. By now, the group should be most productive. Individual members have become self-assured, and the need for group approval is past. Members are both highly task-oriented and highly people-oriented. There is unity: group identity is complete, group morale is high, and group loyalty is intense.

The task function becomes genuine problem solving, leading toward optimal solutions and optimum group development. There is support for experimentation in solving problems and an emphasis on achievement. The overall goal is productivity through problem solving and work. The high degree of comfort means that all the energy of the group can be directed towards the task(s) in hand. Teams begin to operate on higher levels of trust as loyalty and relationships develop. Decision making becomes easier. Some decisions are delegated to sub-groups or individuals. This is the reaching the team goal stage. The team is able to manage more complex tasks and cope with greater change. This stage can lead to a return to the former stage as group membership changes or a new forming stage as the group gets competent. On the other hand it may lead to the adjoining stage as the group successfully reaches its goals and completes its work. This stage may not be reached in the PBL tutorial.

5. Adjoining Stage

Tuckman added this final stage ten years after developing the four stages. Tuckman's final stage, adjourning (Tuckman & Jensen, 1977), involves the termination of task behaviours and disengagement from relationships. A planned conclusion usually includes recognition for participation and achievement and an opportunity for members to say personal goodbyes. Concluding a group can create some apprehension—in effect, a minor crisis. The termination of the group is a regressive movement from giving up control to giving up inclusion in the group. The most effective interventions in this stage are those that facilitate task termination and the disengagement process.

In the real word, groups are constantly forming and changing. Each time that happens, the groups move to a different stage. A group may be happy in the norming or performing stage, but a new members' arrival may force the group back into storming. Leaders should be aware of this and try to help the group to get back to performing as quickly as possible.

References

Risdon, C., Braley, D., & Gordon N. (2002). *Facilitating small groups: PBL learning. Desired tutor competencies.* Retrieved from http://www.fhs.mcmaster.ca/facdev/Small%20group%20tutoring%20competencies.pdf

Tuckman, B. (1965). Development sequence in small groups. *Psychological Bulletin, 63,* 384-300.

Tuckman, B., & Jensen, M. (1977). Stages of small group development. *Group and Organisational Studies*, 2, 412-427.

Appendix 11k: Guidelines for Effective Group Process

Group exists on two levels; the task (what the group is trying to accomplish) and the interpersonal process (how they communicate and function whilst going about the tasks) (Ridson et al., 2003). Group process is how members work together to get things done. Through group process, observation and analysis can help identify problems early to avoid the need for a major overhaul as the group progresses. Process refers to how a group works together. Process includes how members talk to each other, how they identify and solve problems, how they make decisions, and how they handle conflict. Group processing activities help to build team skills, allow students to reflect on their own learning process and outcomes. It also provides tutors with continuous feedback.

Group processing involves elements of leadership, communication, decision making, and conflict resolution. In PBL, it is important for tutors and students to monitor individual and group progress. According to Creighton (2005), there are group processes techniques designed that can help groups to work more effectively in meeting. Creighton believes that groups that use group process procedures are more satisfied with their decisions and more committed to their implementation.

Effective group takes a closer look at how members of a group work together, which roles they fill and whether members are contributing equally. Features of an effective group are:

- All members work toward the goals of the group. All have a shared vision and constantly work to have a good process that they believe leads to maximised learning for every member of the group.
- The working atmosphere is comfortable where there is no obvious tension.
- The task of the group is well understood and accepted by all members.
- Members should do self-critiques.
- Members should do their homework. Prepare in advance for meetings.
- Members of the group are attracted to each other and are loyal to each other.
- Recognise that diversity of a group is one of its strengths.
- The group has a timeline for the project.
- Sharing responsibility for outcomes throughout the group.

- A shared belief in the value of collaborative practice and collaborative learning.

- Members of the group are highly motivated to abide by major values and to achieve important goals of group.

- Members will do all they can at all times to help the group to achieve its central objectives.

- The group is eager to help other members of the group to develop their full potential.

- Where members feel free and secure to make decisions that seem appropriate to them because the goals and philosophy of operation are clearly understood by each member and provide a solid base for making decisions.

- Where everyone participates.

- Where the group plans for meeting, record decisions and keep records of progress.

- Where the group confronts difficulties.

- Share success and celebrate achievements.

- Members have a high degree of trust and confidence in each other.

- All interaction, problem solving, decision making activities of the group occur in a supportive atmosphere.

- Other members of the group will give a member the help need to accomplish successfully the goals set for that person.

- Group knows and uses group process behaviour such as:

  - Group members value differences.

  - Ensure commitment levels remain high.

  - Members focus on content and process.

  - Members communicate directly and clearly with each other.

  - Learn and practice specific roles.

  - Members sense when things are not going well and make efforts to self-correct.

  - Members stay systematic and focused.

  - Ask for clarification instead of letting discussion go on.

  - Members do not pre judge each other.

  - Decisions are made by a kind of consensus.

  - There is little evidence of a struggle for power.

  - Group constantly examines how well it is going and tackles problems that are interfering with its operation.

- Valuing each others contribution, consciously learning from each other.

- Members feel free to express their feelings.

- Check on progress.

- Each member of the group has the right to be heard without interruption; the right to ask questions: the right to his or her opinion; the responsibility to respect others; the right to confidentially and the right to be silent.

- Establish and agree on ground rules for participants.

Ground Rules for PBL Participants

Many students have had negative experiences of group work. They generally perceived it as they do the work and others get the credit for it. It is important that each student be held individually responsible for his or her own performance. When each student group takes this seriously, "free riders" are discouraged and contributors to the group effort are rewarded. To do this requires that there should be ground rules concerning group work that all students must adhere to. These are:

- Come prepared with work done during self-directed learning.

- Be punctual.

- Turn off all mobile phones.

- Be courteous.

- Respect each other's ideas.

- Show respect for each other.

- Show professional behaviour.

- Ask questions of each other.

- Share knowledge.

- Keep discussions focused.

- Give a brief of a copy of learning issues to each member of group.

- Come prepared to discuss what is known and raise questions.

- Be cooperative.

- Listen attentively to the others when they speak.

- Be prepared to contribute equally with other members.

- Make decisions by consensus.
- Disagree openly with any group member, but in an agreeable manner.
- Give credit to other people's ideas.
- Actively participate in all discussion.
- Do not dominate the discussion.
- Allow other members to speak and contribute.
- Speak clearly.
- No negative comments regarding other thoughts/ opinions, especially with regard to expressed values.
- Value differences.
- Be sensitive to learning needs of other group members.
- Listen carefully to what is said, do not take concerns expressed by tasks personally.
- Complete assignments thoroughly and on time.
- Notify group members of absences.
- Do not rush others when they speak.
- Do not compete, but share learning.
- Ask what is confusing to you.
- You can disagree intellectually, but must not take it personally.
- Argue on points based on the overall goal of the group, not for serving self-interests.
- Help to make the group a functional one.
- Be prepared to give honest feedback and constructive criticism of performance in group and preparation for group activities.
- Attempt to make the suggested changes, ask for feedback on redirection.
- Do you very best to make each session function well and productive.
- When ground-rules are violated by one or more students, the group will not ignore it, and will invoke the appropriate consequences.

Besides the above ground rules there should be roles for each of the student in the group. This means that everyone should be a Researcher, Communicator, a Questioner, and a Supporter.

- Researcher (the role every one takes). A researcher's role is to locate resources, read, analyse, and evaluate the information by referring back to the learning issues identified to sort the relevant information from the useless information. Each week, learning objective(s) are identified for research.

- Reporter (all students take part). Each member of the group is responsible for reporting back what he or she has learned from their research to the group.

- Questioner (everyone). Each student is expected to ask questions that challenges group consensus, and calls for alternative ideas.

- Supporter (everyone). This is the role for everyone of the group. The role involves looking after people in the group, being friendly and approachable, and ready to help out when someone is in trouble.

There are also roles that some of the members have to carry out to facilitate the group process for it to work effectively. There are two students taking different roles during the tutorial process. These are the roles of Facilitator and the Scribe. Each group member should perform the other roles as a Researcher, Communicator, a Questioner, and a Supporter.

- Facilitator (one person nominated each tutorial). The role of the facilitator is to maintain the group's focus, motivation, and drive. The Facilitator also has a reflective role. It is the role of the facilitator to summarise and evaluate the work already done. He or she also checks that everyone in the group understands and is involved with the problem. The facilitator should make sure that objectives are met and each person is clear about what decisions have been made, and what their individual responsibilities are. It is the responsibility of the facilitator to watch how the group works together to solve the problem using the PBL chart. The process observer also notes how well the PBL steps were followed, and notes where the group's behaviour is unsatisfactory. At the end of the meeting, the facilitator will briefly summarise his/her observations and ask for strategies that the group can implement to improve the performance.

- Scribe (one person is assigned this role). The Scribe acts as reporter by writing the group's thoughts, decisions, and processes. He or she is responsible for confirming that the group agrees on what is written, and for checking back on decisions that have already been made. The Scribe also keeps information about assignments, strategies, important issues, data, and group records.

Dealing with members of a group is a complex process, because each individual has a particular and unique personality style that has been shaped by their experiences in life. It is important for tutors of PBL to understand group process in order to resolve conflicts within the groups.

Getting to know each other is crucial in group process and it is not a fast process. A healthy group has a balance between task and process. If there is mostly task and little process, the friction between members will erupt into communications problems and the resulting conflicts keep tasks from moving forward. Conversely, too much process and everybody spends much of their time in meetings and the tasks that need doing languish (Sandelin, 1997). According to Sandelin, we need process to determine the direction to go and how to work together, and task orientation to accomplish all the jobs needed.

Also, according to Sandelin (1997), conflicts arising between processes and tasks come from personality styles. A task oriented person is a person who gets great pleasure in getting results, whereas a process oriented person is one who gets pleasure from working with people. Sandelin believes that an ideal group should have a mixture of styles.

One of the essential issues concerning group process is that of sharing feelings. There may be bad feelings, as they do not get talked about. Sandelin (1997) suggests a feeling cycles dialogue to help everyone express how they are feeling.

Active listening is another important skill in group process as it can enhance communication. In active listening, one listens carefully and then paraphrases back what has been heard, with the goal of supporting and drawing out the feelings of the speaker. It validates a person's feelings and encourages them to fully communicate. The goal of active listening is to help clarify the feeling and behind the words. Active listening creates a supportive bond between the speaker and the listener. The speaker is encouraged to express feelings honestly because there is no threat of criticism or judgement.

Another issue of which groups should be aware is triangulation; that is, talking about others when they are not present. The aim of triangulation is to degrade the person not present. Malicious triangulation is a very dysfunctional behaviour and one of the worst things that can happen in a group. It undermines relationships in a huge way and creates an atmosphere of distrust, disrespect, and paranoia. Malicious gossip and character assassination must be avoided at all costs in group processes.

Resolving Conflicts

It is inevitable that groups meet conflicts and miscommunication. However, it is important to define a process that resolves problems and encourages members to talk about the issues under conflict in a controlled and reasonable way. Ignoring conflicts between individuals will find conflicts coming into meetings as hidden agendas. Interpersonal conflicts usually start out as poor communication. According to Sandelin (1997), the more frank and open we are whilst communicating, the less conflict will exist and less severe it will be. Some conflicts are not resolvable and it is important to simply respectfully accept the differences. Following are some conflict resolution strategies, adapted from Sandelin (1997):

- Learn to identify what is needed by another person and learn how to gracefully ask another person to define what they need.

- A key question in working with conflict is "Why?" Why are you so angry? Why do you feel so strongly about this? Learn to ask for clarification when an issue becomes conflict.

- Determine whether the disagreement is over facts, or the respective feelings about the facts. Ask questions to discover the underlying assumptions, values, and attitudes.

- Do not make it personal. If you disagree about an idea or concept, frame the discussion around the idea, not the person.

- Try reversing the roles. Agree to argue the other side for fifteen minutes and then express the other viewpoints as persuasively as you can.

- Is it really an either/or issue? Put both sides away and brainstorm other ideas.

- Do a deliberate defocusing by temporarily adjourning the meeting for two hours.

- Rather than try to find the right answer, throw out the bad answers—the things you agree will not work. This might narrow the focus and also bring out something you had not thought of before.

- If personal behaviour problems occur in a group, it is a good idea to have a mediator to help the group.

References

Creighton, J. L. (2004). *Using small group process techniques to improve effectiveness*. Effective Meeting Com. Retrieved from http://www.candclnc.com

Risdon, C., Braley, D., & Gordon, N. (2002). *Facilitating small groups: PBL learning Desired tutor competencies* Retrieved from http://www.fhs.mcmaster.ca/facdev/Small%20group%20tutoring%20competencies.pdf

Sandelin, R. (1997). *Interpersonal skills and conflict resolution.* Community Resource Guide.

Appendix 11l: Group Formation

Group size varies between four and seven members. We recommend a group of no more than six, although four would be our ideal size. Four is ideal because it is large enough to contain students who will bring diverse experiences, opinions, and learning styles to the group. The size is not so big that a member can hide and do nothing. All should carry out their fair share of the workload. A group of four also has the benefit of easy pairing formation within the group.

It is our belief that a group should be heterogeneous in ability. The disadvantages of having only weak students are obvious. A group of only strong students is equally undesirable, as this group would have an unfair advantage over other groups in the class. We found that there were more interactions between students of a mixed ability. The weaker students gained from seeing how better students studied and approached problems. The stronger students gained a deeper understanding of the subject by teaching it to the others. Group formation should promote course goals, sound learning theory, and philosophical convictions (Mills & Cottell, 1998).

Besides the reasons given for heterogeneity in ability, we believe that it is also important to deliberately mix students based on achievement level, gender, ethnicity, and cultural background. Such grouping will permit students to work constructively with varied individuals who will bring different strengths and approaches to solving problems. Besides success with immediate tasks, positive interactions with the diverse members of the group also prepare students for the modern workplace and society as a whole.

Although students would prefer to choose people they know and like for members of their groups, it is important to explain to the students our rationale for grouping them as we do. Our own procedure for placing students in groups is firstly to determine the make up of the group. A group of four to six is our choice. If possible we always make sure that there will be a female among the group. From our experience we found that a female presence had a positive impact on the group as a whole. It should be noted that in computing and engineering subjects the number of females to males is usually quite small, so it is not always possible to put a female into every group. In other subject areas, the reverse may be true. We would strongly resist the temptation to form an all-female group from the few females we have in our classes.

As our students came from different countries and cultures, we decided to reflect this in our groupings by choosing members from each of the cultures and nationalities. For example, we might have a local English student, a Greek, a Chinese, and an Indian, any one of whom may be female. In traditional lecture-based learning, these different cultural groups seldom mix, each preferring to form groups of their own particular background. Initially students resisted the formation of the groups in this manner. It was important to explain to the students why we had taken the action we had. With our encouragement, the students reluctantly adopted the groups.

Another useful factor when choosing members for a group concerns age. We found it useful to put people of different ages together. Having a member of the team who is more mature helps to keep the group motivated and stimulates learning.

Having different members of the group from different cultures also helped students to see problems from different perspectives. Students found the experience of working in a heterogeneous and diverse group enhanced their academic as well as cultural aspects of their lives.

Reference

Mills, B. J., & Cottell, P. G. (1998). *Cooperative learning in higher education faculty.* Phoenix: American Council of Education/Oryx Press

Appendix 11m: Ways to Improve Social Support in Groups

(Adapted from Neil & Dias, 2002).

- Establish a code of conduct developed by the group.

- Discuss group issues only—only discuss problems concerning group issues, not individuals in the group. If there are any problems between individuals, then these should be sorted out before or after group discussions, on their own or with the tutor. Positive comments about individuals are acceptable.

- Model supportive behaviour—it is important to show students how tutors behave.

- Make positive comments during sessions. Complement individual members for their contributions when facilitating.

- Early intervention—when negative social behaviour starts to develop, act to change the pattern earlier rather than later.

- Individual counselling—take someone who is not socially supporting the group aside and talk with them about ways in which they can be more positively involved through the program.

- Identify strengths and challenges—ask students to identify the strengths of a group and draw these in a wide circle. Then ask students what challenges the group faces and write them in the middle. Explain that the group has enough strength to hold itself together and to solve the challenges. The challenges the group faces are opportunities (in the middle). As each of these opportunities is dealt with, it becomes a strength of the group.

- Line up—a very controversial and socially challenging task. Ask the students to line themselves up in order from the student who is contributing most to the group through to the one who is contributing least. Once the students agree on a line-up, then say that each student will get a chance to choose another student whom they believe should move further up towards the student who contributes most. Debrief.

- Anonymous Positive Feedback—have everyone stick a blank sheet of paper on their backs. Students are then asked to mill around and write honest, positive feedback onto these sheets of paper. Students can later read and discuss the feedback they received.

- Social Gathering—suggest to students what they would like to do together socially and how they could get to know one another better.

Reference

Neil, J. H., & Dias, K. L. (2002). *Social support helps people grow.* University of New Hampshire and Northern Territory University.

Appendix 11n: Effective Communication

To understand effective communication, it is useful to have some knowledge of the sender and receiver in the communication process. The sender of the information has to be aware of certain variables when communicating with another person. We believe that the crucial variables to the PBL process are: the sender's communication skills, the sender's attitudes, and the feedback received by the sender. The communication skills of the sender that are important for effective communication include listening and speaking.

Listening Skills

Listening skills are important for effective communication to occur. According to the Foundation Coalition (2004), effective listening involves the following skills: Active listening, perspective taking, understanding the message, maintaining neutrality, understanding position vs. interests and managing one's emotions.

Active listening is a communication procedure wherein the listener uses non-verbal behaviour, such as eye contact and gestures, as well as verbal behaviour, including open-ended questions, tone of voice, restatements and summaries to demonstrate to the speaker that he or she is being heard.

Perception is one's viewpoint or understanding of a situation. Perspective taking is being able to understand (but not necessarily agree with) another's point of view. Understanding the message is necessary because we think four or five times faster than people talk, therefore we can invest additional capacity while listening to interpret what we hear and look for underlying meaning.

Maintaining neutrality means listening without judgement. It is a valuable skill. Understanding positions is another skill in effective listening. A position, point of view, or a specific solution that a party proposes to meet their interests is likely to be concrete and explicit, often involving a demand or threat and leaving little room for discussion. An essential activity is for people to move beyond positions in order to understand one another's underlying interests and needs.

Managing emotion is important because emotion can enhance the communication process or get in the way of effective communication.

Effective listening involves:

- Listening openly and with empathy to the other person.
- Attending to non-verbal clues such as body language, listening between the lines.
- Using multiple techniques to understand the speaker (ask, rephrase, and repeat).
- Communicating your feelings.
- Acknowledging what is said, but not totally controlling the conversation.
- Learning supportive, not one-way listening.
- Judging the content, not the sender.
- Comprehending before making judgement.
- Asking the other person for as many details as they can provide.

- Paraphrasing what the speaker is saying to make sure you understand what is said and checking for understanding.
- Not reacting to emotional words, but interpreting their purpose.

Constructive Feedback

Feedback is critical for all members of groups. There is a big difference between constructive and destructive criticism. Effective feedback is essential for group effectiveness. Effective feedback can be reinforcing if given properly. Some people are reluctant to give feedback for fear of causing embarrassment, fear of an emotional reaction, discomfort and an inability to handle the reaction. Providing feedback to a member of the group who has presented and idea can be a valuable exercise. When communicating, it is important that we learn to be effective, both in the way we receive feedback from others and the way we give feedback. No person wants to have others disagree with them. However, part of effective communication is being able to productively engage in conflict and to be able to give and receive constructive criticism. According to the Foundation Coalition (2004), there are four things we can do when someone disagrees with us, our opinion, or a proposed solution:

- Evaluate if we are taking the constructive criticism personally.
- Get ourselves involved in "continuous improvement mode," that is, this feedback is information that can help us become better—better at the substance of the issue, or better at interpersonal skills.
- Find something that we can agree upon and express that agreement.
- Do not assume that you know what the other person thinks or feels.

Giving Feedback to Group Members

- When giving feedback to group members, start with something supportive. Point out where we agree with him/her.
- State our opinion using "I statements" I statements are always carefully phrased so that we are acknowledging our point of view with no hint of negativity toward the opinion of the recipient. An example of an "I" statement is: "When you interrupt" (specific behaviour), "I feel you do not value my input to the group," (expression of your thought or feelings) "and I would like you not to interrupt me when I am speaking." (behaviour-change request).
- Monitor our tone of voice and body language.

It is important to remind students of the above communication information and skills that they need in order to communicate effectively with the members of their groups. Students must make conscious efforts at continually practising these important communication skills.

Reference

The Foundation Coalition (2004). Effective interpersonal/intrateam communication. Retrieved from http://www.foundation.org

Appendix 11o: Ways to Enhance Motivation

To encourage students to become self-motivated independent learners, tutors can do the following:

- Cultivate a relationship that allows students to trust you.
- Give frequent positive feedback that supports student belief that they can do well.
- Help students relate to the material and connect it to real life.
- Provide students with a sense of belonging.
- Be enthusiastic about your subject.
- Emphasise mastery and learning instead of grades.
- Create an open and positive atmosphere.
- Assign tasks that are neither too easy nor too difficult.
- Find out what motivates students.
- Help students to feel that they are valued members of the group.
- Determine why students are not working.
- Encourage students to take active participation in learning.
- Help students set achievable goals for themselves.
- Make learning fun and exciting.
- Create a caring and supportive environment for learning.
- Find out about students' interests, hobbies, career goals and experiences.
- Challenge students with higher-order thinking activities.
- Strengthen students' self-motivation.

- Encourage interaction among students.
- Make learning visible.
- Help students clarify and reflect upon their ideas.
- Let students have a say in choosing what will be studied.
- Provide opportunities for students to evaluate their own performance.
- Avoid giving in to students pleas for the answer to a problem.
- Satisfy student needs.
- Provide ongoing constructive feedback.
- Relate content to students' interests.
- Make assignments or problems interesting and fun in order to encourage participation.
- Challenge students' ideas.
- Provide students with a sense of achievement.
- Encourage students to make decisions about their own learning.
- Encourage students to think.

Appendix 11p: Extract from Students' Feedback; 2004/5 Cohort

Scott Dow

BSc (Hons) Computing Science

The PBL module taught me a completely new way to teach and learn. Using PBL is a very difficult concept to grasp early-on but, having learnt it, the value of it is immediately apparent. For the basis of our module we were split into groups along with students with many differing backgrounds and cultures. We were then set a task that would ordinarily be much too difficult to complete on our own. This forces the group to work together to solve that task.

My own project was implemented using PBL in the structure. This allowed me as an individual to also apply this model to my own work. In doing so I feel that I was able to produce a project that was far above anything I could have produced without PBL. It is my opinion that this module should be compulsory for every entry student at university as, equipped with this knowledge from the beginning; students would be able to perform much, much better throughout their time in education.

PBL also allows for much better retention of the course materials. During the exam I had little or no difficulty in recalling what I needed to know to answer the questions. Speaking to my fellow students they also felt the same way. It seemed as if the exam was easier, when in fact, with hindsight it was just that our knowledge was better having learnt it for ourselves.

So, as a final thought I would recommend PBL to anyone considering taking the subject. It will equip you with a means to learn that is very different, but also much better than anything you will have experienced previously. Although it involves much more work, in the long-term you will reap the benefits of this method. Already, the courseware I implemented using the methods discussed have seen improvements in the students using it at technical high school. I will continue to use the methods, not only in teaching but in my own personal and professional development. This is, without a doubt, the single most valuable subject I have studied at university in four years and anyone not taking it has truly missed out on a very valuable experience.

Mathew Cartwight

BSc (Hons) Computing Science

From a more personal opinion this module has helped me complete my final year dissertation at university. My background has not been in computing and it was a struggle to meet the standards required of me, but after undertaking the PBL module, I have now completed a final year dissertation which I honestly did not think was possible.

Sajid Bashir

BSc (Hons) Internet Technology student

Overall I can confidently say that I have acquired a skill that I will use for the rest of my life. I knew that when I came to university I will walk away with many skills but not such a beneficial skill as PBL. PBL has provided me with a skill that has made me a confident person, it has provided me with the required knowledge I needed before I undertake a full time job. One of the things I was dreading after university was taking on a job, I thought I might not be able to achieve the tasks that were given to me. However, now that I have acquired this skill of PBL I can confidently say that I am looking forward to the working world.

Asif Khalil

BSc Computing Science Student

At first this method of learning seemed very difficult and challenging because it was a completely new approach. At that time I did not realise how useful PBL will be, not only for the given problem but also how the same method could be applied to other areas of my studies, fundamentally in tackling my final year project. The research was then challenged by being thoroughly questioned in every aspect, this demonstrated what knowledge I had learned and understood. I found this method of learning very effective in increasing self motivation as I enjoyed facing the challenge, as well as increasing the knowledge gained on a wider scope.

My final year project which was an "Interactive Training Package" for Hanson Building Products—Hoveringham, adopted the PBL method. My final year project supervisor challenged me on the research around the problem area which resulted in a successful project.

As I found this learning environment very beneficial and interesting, I proposed this method of PBL to the senior staff at Hanson Building Products—Hoveringham. They seemed very keen in adopting this approach in the development of their production team "Problem Based Learning is considered to be a very useful learning method for students. At Hanson-Hoveringham we can adopt the PBL method, integrating it with our current training at different levels of management including the production team" (Orr, 2005). Works Manager, Hanson Building Products Hoveringham. Training new or existing employees is another area that was recognised to be benefited by PBL. "At Hanson-Hoveringham we are always exploring new methods and techniques to improve our existing training system, I feel a learning environment such as Problem Based Learning would be excellent to incorporate in the learning process involved in training employees, as greater knowledge and understanding will be gained" (Zar, 2005) . Quality Development Manager, Hanson Building Products Hoveringham.

On reflection PBL has helped me to improve many of my existing skills including; independent research and linking different areas of research by recognising the key factors. This has aided in good time management and improving my organisation skills as I was able to recognise at a very early stage what type of research was required to solve the problem hence, resulting in solving the project efficiently and effectively. As my first PBL project was in a team environment, good communication between team members was essential, as a result my communication skills have improved and I feel I am more confident in expressing my views and sharing my knowledge with my colleagues.

I feel PBL can be easily adapted into any field of learning; learners will be benefited by increasing their knowledge with new skills as well as improving existing skills. This change was recognised as my own average grade increased in my final year compared to the two previous years at university.

Khoo Kok Lung

BSc (Hons) Computing Science

Unlike other module class that I have attended before, I felt that this module is not only talking about a particular subject area but it broadly teaches doing proper research, guides me in handling my FYP wholly and helps me to find and improve the way I learn and study. Having attended this lesson I also have learnt articulating with a group of my friends and the lecturer, giving me a lot of knowledge in gaining and improving critical thinking skills in the process of struggling with the actual problem. During the project development, PBL have helped me to develop critical thinking skills where I can:

- *Clearly define a problem.*
- *Develop alternative theories.*
- *Access, evaluate, and utilize data from a variety of sources.*
- *Alter theories given new information.*
- *Develop clearly stated solutions that fit the problem and its inherent conditions, based upon information and clearly clarified reasoning.*

Chapter XII

Postscript

Keep it exciting and fun! If you want some real advice, look at how young children learn or how your students learn new skills, knowledge, etc. outside the classroom in their hobbies and personal life. It's all problem-based! (Ranald Macdonald)

We hope that by the time you have reached this chapter, you will have become enthusiastic to incorporate principles and practice of PBL into your teaching.

In the chapters of this book, we have tried to explore issues that are central to successfully implementing PBL. There are clearly many differences from the traditional transmission model of teaching, since PBL is fundamentally a different philosophy, based on student enquiry. However, if we set aside labels, it is also clear that there are principles and aspects of PBL practice that are often incorporated in many courses and we would argue that there is a continuum of pedagogical approaches from what might be regarded as *pure* transmission, in the archetypal lecture, through to *pure* research. Problem-based learning is somewhere near the research end.

Analysing and deconstructing problem-based learning in the way that we have in this book is useful in order to explore aspects of the method in some detail. However, it also has some inherent dangers: PBL is a closely coupled system and the components that we have explored in previous chapters are interdependent. The interdependencies within PBL are not the only ones to be considered, unless you are implementing PBL throughout the entire curriculum, it is part of a wider teaching and learning context in your institution, and consequently there are also significant influences from that environment into the problem-based elements.

Since learning is complex, institutional contexts differ widely and PBL changes many aspects of the learning system. We posed the following question to a wide range of PBL researchers and practitioners:

What is the Most Important Advice You Could Give Someone Just Starting to Use PBL?

We received replies from locations as diverse as Australia, Finland, Mexico, Alaska, and the UK, which provided a global perspective.

There were three themes that were prevalent: the importance of preparation; the likelihood of criticism and difficulties; and the need to adapt to your local situation.

Preparation and Planning for Change

Perhaps unsurprisingly, preparation and planning were cited as essential.

Pedro Gordan helpfully identifies four areas for preparation and planning: goals, people, information, and resources, which are also supported by other respondents.

The goals for PBL are usually broader than cognitive objectives, encompassing process skills.

"Be clear about the purpose for introducing PBL and the learning outcomes," recommends Jim Wood.

Linda Dislehorst further emphasises the importance of the learning outcomes in the design of PBL: *"Knowing those outcomes will determine every other piece that goes into the structure of the PBL experience."*

The people dimension is reported as being one of the most problematic: "People have been used in traditional way of teaching for a few thousand years," points out Markku Suni. "Thus, it is rather natural to expect teaching going this way." So, preparing the stakeholders for the change—both staff and students—is critical to success.

The biggest difficulties were reported as being the adaptation of staff, rather more than students. According to David Rawcliffe, "It is difficult for teachers to change, especially for the "experienced" teacher who believe what they have been doing is right."

When implementing curriculum change there is a lot to learn and gathering information from others who have managed this change avoids reinventing the wheel (and overcoming the same difficulties). This can be obtained from published case studies and personal contact through visiting other institutions and inviting consultants into your organisation.

Finally, resources are particularly practical consideration, so preparation and planning the physical resources (rooms), learning resources (library), and financial resources are necessary.

Expect Difficulties and Criticism

The second theme concerned criticism and difficulties, most of which are concerned with the people aspect identified above. PBL is challenging to students and staff alike. Change can bring feelings of insecurity and this can manifest itself as hostility and criticism from both faculty and students.

PBL is utterly unlike most other education [students] will ever have encountered. It entails real engagement and it is pretty well impossible to drift or mug up at the very end of the semester. Students like everything in bite sized chunks these days and PBL gives them an oxen rather than a beef burger. (John Bradbeer)

Faculty resistance can be based on change of role or on concerns that students may not learn particular subject matter unless they are told. Pedro Gordan (personal communication, August 29, 2004) provides a dean's perspective and reports that faculty education can be effective at overcoming these issues:

Case studies are an excellent method of gathering relevant information about PBL. We have done it by using the PBL method to introduce its principles, in a "metalanguage" format, so faculty can learn its fundamentals by experiencing the method.

However, the change of role is not easy, and the difficulty of becoming an effective PBL facilitator was highlighted, but Maria Hirose also identified it as a particularly satisfying aspect for tutors.

Adaptation and Variety

It can be tempting to implement an existing model of PBL by taking it off the shelf from another institution. We have seen examples of this. After all, there would appear to be a good rationale for it: if you adopt a tried and tested approach you would expect to encounter fewer difficulties and save a considerable amount of development time.

However, one of the strongest recommendations from our respondents was to avoid wholesale copying of a model from another institution. There are a number of reasons for this. First, from a change management perspective, ownership of the change by faculty is critical for a successful outcome and this is difficult to achieve if a curriculum and model are transplanted from another institution.

There are many varieties of PBL, but they do not come a la Carte. (Derek Raine)

The second reason for modifying and adapting a PBL model is to make it appropriate for the particular context that you are in. The subject, the institutional culture and resources, and the experience and ability of students are all factors that are important in devising learning experiences that are effective. After all, PBL is consistent with constructivism, which places a strong emphasis on prior experience of the learner.

This does not mean that you should always reinvent the wheel, but adaptation is important so that the teaching and learning model is appropriate and relevant for your students and your faculty.

PBL is not a tool, it is a philosophy. It should not conflict with the learning environment. Thus, workloads and timetables must be consistent; the physical environment must be consistent. (Derek Raine)

Part of the adaptation to the local context involves integrating PBL with other teaching and learning methods. After reading some glowing accounts of the benefits of PBL, you could be forgiven for thinking that all learning should be conducted this way. However, experience would suggest that variety is not only the spice of life, but is good for learning too. Peter French warns:

Be sure that you are not adding to the list of errors from using the method as the only method. True teaching must involve a cross section of educational technologies.

Ranald Macdonald relates this back to the fundamental motivation for examining teaching and learning:

My advice would be not to get too hung up on models, but to look at learning and how best to improve it. This often means include a variety of experiences, including of assessment, rather than some of the rather dry, formulaic approaches to PBL that have appeared, with which students (and staff) readily get bored.

We see this as a critical point; problem-based learning arose out of the aim to improve learning and dissatisfaction with traditional methods. Quite often, when labels are attached to a new method, the original aims can almost be forgotten, and a cult can grow up around the label.

We view PBL as one of the core components of an effective teaching and learning system, a system that is devised and owned by the faculty, adapted from experiences of others to be suitable to their particular environment. We hope that you will have found ideas within this book that you can take and adapt to improve your own practice and your student's learning and enjoyment.

References

Gordan, P. (2004). A *new medicine curriculum in Londrina: The Dean's perspective on the change process*. Personal communication.

Annex A:
Internet Resources

Introduction

This annex contains some useful Internet resources on PBL. This list is by no means an exhaustive one. The aim of listing some useful resources here is to giver readers an idea of where to find institutions that are implementing PBL and to give examples of how PBL is used in different subjects and levels of education.

Useful Reviewed Web Sites

The PBLI site: http://www.pbli.org

Howard Barrows is the director of PBLI. This Web site contains useful information on PBL from the medical school where Barrows worked. It contains useful information for introduction to PBL across various disciplines and educational levels.

Illinois Mathematics and Science Academy: Centre for Problem-Based Learning: http://www.imsa.edu/team/cpbl/cpbl.html

This is an extensive site which contains a large collection of resources, including an interactive problem-based learning experience.

Queen's University at Kingston, Ontario, Canada, K7L 3N6., School of Medicine Problem-Based Learning: http://meds.queensu.ca/medicine/pbl/ pblhome.htm

The school of medicine at Queen's university in Ontario, Canada is a good example of how PBL is used in health science. It provides useful information to how to set up PBL support, student's guides and tutor's guides. There are also PBL links and resources.

Samford University PBL site: http://www.samford.edu/pbl/resources.html

This Web site provides information on the background and development of PBL, the PBL process and links to useful PBL listservs, publications and audiovisual materials together with conferences and other staff development events. It provides a glossary of information about PBL. There are many excellent PBL peer review on-line portfolio that features PBL practitioner's reflection on the design of courses, student learning and evaluation

UK Problem Based Learning Initiatives: http://www.hss.coventry.ac.uk/pbl/

This Web site hosts some trigger materials learning is being used in the UK, together with information about where problem-based learning is used

Universiteit Maastricht PBL-site: http://www.unimaas.nl/pbl/

The University of Maastricht is one of the pioneers of PBL, and this Web site contains a collection of resources including publications, courses , videos , educational projects, consultants, international networks, PBL concepts and Frequently Asked Questions

University of Delaware PBL site: http://www.udel.edu/pbl/

The University of Delaware in Colorado has materials concerning with PBL for Higher education. This site contains a number of resources; sample problems; links to other Web sites, articles, conference announcements. There is a PBL Clearinghouse that offers access to many different PBL problems for various subjects.

Other Useful PBL Web Sites

1. **Deliberations (electronic journal on teaching and learning—follow site to PBL):** http://www.lgu.ac.uk/deliberations/home.html

2. **Distributed Course delivery for Problem Based Learning (San Diego State University):** http://edweb.sdsu.edu/clrit/home.html

3. http://www.dlsweb.rmit.edu.au/eng/beng0001/PBL-LIST/PBL/index.html

4. **McMaster University, Faculty of Health Sciences:** http:// www.fhs.mcmaster.ca/mhsi/problem-.htm

5. **PBL and Engineering Education (some good general information):** http://cleo.eng.monash.edu.au/teaching/learning/centre

6. **Problem-Based Learning in Business Education: Curriculum Design and Implementation Issues:** http://mbawb.cob.ohiou.edu/papers.html

7. **Problem Based Learning Assessment and Research Centre:** http://www.newcastle.edu.au/services/iesd/learndevelop/problarc/index.html

8. **Queen's University, Canada, Problem-Based Learning home page, contains a useful and detailed handbook on PBL:** http://meds.queensu.ca/medicine/pbl/pblhome.htm

9. **South Illinois University School of Medicine—PBL Page:** http://www.pbli.org/

10. **University of Hawaii, John A.Burns School of Medicine:** http://medworld.biomed.hawaii.edu/

11. **University of Mississippi School of Pharmacy Problem-Based Learning Home Page:** http://www.olemiss.edu/courses/pbl/

Useful Mailing Lists and List Servers

There are a number of PBL mailing list servers that provide forums for discussion and sharing of PBL issues. Examples are:

- JISCmail PBL List
  - List Name: PBL
  - List site: http://www.jiscmail.ac.uk/mailinglists/index.htm
- University of Delaware
  - List Name: UD-PBL-UNDERGRAD
  - List Site: http://www.udel.edu/pbl/ud-pbl-undergrad.html
- RMIT
  - List Name: PBL-LIST
  - List Site: http://www.dlsweb.rmit.edu.au/eng/beng0001/PBL-LIST/PBL/index.html
- University of Delaware
  - List Name: UD-PBL-UNDERGRAD
  - List Site: http://www.udel.edu/pbl/ud-pbl-undergrad.html

Annex B: Ace Training Ltd. – Complete Case Study

Introduction

In this annex we collect together the documents relating to the main case study used throughout the book (Ace Training Ltd.). Although much of this material has been incorporated in a number of chapters, collecting all the components together provides coherence. We hope that this example will stimulate you to design your own triggers, and adapt them to your own teaching and learning situation.

The following PBL example occupies the first semester of a second year undergraduate module on computer networking for students studying B.Sc. Information Technology. It reflects work that a network analysts/ designers would be expected to do, though in practice the work would be distributed over a number of different employee roles.

The entire module is designed for a study time of 150 hours, over a 12 week semester. It is designed for teams of four to five students. Student are novices at PBL and are prepared with workshops introducing PBL and team working skills within the first week, prior to introduction of the Problem Statement.

The module comprises three PBL cases:

- PBL1: Requirements Analysis
- PBL2: System Specification
- PBL3: System construction

For each of these PBL cases, we have included the problem-statement as given to students, the facilitator guide and the assessment criteria. The subject-specific learning outcomes related to this case are as follows:

1.   Critically analyse the requirements for a small-scale network.
2.   Synthesise and evaluate a design for a solution to a network requirement.

Since this is the first experience students have of Problem-based Learning, the case is presented as a role play; students initially identify questions that need answering to produce a specification that is complete and unambiguous. The PBL case fits in the "PBL for professional action" model category (Savin-Baden, 2000) though there is quite a large knowledge component in the subject area of computer networking.

Students obtain the information by identifying suitable employees to interview and carrying out the interviews. The employees are role-played by faculty members. Feedback is provided at the requirement specification stage to ensure that they can work from a reasonable set of requirements.

The draft system specifications are also formatively assessed. Summative assessment comprises: Examination (multi-choice questions), Final Proposal, team presentation, practical network demonstration, Individual research hand-outs and peer assessment of team working.

PBL Case 1: Ace Training Ltd.

Problem Statement

Ace Training Ltd. is a small company, which delivers technical computer-training courses at its training centre in Manchester, and on customer premises throughout the UK. It employs a Sales manager, 10 sales staff, two marketing people, and two accounts staff in its head office in Liverpool. The Managing Director (MD), his secretary and switchboard/receptionist are also located there.

At the training centre there are the following employees: a manager, two administrators, one technician and ten instructors.

The sales representatives make the vast majority of sales over the telephone. There is very little use of information technology in the head office. The marketing department has one Apple Macintosh® computer, the accounts department uses one PC running *Sage*® accounting software and the Sales department has one PC for preparing quotes. The MD's secretary also has a computer.

The Managing Director views the current system as inefficient. He has called in your team, as consultants, to advise him. He believes a network for the head office will improve sales performance significantly. Your terms of reference are:

To design and present proposal for purchase, implementation and support of new network for Sales tracking, accounts, and general administration.

This is a sizeable task, despite the small scale of the company. Clearly such factors such as cost of the solution, training and support are required for a comprehensive solution.

There is insufficient information given above to specify the solution precisely. You will need to find out additional information by arranging interviews with appropriate people in the company. You are restricted to two twenty-minute interviews.

Deliverables

1. At the end of the fist session (*week 1*): Submit a *plan* to your tutor, outlining Information you need to obtain from the interviews and learning issues you have generated.

2. Your team should produce a *User Requirements Specification in Week 3* of the module (end of PBL1). The information for this document should be obtained from the problem statement; together with information you obtained by interviews. A template for this specification is available (see module Web site PBL1 information page).

3. Your team should produce a *final proposal in week 11* according to the proposal template (see module Web site PBL1 information page). This will comprise your requirements from PBL1, and solution from PBL2. Your team should present your solution to the board of Ace Training Ltd in week 12. A short *PowerPoint presentation* is expected as well as the written report. The presentation should last 15 minutes, with a further 5 minutes for questions.

4. Your team will demonstrate the network you have constructed after PBL3, in week 11.

Assessment Criteria/Weightings

Assessment criteria will be available from the module Web site.

Further Information

Ace Training Ltd. Business Issues

1.   The company has grown rapidly and a number of problems have arisen that have caused serious inefficiencies in the sales processes. For example: All customer sales records are all kept on paper. Each sales rep keeps a diary and card index of the customers that they are responsible for. This means that the information on a particular customer is difficult to find—especially if their sales rep is not in the office. This inefficiency has led to a number of lost sales opportunities. Since the sales people are largely paid on commission, this has caused low moral (and limited profits). The *ACT!* ™ Contact management software from Sage® group plc. (http://www.sage.com/) has been selected as the preferred product.

2.   A consequence of the new way of working is that maximum downtime of the system must be 2 hrs.

3.   The Training Centre manager often exchanges faxes with the Sales manager.

4.   The Accounts department has an old version of Sage® Accounts, which does not cope with multiple currencies (in particular the Euro).

Scope

The Manchester training centre does not require networking, but the training centre manager will need access to e-mails (via the Internet).

Advice

1.   Analysing information is an important skill. Follow the PBL stages (see module guide); identify issues to clarify from the problem statement, identify information you need to obtain from the company to complete your requirement specification, identify any learning you need to undertake before the interviews. Create a plan, which should be submitted to your tutor at the end of the class.

2. Elect a team leader for this PBL case, and a scribe (secretary).

3. You should also keep records of all meetings (see PBL guidance).

4. Remember team working principles you learned in the PBL introduction workshop and the roles of team leader and scribe. Make sure you involve everyone!

Resources

There are a number of resources available to you:

1. For information about networking technology and terminology, see the course text and resources available on the module Web site.

2. For resources about interviewing skills and information about Ace Training, consult the module Web site.

3. Template for requirement specification (see module Web site).

Facilitator's Guide: Ace Training:
PBL Case 1 – Requirements Analysis

Trigger: See Student's Guide to PBL1

Schedule

See Example 1.

Example 1.

	Class activities	Independent study / submissions
Week 1	Intro to course (plenary lecture) **Intro to PBL1: Requirements Analysis** Explore scenario, generate list of questions / information required for interviews next week. Create plan	Plan interview, locate resources.
Week 2	Role play interviews View, analyze and evaluate Video interviews (technique and information content) Interview Managing Director (20 minutes): receive oral feedback Interview Sales Manager (20 minutes): receive oral feedback	Review findings, construct requirements specification.
Week 3	Sharing/ meeting Review progress; identify any other information required / request from tutor. Finalize requirement specification Review team performance to date	Submit draft requirement specification

Resources

The Module Web site identifies a long list of suitable resources, linked to the PBL case. There are:

- PBL process documentation in the module guide.
- Notes on interviewing techniques.
- An example template for a Requirements Specification.
- Ace Training's software and hardware inventory.
- Ace Training's organization chart.
- Layout of Liverpool office and details of construction.
- Some example forms (invoices, orders) which were once requested by a team. (These are irrelevant.)
- Video of interviews (good and bad technique) with the Accounts department manager.

Background

Following is summary of requirement as an aide memoir for the role plays. Students should work from their own requirements generated at the end of PBL1. Assessment criteria are in the module guide and Web site.

Role play information is included for faculty in *Guide for Sales Manager* and *Guide for Managing Director*. Note, there is a conflict: MD does not want internal email, Sales manager and Accounts Manager do. Students need to acknowledge and discuss approach to resolve this. Different client views are realistic.

Requirements

See Example 2.

Week 1

Aim: Today the aim is to ensure they have explored the problem statement and

1. Elected team leader and scribe for PBL1.
2. Analyzed the problems statement and background to produce an outline list of requirements.

Example 2.

Sales		
1. Contact mgt software, enabling all sales reps to access all client details from their own PC.	2. PC per sales person inc mgr.	
3. E-mail to Manchester via ISP	4. Web site with email enquiry (not e-commerce)	
5. High speed printer	6. Facility for sales reps to produce own quotes / letters	
Accounts		
1. Update Sage to latest Line50 Accounts (Euro & performance issues)	2. 2 x new PC	
3. Printer replacement		
Marketing		
1. Keep iMac / printer, not networked	2. Mailing list in-house (use contact mgt software to generate it).	
General		
1. PC for all staff except Marketing.	2. Security - Personnel data / Sales/ Accounts kept separate. Internet security needed.	
3. All PCs to be networked, current ones to be included if possible.	4. Budget - within GBP40k	
Training Requirements		
1. On-site training for sales, in small groups. Cannot release more than half at a time.	2. General PC training in-house.	
3. Training schedule & plan required.		
Installation requirements		
1. Outside working hours		
Support requirements		
1. Specification for a technician / Web Developer, Inc. qualifications & salary.	2. Maximum down time is half an hour during working day	

3. Identified a list of information that they will need to find out from interview.
4. Explored the Module Web site for resources.
5. Created a plan of who does what and by when.

This is the first time they have done this you need to make sure:

- You give them lots of encouragement.
- They follow the PBL stages systematically (see module guide).
- Everyone is involved.
- They discuss feelings as well as task (at start or end).
- A plan is produced.
- Times are arranged for interviews next week.

Prompt them towards considering the following without directly giving them the topics. If they cannot get there, they need to investigate what is needed in a network.

Possible questions to ask:

1.   What do they need to know about the company? Why?

   •   Company processes, communication, decision making, services & product lifecycles, organisational structures, future plans/ acquisitions, Customer/ partner/ vendor relationships

2.   What sort of things will they have to specify eventually—does this affect questions they will ask?

   •   System software, choice of O/S: what facilities they will require.

   •   Applications: what needed?

   •   Resilience: what does it mean?

   •   Security issues

   •   Networking: Cabling compatibility

   •   Hardware: to support software. Server (see notes on WebCT under resources), Printers, clients.

   •   Training—application

   •   Installation: costs, cable runs, time etc.

   •   Support—after identified O/S

3.   Interviewing—how to do it well?

   They need to think about interviewing.

   •   Is the purpose just to get information? (e.g., impress with your professionalism)

   •   Who should they interview? (They should identify a number of peoples, for different perspectives. It is limited to two so who would be most appropriate?)

   •   What is a good or bad interview?

   •   What sort of questions will you ask?—Do you ask the same questions to all clients? (Would you ask the MD what operating system he wants to use, Linux or Windows?) Why not?

   •   What structure should there be to the interview?

   •   How will you record answers?

I would expect them to plan a meeting to finalize interview questions prior to the interviews. Emphasize that all students must participate in the interview.

Week 2

Aim: Today the aim is for students to practice interview technique, collect useful information and receive formative (oral) feedback on their interview performance.

Video of Accounts Manager Interviews (lecture theatre)

1. Play bad interview and ask students to identify poor technique
2. Play good interview and ask students to identify improvements, in particular the structure (general situation to client problems, to impact of those problems and the value of resolving them)
3. Students can borrow copies of the video to extract information about the Accounts department requirements.

Role Play Interviews

1. Collect role play advice guides for your role as Managing Director or Sales Manager.
2. Use the Interview checklist during interview to determine if they have elicited the appropriate (complete) information, have all taken part, followed a systematic structure, and behaved professionally.
3. Ask them to self assess (briefly) their impression of their performance.
4. Provide oral feedback at end of interview based on your notes.

Grading Criteria: Communication:	Pass	Good Pass	Excellent
C2 Collect appropriate information in a structured manner during an interview.	Asks clear questions in logical manner, mostly open questions.	Clear structure to interview, follows up answers with more detailed exploration.	Includes checkpoint summaries, uses suitable interview model.

Week 3

Aim: Today the aim is for students to review and finalize their requirements specification and to conduct a preliminary team reflection on performance.

Resources

*   Group work checklist for reflection

During facilitated PBL team meeting:

1. Ask them to explain their requirements and to identify any weaknesses and corresponding actions.

2. Conduct discussion about group performance, using the group work feedback sheet.

3. Team to provide constructive feedback to team leader.

4. Elect leader for next PBL case.

5. Ask them to identify and document points for improvement.

6. Refer them to the assessment criteria for the requirement specification.

Grading Criteria:	Pass (threshold)	Good Pass (GP)	Excellent
LO2 Critically analyse the requirements for a small-scale network.	Key appropriate functional and non-functional requirements correctly identified and in appropriate format.	Most requirements identified correctly and in appropriate format, and prioritised appropriately.	Comprehensive list of functional and non-functional requirements unambiguously and correctly identified and in appropriate format, and prioritised appropriately.

M21661A Computer Networks: PBL Case 2: Network System Specification

Introduction

This case follows logically from the first. You should now have a good idea about Ace Training's requirements. These should be documented and form a basis for choosing a system. There are likely to be some minor details that you have not yet pinned down, but you have enough to be able to start identifying a suitable system.

For this case you should choose new chairperson and secretary/ scribe.

Your Problem

To design and present a fully costed and justified proposal for purchase, implementation and support of new network for Sales tracking, marketing and accounts.

Deliverables for PBL2

1. *Each week at the end of class you must submit a plan* to your tutor, showing learning issues, who they are assigned to and target completion date.

2. In PBL2 you will research and develop a solution to meet these requirements and you will submit a *Draft proposal in week 6* according to the proposal template (see module Web site PBL1 information page). You will receive feedback on this and submit a *Final proposal in Week 11*. You will present this proposal to the board of Ace Training Ltd (15 minute PowerPoint presentation) in Week 12.

3. Individual Research Handout (Week 6).

Assessment Criteria/Weightings

Assessment criteria will be available from the module Web site.

Advice: PBL Process (Steps 1-5)

*   Step 1: Make a list of issues that need clarifying. This concerns the outputs from PBL case 1 - is your requirements specification complete, correct and unambiguous? Are you sure?

*   Step 2: Define the problem—This is stated for you above.

*   Step 3: What do you know about the subject (networks) already? In your team, hold a brainstorming session to identify what you know about network systems that is relevant to Ace Training's needs. For example, how can hardware be interconnected to form a network? Are there any alternatives? Similarly, what do you know about software (operating systems and applications) that will met their needs? Are there alternatives here?

*   Step 4: Make a systematic list of what you know. Examine the suggestions the group has produced. Organise the connections and categories, value and sort out what is irrelevant.

Identify what you do not know, and what you need to learn or understand to solve the problem. In order to specify a solution, you need to know about the components and alternatives.

Learning

→≫ Important!

- Step 5: Formulate learning issues (Make a plan)

This is a critical point. It is worth spending some time on this part: if you do not identify clearly constructed research questions as the learning issues, you can waste huge amounts of time.

After identifying what you do not know or what you need to know, you will create a study or work plan that will include all or part of the following steps.

1. Prioritise learning needs
2. Set learning goals and objectives
3. Decide **who will do what, and by when**. *This must be checked by your Tutor before you leave the class.* Decide how/when the individual learning will be shared with the rest of the group.

- **Step 6:** Individual work. You are now ready to complete your study plan. Each member of the group should decide her/his knowledge and learning needs. She/he should organise her/his own way to the new knowledge. Members can work individually or within groups. Again the timescale is tight. You need to clarify your solution to a point that enables you to start building a demonstration system. The class next week will provide you with time for your team meetings, to report back, share and refine any further research you need to do.

End of Class Check

Check and submit a copy of your plan to your Tutor before you leave.

Resources

There are a number of resources available to you:

1. For information about networking technology and terminology, see the course text and resources available on the module Web site.
2. Template for proposal—see module Web site.

Facilitator's Guide: Ace Training: PBL Case 2 – System Specification

Trigger

To design and present a fully costed and justified proposal for purchase, implementation and support of new network for Sales tracking, marketing and accounts.

Schedule

	Class activities	Independent study / submissions
Week 1 (sem week 4)	**Intro to PBL2: System Specification** Generate Learning Issues (using outcome from PBL1 requirements) Create plan	Individual research Produce individual research handout
Week 2	**Sharing/Teach meeting** Review progress, share handouts/ apply to problem. Select next learning issues Create plan	Submit individual handout
Week 3	**Sharing/ Teach meeting** Review progress, share handouts/ apply to problem. Allocate work for proposal Create plan	Submit individual handout
Week 4	**Review proposal & Reflect on progress** Finalize proposal Peer and self assessment.	Submit Draft proposal

Resources

The Module Web site identifies a long list of suitable resources, linked to the PBL case. The course book (Introducing Computer Networking) is also appropriate to sort out the fundamental networking choices and knowledge.

Background

Following is summary of requirement as an aide memoir for the tutor. Students should work from their own requirements generated at the end of PBL1. Assessment criteria are in the module guide and Web site.

Requirements

Sales	
1. Contact mgt software, enabling all sales reps to access all client details from their own PC.	2. PC per sales person inc mgr.
3. E-mail to Manchester via ISP	4. Web site with email enquiry (not e-commerce)
5. High speed printer	6. Facility for sales reps to produce own quotes / letters
Accounts	
1. Update Sage to latest Line50 Accounts (Euro & performance issues)	2. 2 x new PC
3. Printer replacement	
Marketing	
1. Keep iMac / printer, not networked	2. Mailing list in-house (use contact mgt software to generate it).
General	
1. PC for all staff except Marketing.	2. Security - Personnel data / Sales/ Accounts kept separate. Internet security needed.
3. All PCs to be networked, current ones to be included if possible.	4. Budget - within GBP40k
Training Requirements	
1. On-site training for sales, in small groups. Cannot release more than half at a time.	2. General PC training in-house.
3. Training schedule & plan required.	
Installation requirements	
1. Outside working hours	
Support requirements	
1. Specification for a technician / Web developer Inc qualifications & salary.	2. Maximum down time is half an hour during working day

Week 1

Aim: Today the aim is to ensure they have generated appropriate learning issues and have created a plan of who does what and by when.

- The requirements are wide ranging; You will need to make sure that they achieve some focus, for example get them to consider what order the problems need solving: IT IS NOT ACCEPTABLE for them to divide work along the lines of Software/ Hardware/ training/ Installation.

- Check that they discuss in some detail the issues around and have generated learning issues, including underpinning theory. Help them to phrase the research questions at this stage. *This is critical for good learning.*

- **Suggested Learning Issues for week 1 that they may generate are:**
  1. *How can computers be connected in a network to share data?* This is the main question at the start. They need to look at alternatives, brainstorm what they know.
     a. Are there different kinds of network?
     b. What are the key characteristics of networks (performance etc)
     c. How can computers be connected together? (Wireless and wired)
     d. What software is needed to connect computers together?
     e. How can a computer direct messages to another computer?
  2. What versions of Act! And Sage Accounts will meet Ace's needs?
     a. What operating systems do they work on?
     b. What alternatives are there?
     c. What hardware requirements do they have?
     d. What network versions are available?
  3. What options are there for E-mail connections?
     a. What ISP connection alternatives (ISDN, DSL, Dial up)
     b. What criteria are important for selection
  4. How can resilience be achieved?
     a. What sort of threats are there?
     b. How can they be dealt with?
- They should be able to reflect on their experience with the university network and identify possible operating systems to investigate, and alternatives (Novell NetWare, Windows, Linux)
- *Make sure they hand you a copy of the plan before they go, and check it has appropriate detail.*
- *Make sure they know the format of the individual research handout, and stress it must not be cut/ paste from Google search!*

Next week we will challenge them on their understanding as they explain it to each other.

Week 2

Aim: The teaching and sharing of knowledge and application to problem scenario if sufficiently clear conclusion can be made.

Possible questions to explore knowledge

1. Networking Technologies (Layers ½) Ethernet/Token Ring, Wireless LAN, ATM

   a. How does it work (CSMA/CD, etc.).

   b. What speeds do they operate at?

   c. What is meant by the term bandwidth?

   d. What cabling does it use? (Cat 1-6, Fibre, STP).

   e. What components are used (hub/switch , MAU).

   f. How are frames/cells addressed?

   g. Advantages/disadvantages?

   h. What layers of OSI model?

2. Interconnecting devices: Switches and Hubs

   a. What is the Difference?

   b. Half/Full duplex?

   c. Speeds/Networking technologies.

   d. Cut through vs. Store and forward.

   e. Layer of OSI model.

   f. How do you combine?

3. Connecting to the Internet

   a. What options are available?

   b. What components needed?

   c. What is a router? How does it differ from switch and hub?

4. Operating Systems

   a. Client/Server or Peer to Peer?

   b. Will it run the applications (Sage Line50, Act!, Office apps).

   c. Security domains (able? How?)

   d. Client OS.

5. Resilience

   a. What does it mean? What threats?

   b. How is it achieved Tape backup/ RAID/ Mirror / clustering/ UPS discussions.

Learning Issues

I expect that the exploration of the previous Learning Issues will require further depth and splitting up. I would have expected them to resolve: Peer to peer vs. Client server for this case.

I would expect them to be considering:

1. *Networking:* Ethernet, Token Ring, Wi-fi for the LAN. They can therefore clarify the key info needed about these to decide next week: i.e. relative cost & performance: How do they work? What are the key features? What standards? What data rate? Which would be suitable for Ace Training & Why?

   Interconnections: If wired what options for cable types? Compatibility? What options to connect the computes (Hub? Switch? Routers? Network cards?)

2. *What versions of Act! And Sage Accounts will meet Ace's needs?* They should have identified a number of versions of Sage and Act, and identified a suitable network version of each and the O/S & Hardware requirements. This should be decided.

3. ***What Operating Systems are suitable?*** Having identified Client/Server (or P2P) and the O/S that Sage Line 50 / Act can run on, they can now investigate the alternatives for the O/S. Linux is out (App S/W will not run on it). Alternatives are Server: NetWare v 6.0, Windows Server 2003. Client Windows XP. Research into relative merits of Netware and Windows. They need to identify the selection criteria: (Cost/Performance/security/resilience)

4. How can resilience be achieved?

   a. They may still be struggling with the options and different effects. Help them to consider threats such as Fire/Flood. Disk failure, Power failure and server hardware failure. They should discover Tape, RAID, Mirroring of servers/ Clusters and UPS at some stage. Likely to need help phrasing research questions here.

5. *E-MAIL/ISP:* Should be finished by now: Expect comparison of ISDN and DSL. DSL performance needs questioning (e.g. data rate, contention ratio, ADSL vs. SDSL). ISP email provision and Web space criteria should have been identified.

Week 3

Aim: The teaching and sharing of knowledge and application to problem scenario.

By end of today:

1. Selected network topology, idea of cabling type / wireless, speed
2. Drawn provisional network diagram
3. Decided how email provided
4. Chosen server O/S & clients

Learning Issues

1. Security Issues: Internet (Firewall), Virus, O/S security to protect data. How can groups of user's data be protected from other users?
2. Resilience issues as ongoing.
3. Hardware: To support software. Server, Printers, clients. Costs.
4. Training: Applications and systems training—what might be needed? Have you enough information to create a training plan?
5. Installation: Costs, cable runs, time etc, installing structured cabling, face plates, patch panels.
6. Support: Skills, qualifications and salary a technician could expect.

Plan should include the synthesis of the draft proposal. Minimum requirements are selection of networking technology, operating systems and application software.

Week 4

Aim: The teaching and sharing of knowledge and application to problem scenario.

1. Allow half an hour for team review of their proposal.
2. Allow 45 minutes for the sharing of learning
3. Allow half an hour for reflection and review of team performance, identifying group actions for next stage.

M21661A Computer Networks: PBL Case 3 – Network Construction

Introduction

This case follows logically from the second. This is where you get your "hands dirty." You should now have a good idea about the system that you will be proposing for Ace Training. This should be documented and form a basis for constructing a system. There are likely to be some details that you have not yet finalised, but you should have determined which operating systems you will propose.

For this case you should choose new chairperson and secretary/ scribe.

Your Problem

How do you build a demonstration network for Ace training (comprising a Server and 2 clients), using the software you have selected, to demonstrate your solution?

Once you have identified *what* to do, and *how* to do it, then you need to construct the network

Deliverables

1. This week: A plan of how you intend to use the lab time in the next 3 weeks, i.e. what you will install and configure in a particular week and the software, hardware you need from the technician at each lab. You are unlikely to be able to stick precisely to this, but you will be able to reflect on how well you estimated time required.

2. In PBL3 you will research and construct a small network to meet these requirements. You will demonstrate this to your tutor on week 11 of the Semester (see schedule on Web site for actual date). You must show a plan of what you are going to demonstrate to your tutor. This should show access to shared network folders and applications with appropriate security [e.g. Sales people should not be able to use Sage Accounts] Evidence of printing from applications should ideally be provided also.

3.   You will present the final proposal to the board of Ace Training Ltd in Week 12. Your presentation should be approximately 15 minutes, all members of the team should be involved and a PowerPoint slide show should be used. The presentation should summarise the proposal. In your presentation, you should include the following:

   a.   Introduce your company to build confidence in your company's ability to meet the customer's needs.

   b.   Identify the needs.

   c.   Explain your solution.

   d.   Explain the benefits of the solution, and in particular why you should be chosen.

   The presentation should be business focussed (on the customer's needs) rather than very technical. Do not discuss the details of faceplates used for cable connections! (As one team did a couple of years ago.)

4.   You will submit the final proposal in week 12. Proposal template and checklist are available from the Web site

5.   Individual Reflection & peer assessment (Week 12). The individual reflection should clearly demonstrate your part in the network construction, and should evaluate the approach you have taken in this PBL. You should identify your learning and action points for improvement in the future.

Assessment Criteria/Weightings

Assessment criteria will be available from the module Web site.

Advice: Applying the PBL Process (Steps 1-4)

-   Step 1: Make a list of issues that need clarifying. What do you intend to demonstrate in the network? What will the network comprise (hardware & software)? Make a list of the components you will need from the technician.

-   Step 2: Define the problem. What is the problem you are solving in this PBL case? Are there any sub-problems that need solving before the larger problem can be solved?

-   Step 3: What do you know about this already? In your team, hold a brainstorming session to identify what you know about building a network. What activities are needed?

Important!
• Step 4: Make a systematic inventory. Examine the suggestions the group has produced. Organise the connections and categories, value and sort out what is irrelevant.

Identify what you do not know, and what you need to learn or understand to solve the problem.

Learning

- Step 5: Formulate learning objectives. After identifying what you do not know or what you need to know, you will create a study or work plan that will include all or part of the following steps.
  1. Prioritise learning needs
  2. Decide *who will do what, and by when.* Decide how / when the individual learning will be shared with the rest of the group.
- Step 6: Individual work. You are now ready to complete your study plan. The seminar time next week will provide you with time for your team meetings, to report back, share and start constructing the network. You are also likely to need to refine any further research you need to do.

NB It is essential that you have a plan of what practical tasks you will be undertaking, and have read up about them BEFORE you start installing software / hardware. Everyone in the group must be able to explain what you are doing, why, and what you expect to happen before you carry out any practical work.

You should allow sufficient time to install and re-install the software. Do not expect it to go perfectly the first time around. You often learn more by repeating something!

Resources

Before you install software you must research information to perform the task successfully. This means finding installation notes for:

1. The operating system.   The module Web site has some notes for partitioning hard disks, installing Windows2003 Server, setting up an Active

Directory Domain, Adding Users, security groups and client computers to the domain, configuring a file and print server. There are also lots of Web sites that will provide this information. Find suitable notes and print them out. Go through them in advance to identify any confusing terms or procedures and resolve them before you start. Suitable sites for Windows 2003 are:

Habraken, J. (2003). *Installing Windows Server 2003* Sams. Retrieved February 14, 2004, from http://www.samspublishing.com/articles/article. asp?p=98829&seqNum=1

Petri, D. (n.d.). *How can I install Windows Server 2003 on my server?* Retrieved February 14, 2004, from http://www.petri.co.il/install_windows_2003.htm

These links are available from the Web site (page labelled Network Theory Links, etc.)

2.   Installing the application software. The module Web site has installation and configuration notes for Sage Line50 and Act! You can also obtain more detail from the Sage Line50 installation manual that you can borrow.

3.   You are setting up a small network which will need IP addresses. Use the private addresses: 192.168.0.1, 192.168.0.2, 192.168.0.3 with subnet mask 255.255.255.0. You will also need to invent a name for your network domain.

Facilitator's Guide: Ace Training: PBL Case 3 – System Construction

Trigger

How do you build a demonstration network for Ace training (comprising a Server and 2 clients), using the software you have selected, to demonstrate your solution?

Schedule

	Class activities	Independent study / submissions
Week 1 (seem week 8)	Intro to PBL3: System Construction Generate Learning Issues Create implementation plan	Submit Plan Individual research Produce individual research handout
Week 2	Sharing/Teach meeting/ Lab implementation Obtain resources, construct hardware and start software installation Monitor progress against plan	
Week 3	Sharing/Teach meeting/ Lab implementation Obtain resources, construct hardware and start software installation Monitor progress against plan	Submit individual handout
Week 4	Demonstrate network	Submit final team proposal
Week 5	Presentation Peer assessment.	Submit Reflection and Peer assessment

Resources

The Module Web site identifies a long list of suitable resources, linked to the PBL case. There are installation and configuration notes for MS Windows 2003 server, Domains, users/ groups, shared folders, drive mappings, Sage Line 50 and Act! There are also notes on establishing network connectivity.

Week 1

Aim: Today the aim is to ensure they have generated appropriate learning issues and have created a plan of who does what and by when.

- *Suggested Learning Issues for week 1 that they may generate are:*
  1. How do you configure the network so that the computers can send messages to each other?
     a. This should raise issues of addressing, in particular IP and Subnet masks. If not, they will encounter this when investigating the network setup.
  2. How do you install Microsoft Windows 2003 Server® and XP® client
  3. How do you add users?
  4. How do you configure security to restrict access to certain folders?
  5. How do you install Sage Line50 and Act! so that all network users share the same database?

6.   How do you configure Printers?

* *They should create a plan for the next four weeks, which they will monitor. Make sure they hand you a copy of the plan before they go, and check it has appropriate detail.*

Week 2 and Week 3

Aim: The sharing of knowledge, construction of the network and monitoring progress against the plan.

Preparation of a plan for the demonstration, related to the client requirements.

Week 4

Aim: Demonstration

1.   Refuse to start until you have seen their demonstration plan.
2.   Allow them to complete the demonstration.
3.   Ask the team questions, particularly related to the sharing of folders, drive mappings and security groups.
4.   Teams complete peer assessment from template
5.   By next week, complete reflective report as per the template on the Web site.

Grading Criteria	Pass	Good Pass (GP)	Excellent
LO4 Construct, install and use a range of administration tools for a small LAN.	Demonstration shows evidence of planning, all team involved, Shared / restricted access, User login and applications demonstrated. Questions answered showing some correct knowledge. Likely to need significant prompting.	As Pass and evidence of thorough organisation of the demonstration, relates to client requirements. Questions answered correctly, may be some prompting.	As GP and all aspects of demo systematically related to client requirements. Questions answered confidently, correctly and comprehensively

Week 5

Aim: Presentation

1.	*Presentation skill (individual)*	Presentation within 5 minutes of agreed time & Logical structure. Clear speech, some eye contact. Co-ordinates with other team members. PowerPoint uses appropriate text and graphics.	As Pass and clear introductions / summary / signposting. Answers questions knowledgeably. Explains slides.	As GP and confident, enthusiastic, persuasive, does not read from a script, relates to clients
2.	*Presentation content (team)*	Presentation is consistent with, and relates to report.	Presentation is balanced and discusses key points	Presentation is persuasive and clearly links features/ benefits of solution with client needs and problems.

Glossary

Anchored Instruction: Developed by the Cognition and Technology Group at Vanderbilt [CTGV] (1993), based on the concept of creating a semantically rich "anchor" that illustrates important problem-solving situations. These anchors create a "macrocontext" that provides a common ground for experts in various areas, as well as teachers and students from diverse backgrounds, to communicate and build collective understanding (CTGV, 1993). Macrocontexts can be used to integrate concepts across curriculum in which meaningful authentic problems can be posed. The anchors can serve as contexts for collective inquiry in classrooms and research on learning.

Assessment: Term used for evaluating student achievement of learning outcomes in some way. For example, this may involve indicators of performance of a task or skill; behaviours, attitudes or assessment of knowledge (understanding, application).

- **Norm-Referenced Assessment:** An assessment method that designed to measure and compare individual students' to those of their peer group (that is, *norm group*). It measures relative performance rather than absolute achievement.

- **Criterion-Referenced Assessment:** An aassessment method that measures student knowledge and understanding in relation to specific *standards*. It measures students' performance in relation to standards, not in relation to other students; all students may earn the highest grade if all meet the established criteria.

- **Reliability and Validity:** A valid assessment is one that measures "what it is supposed to measure" (Biggs & Moore 1993, p. 409). In designing assessment we often rely on expert judgment of validity, that is, whether the success at the assessed task implies achievement of the learning outcome. Validity is a large and fascinating topic in its own right, trying to establish validity in an objective way is by no means trivial. Biggs (1999, p. 152) argues that valid assessment "must be of the total performance, not just aspects of it." Reliability concerns how consistent the results of some assessment can be made buy different assessors, on different occasions. It is vital that summative assessments are both reliable and valid. This generally requires large amounts of time and often moderation by other assessors. Formative assessments on the other hand should be valid, but need not be reliable, the feedback is more important than the accuracy of the grade.

Asynchronous Tools for Communication: Those which do not rely on participants being available at the same time in order to communicate. Examples include e-mail and electronic forums (often called conferences or bulletin boards).

Attitudes: Complex mental states of human beings that affect their choices of personal action toward people, things and events. Learners have an attitude when they make consistent choices in repeated situations.

Authenticity: Used to indicate that the problem occurs in a sufficiently real-world context so that it is "true-to-life." This real-world nature can be motivational for the student. However, authenticity is a relative term that varies with student experience: what is authentic to a 15-year-old and relevant to their experience is likely to be very different to that of a post graduate student.

Behavioural Learning: Described as a change in the observable behaviour of a learner, made as a function of events in the environment. The primary focus of the behavioural perspective is on behaviour and the influence of the external environment in shaping the individual's behaviour (Newby et al., 1996). Learning in behaviourism is equated with changes in either the form or frequency of observable performance. The learner, in behavioural learning, is characterised as being reactive to conditions in the environment as opposed to taking an active role in discovering the environment.

Blended Learning: A relatively new term, used to denote the combination or integration of e-learning with traditional face-to-face learning. LittleJohn (2004) argues that there is not a precise definition and the term blended learning is often used to include integration of electronic forms of learning administration as well as electronic content delivery.

Blogging: see Web log

Bloom's Taxonomy: Benjamin Bloom (1956) developed a taxonomy for categorizing level of abstraction of questions that commonly occur in educational settings of intellectual behaviour in learning. This taxonomy contains three overlapping domains: the cognitive, psychomotor, and affective. Cognitive is for mental skills (Knowledge), affective is for growth in feelings or emotional areas (Attitude), while psychomotor is for manual or physical skills (Skills). Within the cognitive domain, he identified six levels: knowledge, comprehension, application, analysis, synthesis, and evaluation. These domains and levels are very useful to help the development of critical thinking skills of students.

Bruner Discovery Learning: Bruner (1965) believes that learning is an active, social process; in which students construct new ideas or concepts based on their current knowledge. To Bruner, learning is a continual process that occurs in three stages. The first is Enactive in which children need to experience the concrete, such as manipulating objects in their hands, or touching a cat, in order to understand. Iconic is the second stage when children are able to represent materials graphically or mentally. They can do basic additions in their heads. Finally, Symbolic, children are able to use logic, higher order thinking skills and symbolic systems such as using formula. Bruner believes that knowledge is best acquired through discovery (Bruner, 1961). Interaction between students and instructors is necessary for discovery learning. Tutors should try to encourage students to discover principles by themselves. The tutor and student should engage in active dialog. Bruner also believes that the curriculum should be organized in a spiral manner so that students continually build upon what they have already learned.

Case-Based Lectures: When students are presented with case vignettes, or more complete case histories before the lecture. The cases highlight material to be covered. The students have to analyse the case using their prior knowledge, before any new knowledge is provided. This effect causes some oriented structuring of information provided in lectures, as opposed to possible restructuring of information already provided, as may occur in the lecture-demonstration method above. This is not self-directed learning.

Case Method: Where students are given a complete case for study and research in preparation for subsequent class discussion. The subsequent interactive case discussion in class with the teacher combines both student-directed and teacher-directed learning. There is a stronger challenge to hypothesis generation, data analysis and decision making with more active structuring of information. The method is also more motivating. However, the case study is already organised and synthesised for the students, thus limiting the amount of reasoning that will occur.

Cognitive Apprenticeship: A model of instruction developed by Collins and colleagues (1989) that makes thinking visible to students in learning. These authors believe that Cognitive Apprenticeship can be adapted to the teaching and learning of cognitive skills.

Cognitive Domain: Defined as learning that involves instinctual skills such as knowledge, concepts, rules and principles.

Cognitive Engagement: Observable when the learners are giving sustained, engaged attention to a task requiring mental effort; and authentic, useful learning is produced by extended engagement in optimally complex cognitive activities (Corno & Mandinach, 1983). Cognitive engagement and motivation are inextricably linked together through mental representations, monitoring, and evaluation of responses and strategic thinking (Stoney & Oliver, 1999). The highest form of cognitive engagement is self-regulated learning, where learners plan and manage their own learning and have a high degree of personal control and autonomy.

Cognitive Flexibility Theory (CFT): An integrated theory of learning, mental representation and instruction. It provides a number of heuristics to design instruction that avoids over-simplifying instruction by providing real-world cases, using multiple representations of content in order to enhance transfer and requiring knowledge construction by the learners, not knowledge retrieval. A central tenet of the theory is that revisiting the same material at different times, for different purposes, and from different conceptual perspectives is essential for attaining the goals of advanced knowledge acquisition (Spiro et al., 1991)

Cognitive Learning: Equated with discrete changes between states of knowledge rather than with changes in the probability of response. In cognitive learning, the issues of how information is received, organised, stored and retrieved by the mind is important. Learning is concerned not so much with what learners do, but with what they know and how they came to acquire that knowledge (Jonassen, 1991). The most dominant of the cognitive learning theories is based on an information-processing approach.

Cognitive Strategies: Learners have acquired cognitive strategies when they have developed ways to improve the effectiveness and efficiency of their own intellectual and learning processes; when they can learn independently; when they can propose and solve original problems. This is the highest form of learning.

Computer Supported Collaborative Learning (CSCL): Refers to the practice of using computer technology to support communication between learners in order to help them construct meaning. It is therefore based on social constructivist theories of learning.

Constructivist Learning: Theory is based on the assumption that knowledge is constructed by learners as they attempt to make sense of their experiences. Learners actively construct knowledge, based on prior experiences, and they are not empty vessels waiting to be filled. In constructivism, constructive processes operate and learners form, elaborate and test candidate mental structures until a satisfactory one emerges (Perkins, 1991).

Critical Thinking Skills: Ability to use logic and reasoning in solving problems In order to help students to acquire critical thinking skills, students should be provided with environments where thinking skills can be learned and then practised in realistic situations. A strategy for teaching critical thinking skills includes: identifying the problem, deciphering the purpose, uncovering the assumptions, recognising and using different paradigms, demonstrating different methods of reasoning, examining data, creating alternative solutions and evaluating one's thinking to improve it (Chubinski, 1996).

Discovery Learning: An instructional method that uses an inductive approach to find answers by students through the use of trial and error in problem solving strategies.

Distributed (Virtual) PBL: Distributed PBL (dPBL) refers to the situation where the participants in the PBL team are dispersed geographically. Typically communication and collaboration between team members during the PBL cycle is conducted using electronic means. Hence the term "virtual PBL" has been used to describe the same conditions. Distributed PBL may occur where all participants are dispersed, or there may be variations where sub-teams are located in the same location. Such situations can mirror the modern work practice of employing globally distributed teams.

E-Learning (JISC): "Defined as 'learning facilitated and supported through the use of information and communications technology', e-learning may involve the use of some, or all, of the following technologies:

- Desktop and laptop computers;
- Software, including assistive software;
- Interactive whiteboards;
- Digital cameras;
- Mobile and wireless tools, including mobile phones;
- Electronic communication tools, including e-mail, discussion boards, chat facilities and video conferencing;
- Virtual Learning Environments (VLEs); and
- Learning activity management systems."

Much has been promised about the potential of technology to revolutionise learning, with benefits identified in six key dimensions:

- Connectivity: Access to information is available on a global scale.
- Flexibility: Learning can take place any time, any place.
- Interactivity: Assessment of learning can be immediate and autonomous.
- Collaboration: Use of discussion tools can support collaborative learning beyond the classroom.
- Extended opportunities: E-content can reinforce and extend classroom-based learning.
- Motivation: Multimedia resources can make learning "fun" (JISCa, n.d).

Facilitator's Guide: A document that replaces the traditional lesson plans and scheme of work. It is particularly necessary if there are a number of tutors running the course to help achieve a level of consistency. Typical contents include: A schedule for the PBL case, identifying milestones, activities, deliverables; Sample questions to ask at each meeting; Assessment criteria; Details of what you expect students to achieve at each stage. E.g.: After the first session the key learning issues/appropriate resources.

FIRO-B®: (An abbreviation for Fundamental Interpersonal Relations Orientation-Behavior). The FIRO-B is a proprietary psychometric tool for helping people understand themselves and how to work with others. There is a 54-item personality questionnaire to measure dimensions of interpersonal relationships: inclusion, control and affection.

Formative Assessment: "*Formative assessment* is designed to provide learners with feedback on progress and inform development, but does not contribute to the overall assessment" (QAA, 2000, p. 4).

Group Dynamics: Implies that individual behaviours may differ depending on individuals' current or prospective connections to a group. It is also Phenomena that occur in groups based upon their interactions and interrelations.

Guided Design: Name for a scaffolding technique where students are prompted through the decision making process by a set of printed instructions, their answers are checked by the tutor and sample feedback answers are provided at appropriate times. Students are asked to reflect on any differences. This approach constrains the student, reduces their ownership and also requires a large amount of preparation by the tutor. It can be a very good way to introduce aspects of PBL, and the degree of guidance can be relaxed in later cases.

Holistic Assessment: Recognizes *overall performance* on the task, rather than analyzing and giving marks for each component part. In the latter it could be possible to achieve a pass by knowing very thoroughly several components of the solution, but being incapable of evaluating it in context and synthesizing a viable solution. This holistic approach corresponds to a qualitative view rather than a quantitative view; judging how well the knowledge and skills are integrated, rather than how much the student knows.

Information and Communication Technologies (ICT): "The building blocks of the Networked World." ICTs include telecommunications technologies, such as telephony, cable, satellite and radio, as well as digital technologies, such as computers, information networks and software." (Harvard Center for International Development, n.d.) http://cyber.law.harvard.edu/home/

Information Processing: Views the learner as a processor of information in the same way as a computer. Learning occurs when information is input from the environment, processed and stored in memory and output in the form of some learned capability. Learning is therefore perceived as information processing.

Instruction: Concerned with teaching. It makes use of deliberate arrangements of learning conditions to achieve an intended goal. Newby and others (1996) defined instruction as the selection and arrangement of information, activities, approaches and media to help students meet predetermined learning goals.

Intellectual Skills: Individuals use intellectual skills when they show competence, or interact with the environment using symbols or language. They demonstrate that they know how to do something of an intellectual nature.

Intelligent Tutoring System (ITS): "ITSs are computer-based learning systems which attempt to adapt to the needs of learners" (self, 1998). This involves the application of artificial intelligence techniques to model aspects of the learning process, such as domain knowledge, learner's knowledge and teaching knowledge.

Kolb Experiential Learning: (1984) Suggests that learning is the process whereby knowledge is created through the transformation of experience. His theory provides a way of structuring and sequencing the curriculum and indicates how a session or whole course may be taught to improve student learning. Kolb's experiential learning structures a session or a whole course using a learning cycle. The different stages of learning are associated with the different learning styles. The core of Kolb's four stage model is a simple description of the learning cycle that shows how experience is translated through reflection into concepts, which in turn are used as guides for active experimentation and choice of new experiences. The four stages are: concrete experience (CE), reflective observation (RO), abstract conceptualization (AC) and active experimentation (AE). Because learners have to go through the cycles several times, it is best thought of as a spiral of cycles. The different stages are associated with distinct learning styles. Kolb believes that student develops a preference for learning in a particular way.

Learner-Based Cases: Where the teacher presents the students with information in lectures and then a case or two, usually vignettes, to demonstrate the relevance of the information. Learner-based cases are typically used by teachers in their teaching and often referred to as PBL. However, this method does not directly foster any of the objectives required of PBL. Students are typically asked to understand the case presented in terms of information in the lectures and some of the information may be restructured by students. Although some hypothesis generation, data analysis and limited decision making may be required, there is no inquiry or case-building skills involved.

Learning: Defined as a persisting change in human performance or performance potential. There should be a change in performance brought about as a result of the learner's interaction with the environment Driscoll (1994). It is measured by the amount of change that occurs in an individual's level of performance or behaviour. This change occurs over time and results from specific experiences such as practice (Newby et al., 1996).

Learning Companion System (LCS): (Chou et al., 2002) An LCS is a development of an Intelligent Tutoring System (ITS) but whereas an ITS is built around a pedagogical model of instruction, educational software agents within an LCS can have a variety of roles, for example: a competitor, collaborator, troublemaker or critic.

Learning Environment: The physical surroundings in which learning takes place.

Learning Issue: A topic that requires further study outside of the tutorial meeting.   Learning Issues are critical for successful development of self-directed learning. A good learning issue is presented in the form of an answerable *question*; is *focused, requiring specific information*; pursues information that is *relevant* to the problem; goes beyond superficial knowledge to probe *conceptual* issues and is often set in a *context* that provides direction (UDEL).

Learning Outcomes: These define the *knowledge, skills,* and *abilities* that students will attain as a result of their successful completion of a particular set of learning experiences. Thus they are learner centred, rather than teacher-centred and define what a student will know, and what a student will be able to do at the end of the course. Quite often we use the terms *Learning Objectives* and *Learning outcomes* interchangeably. However, strictly we can differentiate between them in terms of specificity Objectives are usually detailed *behaviourist* statements which specify *exactly* the action that is to be assessed. Outcomes tend to be more general descriptors.

Learning Team Coach: The term we have used to refer to a student PBL team facilitator. The term coach is also used by Woods(1994). We believe it carries more positive associations than the term facilitator, the metaphor of a sports team coach, implying active involvement, being dedicated to improving performance of the team, calling to account individuals who do not perform, helping the team keep focus, celebrating success, but standing on the sidelines while the team performs (solves the problem) without doing it for them.

LTM: Long term memory

Metacognitive Skills: Are "thinking about thinking." They are required when we are confronted with a difficult, unexpected or puzzling problem or situation. It is the conscious monitoring and direction of problem solving or reasoning activities (Barrows, 1988).

Motor Skills: Learners have developed motor skills when they perform a physical task utilising equipment or materials according to a routine procedure. Driving a car, throwing a ball or typing a letter are all examples of motor skills.

OPV: Other person's viewpoint

Patchwork Text: (Winter et al., 1999) "This is a way of getting students to present their work in written form. Students build up text in course work over a number of weeks. Each component of work is shared with other students and they are expected to use different styles, such as a commentary on a lecture, a personal account, and a book review. This kind of assessment fits well with PBL because of its emphasis on critique and self-questioning." (Savin-Baden & McDonald, 2004 p. 12)

Peer Assessment: Refers to the situation where students make judgments about each others' work or performance. There are a number of different ways this can be used: Students can identify their own criteria to assess each other, though a more common approach is for students to assess each other with criteria devised by faculty. The former method fits with the PBL approach of empowering students. Faculty often feel more comfortable with criteria they have devised, though this does have a disadvantage that students may not interpret them in the way that faculty had intended. Any form of peer assessment requires preparation of the students. It is also important to consider how results are fed back and the weighting involved. Nevertheless, it can be a valid approach to assessing student contribution to a team.

Portfolios: Have been used in assessment for many years, usually consisting of a collection of samples of work over a period of time. Recently, Nicky Guard reports (guard, n.d.) that "portfolios are finding a wider application as a form of educational assessment, especially in the USA. Even though they may vary in format, educational portfolios distinguish themselves from other portfolios by including reflective elements. They are therefore not merely a collection of best practice or artefacts but are also intended to document the learning process and involve students in actively reflecting on their learning."

Prior Knowledge: Often characterised metaphorically as schemata—organised networks of prior knowledge. According to Bartlett (1932), *schemas* or *schemata* are the basis of *all* knowledge. Schemata provide means by which learners can compare and contrast to-be-learned information with existing knowledge, to assimilate new information meaningfully within existing knowledge and to continually restructure knowledge accordingly (Hannafin & Hooper 1993).

Problem-Based Learning (PBL): According to Barrows (1988) is "... the learning that results from the process of working towards the understanding of, or resolution of a problem." Barrows describes the main educational goals as: to develop students' thinking or reasoning skills (problem solving, metacognition, critical thinking) and to help students become independent, self-directed learners (learning to learn, learning management).

Problem-Solving Learning: The situation where students are provided with a problem (usually of a restricted nature) that they solve with knowledge that has been provided previously.

Problem-Solving Skills: In the context of PBL, these are identified by Woods Woods (1994,1996) and comprise: Awareness of problem solving processes; analysis of problems for issues; demonstrating a systematic approach; creativity; use of knowledge appropriately; generating & testing hypotheses; confidence in own ability.

Problem Statement: This is the initial statement that students are given. It is formulated as a problem or query or puzzle that the team has to investigate. The aim is for students to learn, not necessarily to solve the problem; however in many cases solving the problem achieves the same end. A problem statement is not merely an exercise; ideally it should be authentic and messy, providing a number of avenues for investigation.

Programmed Learning: An "educational technique characterized by self-paced, self-administered instruction presented in logical sequence and with much repetition of concepts. Programmed learning received its major impetus from the work done in the mid-1950s by the American behavioural psychologist B.F. Skinner" (Encyclopaedia Britannica on-line).

Project-Based Learning: Typically uses a production model. It consists of:

1. Identify the purpose for the creation of the end product and their audience,
2. Research the topic,
3. Design the product, and
4. Create a plan for project management. (Esch, 2000)

Reflection: A term that is widely used today in education to describe an active process of self-analysis of performance where the learner attempts to make some sort of sense of their experiences. Dewey (1933, p. 9) defined reflection as: "An active persistent and careful consideration of any belief or supposed form of knowledge in the light of the grounds that support it and the further conclusion to which it tends." Boud et al. (1985, p. 19) explain reflection as "a generic term for those intellectual and effective activities in which individuals engage to explore their experiences in order to lead to a new understanding and appreciation." Schön (1987) is well known for his suggestion that there are different levels of reflection: these are reflection-in-action (a characteristic of experts) and reflection-on-action (after the event).

Reflection: Means the pulling together of a broad range of previous thinking or knowledge in order to make greater sense of it for another purpose that may transcend the previous bounds of personal knowledge or thought (Moon, 2002). It normally involves complicated mental processing of issues for which there is no obvious solution (Dewey, 1933). This suggests that reflection implies a form of mental processing with a purpose and/or an anticipated outcome that is applied to relatively complicated or unstructured ideas for which there is not an obvious solution. Reflection therefore has close association with, or involvement in, learning and the representation of learning. There may be an overlap between the use of the words "reflection" and "thinking." These words can refer to the same activity as in the notion of the "reflection practitioner" (Schön 1983). An example of this is that of taking an overview or "sitting back" from a situation to review.

Reflective Journal: A reflective journal enables the documentation of experiences, thoughts, questions, ideas and conclusions during the learning experience. By recording such information on a regular basis we reduce the chance of omission and we encourage a regular cycle of action planning. A journal can also provide a detailed evidence base when analysing and reflecting on a course as a whole.

Resource-Based Learning (RBL): Resource-based learning is an approach to learning where students are exposed to a wide variety of resources. PBL can be regarded as a specialised form of RBL, with a particular defined process, and particular requirements for the characteristics of the problem-statement.

Scaffolding: A term originally used by Bruner to describe tutorial interaction between an adult and a child. It is a metaphor of a *temporary* support for learning that is gradually removed. In this book it is used to refer to all forms of learning support, whether or not they be cognitively-based, logistical or emotional. It broadly refers to the range of services provided to assist students' progress towards independent learning.

Seen Examination: A seen examination is one in which the questions are provided to students in advance of the examination. They are sometimes referred to as "pre-seen" examinations. Advantages of seen examinations are that they reduce the stress on students and remove the element of luck in "revising for the right question." From a perspective of Problem-based Learning, they can be problem-statements that are individually assessed, which complements team assessment in PBL. Seen examinations also enable more complex questions to be set, since students have more time to explore and answer them. They also have the opportunity to clarify any aspects of the question that they are unsure of: you cannot answer a question you do not understand.

Self Assessment: The process by which students assess their own work. This may be using criteria they have developed, or by interpreting criteria developed by the tutor. It is well aligned with PBL, and is particularly easy to use for formative assessment. However, it is essential that students are prepared well for self-assessment; especially if they do not generate the criteria themselves.

STM: Short-term memory

Student-Centred Learning: When students take control of their own learning. Students should be actively involved in determining what their own learning needs are and how these needs are best met.

Summative Assessment: "*Summative assessment* provides a measure of achievement or failure made in respect of a learner's performance in relation to the intended learning outcomes of the programme of study" (QAA, 2000, p. 4). Thus, work that is submitted during the module, and which is graded, counting towards the final mark is still classified as summative assessment.

Synchronous Communication Tools: Those that require participants to be communicating at the same time, though they may be separated geographically. Telephones, Web-cams, video-conferencing and instant messaging are examples.

Trigger: see problem-statement

Tripartite Assessment: (Savin-Baden, 2003) This is a method of assessment that balances individual and team marks as follows. There are three components: Firstly the team submits a report for which they receive a mark in the normal PBL manner. Secondly each individual submits the piece of work they researched. Finally the individual writes an account of the group process that is linked to the theory of group work.

Triple Jump: (Painvin et al., 1979) This is an assessment that has been specifically developed for PBL, but it is very time consuming. As the name suggests, the "Triple jump" exercise has three phases: hop, step and jump. In the hop phase the tutor questions the student. The step phase allows the student time to research the questions that have emerged from the first phase. In the final jump phase the student is provides the tutor with a written report of their findings.

Tutor or Teacher: These terms are used interchangeably to denote any person who is conducting the teaching or the tutorial process. In traditional classrooms, the tutor is usually the professor who is delivering the lectures. In the tutorial session, the tutor could be the professor or teacher or instructor facilitating the students in their studies.

Undergraduate: Refers to university students studying for their first degree. In the British educational system there is no direct equivalent to "high school graduates."

Virtual Learning Environment (VLE): A useful working definition is provided by JISC: "A Virtual Learning Environment is a collection of integrated tools enabling the management of on-line learning, providing a delivery mechanism, student tracking, assessment and access to resources." These integrated tools may be one product (e.g. BlackBoard, WebCT) or an integrated set of individual, perhaps open-source, tools" (JISC n.d.). A VLE may link to administrative systems, both in-house and external. Such an integrated system is sometimes called a Managed Learning Environment (MLE).

Viva: An oral examination (shortened from Viva Voce).

Weblog: "A public Web site where users post informal journals of their thoughts, comments, and philosophies, updated frequently and normally reflecting the views of the blog's creator." (glossary of on-line education terms)

Wiki (pronounced "wicky" or "weeky") or **WikiWiki:** As defined by the Wikipedia[1] is a Web site (or other hypertext document collection) that gives users the ability to add content, as on an Internet forum, but also allows that content to be edited by other users.

References

Barrows, H. S. (1988). *The tutorial process.* Springfield: Southern Illinois University, School of Medicine.

Biggs, J. B., & Moore, P. J. (1993). *The process of learning.* Sydney: Prentice Hall of Australia.

Boud, D., Keough, R., & Walker, D. (1985) *Reflection: Turning experience into learning.* London: Kogan Page.

Bruner, J. S. (1961). The act of discovery. *Harvard Educational Review, 31*(1), 21-32.

Bruner, J. S. (1965). The growth of mind. *American Psychologist, 20,* 1007-1017.

Chou, C. Y., Chan, T. W., & Lin, C. J. (2002). Redefining the learning companion: the past, present, and future of educational agents. *Computers & Education, 40,* 255-269.

Chubinski, S. (1996). Creative critical thinking strategies. *Nurse Educator, 21*(6), 23-27.

Cognition and Technology Group at Vanderbilt [CTGV] (1991). Technology and the design of generative learning environments. *Educational Technology, 31,* 34-40

Cognition and Technology Group at Vanderbilt [CTGV] (1993). Designing learning environments that support thinking: The Jasper Series as a case study. In T. M. Duffy, J. Lowyck, & D. H. Jonassen (Eds.), *Designing environments for constructive learning.* NATO-ASI Series, London: Springer-Verlag.

Dewey, J. (1933). *How we think.* Boston: D.C. Heat & Co.

Driscoll, M. P. (1994). *Psychology of learning for instruction.* Boston: Allyn & Bacon.

Encyclopaedia Britannica on-line (n.d.). Retrieved April 23, 2005, from http://www.britannica.com/

Esch, C. (2000). *Project-based and problem-based: Same or different?* Retrieved March 30, 2005, from The multimedia project: Project-based learning with multimedia, http://pblmm.k12.ca.us/PBLGuide/PBL&PBL.htm

Gagné, R. M., Briggs, L. J., & Wager, W.W. (1988). *Principles of instructional design* (3rd ed.). London: Holt, Rinehart & Winston.

Glossary of online education terms (n.d.). Retrieved April 23, 2005, from www.geocities.com/Athens/2405/glossary.html

Guard, N., Richter, U., & Waller, S. (n.d.). *Portfolio assessments, higher education academy subject. Centre for Languages, Linguistics and Area Studies.* Retrieved April 10, 2005, from http://www.lang.ltsn.ac.uk/resources/guidecontents.aspx

Hannafin, M. J., & Hooper, S.R. (1993). Learning Principles. In M. Fleming & W. Levie (Eds.), *Instructional message design: Principles from behavioural and cognitive sciences* (2nd ed.). Englewood Cliffs, NJ: Educational Technology Publications.

Harvard Center for International Developmen (n.d.). Retrieved April 23, 2005, from http://cyber.law.harvard.edu/home/

JISC (n.d.). *Effective use of virtual learning environments,* Retrieved on April 18, 2005, from http://www.jiscinfonet.ac.uk/InfoKits/effective-use-of-VLEs

JISCa (n.d.). *Starting point: Definition.* Retrieved on April 18, 2005, from http://blackboard.sihe.ac.uk/support/jisc/html/start_defin.htm

Jonassen, D. H. (1991). Objectivism vs. constructivism: Do we need a philosophical paradigm shift? *Educational Research & Development, 38*(3), 5-14.

Kolb, D. (1984). *Experiential learning as the science of learning and development.* Englewood Cliffs, NJ: Prentice-Hall.

Kolb, D. A. (1984). *Experiential learning: Experience as the source of learning and development.* Englewood Cliffs, NJ: Prentice Hall.

Littlejohn, A. (2004. *Blended learning: The "best of both worlds?"* Retrieved April 23, 2005, from http://kn.open.ac.uk/public/

Lowyck, D. H., & Jonassen (Eds.). *Designing environments for constructive learning.* NATO-ASI Series, London: Springer-Verlag.

Macdonald, R., & Savin-Baden, M. (2004) *A briefing on assessment in problem-based learning, LTSN Generic Centr.* Retrieved April 10, 2005, from http://www.heacademy.ac.uk/

Moon, J. A. (2002). *Reflection in learning and professional development: Theory and practice.* London: Kogan-Page.

Newby, T. J., Stepich, D. A., Lehman, J. D., & Russell, J. D. (1996). *Instructional technology for teaching and learning: Designing instruction, integrating computers, and using media.* Englewood Cliffs, NJ: Merrill/Prentice-Hall.

Painvin, C., Neufeld, V., Norman. G., Walker, I., & Whelan, G. (1979) The "triple jump" exercise: A structured measure of problem-solving and self-directed learning. *Proceedings of the 18th Annual Conference on Research in Medical Education.*

Perkins, D. (1991). Technology meets constructivism: Do they make a marriage? *Educational Technology, 35*(5), 18-33.

Quality Assurance Agency (2000). *Code of practice for the assurance of academic quality and standards in higher education, Section 6: Assessment of students.* Retrieved April 10, 2005, from http://www.qaa.ac.uk/academicinfrastructure/codeOfPractice/section6/default.asp

Savery, J. R., & Duffy, T. M. (1995). Problem-based learning: An instructional model and its constructivist framework. *Educational Technology, 35,* 31-37.

Savin-Baden, M. (2003*) Facilitating problem-based learning in higher education: Illuminating perspectives.* Buckingham: SRHE/Open University Press.

Schön, D. (1983). *The reflective practitioner.* San Francisco: Jossey-Bass.

Schön, D. (1987). *Educating the reflective practitioner.* San Francisco: Jossey-Bass.

Schunk. D. (1989). Self-efficacy and cognitive skill learning. In C. Ames & Ames (Eds.), *Research on motivation in education: Goals and cognition, 3,* 13-44. San Diego: Academic Press.

Schunk, D. H. (1991). *Learning Theories: An educational perspective.* Englewood Cliffs, NJ: Merrill/Prentice-Hall.

Self, J. (1998) The defining characteristics of intelligent tutoring systems research: ITSs care, precisely. *International, Journal of Artificial Intelligence in Education* (1999), *10,* 350-364

Spiro, R. J., Feltovich, P. J., Jacobson, M. J., & Coulson, R .L. (1991). Cognitive flexibility, constructivism, and hypertext: Random access instruction for advanced knowledge acquisition in ill-structured domains. *Educational Technology, 31,* 24-33

Stoney, S., & Oliver, R. (1999). Can higher order thinking and cognitive engagement be enhanced with multimedia? *Interactive Multimedia Electronic journal of Computer-Enhanced Learning, 1,* 2.

UDEL (n.d.). *Characteristics of good learning issue.* Retrieved April 10, 2005, from http://www.udel.edu/chem/white/teaching/CHEM643/LrnIssue.html

Winter, R. Buck, A., & Sobiechowska, P. (1999). *Professional experience and the investigative imagination.* London: Routledge.

Woods, D. R. (1994). *Problem-based learning: How to gain the most from PBL.* Hamilton, Ontario: Donald R Woods.

Woods, D. R. (1996). *Problem-based learning: Helping your students gain the most from PBL* (3rd ed.). Hamilton, Ontario: Donald R Woods.

Endnote

[1]   http://en.wikipedia.org/wiki/Main_Page

About the Authors

Lorna Uden is the senior lecturer in the Faculty of Computer, Engineering, and Technology at Staffordshire University, UK. She received a BSc from Aston University, UK (1981), a BA from the Open University (1982), and a PhD from Staffordshire University (1999). She has published more than 70 papers in conferences, journals, book chapters, and workshops. Her research interests include learning technology, Web engineering and technology, human computer Interaction, groupware, activity theory, e-business, knowledge management, and problem-based learning (PBL). Dr. Uden is a member of the Higher Education Academy and ACM. She has been researching and using PBL in her teaching since 1996. She is editor of the *International Journal of Web Engineering and Technology (IJWET)* and the *International Journal of Learning Technology (IJLT)* (Inderscience, UK). She also serves as an editorial board member for several international journals.

Chris Beaumont is a senior lecturer for the Department of Computing at Liverpool Hope University, UK. He is currently programme leader for Internet technology, where he teaches on undergraduate and MSc computing programs. After graduating as a senior scholar in computer science from Trinity College, Cambridge, he worked in industry with GEC-Marconi (General Electronic Company of England) and Digital Equipment Corporation before returning to higher education. He is a member of the Higher Education Academy, the Society for the Research into Higher Education, and the ACM SIGCSE. He has also held a number of external examiner posts within the UK. He has been practicing and researching problem-based learning since 1997 and has published and presented several papers on PBL.

Index

Challenges of Teaching with Technology Across the Curriculum:
Issues and Solutions

Lawrence A. Tomei,
Duquesne University, USA

Teachers are looking for a text that will guide them in the selection of appropriate educational software and help them make decisions about the myriad of available Internet sites. They want to know how all this material can help their students learn better. *Challenges of Teaching With Technology Across the Curriculum: Issues and Solutions* integrates both theory and practice with assessment to make learning outcomes possible. This text will become an invaluable reference for any teacher who develops their own instructional materials or is asked to select software and Web sites for their students.

ISBN 1-59140-109-7 (h/c); eISBN 1-59140-117-8 • Price: US $74.95 • 340 pages © 2003

"Technology is embarking on a new phase in the classrooms of the future. Gone are the days when teachers were forced to rely on technologists to prepare their instructional materials."
–*Lawrence A. Tomei, Duquesne University, USA*

It's Easy to Order! Order online at www.idea-group.com or call 717/533-8845x10!
Mon-Fri 8:30 am-5:00 pm (est) or fax 24 hours a day 717/533-8661

Information Science Publishing
Hershey • London • Melbourne • Singapore • Beijing